Adaptive Mentalization-Based Integrative Treatment

Adaptive Mentalization-Based Integrative Treatment
A guide for teams to develop systems of care

Dickon Bevington
Peter Fuggle
Liz Cracknell
Peter Fonagy

OXFORD
UNIVERSITY PRESS

Great Clarendon Street, Oxford, OX2 6DP,
United Kingdom

Oxford University Press is a department of the University of Oxford.
It furthers the University's objective of excellence in research, scholarship,
and education by publishing worldwide. Oxford is a registered trade mark of
Oxford University Press in the UK and in certain other countries

© Oxford University Press 2017

The moral rights of the authors have been asserted

First Edition published in 2017

Impression: 1

All rights reserved. No part of this publication may be reproduced, stored in
a retrieval system, or transmitted, in any form or by any means, without the
prior permission in writing of Oxford University Press, or as expressly permitted
by law, by licence or under terms agreed with the appropriate reprographics
rights organization. Enquiries concerning reproduction outside the scope of the
above should be sent to the Rights Department, Oxford University Press, at the
address above

You must not circulate this work in any other form
and you must impose this same condition on any acquirer

Published in the United States of America by Oxford University Press
198 Madison Avenue, New York, NY 10016, United States of America

British Library Cataloguing in Publication Data

Data available

Library of Congress Control Number: 2017937060

ISBN 978–0–19–871867–3

Printed and bound by
CPI Group (UK) Ltd, Croydon, CR0 4YY

Oxford University Press makes no representation, express or implied, that the
drug dosages in this book are correct. Readers must therefore always check
the product information and clinical procedures with the most up-to-date
published product information and data sheets provided by the manufacturers
and the most recent codes of conduct and safety regulations. The authors and
the publishers do not accept responsibility or legal liability for any errors in the
text or for the misuse or misapplication of material in this work. Except where
otherwise stated, drug dosages and recommendations are for the non-pregnant
adult who is not breast-feeding

Links to third party websites are provided by Oxford in good faith and
for information only. Oxford disclaims any responsibility for the materials
contained in any third party website referenced in this work.

This book is dedicated to the courageous and resilient young people, families, and carers, and the many passionate, committed, and endlessly creative workers in AMBIT-influenced teams who work with them and learn from them. A community of practice, indeed.

Preface

This book describes AMBIT, an approach to working with people—particularly young people and young adults—whose lives are often chaotic and risky, and whose problems are not limited to one domain. In addition to mental health problems, they may have problems with care arrangements, education or employment, exploitation, substance misuse, offending behaviors, and gang affiliations; if these problems are all occurring simultaneously, any progress in one area is easily undermined by harms still occurring in another. Furthermore, the problems in which we are particularly interested include our clients' responses to the help on offer: they rarely knock on a professional's door asking for help with an expectation that this will be delivered (and, perhaps, even less that any help will actually be helpful). These people have been described rather pejoratively as "the hard to reach." AMBIT is a serious attempt to improve the way we help those who are most neglected, excluded, exploited, and underserved in society.

Who is this book for?

This book is primarily directed at all those who work in this difficult area, who manage such work, and who commission it. This implies a wide range of professionals: youth workers, social workers, police officers, psychologists, therapists, psychiatrists, and more. In addition, there are many workers who may not have professional qualifications but whose detailed local knowledge, perhaps as "experts by experience," is often invaluable to the teams in which they work. The authors of this book include a child and adolescent psychiatrist, two psychologists (one primarily a clinician, the other primarily an academic), and a nurse, but the book could not have been written without the contributions of hundreds of workers in the many teams with which we have had the privilege of working in training events. While in some sections we do not hold back from explaining the theory and science underlying AMBIT, we have tried to hold to a rule of writing in an accessible way. Above all, we have tried to write in a way that could speak to the enthusiastic worker who wants to learn why the things that they already do work (which they often do) and how to improve the things that sometimes don't work or seem to work only at great cost to their peace of mind. This is not a book of theory; it is a book about practice, and how theory can help.

What is AMBIT?

AMBIT is no thing. This is not to say it is nothing at all (we have no wish to waste the reader's time), but it is absolutely not designed to be a thing-in-itself; it is neither a polished product ready to roll out as seen, nor a set of defined steps to follow that promises to make everything better. AMBIT is an amorphous, expanding (and sometimes contracting) set of orienting principles and practices, which pivot around the core theory of mentalizing (which we describe in some detail in Chapter 2), its links to learning, and our belief in an ethical mandate to share such learning. "There is nothing so practical as a good theory," said the sociologist Kurt Lewin (1951, p.169), and given the explosion of creative applications of mentalizing over the past 20 years, this pithy statement certainly seems to hold true here.

Like any child, AMBIT has followed its own developmental trajectory. Starting in the late 1990s, it was developed first as a kind of "thought experiment" by a group of clinicians and academics connected to the Anna Freud Centre (now known as the Anna Freud National Centre for Children and Families) and the Marlborough Family Service in north-west London. Initially, it was called integrative multimodal practice (IMP) and focused exclusively on adolescents with early-onset psychosis or emerging personality problems who were avoiding conventional helping services and required an innovative outreach approach to engage them.[1] In response to early trainings—first with individual practitioners, and from then on with whole teams—the model began to be reshaped in the light of practical experience in real-world applications. Later, we realized that we had stumbled upon a method of treatment development very close to that which had been so elegantly described by Weisz and colleagues (Bearman et al., 2010; Weisz et al., 2006; Chorpita et al., 2005) as the "deployment-focused" model of innovation. This approach involves a process of making iterative adjustments to an evolving model in the light of multiple real-world field applications, a complementary approach to the "pharmaceutical" model of development via conceptualization in a laboratory (or academic ivory tower), a controlled trial or two (often involving very different clients from those who appear in local services), and subsequent roll-out of a package as "evidence-based practice."

Successive trainings in early versions of the model brought new insights and learning about the applicability and effectiveness of these emerging ideas and core practices from workers in the field. For example, an early milestone was

---

[1] The original authors of IMP were Peter Fonagy, Mary Target, Eia Asen, Dickon Bevington, Peter Fuggle, Neil Dawson, and Rabia Malik.

the realization that although this approach places considerable emphasis on the creation of powerful individual worker–client relationships, it is completely unworkable without an equally strong team focus to support such relationships. Thus, individual trainings (which are easier to deliver because individuals sign up individually, out of personal motivation) were replaced by an exclusive focus on team trainings (where it is a given that not everyone present is motivated to be there—some, mandated to attend, inevitably feel that their time would have been better spent getting on with their work than diverting themselves with the machinations, musing, and amusements of training). The project has continued to move forward thanks only to the positive, frank, and creative responses given by so many teams (at the time of writing, approximately 200), and their own contributions and outcomes.

The model has changed. When IMP was renamed adolescent mentalization-based integrative treatment—or "AMBIT"—in 2009, the acronym marked the recognition of two factors: first, that the use of mentalizing had shifted from being just one of a wide range of modalities taught to become the integrative theoretical "hub," and second, the assumption at that time that this work would continue to be directed exclusively at adolescents. The pivotal role of mentalizing has stood the test of time, but the use of AMBIT as an acronym (rather than just the word) is rapidly falling by the wayside, as teams working with non-adolescent populations—young and even middle-aged adults, younger children, vulnerable mothers with infants, and so on—also use the approach. "AMBIT" is increasingly now used simply as the name of the approach—a single word that means one's "sphere of influence"—and this is quite apposite. It is often very unclear to workers where this sphere starts and ends, and how to increase this without causing more problems across the complicated systems they are part of. Nor is the assumption that AMBIT is exclusively for teams providing outreach interventions still particularly helpful—it is now being applied in prisons, care homes, and inpatient and day-hospital settings, too. So the goalposts continue to move, which is exactly as it should be.

The AMBIT project at the Anna Freud National Centre for Children and Families in London coordinates this work, and is responsible for developing and delivering trainings in AMBIT in a number of different ways that have been driven by demand.

The AMBIT project adheres to a few clear principles:

1. **Helpfulness and adaptability.** AMBIT must be helpful rather than harmful to the clients that teams work with. This may seem like stating the obvious, but it means that where evidence exists it is followed, and where it does not (or is found to be inapplicable, or to carry unintended harmful consequences)

then serious attempts to find new evidence, starting from local outcomes and ideally well-conducted trials, should be made, and principles and practices should be adapted in light of this. In other words, AMBIT is unfinished by design; this is an open system for encouraging continual step-by-step improvement.

2. **Open source and free access.** AMBIT must work toward making its learning as widely and easily accessible as possible, avoiding the creation of barriers to dissemination through paywalls and other avoidable costs, or through over-zealous defense of "intellectual property." We recognize that AMBIT has not arisen from nowhere, but from the intellectual efforts, research, and generosity of previous generations of workers. The AMBIT manual, which includes instructions for all its training exercises, as well as video of role plays, didactic teaching, and links to training slides, must remain openly and freely available to all via the internet. AMBIT uses open-source technologies, and releases all its online manualized materials under a Creative Commons license so that any of these materials can be copied, adapted, and shared freely by others, under two conditions—that the original authorship/source of content is acknowledged, and that the same non-commercial terms for sharing this content are applied.

3. **Collaboration.** AMBIT seeks to bring together the knowledge and expertise of local practitioners, service managers/commissioners, and academic researchers, along with service users, on the understanding that improving the quality of help requires recognition of these multiple perspectives, and that inclusivity is critical. Our web-based "wiki" manual allows for pages to spawn sub-pages, and these allow for different perspectives on a contentious subject to be acknowledged and for links to be drawn out that might increase reciprocal understanding and integration. In Chapter 7, we explain the unique structure of our wiki manual, which allows multiple authors and layers of ownership, and makes clear how profoundly AMBIT is, by design, a collaborative endeavor.

AMBIT encourages the active involvement of a large community of practice, and its adherence to open-source principles means that, theoretically, any team anywhere could use its free web-based resources (see below) to self-train at no cost. This would constitute a triumph if it really came to pass, as the cost of training is often a barrier to uptake, but we do recognize the desire for, and helpfulness of, external trainers. The online resources include a number of questionnaires developed to probe existing practice and encourage teams to reflect on their own training needs and readiness and energy for change. Over the years we have consistently reflected on how we have underestimated the amount of pre-training preparation that is useful, despite consistently increasing it. In Chapter 11 we also lay out the different methods of training that are currently in operation.

Finally, we have an admission to make: because AMBIT is designed to change, adapt, and develop, and is the work of an increasing number of contributors, this book is already out of date. The web-based manual, where AMBIT has been and continues to be developed (to see the manual, visit https://manuals.annafreud.org and follow the links to AMBIT[2]), is the live and fullest expression of this approach. In this resource, the large community of practice can document their own local learning in locally owned and adaptable versions of the core AMBIT manual, and these pages can be accessed via any other localized manual via a "compare and share" facility. Every month a fascinating range of pages is authored, and content arising from one team can easily be cloned and customized by another, so that emerging best practice can disseminate quickly. However, it is not all dizzying change; after some years of rapid change and development, the core AMBIT content has now largely stabilized (although there is constant effort to simplify, clarify, and integrate the rich collection of material available). This book is an attempt to capture some of the core ideas and experience of AMBIT in a single narrative, in the hope that readers finding something helpful in these pages will explore the model further, and might perhaps themselves contribute to the next iterations of this project online.

How to read this book

Writing this book was a pleasure and a pain: a pleasure to create a clear (and we hope coherent) narrative; a pain because that is not in the least how AMBIT was developed or is used in real life. AMBIT has been developed incrementally over well over a decade, using a web-based wiki manual (for which we were proud winners of *The Guardian*/Virgin Media Business "Innovation Nation" award for collaboration in 2012). This online resource is purposefully "non-linear" in structure—as is much of the work that we do with our clients. Writing a new page in our wiki manual involves not just the creation of content, but the explicit linking and integrating of that content with pre-existing content across

---

[2] https://manuals.annafreud.org is a "signposting" site through which visitors can quickly obtain links to the core content of the AMBIT manual and the many locally adapted versions of this content (see Chapter 7), as well as to the manuals for other therapeutic approaches under development that have chosen to use the same "wiki" format for their manuals. It aims to provide a "one-stop shop" to help users find the correct link to the treatment manual that they seek.

the whole of the wiki, using hyperlinks and tagging. This can be thought of as "writing in three dimensions," so that the reader can read across the text, or *into* it, delving deeper into areas of particular interest.

The online manual is read by clicking links or following tagged content, so that the reader ends up generating the "chapter" they need at that time out of a densely interlinked network of pages. There has been a gradual realization of the extent to which this novel format for recording innovations in theory and practice has itself shaped the development and even some of the content of our thinking, and we are hugely grateful to the lively and generous community of open-source programmers gathered around the TiddlyWiki project (http://tiddlywiki.com/), without whom this fruitful collaboration would have been quite impossible. We describe more about our online manual(s) in Chapter 7. Turning our hyperlinked content into a story with a beginning, middle, and end has been a challenge, and we have often wished for the paper-based equivalent of the hyperlink or tag that would open a theoretical explanation or a practice description that is used in numerous different places and ways. As a result, the reader will find a certain amount of retelling (we will avoid calling it repetition, because in the retelling there may be additional nuances that can be added in different contexts, and the possibility that this will help with learning) and references to other chapters where an idea is explained in more depth. Some readers may find that they are happy to jump about within the book, but we have written it to be read as a single narrative, for those who prefer to know how many more pages they have to go until the end.

What this book covers

We expect that different chapters will be of greater or lesser interest to different readers, and here we describe the simple bones of the book's structure. In Chapter 1 we start with an overview of what we see as the problems that face workers in the field, and conclude with an overview of AMBIT's proposed solutions. If you do not recognize the problems that we describe here, this book may not be for you. Next, some may be tempted to skip the chapter on our core theory, mentalizing (Chapter 2), and jump straight into the coverage of work with clients (Chapters 3 and 4) to get to the "meat." Others may consider avoiding the chapters that follow (Chapters 5, 6, and 7) on the broader structure that AMBIT emphasizes to support this face-to-face work ("Working with your team," "Working with your networks," and "Learning at work," respectively). Of course, we believe that the chapters on face-to-face work (Chapters 3 and 4) are interesting and useful in their own right, but we hope that readers will persevere first with the theory in Chapter 2, while recognizing that it is the most explicitly "academic" in tone and may thus be seen as the most difficult to read—but the whole book is really about putting these ideas to work in practical ways. Though it is a terrible idea to talk one's own book down in the preface, we also suspect that experienced practitioners may find that Chapters 3 and 4 are the least novel in one sense—after all, working with clients is what they do every day—so we strongly encourage readers to read on and consider the whole. AMBIT places enormous stress on the need to balance face-to-face work with balanced attention to the three other "quadrants" presented in Chapters 5, 6, and 7, which collectively make up the AMBIT "wheel" (introduced in Chapter 1) and without which we suggest the work is not only likely to be faltering or risky, but above all, perhaps rather similar to current practice.

After the chapters covering the core features of AMBIT, there follow two chapters that are, in ways, the most important ones in the book, as they represent accounts from users in the field. In the first of these (Chapter 8), a young person and his keyworker reflect on the client's perspective. We are incredibly grateful for the generosity that this extraordinarily frank and articulate young man has gifted us through his time and thoughtfulness. In Chapter 9 there is a collection of short field reports from a selection of teams working under the influence of AMBIT. Chapter 10 is more directed at commissioners and those with an interest in developing services that are fit for purpose, and attempts to find a balance between challenge and aspiration.

Finally, Chapter 11 offers some concluding reflections along with a brief description of the project's experience (and privilege) of working with a very large variety of teams, mainly in the UK but spanning the globe, developing a range of different ways to disseminate learning and, in a reciprocal exchange, collecting the ground-level feedback that continues to shape and enrich the model.

What's in a name? A note on terminology

AMBIT is designed to be a flexible platform that recognizes the wide variation in teams that work under the influence of its principled stance and core practices with heterogeneous client groups. We are aware that, although AMBIT was initially developed in response to an adolescent population, it is now being applied to populations that are both older and younger than this original client group. For this book we have therefore made the decision to refer mainly to "clients" rather than "young people," although we are aware that many of our examples are drawn from our core "constituency" of adolescents. We are also aware of the fact that, for some people, being referred to as a "client" is just as aversive as being referred to as a "young person" or a "patient." Our choice of terminology is a compromise, and we recommend that workers in the field talk to individual clients about how they would like to be addressed.

We have also taken this opportunity to change the name of this intervention. We are sticking with AMBIT, but for some time have preferred to use this as the word, rather than to speak of the original "adolescent mentalization-based integrative treatment," precisely because this approach is increasingly being adapted for use in non-adolescent populations. Recognizing that adaptation lies close to the heart of AMBIT, we acknowledge that if it stands for anything, then *adaptive* mentalization-based integrative treatment is a truer description.

We also resist too concrete a definition of the precise pathways and mechanisms by which new clients are helped. Some workers and clients object to the use of terminology such as "treatment" or "therapy," which can be seen as pathologizing. Although there are certainly occasional references to "treatment" or "therapy" in this book, in the context of our client group we agree that while "treatment" evokes the notion that this work is about the way we treat the young people in our care, a better way of referring to the work is simply as "help" or a "relationship of help." Youth workers who are reaching out to excluded young people through youth activities or street-level meetings will inevitably engage and take on new clients in very different ways, and with very different offers, compared with an intensive specialist mental health outreach service targeting specific young people who have been referred by other professionals concerned about their mental health. Examples of both such services co-exist in the AMBIT community of practice.

References

Bearman, S. K., Ugueto, A., Alleyne, A., & Weisz, J. R. (2010). Adapting CBT for depression to fit diverse youths and contexts: Applying the deployment-focused model of treatment development and testing. In: J. R. Weisz, & A. E. Kazdin (eds.), *Evidence-Based Psychotherapies for Children and Adolescents*, 2nd edn, pp. 466–81. New York, NY: Guilford Press.

Chorpita, B. F., Daleiden, E. L., & Weisz, J. R. (2005). Identifying and selecting the common elements of evidence based interventions: A distillation and matching model. *Mental Health Services Research* 7: 5–20. doi: 10.1007/s11020-005-1962-6

Lewin, K. (1951). *Field Theory in Social Science: Selected theoretical papers* (New York, NY: Harper & Row).

Weisz, J. R., Jensen-Doss, A., & Hawley, K. M. (2006). Evidence-based youth psychotherapies versus usual clinical care: A meta-analysis of direct comparisons. *American Psychologist* 61: 671–89. doi: 10.1037/0003-066X.61.7.671

Contents

1 Setting the scene *1*

2 How the engine works: Trust and making sense of each other and ourselves *42*

3 Active Planning: Mapping the territory and navigational skills for AMBIT-influenced work *67*

4 Working with your client *123*

5 Working with your team *170*

6 Working with your networks *210*

7 Learning at work: Toward a learning stance in teams *263*

8 "It was somebody I could trust": A descriptive case study of one young man's experience with an AMBIT-influenced team *299*

9 There is no such thing as a standard AMBIT team *327*

10 Adopting the AMBIT approach to changing wider systems of help *351*

11 Future ambitions for the AMBIT project *374*

Index *393*

Chapter 1
Setting the scene

Introduction: What is AMBIT, and what is it for?

This chapter lays out the authors' basic argument. Working with the kinds of human suffering and complications that AMBIT (adaptive mentalization-based integrative treatment) is designed to help with is, we argue, a better yardstick for complex, difficult work than the proverbial "rocket science". First, we plot out the complicated and fraught background of reorganizations and shifting priorities, alongside changing needs and resources, that provide the backdrop for workers in this field. Then we offer a series of four extended case studies that draw out some of the gnarliest problems encountered by practitioners involved in such work. On the one hand, if these scenarios are not recognized by readers, then we will have saved them the bother of reading further. On the other hand, if they do speak to their own condition as workers, we hope the AMBIT "diagnosis" that follows will be of interest and will make sense.

Next, we lay out in the broadest terms the solutions that AMBIT tries to offer. We introduce the overarching structure of AMBIT, summarized in diagrammatic form in the "AMBIT wheel," which suggests four key areas of activity and eight elements of a principled stance for workers. At its center—the load-bearing axle, as it were—is the core theory that underpins AMBIT: mentalizing. AMBIT is in many ways a systematic approach to applying this theory across the fullest range of practices required for this work, extending beyond simply what happens in the private space between worker and client.

In subsequent chapters we will explore in greater detail the constituent parts of AMBIT, starting with a fuller explanation of mentalizing in Chapter 2. As much of AMBIT concerns placing things in context, though, this chapter exists to provide a first pass over the whole.

A new kind of rocket science

For a long time rocket scientists have grabbed all the glory, and we mean to change this. "Rocket science" has become the yardstick for describing mind-blowingly complicated, risky, clever, creative, and daring work. However, in many ways rocket scientists have it quite easy. They do not work in the circumstances in which frontline mental health workers have to operate: the resource constraints; the levels of uncertainty and of unevidenced certainty we must confront and keep our balance between; the opportunities not just for spectacular disasters, but for slow-motion crashes that take decades to work their way through; and the sheer number of lives at stake. These all create an unstable and precarious backdrop to everything we do. To this we can add the many different ingredients that "we"—the workers in this field—are made up of: our different professional trainings, remits, and commissioned priorities. Add to this the divergent (and, all too often, unhelpfully tribal and competitive) theoretical models for making sense of the problems we tackle (genetic, neuroscientific, cognitive, behavioral, psychodynamic, social-ecological, systemic, educational, political …) and we begin to look quite good compared with the whizz-bangs of rocket science. We haven't even added to this mix the public image of services, the corrosive influence of stigma, and the twists and turns of political leadership that set the context for our heroic work.

What follows is a description largely based on experience in the UK, but our international collaborators, colleagues, and friends have not substantially contradicted this picture.

The state of services

The current state of children's services brings constant negative publicity: an unrelenting tale of crises, scandals, and public and media outcry. Services are endlessly being transformed, recommissioned, or cut. Some workers have been "transformed" so often it comes as a shock that they remain familiar to themselves. News headlines decrying the state of services are, often quite rightly, commonplace: "Alarm over children's mental health services" (*The Times*, 7 January 2016); "A&Es hit by children's mental health crisis" (*The Guardian*, December 26, 2015); "One in five mentally ill children refused help" (*The Mirror*, October 12, 2015); "A third of mental health trusts in England who replied to *ITN News* said they had no inpatient beds available for children in a 48-hour period" (*ITN News*, February 8, 2016).

Meanwhile, there is a sense of ever-growing need. Teachers, for example, are experiencing unprecedented levels of pressure in dealing with rising rates of mental health difficulties among their pupils, with three children in every classroom reported to have a diagnosable mental health disorder. The recently conducted Adult Psychiatric Morbidity Survey in England (McManus et al., 2016) found that one in four (25.7%) young women and one in ten (9.7%) young men aged between 16 and 24 years reported having self-harmed at some point.

The government responds; working parties are set up, and inquiries and select committees gather. In 2004, the UK's Department of Health published *The Mental Health and Psychological Well-being of Children and Young People* (Department of Health, 2004) as part of the *National Service Framework for Children, Young People and Maternity Services*. The vision set out in this report stated: the importance of early intervention for children and young people with mental health disorders; the importance of meeting the needs of children and families with complex needs; and that "all children, young people and families have access to mental health care based upon the best available evidence and provided by staff with an appropriate range of skills and competencies." Its standard was that "all children and young people, from birth to their eighteenth birthday, who have mental health problems and disorders have access to timely, integrated, high quality, multi-disciplinary mental health services to ensure effective assessment, treatment and support, for them and their families." This was part of the "Every Child Matters" program of the then government, which sought to set out the core framework for the complete reform of children's services in the UK. However, after the change in government in 2010, this model was superseded by a different approach, with a renewed interest in supporting localism and parental choice.

In 2008, the National CAMHS (Child and Adolescent Mental Health Services) Review found that, despite significant progress having been made since the 2004 report, "improvements in mental health and psychological well-being are still not as comprehensive, as consistent or as good as they could be" (National CAMHS Review, 2008). The review, again convincingly, presented the case for the need for more joined-up working across children's services to provide integrated child and family support for mental health, with specialist services being accessible across the country, readily available, and based on the best evidence. It recommended that young people approaching the age of 18 years should be better prepared for and supported across their transition to adult services.

In February 2011, the UK Government published another key report: *No Health Without Mental Health: A cross-Government mental health outcomes strategy for people of all ages* (Department of Health, 2011). This report emphasized the value of early mental health intervention, particularly for vulnerable children and young people, and listed "the early years, children, young people and families" as one of the critical priorities for the role of government. Following on from this, in 2012 the government established a Children and Young People's Health Outcomes Strategy. As part of this, a Children and Young People's Health Outcomes Forum was set up, and included a mental health subgroup. The strategy set out six objectives: that more children and young people will have good mental health; that those with mental health problems will have better recovery rates, positive experiences of care, and improved joined-up physical and mental health care; and that fewer children and young people will suffer avoidable harm and also stigma and discrimination (Children and Young People's Health Outcomes Forum, 2012). In 2013, the government responded to this forum by signing a pledge, *Better Health Outcomes for Children and Young People*, committing to do everything it could to improve the health of children and young people, improve services from pregnancy to adolescence and beyond, and reduce avoidable deaths. The pledge stated: "Children and young people will be at the heart of decision-making, with the health outcomes that matter most taking priority" (Department of Health, 2013). A new Children and Young People's Health Outcomes Board was also established, led by the Chief Medical Officer.

In 2014, the Health Select Committee held an inquiry into the state of CAMHS, and in September of that year the Children and Young People's Mental Health Taskforce was set up. In 2015, this group published the report *Future in Mind: Promoting, Protecting and Improving Children and Young People's Mental Health and Wellbeing* (Department of Health, & NHS England, 2015). This again highlighted the fact that children and young people were still, far too often, not receiving help for diagnosable mental health conditions (less than 25–35% of this group accessed help). Waiting times were increasing, and lack of leadership across agencies meant that too many children and young people were still slipping through the net. Highly complex commissioning arrangements were adding to problems of accountability and leadership. Sometimes different teams in the same local network found themselves rivals in local tendering processes while simultaneously trying to collaborate in a young person's care. Access to out-of-hours and crisis care was highlighted as a particular problem, with some parts of the UK having no place of safety for under-18s recorded by the Care Quality Commission. Highly vulnerable groups were particularly likely to find it difficult to access services. The report set out ten aspirations that the government wished to see made a reality in relation to children and young people by 2020, including: improved public awareness; availability of timely access to clinically effective mental health interventions across the country; a system based around the needs of children and young people and their families, rather than based on tiers of need; the use of evidence-based treatments; more visible and accessible mental health support; improved access to crisis care; improved access to parenting interventions to support early care and development; a "better offer" for the most vulnerable children and young people; improved accountability and transparency in the system; and more effective training of mental health professionals in child development and mental health. Delivering these national changes will partly be effected locally through the development and agreement of Transformation Plans for Children and Young People's Mental Health and Wellbeing, which will mostly be drawn up by Clinical Commissioning Groups, in association with local partners. These plans will articulate what is to be made locally available, in line with national aspirations.

All this policy work—the reports, inquiries, and hearings—points to both our awareness that child and adolescent mental health is inadequately supported, and an admirable desire to change this situation. But for professionals working in the field, it is easy to feel that, after all this reporting and inquiring, the situation at ground level remains largely unchanged: child and adolescent mental health problems are woefully undiagnosed, undertreated, and undercatered for. Service provision is inadequate, and the services that are provided are too often of disappointing quality—not joined-up, with too many children and young people who are in need of help remaining out of reach, and too many cries for help going unheard. In particular, the most vulnerable children, with the most complex difficulties, are still far too unlikely to have their needs met.

This description has focused mainly on mental health, but we are confident that readers working in services for young offenders; for educational inclusion; for exploited, abused, neglected, or looked-after children and young people; or for young adults with these difficulties in their pasts requiring adult services will recognize the story. Versions of AMBIT have been developed with workers in all of these fields, who know that very often they are working for the self-same clients.

And so, while we do not wish to appear in any way disrespectful toward rocket scientists, we would suggest that the kind of work this book describes involves a level of challenge that would justify it in usurping rocket science as a byword for byzantine complexity and heroic struggle. So, the purposes of this book are really twofold: first, to use the AMBIT approach to make sense of the maze of complexities that opens up before workers in many settings when it comes to the field of mental health in the midst of multiple other social, educational, and legal problems; and second, to explain how the AMBIT approach can set out ways of tackling this work that are more effective, creative, and secure in this highly demanding environment.

By way of introduction, in this chapter we will lay out a general "AMBIT diagnosis" of the kinds of problems that beset work with hard-to-reach children, adolescents, and young adults, and then set out a tentative "AMBIT solution"—ways of working to overcome the difficulties that have undermined attempts to create a system capable of providing the level of care that the many highly motivated and able professionals working within it would dearly love to be able to provide.

The AMBIT diagnosis

Here, we focus on child and adolescent mental health, as these were the roots for AMBIT, but we firmly believe that the same issues are applicable across other age groups. First, the proposition that the problems facing child and adolescent mental health are related to the provision of funding is one with which we wholeheartedly agree. In January 2015, official figures for the UK revealed there had been a 6% cut in real terms (amounting to nearly £50 million) since 2010. More money is needed in the system.

But this is not the only issue; more money brings new initiatives, and new initiatives risk further complicating a system already overburdened with initiatives. The problem is not so much a lack of initiatives but a lack of connection between them. Within most services as they currently operate "at ground level," resources are currently directed toward solving individual problems. However, each professional in each service recognizes that almost none of the problems they are responding to has a single cause. In most situations, workers want to link to other systems, but the infrastructure to create links, or the culture to support them, is often absent. This is, in most cases, the result not of a lack of motivation, but of the challenges of creating such an infrastructure and sustaining such a culture—which are substantial. A challenge for the future (let's imagine a brighter future!) might be: "How would we spend the money, when it flows again, in a way that doesn't generate a new frenzy of empire- or silo-building?"

We now introduce a series of four case studies as examples that encapsulate the kind of difficulties encountered in work scenarios, as revealed by an AMBIT diagnosis. These case studies are composites, based on conversations we have had with more than 1,500 workers who we have trained, in approximately 200 teams—mostly in the UK, but increasingly worldwide. There are of course other difficulties, but these are the four common themes that have "stood the test of time" as the AMBIT approach to this work has been developed.

1. Network complexity

To address the many interacting roots of their problems, the young people encountered in AMBIT work almost inevitably require—and frequently attract—complicated networks of multi-agency and multi-professional efforts to provide help. The multi-professional approach has many strengths, but it also brings its own set of very particular difficulties. We will argue that the natural resting state of such networks is to be "dis-integrated". This is in contrast to the idealized state of coordinated, integrated, or joined-up working that almost every official report or inquiry ever written has offered as the proposed or expected ideal (from which state of grace it is easy to feel we workers in the field have somehow fallen).

Amir

Amir is 14 years old. He is the youngest of six children whose parents emigrated from Bangladesh 20 years ago, and who have worked in the clothing trade since. There are concerns about Amir's proneness to violence, his determined truanting from school, his use of a range of substances, and his increasing identification with a local gang, for whom he is suspected to be working as a "runner," delivering drugs across the local neighborhood.

Amir's mother died two years ago in a road traffic accident, when she was being driven by his eldest brother, Hamid. The other driver involved in the crash also died. Hamid subsequently served an 18-month prison sentence after admitting he was intoxicated at the time of the accident. Following Hamid's release to a local hostel, the family home has been riven with conflict, with Amir and one other brother siding with Hamid against Amir's three sisters and his father, whose own depression has meant that he has been unable to work since his wife's death. Hamid is suspected of having links to the same local gang in which Amir is thought to be involved. Their father has repeatedly stated that he has disowned Hamid, and threatens to do the same to Amir.

A wide variety of agencies and workers are involved, either nominally or actively, in Amir's case: the local Youth Offending Team, which has allocated Amir to a project specially designed to target young people at risk of offending and who are suspected of having gang connections; the local educational welfare service, which has been engaged in trying to reconnect Amir to his local school and to reduce his number of unauthorized absences; and the local CAMHS, which has offered parenting sessions for Amir's father and family therapy, and previously provided some individual work with Amir, centered on helping him to manage the after-effects of his traumatic bereavement. The local children's social services have registered Amir and two of his sisters as "children in need" whose emotional and developmental needs are at risk of not being met without additional support for the family. They have provided a family support worker to support the day-to-day administration of family life, focusing on practical issues such as budgeting and health and hygiene at home. The father has for many years been involved with the local mosque; the imam there knows the family very well and is actively involved in informal attempts to mend the rifts between family members. A young people's substance use service has offered Amir several appointments, but has not yet persuaded him to make contact.

Amir's most frequent response to the workers in these agencies is to complain that he does not have time to see them all, and that anyway he "can't see the point" of their offers of help, as he is "coping fine" without them. He draws attention to the smallest perceived contradictions or frictions between agencies and workers, and occasionally uses these to defend, justify, or persuade others to overlook his non-engagement ("None of you agree, so why should I?"; "You said that meeting with those people wasn't very important, so I didn't go"). For example, he frequently answers requests to attend school from his Educational Welfare Officer or the Head of Year with somewhat triumphant declarations about the important appointments that he has to attend with other teams, which make it impossible for him to fulfil their requests (even though his attendance at such appointments is at best patchy). It is noted that Amir appears keenly aware of how frustrated school staff are about the number of other appointments that he is "required" to attend for other helping services, which tend to be scheduled in school hours; this is seen as only adding to the patchiness of his attendance at lessons.

Similarly, Amir is aware of tensions between his local imam and some of the statutory services involved in his care. Although Amir does not regularly attend his mosque and is not obedient to many of the practices it teaches, he frequently claims that his imam disapproves of social services and the Youth Offending Team on the basis of rather generalized reports of perceptions that they take an overly laissez-faire approach to youth behavior. Repeating such negative opinions in front of his father seems in turn to increase resistance in the wider family to adhering to plans made in these other parts of the network.

Even without Amir's involvement, there are times when different elements of the network appear to be pulling in different directions. At one point there was a rather intemperate exchange of e-mails between workers in CAMHS, social services, and the Youth Offending Team, following the non-attendance of a CAMHS worker at a planned multi-agency meeting. The CAMHS worker justified their non-attendance on the grounds that Amir and his family have made it clear that at present they are not willing to accept therapeutic interventions, and that there seemed to be some magical thinking in other parts of the multi-agency network about the way that therapy could solve this young person and his family's problems, which in their opinion were more social and legal. This message was perceived by the other parts of the network as unnecessarily blunt, and a misrepresentation of their own positions and of the problem they had actually complained about—that is, the lack of communication by the CAMHS worker about their planned non-attendance.

Amir represents a significant challenge in his own right for a worker or a team, but in our discussion here we focus on the intersecting professional, organizational, and personal relationships that together create the multi-agency network that has gathered around Amir and his family.

Numerous challenges arise in trying to bridge the tension between the need to access sufficient expertise to address the multiple different and interacting problems that Amir faces and the need to avoid overwhelming a young person whose confidence in forming working relationships with even one worker or team is likely to be low. Expecting him to make four, five, or even six relationships with representatives of different teams is a task that might be expected to tax even the most gregarious and socially confident individual.

Practitioners in different teams and from different professional disciplines have often spent years training in quite specific areas of learning and practice. The sociologically trained social worker may emphasize access to opportunities or divergence from social roles and responsibilities such as parenting; the biologically inclined psychiatrist may focus on the genetic heredity of behavioral traits or diagnostic vulnerabilities; the psychoanalyst may focus on the operation of emotional transferences or powerful defenses; the cognitive-behavioral therapist on the repetitive "negative attributional thoughts" by which experiences are labeled; the family therapist on the reciprocal effects of patterned interactions on different parts of the wider system; and so on. While in the details it is usually possible to "translate" explanations or interventions from separate theories into the language of others, this is not always the case; this calls to mind the (pleasingly transcultural) tale of the Tower of Babel, where collaborative industry was halted by the introduction of different tongues. More critically, the effect of adding multiple workers and treatment models—however well-intentioned each may be—risks inadvertently creating an experience of care for the young person or family that is actually aversive ("It's like being set upon by a flock of birds!").

In many cases, such multi-agency networks function effectively enough, but perhaps more often the work is delivered in more or less "dis-integrated" ways. We will expand further on what we mean by this in Chapter 6, but, for now, we mean that different teams or professionals may hold very different ideas about the nature of the "problem" or "challenge" they are addressing—either because they have gathered different understandings from Amir, or because they have different professional roles or remits to fulfil. A Youth Offending Team worker may see their primary role as reducing the risk of Amir escalating his offending and requiring incarceration, whereas the local imam may see his primary role as addressing the spiritual needs of Amir and his family, alongside supporting his hard-pressed community. The local psychiatrist may see their role as providing specialist assessment for Amir, identifying and treating severe psychiatric disorders such as depression, posttraumatic stress disorder, pathological bereavement, or substance use disorder, while the Educational Welfare Officer and the school's primary concern is to address Amir's poor school attendance. In some cases the fulfilment of one role may create specific problems for the fulfilment of others—for instance, Amir's school sees his attendance at other appointments during school hours as directly undermining of their key concern, which is to improve his attendance and reintegrate him into the prosocial setting of school.

Alternatively, teams or professionals may agree on the nature of the problem(s) but have divergent ideas about the most appropriate solutions (e.g. psychotherapy as opposed to medication, or school attendance versus reparative justice work).

Finally, teams may agree on the problem(s) and the most helpful solutions, but find themselves disagreeing about which person or team holds responsibility for delivering those solutions. For instance, there may be agreement across agencies that Amir would benefit from some education on the risks of substance use, but while the school and Youth Offending Team may want a worker from the specialist substance use service to deliver this, workers within that team may feel that this is something that a worker already well known to Amir could do just as well—or even better—given the existing trust they have earned, especially if they are given some support and specialist guidance. Meanwhile, Amir is not experiencing the kind of helping relationship that he would ideally have at this critical stage of his development.

Thus far, our experience of the teams we have trained suggests that cross-professional misunderstandings, frank disagreements, or overcrowded delivery systems such as those outlined in this case study occur frequently enough to justify targeted work and specific, focused disciplines and practices to identify and address such barriers, in order to minimize their potential for undermining progress or even causing harm.

2. Hard-to-reach young people and families

The next element of our AMBIT diagnosis is the problem of reaching young people who are, perhaps unhelpfully, regarded as "hard to reach." This phrase often carries judgmental implications, but while it is true that in many cases such young people *are* hard to reach, this is generally *for a reason*: their rejection of professional attempts to help them is often quite purposeful and deliberate, rather than simply occurring by accident, because of intrinsic cussedness, or because of some mutual misunderstanding or misinterpretation. Conversely, however, it may often result from the failure of services and workers to show an authentic understanding of a young person's dilemma, or to have practical strategies and resources to address the harsh realities that render such young people "hard to reach." It is certainly the case that there are often other members of the community (drug dealers, gang members, pimps) who, in contrast, find it relatively easy to reach such young people.

Dan

Dan is 15 years old. At the point of referral to this service there are concerns about recent self-injurious behavior (multiple shallow lacerations to his forearms) and statements that he has been making about wishing he were dead.

Dan has a long history of professional concern and attempts at intervention, dating back to when his parents first complained of his high levels of activity and aggressive impulsivity, at age 6. At that time his primary school was complaining that his behavior in class was disrupting other pupils, and he was already falling behind in basic literacy and numeracy. He was diagnosed with ADHD (attention deficit hyperactivity disorder); attempts to support his development with medication were hampered because of poor adherence to prescribing instructions, poor attendance at review meetings by his parents, and (unproven) suspicions that his medication may have been misused or illegally sold by his parents. Medication was finally abandoned as a strategy when Dan was age 10, and his parents stopped attending mental health services thereafter.

Neither of Dan's parents is currently in work. There are concerns that both parents are prone to binge drinking and both are long-term cannabis users. Dan's father has recently returned home from a short prison sentence for burglary. Both parents are known to have been raised partly in the care system during their own childhoods, and have been noted to have rather fixed ideas about the unhelpfulness of social services in general, relating this stance to their own very negative past experiences. There are four younger siblings in the family home, and social services have designated these children (but not Dan) as "children in need." However, the support on offer (a family support worker, access to a day nursery, parenting classes) is at best only partially effective, as both parents are prone to missing or refusing appointments and the younger children's attendance at nursery and primary school is unreliable.

Dan's own school attendance has been peppered with exclusions, mainly owing to his increasingly worrying levels of aggression, and he has been moved to different schools three times over the past five years. He is currently attending a school for children whose emotional and behavioral difficulties intrude upon their learning. Here he has made one or two positive links—with a teaching support worker (TSW) in the mechanical engineering workshop, whom he feels "has something to teach me," and with his course tutor, who "sort of gets me." However, in spite of these positives, he has begun to miss school more frequently, and when he is present, his comments about life being pointless and references to there being a way out are increasingly worrying staff. Many shallow lacerations on his forearms were first noticed in the workshop, but when these were pointed out (the TSW felt this had been done quite sensitively), Dan reacted furiously, shouting at the TSW while holding a hammer in his hand. This was perceived as physically threatening by the TSW, although Dan categorically denied any such intent, and said that once again he felt like he was being "fitted up" because the school wanted to exclude him.

Approached later that day by his tutor, Dan vigorously refused to see any other mental health professionals, exclaiming that he has seen enough of them already and that "they won't do anything useful anyway!" The school feels it has no option but to impose a temporary exclusion on Dan, in order to be consistent about the message that aggression (particularly in the workshops) is completely unacceptable. The school organizes to meet him later the same day to explain this, but at the appointed time they find he has already absconded. It later transpires that Dan left to spend time with an older group of young men who he has described as his "real family" and who are believed to be involved in a gang.

In Dan's case, although on the face of it there seem to be many good reasons for professionals to be appropriately concerned about him, his own reaction is to push those workers away or place himself beyond their reach. This is a common feature among young people for whom AMBIT would position itself as being an appropriate intervention. Dan's apparently contradictory response to what looks like a perfectly reasonable offer of help makes sense to him: in his eyes, the helpers won't do any good anyway, or worse, they may be conspiring to identify vulnerabilities and use them to justify excluding him from positive aspects of his life or to hurt him. Of course, in addition to these reasons there are likely to be many further factors, less immediately apparent to him or others, that also influence his behavior.

Dan's rejection of help likely mirrors the pattern of his parents' behavior over the years, and perhaps may even have partly been "taught" by them quite explicitly; he may have repeatedly heard warnings about the perils of getting involved with social workers, doctors, psychologists, the police, etc. A frequently noted feature of the young people for whom AMBIT is designed is the lack of supportive structures around them that could help or encourage them to attend appointments. We need to be careful to avoid over-simplistic and parent-blaming accounts: of course Dan's parents' own expectations about how agencies behave are based in part upon their own experiences, and in part upon the kinds of narratives—factual or mythological—that attach themselves to groups that are considered to have power, in every culture or sub-culture. Critical in this account, however, is the fact that Dan's rejection of help appears to be active and intentional; it is an expression of his *agency* in the world—his capacity to influence events—even if most benign observers might regard his stance as mistaken or self-defeating.

The active rejection of help is the issue we want to highlight in relation to our discussion of Dan's case (while of course accepting that there are many other elements to the story that are also important). We can wonder whether Dan's past experience of help has colored and influenced the internal "maps" that he holds, which shape his expectations of the people who claim to be "helpers" of one sort or another (these expectations are what the field of attachment would refer to as his *internal working models* of attachment). For instance, we can hypothesize that Dan's earliest childhood experiences of asking for help from his parents may have triggered unpredictable responses, depending, among other things, on whether or not his parents were intoxicated at the time of asking. For a young child, some parental responses may have been exasperating (being ignored, for instance), forcing him to learn to cope on his own and perhaps to cope by becoming quite scornful toward his own experiences of neediness. Instead of acknowledging his own needs, which would again confront him with his vulnerability, he might instead have learned to "tough it out." Alternatively, some of his parents' responses may have been quite terrifying to a young child—flaring rage in response to his fearful toddler screams, for instance. Such reactions, especially if they were reasonably frequent, might be expected to create a great deal of anxiety in a child, but perhaps also feelings of fury toward the helper—and also toward the help-seeking self. We will cover some of these emerging patterns of response in more detail in Chapter 4.

When their interactions are observed in great detail, most parents who are judged to be perfectly "good enough" (those who demonstrate secure attachments to their child) are actually found to "misread" their children's emotional needs a fairly high proportion of the time. Studies suggest that 70% of parent interactions "fail" in this way. However, in most of these cases the misreading is quite slight and is corrected—often in a matter of moments—when the parent realizes their mistake and makes amends (Tronick & Beeghly, 2011). The earliest relationships of many young people for whom AMBIT was designed may have been much more challenging, with such misreadings not only going uncorrected, but amounting to frank emotional abuse or neglect; not infrequently this may have been accompanied by physical or sexual abuse. Misreading or ignoring the child's mind entirely is likely to have been more common in these young people's past histories than most; their early lives may have been marked by very few moments where they had access to the kind of sensitive attunement that is one of the common features shared by parents with securely attached children.

So, the worker in this situation is faced with a paradox: the more they and Dan develop a relationship where help can be asked for and given, the more risk there is that precisely in these very intimate moments (there is little more intimate than the revealing of a wound), Dan's long-standing anxieties will be triggered. The closer the attachment bond between client and worker becomes, the more risk there is that with this intimacy intentions will be misread, tempers will fray, and unplanned things will happen—just as Dan predicted—confirming once again his inclination to steer clear of any adults who claim they are there to help him.

Even before getting to this point, though, there are many other pitfalls to negotiate. For instance, a client's initial, reflexive rejection of their worker's well-intentioned and carefully designed offers of assessment or practical help may be blunt: "You couldn't ever understand me!"; "I don't need that!"; or "That won't work!" (Experienced practitioners will know that these examples would, in reality, often be expressed in more colorful language.)

It is very easy for a worker to respond to such statements by restating or elaborating their own arguments: "Try me! I am really good at this work, you know! I have done a really thorough assessment, and look, it shows you *are* depressed! . . . But this is an *evidence-based* treatment!" From the young person's perspective, such a reaction from the worker may not really communicate an authentic understanding or commitment to their needs, or the worker's tenacity and seriousness of purpose in trying to help. Rather, the young person may experience this as yet more denial and dismissal of the reality of their world as they know it. By trying so hard to engage, the worker inadvertently risks offering more proof to the young person that "this worker standing before me [where perhaps many have stood before], he/she doesn't get me, either." The offer of engagement becomes an additional burden to shoulder, rather than the relief it is intended to be.

3. Working with worry makes for worrying work

In our next case study, that of Bryony, we show that working with clients who have multiple problems, who are enmeshed in multiple systems, and who frequently present with very significant risks to themselves or to others, quite properly and naturally makes the worker feel anxious at times. We are keen to emphasize that this should not cause professional shame, but instead deserves serious thought and planning.

Bryony

Bryony is a 17-year-old who is known to have been the victim of childhood sexual abuse at the hands of her stepfather at the age of 15. This man is currently serving a prison term for the offense, but Bryony's mother has consistently refused to believe her disclosures and has firmly sided with the stepfather. This has led to a catastrophic breakdown of the relationship between mother and daughter, with violence on both sides, so that an alternative placement was seen as the safest option for Bryony. Bryony is therefore voluntarily accommodated in a supported hostel, which is in an urban setting several hours' journey from the deeply rural location of the family home. Bryony initially struggled to settle into this new setting, and presented alternately as precociously sexualized in appearance and behavior, and as dangerously naive.

Past school reports describe a girl who was initially a diligent student but whose IQ was toward the lower end of the normal range, so that she had always struggled with academic studies, and was vulnerable in large-group settings. As she moved into puberty, there was a marked deterioration in her attendance record, and concerns were raised at school about what was seen as her increasingly sexually provocative dress and behavior. The school nurse had made gentle inquiries, offering advice on safer sex and contraception, but Bryony had repeatedly denied being involved in any physical relationships. Her sexualized behavior at this time was noted as one of the main reasons she was increasingly ostracized by her peer group at school. Her formal education ended with a very poor set of exam results, and it was only after she had left school that the revelations of sexual abuse finally came to light, when Bryony told a worker at the local youth club.

Bryony initially found the transition to living at the hostel very hard; she described feeling homesick and appeared totally overwhelmed and isolated. She regularly refused offers of counseling, saying that she just wanted to forget the past. Over the past six months, however, she had gradually become friendly with a group of somewhat older adults, mostly male, two of whom were known to hostel staff vaguely by reputation as substance users. Details about this group were hard to come by, however; they appeared to avoid any contact with staff in the hostel, and they would wait for Bryony outside rather than coming in to meet her at the reception, where staff would be present. Recently, Bryony had been excitedly showing off a new mobile phone to staff, proudly describing it as a present. It was noticed that she would respond to text messages she received on this phone by leaving the building at short notice, and without giving any details of where she was going. Occasionally, she would not return until the next day, and would be evasive when asked about where she had been. On two occasions she was seen to have bruising on her arms, but on being asked how this had happened she claimed to not remember how it happened and laughed it off.

Her keyworker decided to tackle suspicion that Bryony might be being groomed or sexually exploited head on, and explained her concerns. Bryony reacted to this approach by laughing, playfully accusing the worker of being jealous that she was having more fun than her, and reminding her that she is now above the age of consent. Asked about the bruises again, Bryony answered, "I don't know—when you're partying you can't remember everything that happens! Anyway, I don't want to talk about this anymore now—you're getting boring." The keyworker explained her worries for Bryony's safety in a bit more detail, as a prelude to inquiring further, but Bryony became irritable and walked off.

The keyworker discussed her concerns with colleagues in the hostel and with Bryony's social worker. Most agreed that the story was indeed worrying, but the message Bryony's keyworker got was that she probably needed to accept that professionals were quite powerless to do more than watch and wait at this stage, mainly because of Bryony's age; Bryony was seen as making choices rather than being forced to do anything. One colleague was rather more critical, suggesting that the keyworker herself might be being a little naive in refusing to accept that "the world just works like this—in every city, everywhere."

Bryony's keyworker felt increasingly as though she was the only person in the network who was really worried, who really grasped Bryony's extreme vulnerability in relation to her naivety and low IQ, and her desperate need to feel loved, as well as the immediate risk of sexual violence, being drawn further toward prostitution or entrenched substance use, or being trafficked.

Young people appropriate for AMBIT-influenced work will generally present with risks to the self or others—for example, risks of suicide, self-injury, vulnerability to exploitation or abuse, physical and psychological risks associated with substance use, or dangerous patterns of eating. These risks are not simple to manage even when other positive factors are in place. Workers are frequently placed in the position of having to balance competing risks and select the least harmful of a range of options that all carry some risk. There may be severe constraints on the resources available to make possible a really robust or categorical shift in circumstances; for instance, thresholds for taking a child into care (especially at the upper age limits) may be very high. Hospitalizing a young person for a mental health problem is often achieved only in the face of immediate threat to life, and while this may provide a short-term solution, many inpatient stays are short, allowing only momentary respite for local services.

Potential solutions frequently carry risks themselves. Accommodating a young person in a children's home or psychiatric unit may be a life-saving intervention, but it may also place a vulnerable young person in a social setting where distress, disturbance, and pathological responses to these threats are the norm, where access to unhelpful influences is increased, and where access to protective existing relationships is reduced. Many hostels and children's homes are geographically distant from the young person's home, and taking a child into the professional care system risks reducing the confidence of existing family care networks, who may increasingly see the situation as one requiring professional skills that they do not possess.

Workers may be drawn to this kind of employment for many reasons—personal and reparative, academic, economic, and ethical, to name but a handful. It is (mercifully) very rare that they are *not* motivated by a desire to be helpful and to make a positive difference to the lives of the young people they care for. (Such horrifying possibilities do exist, of course, and are countered mainly by attention to supervisory structures—examples of which are covered in Chapter 5.) A far more common problem is that well-intentioned workers become burned out after seeing up close the desperate trajectories of their young clients, dealing with risks they feel powerless to mitigate, or worse, discovering that their interventions may occasionally and inadvertently cause harm.

In such stressful circumstances, people react in many different ways. Some "up-regulate" their tolerance of risk, becoming blunted to concerns and perhaps appearing hardened or even indifferent to suffering (while often declaring that their stance is based on street-level experience and sometimes expressing a kind of machismo and scorn for naive "do-gooders"). Others prevaricate when action is required, musing at length about potential explanatory theories, as if they could think the young person into safety. Others fall prey to anxiety, becoming forgetful, missing appointments, requiring sick leave, or in other ways becoming less able to provide consistency and rigor in what they offer to their clients. Just as the word "worry" carries a double meaning, referring both to anxious concern and also to something more aggressive (as Tom Main pointed out in his seminal paper "The ailment" (Main, 1957), the dog "worries" a bone), there is a risk that workers subjected to such worry may find justifications for increasingly assertive, or even aggressive, interventions. In part this may be to assuage their own anxiety, allowing them to feel that they are doing everything they can; it may also in part be a punitive response to the bruising nature of such worry.

In later chapters we will examine these responses in more depth, particularly the corrosive influence that anxiety has upon the worker's capacity to think clearly (and therefore safely) about their clients and their own needs.

4. Old dogs, new tricks: Learning at work is hard

The final component of our "AMBIT diagnosis" is the problem of learning and changing at work. In particular, we focus on the importance of "team learning," by which we mean the creation of a culture of open-eyed curiosity that leads to team behaviors that are adapted in step with the evidence—from local experiences or from the work of the wider scientific community. This is especially relevant when it comes to that most inevitable feature of all human interactive endeavor: errors. Acknowledging and learning from errors is especially hard, but of the greatest value. This ideal is very difficult to achieve, not least because of the stresses that are intrinsic to this work, but also because of the overwhelming organizational and economic pressures that bear down on the teams involved.

The Catch-up Crew and Ian

The "Catch-up Crew" was formed 18 months ago with a specific remit to reach out to young people at risk of hospitalization or other statutory accommodation, engaging them and applying a range of home- and/or school-based interventions to stabilize their situation and avoid such outcomes. It serves a large coastal town and the surrounding (rural) area, where there are especially high rates of youth unemployment. The team is led by the local mental health services, alongside therapists and a part-time psychiatrist, and also includes a number of social workers, who, along with three youth workers, are seconded from the local authority.

There has been low-level friction with other pre-existing services since the team was originally formed. The team has been accused of duplicating work already commissioned from these services, as well as attempting to recruit some of the most enthusiastic workers away from their long-standing clinic-based teams. These original teams subsequently felt depleted and somewhat resentful toward this "favored new child" in the "family" of local services. There have been ongoing low-level disputes about the threshold criteria for engaging the Catch-up Crew team in a case ever since. A common theme in informal conversations among workers outside the team is the perceived "preciousness" of the Catch-up Crew team; they are seen as rejecting referrals that are judged to be "not hard enough to reach" and yet also rejecting referrals that are "too high risk," leaving the existing clinic-based services with a sense that they are expected to "pick up all the leftovers." For their part, the Catch-up Crew team feel badly misunderstood by the mainstream services, who they see as being stuck in their ways and so comfortable and secure in their offices that they underestimate the exposure, isolation, and intensity that the Catch-up Crew workers have to deal with when they deliver their outreach interventions.

A new referral brings these frictions to the surface. Ian is a 16-year-old living in long-term foster care after past neglect. His threats to commit suicide and self-injurious behavior (causing multiple shallow lacerations) have pushed his foster carers to the limit and now threaten the security of his placement. Ian's mental health care has previously been provided by a long-established outpatient clinic, but the worker there (who has known Ian for several years) is now retiring, and the team assessing Ian's escalating threats are highly conscious of this impending loss. However, pressed in other directions by several new crises in their existing caseload, the Catch-up Crew team initially reject the referral of Ian without assessing him. They do so on the grounds that nothing substantive is reported to have changed in Ian's mental state; he is evidently already engaged with his existing team, and he has demonstrated over the course of two years that he can attend outpatient appointments reliably without needing outreach interventions. This triggers an angry response from the outpatient clinic workers, who feel that their professional judgment (that the situation has deteriorated, and that more assertive outreach is the most appropriate way to contain the risk) has been challenged. Two days later, Ian is briefly admitted to hospital following a small paracetamol overdose.

At their next team meeting, the Catch-up Crew agree among themselves that it was probably an error to have rejected this referral without first assessing Ian. They engage in animated debate about the qualities of an ideal referral letter; an observer might have described them as becoming "heated" about the extent to which the referral letter for Ian was judged to fall short of these ideals. They agree that face-to-face contact will be arranged to apologize to the outpatient clinic team for their somewhat too-hasty rejection, and that an urgent assessment of Ian is now warranted.

That meeting goes some way to repairing relationships between the teams, and the work proceeds. However, a more powerful "mythology" about the outpatient clinic and its poor-quality referral letters seems to have taken root in the Catch-up Crew. Three months later, a similar scenario plays out after another referral from the outpatient clinic team is rejected—chiefly on the grounds (it seems to the disgruntled referrer) that her letter was simply written in the wrong format. On this occasion a formal complaint is issued, leading to a lengthy and painful process that culminates in the generation of some written protocols; these support shared decision-making about referrals between the two teams, and lay out clear processes for these in the future. Over the next year there is a slow thawing of relations between the teams.

As our clients often demonstrate to us, directly or indirectly, it is very difficult to stimulate the right state of mind—trusting, attentive, and curious—for genuine new learning in circumstances of high stress, conflict, and anxiety. Exactly the same constraints apply to teams engaged in this kind of work. The Catch-up Crew was a new team striving to clarify its remit. In addition, it had to overcome the misgivings of neighboring teams, as well as manage the risks, demands, and frustrations that their work itself carries. It is unsurprising that in this context the team appears to have struggled to notice and fully own up to its own errors, and still less to find the time or space to examine these errors and create improvements in a timely way.

The Catch-up Crew team and its more established clinic-based colleagues were both subject to one of the hazards of working in a multi-agency context— the subtle negative mythologies about neighboring teams that commonly build up across such networks. These may be fed by rivalries, fear, or conflicting briefs and beliefs, as well as the subtle influence of biased negative feedback to which all members of networks are subject. Every referral to one part of a multi-agency network implies, at some level, a "failure" on the part of another to contain the problem; without knowing the number of cases that are managed expertly and effectively by a referring team, it is easy for a worker or a whole team receiving these referrals to confirm their "mythology" that the referring service is failing. Aside from this, young people, and their adult counterparts, may consciously or unconsciously try to evoke additional and more strenuous efforts on the part of a new worker (or team) by listing the shortcomings of a previous service that has attempted to help them. The invitation to improve upon the (reportedly shoddy) work of another service or worker is hard to resist, and it means that workers may be more often exposed to negative reports of other people's work than to positive ones.

The benefit of a strong mythology is that it can help to bind a team, identifying "us" more closely, but only in opposition to "them." As this case study shows, this carries significant risks—mythologies do not carry the same clarity as validated facts, and new learning under such influences is made even more difficult. In this example, the Catch-up Crew team were initially quite unable to reflect upon the position that they were taking in relation to other parts of the wider system.

In the long run, a process was imposed (the complaints procedure) that appears to have generated learning—a clarification of the risks involved in the "cross-border trade" of a new referral, and the development of a series of steps designed to mitigate the most likely failures or misunderstandings in the tricky task of managing referrals.

The Catch-up Crew team was originally established to work in new and different ways in the hope of reaching a group of troubled, worrying (and expensive to reach) young people, and intervening earlier and more effectively with them. In spite of a range of approaches that have some support from well-conducted trials (e.g. Fonagy et al., 2013; Rigter et al., 2013; Liddle et al., 2009; Feigenbaum, 2007; Linehan et al., 2006), this kind of work is still largely conducted in uncharted waters, especially in the uniquely local details and protocols of, for instance, how to transfer a case. Errors are inevitable; learning from these, and combining this learning with lessons from the global research community as evidence creeps forwards, is a difficult—but, we argue, absolutely essential—component of good practice.

Toward a solution?

By the end of this section, the intention is that you will have a basic picture of the AMBIT "vehicle" and some ideas about how to start driving it. As with learning to drive a car, the idea that it might all be taught via a book is absurd, but some basic understandings (where the brake pedal is, how to get the car into gear, locating the indicators and knowing what they are for) are worth grasping. Where and how you drive or modify your car will inevitably be dependent on your context—for example, in some countries people drive on the right-hand side of the road. We discuss this kind of local adaptation in Chapter 7.

Up to this point we have described why working with people with complex needs—particularly with young populations who are less than convinced that professional help is ever helpful, and whose behaviors can make our hair stand on end—is harder than rocket science. Via our case studies, we have highlighted four aspects of the work that make things particularly hard: network disintegration, the challenge of reaching "hard-to-reach" clients, the high levels of worry associated with many cases, and the difficulty of team learning in such circumstances. Now we must sketch the main features of the AMBIT "solution" that has been evolving over the past decade or more through the collaboration of thinkers, academics, managers, and street-level workers to help support this work.

In Chapter 2 we will describe how the "engine" that drives AMBIT works; we define that engine as a particular type of mental activity known as *mentalizing*. Supported by the crowning achievement of human evolution—a part of the brain called the prefrontal cortex—mentalizing takes place in our minds, giving us the capacity to make some sense of each other's behavior, and through that understanding, to repair, reposition, or rebalance our own self in relation to others and the wider world. Mentalizing does not arise through self-reflection alone, but is learned in relationships, and is always much easier to kick-start when one's mind is in contact with another mind—particularly if the relationship with that other mind is a trusting one.

The AMBIT approach seeks to influence teams in order to improve their outcomes in work with hard-to-reach clients who have complicated life problems, including significant mental health difficulties. AMBIT actively avoids positioning itself as just another branded form of therapy, but positions itself more as a systematic approach to improvement that many (often very different) services working in this field can use. It does include a lot of ideas and evidence about effective ways of working directly with clients, but this is just a segment (a quarter of what is involved; see "The AMBIT wheel," presented in the next section of this chapter). AMBIT proposes that outcomes in a team will be improved by nurturing the mentalizing capacity of both clients and workers, and by applying this approach even more widely across the formal and informal networks involved. All of this rests upon developing an explicit culture of learning (and remembering) among the members of the team.

This is a major challenge. The chaotic nature of clients' difficulties, their poorly adaptive help-seeking styles, and the depleted or embattled settings in which many teams must work readily disrupt this process. There is no easy formula for overcoming these difficulties. Simply prescribing a fixed set of protocols and procedures by which a team should operate risks delivering "non-contingent care" (a kind of "concrete" care that does not speak to the situation in which the client or family finds themselves, let alone the worker). Instead, AMBIT provides a set of principles, based on evidence and accumulated experience from other AMBIT-influenced services, backed up by a variety of practices; together, these help workers in a team to sustain a mentalizing stance in their work. The development of these principles has been substantially user-led insofar as they have been developed through multiple "deployment-focused" field trials (Weisz & Gray, 2008), training many teams engaged in this work around the UK and across the world, and iteratively adapting the model in response to learning from these real-world settings. Another way of putting this is that AMBIT simply tries to describe, make sense of, and signpost what it is that effective, lively, and engaged teams are doing that works—and to help push this learning forwards as the world, its young people, and their challenges continue to change.

The next section aims to give the reader an understanding of how the different parts of the AMBIT approach link together. This is like a map of what will follow in the rest of the book. Do not be concerned if there are parts that you feel you have only a partial understanding of at this stage; further explanation will be provided later. Think of it as a photograph where you are beginning to recognize the main features, although if you look closely some of the detail remains a little blurred.

AMBIT is really about taking a systematic approach to using this "engine" known as mentalizing, and applying it in four different directions:

- **Working with your client**, which is where most "therapies" focus their attention;
- **Working with your team**, which is stressed as being equally important for AMBIT; as is
- **Working with your networks**, which are the wider informal, multi-agency, and multi-professional networks that tend to gather around these risky clients;
- **Learning at work**, which supports the whole endeavor—the never-ending task of making sense of why in this team we do things in *this* particular way, and not *that* way.

In addition to these four directions, there is a **principled stance** formed from eight separate elements, which are paired because achieving success in one half of each pair can easily often involve losing hold of the other half. AMBIT repeatedly stresses that being out of balance is common—perhaps even the norm—in this work, and, rather than this warranting professional shame and embarrassment, what is required is a structure to help workers to continue correcting their balance.

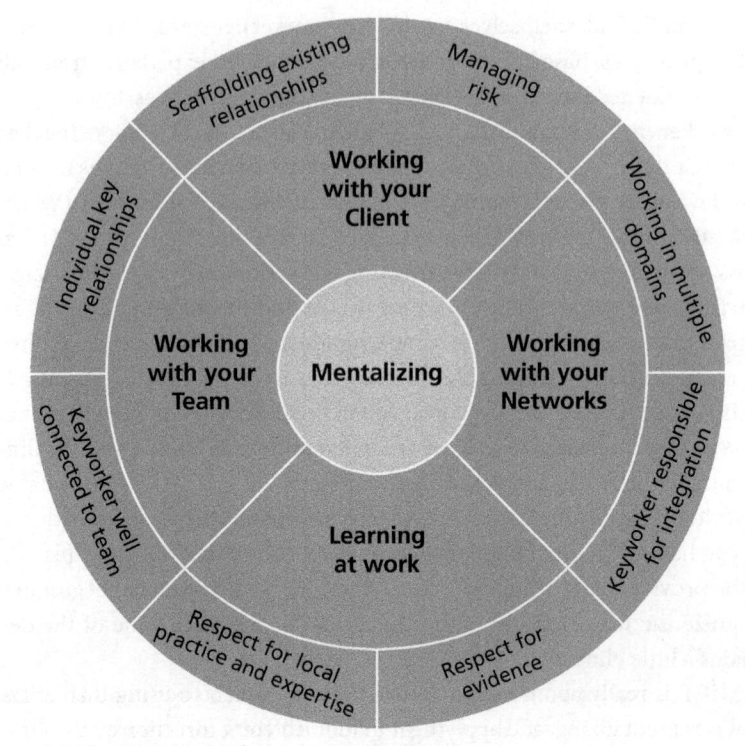

Figure 1.1 The AMBIT wheel.

The AMBIT wheel

The basic structure of AMBIT is summarized in a diagrammatic representation known as the AMBIT wheel (see Figure 1.1).

The AMBIT wheel and whole-systems thinking

The AMBIT wheel is a way of summarizing the basic AMBIT approach. It aims to provide a simple way of reminding workers in a team how the different aspects of the model fit together, and how holding a balance between the elements that push and pull for attention in varied ways is key to success. Although mentalizing holds a pivotal place within AMBIT, the model owes a great deal to systemic ways of thinking. Coherence in the approach relies on fundamental systemic principles of interconnectedness; the role of feedback patterns; the importance of team, network, and family/carer relationships and narratives; and the significance of communication (and its absence) in impacting on the capacity to change (Dallos & Draper, 2010).

The AMBIT wheel emphasizes that helping interventions (of whatever orientation or model) are situated within at least three interconnected systems: the family/care setting, the intervening team, and the wider welfare and educational network. For the worker, one key challenge is to continue working effectively when these interconnected systems create unintended contradictions or negative feedback patterns (what we describe as "disintegration") that undermine the capacity for sustainable change. One of the most striking aspects of our experience of training teams is that this assertion is almost universally acknowledged and agreed by frontline staff. An experience of repeated and often severe inter-system difficulties between family members and team members, and across networks, is almost a universal finding among the more than 1,500 workers trained so far—and this is despite the fact that, clearly, nobody intentionally designed a system to achieve this.

So, although the wellbeing of the client is ultimately at the heart of everything that an AMBIT-trained team is doing, the skill for the worker lies in paying as much attention to the wider context as to the relationship with that client—keeping their balance, as it were. The aspiration for AMBIT is to develop understandings and techniques that work to support a degree of balance between these systems in order to enable change to occur and to be sustainable. These will be elaborated on in Chapters 4 to 7, which focus on the details of practice in working directly with clients (Chapter 4), with teams (Chapter 5), and across wider multi-agency networks (Chapter 6), and on developing systematic approaches to learning at work (Chapter 7).

The AMBIT wheel and balance

The core metaphor of the wheel is *balance*. In order for the wheel to run smoothly, it needs to be balanced, even if the road it runs on continuously knocks it off balance. This also illustrates the fact that undertaking usual casework within AMBIT-trained teams nearly always involves feeling that one is doing several things at once, and often these different tasks present apparent paradoxes and contradictions—that is, a feeling of imbalance. We consider these paradoxes and contradictions as common and ordinary aspects of the work teams take on rather than necessarily being indicators of error or failure. We highlight the fact that workers are often faced with somewhat impossible situations, and the intention of the wheel is to represent some of the core dilemmas, validating frontline experience and assisting workers to regain and maintain the most important balances amid this unpredictable work so as to maintain safe progress in spite of these challenges.

The structure of the AMBIT wheel

The AMBIT wheel consists of three concentric rings: the center, representing mentalizing; the middle, representing the four quadrants of AMBIT practice; and the outer, representing the eight principles that comprise the AMBIT stance. The struggle for balance is represented in all three rings of the wheel.

(i) Center ring: Mentalizing

At the center of the wheel is mentalizing. As we will describe in Chapter 2, one of the key characteristics of mentalizing is that it is a fragile kind of mental activity; humans can never be perfect at it, and it is easily disrupted, at which point non-mentalizing processes become dominant. Mentalizing will be considered as a mental process that is fundamentally about the constant, concerned effort required to hold an adaptive balance between competing components of psychological functioning (such as certainty, "make-believe," or action).

(ii) Middle ring: The four quadrants of AMBIT practice

The middle (second) ring of the wheel describes the four key areas of work in AMBIT that we have listed above, and which broadly address the four areas of particular challenge that the case studies at the start of the chapter aimed to illustrate:

1. Working with your client
2. Working with your team
3. Working with your networks
4. Learning at work.

There is a natural tendency (how could it be otherwise?) for workers and teams to focus most of their energy and time on working with their clients. It is much harder to justify setting aside time purposefully to consider team working, working relationships across the wider professional network, or the process of how the team is learning from its experience and from other emerging evidence; yet, without an appropriate balance of these areas, we argue, the wheel will be lopsided and is likely to come off the road. We assert that the "fecundity" of the theory of mentalizing means that it can be applied at least as usefully in these other rather more neglected quadrants, as well as in working with clients.

The four quadrants represent broad areas of practice, each of which frequently involves addressing at least one of the four dilemmas that are represented in the outer ring as paired (and not infrequently mutually contradictory) principles of an "AMBIT stance" (see below). There are, of course, many other dilemmas in our work, but these four have stood the test of time in the development of the AMBIT model and are sufficiently general to cover most specific dilemmas that may arise. Moreover, they imply a more general principle: that there are few actions that do not carry the risk of unintended consequences. Accepting this reality and finding ways to reflect under pressure in order to make the best judgment possible is a constant reality of our work.

It is the fine details (some drawn from evidence-based practice, others from local practice-based evidence) about the four main areas of practice in the middle ring of the wheel that define how an AMBIT-trained team actually works. These four quadrants are covered in more detail in Chapters 4 to 7.

Our work is never only about the relationship and direct work with the client, family, and/or carers. AMBIT counterbalances the common risk of an over-focus on the client by offering a complementary emphasis on how, for instance, aspects of the network as a whole may or may not be working to support the client; or on how the team may need to help the worker to recognize how heroic and empathic efforts on their part with a client may have drawn them out of the reach of supportive and steadying relationships with colleagues; or on whether there is learning that is more generally applicable from the team in the way that a particular inter-agency misunderstanding arose and was resolved. At its best, AMBIT suggests that balanced practice is achieved when the worker is holding in mind all four of the basic areas of practice around a case. However, above all else, AMBIT suggests that practice in this field is never really in balance; in fact, imbalance characterizes the territory in which workers have chosen to work. Accepting and working with this fact, in order to remain vigilant against the unwanted effects of the most serious losses of balance and to make constant small corrective adjustments toward restoring balance, is at the heart of the approach. We are expected to fail, but what we want to avoid are failures that escalate to the point at which corrective measures are too late. If that sounds too dispiriting, let us turn to the aspirational principles of the AMBIT stance, set out in the outer ring of the wheel.

(iii) Outer ring: The AMBIT stance

The outer ring of the wheel illustrates AMBIT's principled stance—eight paired (and to some extent mutually contradictory) principles that have demonstrated value for workers in the field and the clients with whom they work. These paired principles in the AMBIT stance highlight four core dilemmas that commonly arise. We emphasize that these dilemmas are rarely fully resolved, and workers frequently find themselves challenged (i.e. unbalanced) between the two conflicting sides of the dilemma. One intention in highlighting these dilemmas is to validate the experience of frontline staff; it is rare in the course of working with our clients not to feel as if we are one step behind what is needed. These four dilemmas should not become overly prescriptive or reductive: rather, the aim is to capture some key common issues and offer something akin to the compass dial across which the magnetic needle flickers back and forth—offering if not a precise bearing, then at least a broad orientation.

The first dilemma (located in the left quadrant of the wheel, relating to Working with your Team) lies between the principles of establishing an **individual keyworker relationship** for the client versus that **worker remaining well connected to the team**. Note that in AMBIT it is not assumed that this key relationship must necessarily be with a worker in the AMBIT-trained team—what is most important is that the client has an experience of somebody who "gets" them, in whom they can develop some trust. Later in this chapter we describe the notion of a "Team around the Worker," which explains this in more depth.

Powerful keyworking relationships with clients expose workers to strong feelings that make it difficult to maintain a mentalizing stance in relation to the client, as well as to assess risk accurately and give appropriate responses. So although the successful engagement of the client by the AMBIT worker is one of the cornerstones of effective work, AMBIT emphasizes the need for the worker to maintain *equal* vigilance toward the quality of connectedness between them and other members of their team. The worker's personal skills and surefootedness in face-to-face work can be safely exploited only if they are equally confident in the attentiveness and understanding of team-mates who are "holding their rope" and communicating their separate perspectives on the potentially precipitous path ahead.

The second dilemma (located in the right quadrant of the wheel, relating to Working with your Networks) lies between the principle of **working across multiple domains** and **taking responsibility for integration**. This dilemma focuses on the need to address the complex and multiple problems, their causes, their maintaining factors, and the varied barriers to effective care that blight the lives of highly socially excluded clients—in other words, to treat these holistically. Successfully providing help for a client means addressing the full range of what bothers, harms, or limits them, and helping them access the various resiliencies (which are often conceived of as external, but may equally be internal) that may be available to them. Doing this kind of "wide-angle" work usually requires enlisting skilled and authoritative input from a range of different professionals and agencies. However, for many clients, being approached by large numbers of workers is an aversive experience. The behavior of workers from different agencies is often not as comprehensible to a client as those workers may assume—particularly for a young person whose expectations about authorities or "helpers" (or adults in general) are that, generally, they are far from helpful. Agencies and professionals themselves are not immune to misunderstandings and unhelpful mythologies about one another, either. AMBIT promotes a number of ways in which, within the scope of their influence (their "ambit"), workers can make systematic efforts to reduce the risk of negative impacts from unhelpful or inaccurate assumptions across these systems (e.g. "You just want to take children from their families!" or "Agency X just wants to reduce its caseload!") by working to increase understanding between the minds that make up these systems. One of our assumptions, covered in more depth in Chapters 3, 4, and 6, is that it is important for professionals to broadcast their intentions explicitly to clients and other professionals.

The third dilemma (located in the upper quadrant of the wheel, relating to Working with your Client) lies between the principles of **scaffolding existing relationships** versus **managing risk**. Frontline workers should avoid becoming positioned as unique rescuers, especially if their intervention is time-limited; this approach would store up the risk of further abandonment or feelings of helplessness in the client. Instead, workers try to identify resiliencies and use their own relationship to help support, sustain, and strengthen other existing key relationships (whether professional or informal) in a client's life, particularly those that are likely to remain after the intervention has finished. The systemic aspects of AMBIT mean that although key "existing relationships" will include the client's relationship to their own self (the capacity to mentalize oneself is closely linked to the development of the ability to regulate one's emotional states), work is certainly not limited to this. However, the reality of many of these clients' lives is that their *other* existing relationships often involve adversity and risk; this may include suspected negative interactions (exposure to domestic violence, involvement in criminality, etc.), or longstanding features of low-level (just below "threshold") abuse or neglect. Such dilemmas, although inevitably—and rightly—uncomfortable, are entirely consistent with an overarching safeguarding framework. The counterbalancing AMBIT stance, which serves to place limits on the impetus to engage compassionately with the brutal reality of the client's world, is to pay close and robust attention to the proper management of risk. In doing so, we must recognize that switching to more assertive risk-management protocols may be literally life-saving, but may also put at risk the very relationships of trust that offer hope for positive long-term change.

The fourth dilemma (located in the lower quadrant of the wheel, relating to Learning at Work) is about the tension between **respect for evidence-based practice** versus the practice-based evidence that is born of **local practice and expertise**. AMBIT fully supports the need to work with evidence-based methods as a way of trying to improve the outcomes of services for highly troubled clients. However, as described above, evidence-based practice does not work for all cases, and in the settings and with the populations for whom AMBIT has been designed there are many gaps in the evidence base. Thus, teams need to develop a balance between following evidence-based practice and being able to adapt their practice in response to a lack of benefit to the client when this occurs. AMBIT anticipates that this will occur frequently: partly because of the known limits to the effectiveness of evidence-based methods, partly because the settings (and cultural milieu) where these evidence-based practices are delivered may differ greatly from those where they were tested, and partly because many dilemmas in fieldwork are simply not covered by any scientific evidence at all.

The presentation of the four dilemmas that make up the AMBIT stance is an explicit attempt to articulate the real and constant difficulty in achieving a stable balance between all these considerations. In this way, AMBIT suggests that the usual position for workers with many of their cases is to feel off-balance; a case is rarely exactly in the state that the worker would wish for it to be in. Our assumption is that this sense of being off-balance is often interpreted by workers as indicating that they are not doing their job properly—that is, the default attribution for many staff is that such difficulties indicate a lack of competence on their part, with the potential for consequent feelings of professional shame and anxiety. Shame and anxiety are extremely powerful threats to good mentalizing, and are often drivers of reflexive (as opposed to reflective) and clumsy, or even harmful, actions. The AMBIT approach is, conversely, to suggest that feeling off-balance is the central (normative) experience in much work with most excluded and complex clients—an assertion that has been strongly validated by workers who take part in our trainings.

AMBIT is designed to help workers recognize, articulate, and normalize this sense of imbalance in the work in which they are engaged, creating a non-critical and accepting culture around this experience, and enabling forums within the team, such as supervision or team discussions, in which these imbalances can be explored and addressed. The AMBIT stance outlined in the outer ring of the wheel is not a set of things to *do* but aims to capture eight clear principles grouped as four common dilemmas with which workers are often faced. The intention is explicitly to validate the experience of workers who may feel in the middle of somewhat impossible demands when things are often far from straightforward. The AMBIT stance (or the wheel as a whole) has been described as a set of memorable "grab rails" that workers can use to steady themselves when the terrain is particularly unsteady and the vehicle is bucking and swaying.

In the remaining sections of this chapter, we will cover some of the defining design features of the vehicle itself, which are:

1. That AMBIT is an open, learning system
2. That AMBIT involves a whole team, not just individual workers

3. That, nonetheless, an emphasis on the "team around the worker" supports key individual working relationships; these key relationships are the most likely ambit (sphere of influence) for therapeutic change.

It all rests on learning: AMBIT as a learning organization

Why is it helpful to think of AMBIT as a learning organization? Systematic research on what works in helping children and young people with psychological difficulties has tried to clarify what type of intervention(s) we should use for what sort of problem (Fonagy et al., 2015). That work revealed a number of critical truths. First, research has shown us that most evidence-based psychological treatments are not equally effective for everyone, and that only approximately half of the clients who receive them show improvement (Weisz et al., 2013). This may be an improvement on less evidence-based methods but clearly indicates that, for a significant proportion of cases, we may need to adapt treatments to respond to individual needs. For all forms of psychological intervention, we need to be able to identify people for whom the approach is not proving beneficial, and to change our approach in response. For the group of clients targeted by AMBIT-trained teams, this issue is likely to be even more frequent than for more conventional help-seeking and clinic-attending families and clients, who constitute the majority of participants in most research trials. We also know that standard (evidence-based) interventions are likely to be less effective for populations with greater deprivation and social disadvantage (World Health Organization, 2008) and that some families who have already had the most extensive contact from helping agencies may feel considerable distrust toward them (Ungar et al., 2013). As this is the population typically targeted by the AMBIT approach, we can predict that an important proportion of our clients are unlikely to benefit from standard interventions.

This key observation drives our proposition that it is essential for teams to develop a culture of ongoing inquiry, in which colleagues can learn about what works from each other, as well as from the wider research community. In our view, an effective approach will not be a uniform one: it should be able to adapt to the specific client groups of different teams, to each individual client and their family, and to local cultural norms and variations in networks of provision. Being able to accommodate individual variability is, as we shall see, at the heart of the mentalizing approach and its emphasis on understanding the subjective experiences of individuals. This requires flexibility, individual knowledge, and local expertise. Everything we describe in this book needs to be considered with this in mind. To put this more bluntly, if an "instruction" in this book appears to contradict a worker's common sense and existing knowledge about what might work in their own service and local community, then at the very least they should consult with a trusted colleague before following our advice as you might a recipe book.

In response to the findings we have from a limited evidence base, AMBIT aims to be an open rather than a closed system. An open system allows new ideas and insights that arise from working with clients (or, indeed, pre-existing skills and experience) to become incorporated into an AMBIT-influenced approach, but without cutting adrift from the limited evidence base that we already have. With this balancing act in mind, we have—in concert with workers in the field—developed a set of methods and practices that are designed to encourage teams to learn from their own work and that of others engaged in similar work.

Most teams already have (often well-established) ways of trying to discuss and approach working with difficult cases, so how is an AMBIT-trained team any different in this respect? To some degree it is not; indeed, it would be very strange to find ourselves promoting practices that were not already employed in successful teams. Learning from our casework is clearly central to the whole therapeutic endeavor. However, our belief, backed up by experience of working with many teams, is that much of what goes on for many of us is not always efficient in terms of learning, and that there are opportunities for increasing learning in teams—and these should be nurtured. All too often, reflective practice or setting aside time for team learning is seen as a desirable but ultimately unaffordable luxury. We are not alone in asserting that this is a grave error. Enhancing learning within organizations has been the focus of many writers and studies; one author who has particularly influenced our thinking is Peter Senge (2006) who, from a management and organizational perspective, has articulated a number of principles about how people learn within organizations, which are highly consistent with our mentalizing model. This includes his emphasis on the need to think (and learn) about our role as workers in whole systems, not just as isolated teams. We describe his work in some detail in Chapter 7.

AMBIT as a team approach

AMBIT has been developed as a whole-team approach. It cannot be undertaken by an individual AMBIT-trained therapist delivering "AMBIT therapy" in isolation, because that is not what AMBIT is.

Why is this? First, it serves to emphasize that relationships (in this case, with team members) are crucial to the process of mentalizing itself. As we shall explain in Chapter 2, mentalizing develops from reciprocal interactions and takes place between people (although it can also take place between different parts of one's own mind—"conscious" and "preconscious", as it were, when a person mentalizes their self). The nature of each other's mentalizing will influence how any relationship is experienced. In Chapter 2 we will show how a relationship of trust creates a much more conducive context for mentalizing than relationships characterized by fear or threat. Similarly, our capacity to make sense of the behavior of our client may be enhanced when we can see how some trusted other colleague makes sense of them (or helps us make sense of our own impression of a client, which we have just described to our colleague). This is not a matter of simply agreeing with an alternative view; it is more that in this context it becomes possible to recognize that these are all just "mental maps," and to evaluate the pros and cons of these more openly, rather than arriving at a position with more certainty than the facts actually allow. Nor is this about just being a "supportive colleague" or a "supportive team": we propose that a core aspect of the therapeutic endeavor requires relationships within a team to function in ways that explicitly try to keep active (and benignly insist upon) the capacity of colleagues to make sense of themselves, their clients, and their colleagues. Finally, and perhaps reassuringly to our more action-oriented readers, this is not simply a recipe for endless talking, reflecting, and prevarication. We will show how mentalizing is intimately bound to behavior; it is about making better decisions about what to do.

Second, AMBIT is a team approach because the client group requires it. Working with highly troubled clients with multiple life problems that affect all aspects of their lives is not for the faint-hearted, and is definitely not for solo practitioners, however heroic. (AMBIT does not support heroism as a model of practice.) Work with clients facing the kinds of dilemmas for which AMBIT is designed to help may lead practitioners to "up-regulate" their tolerance for risk, inviting a kind of therapeutic machismo ("perhaps all young people these days do this kind of thing; I should play it cool, not seem to panic …"). This may lead practitioners to collude with risky or illegal behaviors. Clients may even act in ways that are directly seductive, reflecting pathologically sexualized relationships to authority and help. In such situations, if he or she loses the attention of (and links between) professional peers, the lone practitioner is at great risk, and places his/her clients at great risk too. Just as a climber wants the partner who is holding the rope to keep their eyes on them, so it is for the worker with their team-mate.

Third, the AMBIT model of practice places great emphasis on the longer-term task of helping clients to develop a more stable and adaptive relationship to approaching, requesting, and accepting help. One powerful means of social learning is through the modeling of desired behaviors by a trusted other—and, if a worker can develop such a relationship with a client, they also then have the opportunity to model appropriate help-seeking behavior through the way they make explicit use of their own colleagues as sources of help. This will be explained in greater depth in Chapter 5.

Fourth, on a practical level, work with a client will need to continue during periods when a member of staff is on leave. Thus, we often see AMBIT-trained teams working in a similar way to an inpatient team who collectively work out how they cover different tasks related to a particular client in a joined-up way. This is more than just pragmatism, however. There is intrinsic benefit for the client, who experiences (albeit mainly filtered through a single trusted key relationship in the team) a collective approach to considering their needs; in this way they can experience different staff members having different ways of seeing or expressing things, while still being held in a consistent shared approach. This would be similar to processes within reasonably well-functioning families where differences of perspective are tolerated, even welcomed, provided that a basic stance of family loyalty is not broken. To make this explicit to clients, team members are encouraged to refer to other team members (by name) as part of the work, sharing the fact that they have sought help from other team members, and phoning team members when they are uncertain about how to understand a particular situation (sometimes explicitly in front of the client—if need be with the phone switched to loudspeaker mode—allowing the client to listen in on the conversation, much as systemic therapists adopt a "reflecting team" approach).

Fifth, as indicated earlier, a team approach is emphasized in order to recognize the role of team culture in supporting and developing effective practice. Team culture is a slippery concept to define, but we all recognize it when we experience it. How does it feel to be in this team? Do we have our own ways of doing things, and know what these are? This is where AMBIT's emphasis on learning from experience overlaps with team working. In this sense learning is not a solitary endeavor, leading to individual professional development, but instead it is the collective task of developing a "living curriculum" that is built from the shared experiences of workers in the field (Lave & Wenger, 1991), blended with local measures of outcomes, and supported wherever possible on the foundations of evidence from robust science.

Lastly, the AMBIT model asserts that it is a necessary fact that workers feel anxious about their clients at particular times (but not all the time). We are more concerned about workers who find it hard to recognize their own anxiety (or who simply do not feel anxious at all) when working with this client group than workers who show "too much." Anxiety is seen as intrinsic to the context of this work because the target group for AMBIT comprises clients with very considerable vulnerabilities, to whom awful things can and do happen, and who can themselves at times commit serious acts against themselves and others. Thus, anxiety is seen not primarily as an indication that a worker cannot cope with the work, but rather that they are oriented to the realities of the work. With this in mind, the AMBIT approach encourages a team culture in which team members take an active responsibility for responding to their own and each other's anxiety. There are many aspects of AMBIT that directly or indirectly aim to address this core team task.

Building a team approach

How does a team develop this approach? First, AMBIT is a training offered to all members of a team in order to influence team culture around processes of learning. We do not provide training for individuals because the training is essentially a co-production, involving team members together making sense of core AMBIT ideas and adapting AMBIT practices to their specific team context and client group.

The AMBIT training concludes with an invitation for teams to map out their existing team processes and practices. These may include team meetings, supervision arrangements, appraisal systems, mentoring, and away days. Each team is then invited to consider how they could apply AMBIT principles of learning to these existing processes. For example, a manager of an AMBIT-trained outreach team described how, in the staff members' annual appraisal, the issue of how much a team member made use of other team members was included as part of the appraisal process. Staff that were felt to be working very independently were then invited to reflect on this aspect of their practice. AMBIT makes an explicit assertion that asking for help from team members is a positive behavior, and that being explicit about one's uncertainty around a particular case is no cause for professional shame. We are not suggesting that complex staff feelings around their own professional competence can be eliminated by such assertions. However, we do believe that an explicit emphasis on the value and the necessity of professional interdependence provides some protection against the potential for staff members' feelings of vulnerability leading them to feel shame in relation to their work.

Another explicit aim is to reduce the burden on staff that can be associated with the introduction of new practices. Training offers an introduction of perspectives that may (to some extent) be new. However, this newness is marked and stabilized in the fact that it arises within the particular context of a shared whole-team experience of an AMBIT training; conversely, there is an emphasis on the use of incremental rather than radical changes. Training—as with restructuring, reorganization, or any treatment—carries the risk of unwanted effects; for instance, it risks disempowering already skilled workers by implicitly undervaluing their experience, or introducing changes that ultimately disrupt the wider established system. With the rather modest goal of supporting already skilled workers to become more effective and satisfied, rather than simply piling AMBIT-type practices on to already overstretched teams, the approach adopts a respectful position toward existing team cultures based on the assumption that team learning in some form is already happening. AMBIT aims to make the process of team learning much more explicit in order to enable teams to amplify such processes. An example of this incremental and locally adapted approach to changing practice is that of the team that provided a parent telephone support service; after training, the team adjusted their existing daily debriefing meeting along AMBIT lines, which resulted in the meetings being experienced as more supportive—and considerably shorter.

The AMBIT approach also encourages a variety of working practices that highlight the connectedness of the worker to the whole team. These will be described in detail throughout the book. One such example is the use of a disciplined approach to case discussion that we call "Thinking Together" (discussed in Chapter 5); this might involve contacting other team members via mobile phone during a home visit to a client in order to gain an outside perspective on a real-time dilemma. For now, what needs to be emphasized is that AMBIT aims to support purposeful efforts to create an explicit local culture in which the mutual and reciprocal reliance of team members upon one another is accepted as normal and essential to effective practice. For some teams this might seem like a minimal change, while for others it is a shift toward greater intimacy in working relationships. A metaphor frequently used in trainings is of mountaineers negotiating steep and dangerous terrain: as much as the individual skill of the climber out in front counts, so does the quality of attachment between that climber and his or her colleague holding their rope. Knowledge or internalization of the rituals of communication whereby checks are made (that the rope is securely fastened, that it is held, that eyes are on the lead climber at the trickiest parts of the route) are critical to the safety of both parties, and also support their joint progress toward the goal.

Individual relationships: The Team around the Client and the Team around the Worker

Following directly from the above point, the third general aspect of AMBIT highlighted in this chapter again involves what may, for many teams, be a shift in emphasis rather than revolutionary change. The stress here is placed on an individual keyworker relationship. On first impression, this might seem to contradict our emphasis on AMBIT as a team activity. AMBIT is, of course, a team practice, but the whole point of this team is to create safe conditions for the establishment and support of powerful trusting individual relationships between clients and their keyworkers—even if sometimes the keyworker is not necessarily located in the team.

This needs a bit of teasing out to explain what we mean. The reason for privileging an individual keyworker relationship lies in what we know about the development of mentalizing and its recovery when lost; we are aware that we do not describe mentalizing in any depth until Chapter 2, and hope that readers will forgive this running ahead of ourselves. For now, we ask readers to accept that mentalizing can develop when we experience our mind as being held accurately, respectfully, and safely in the mind of a trusted other person. This is something that can be achieved only in individual relationships.

It has become commonplace for services to organize themselves around the idea of a "Team around the Client" (in the UK this is more commonly referred to as a "Team around the Child" (or even simply as a "TAC"), but as AMBIT can be adapted for use in adult populations we have opted to use the more generic term "client"). In its multi-agency approach, AMBIT is unambiguous in its support for the need for staff from different agencies to work together to improve the effectiveness of help for clients and their families. Team around the Client meetings can be very helpful in facilitating such work. In AMBIT we offer an alternative—or rather, a complementary—approach, which is often referred to as the "Team around the Worker."

An unintended consequence of the "Team around the Client" model is that it may prioritize the building of the team (people with the right capacities, skills, authority, etc.) over increasing the capacity of the network to provide help. This is especially the case when the client is giving great cause for concern—a time when referral to multiple expert services is a common and understandable reaction. Being faced with multiple workers, however well-intentioned, may be experienced by a client as oppressive, confusing, and overwhelming. Commonly, clients with the kinds of predicaments described earlier complain explicitly about the number of appointments they are required to attend and the number of different professionals they are expected to engage with—as exemplified in the case study of Amir at the start of this chapter. The potential for these contacts and relationships to remain in a state of passive (or "pretend") compliance is often increased by multiplying the number of workers and agencies involved in a case—which is often exactly what happens, especially when a case is particularly worrying and nobody or no single agency wants to be the one "left holding the baby." In such circumstances, the client may easily feel that their primary task is to comply with high levels of demand coming from such a network, rather than feeling understood and helped by it.

For some clients, perhaps especially those targeted by AMBIT, it may actually work better to *reduce* the number of professionals working directly with them, and for other staff to work indirectly through a "key relationship" or "keyworker" (at least in the early engagement phase). As we will describe in later chapters, AMBIT uses an attachment framework as a way of understanding a client's experience and use of help. The "keyworker," as we define it, is not therefore an administrative role; it is the worker who is, or has the best chance of becoming, the "key" professional *in the mind of the client*—the worker who they *feel most understood by*, and trust the most.

In a large network this keyworker may well be the professional whom the client already knows best; in the absence of such an existing relationship there may be a need to develop a key relationship from scratch. Over time, as the client builds trust in this keyworker, facilitating the introduction of other more specialized workers may become an important part of their role. Of course, when a Team around the Client meeting works effectively, it very often concludes its business having created exactly this kind of "Team around the Worker"—offering ways to support one worker who is recognized as having the relationship that is most valued or trusted by the client, and sequencing or coordinating efforts to introduce input from a range of other workers and agencies so as to avoid overwhelming the client.

This framework also emphasizes that achieving a degree of safety and trust in a helping relationship does not occur rapidly, particularly for clients with very troubled attachment histories. Rather than overwhelm a client with multiple new professional relationships at a point of crisis, the AMBIT approach suggests that it is more productive, at least in the early stages of engagement, to invest in a single key helping relationship that the client can, perhaps over some time, come to trust. Introducing other workers with more differentiated skills, authority, and tasks is much more likely to be successful through (and ideally in the presence of) a trusted keyworker than if they all knock on the client's door independently.

Now we return to the team. The approach outlined above can be offered only if a keyworker is extremely well integrated into, and supported by, a team (and, ideally, a whole network) that not only understands and uses this worker as an important "early conduit" for their collective expertise, but also embraces the maintenance of this worker's own stability (we will later elaborate this as their *mentalizing*) as a shared responsibility. This shift toward the team supporting the keyworker-in-relationship is illustrated in Figure 1.2. Within this approach,

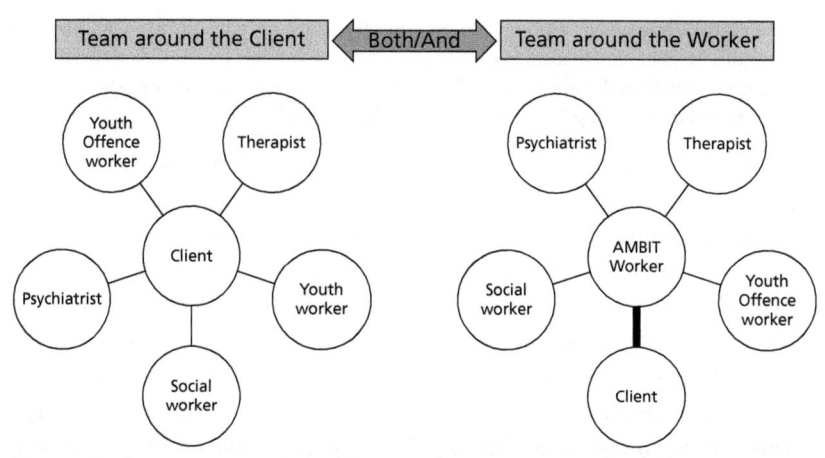

Figure 1.2 The "Team around the Client" and "Team around the Worker."

keyworkers must know that they can call upon a range of expertise and genuine practical or emotional support from their team as needed, and that they are not isolated. In outreach settings this means that mobile phones are an essential tool, allowing keyworkers to access real-time support in the field rather than having to wait for their weekly or fortnightly supervision. Correspondingly, those team members offering such active support are encouraged to see this "working by proxy" as having parity of status with their own face-to-face work; actively supporting our professional colleagues is not a generous (but ultimately optional) extra, but is a core part of the work.

Case example

Simon is a social worker in an AMBIT-trained team and is the keyworker for Dionne, who is 16 years old. Dionne's difficulties were triggered by a recent breakdown of family relationships, leading to immediate concerns for her safety. Simon has been mainly concerned with finding alternative accommodation for Dionne for a while, so that the family might have a chance to calm down and think more fully about where they want to go next. Simon is comfortable in this role. However, it then emerges that Dionne has started cutting herself and has made some suicidal statements. Dionne does not want to see another professional, but Simon does not feel comfortable in managing this problem alone. He discusses the situation with his supervisor and it is agreed that he will make a joint visit to Dionne with the nurse in the team to assess Dionne's self-injurious behavior. Following this assessment, Simon and the nurse have a brief consultation with the team psychiatrist. It is agreed with Dionne that communicating more with others (including Simon) about her self-injury should be one of the goals for her to work on, and that Simon will monitor her self-injurious behavior. If this worsens, he will be able to ask for further help or advice from his team. During this process, from the team's perspective the aim is to work via Simon and the relationship he has established with Dionne rather than to increase the number of professionals involved directly with her as an "automatic reflex."

The AMBIT-trained team around Simon works both to support his anxiety and to extend his skills in relation to managing a problem that he was initially less confident about dealing with, even though, from his client's perspective, he is the worker she feels she can trust. This would be an example of a "Team around the Worker."

There is no precise prescription for how a Team around a Worker may be configured, as this will vary from case to case. The organizing principle is to think more about the quality of relationships that exist between clients and their professional helpers, and their experience of what it is to be helped. Of course, this approach needs to be balanced against the formal roles and skills of individual practitioners. In traditional ways of offering help, formal roles tend to override considerations of the quality of relationships. In AMBIT, the emphasis shifts to consider the importance of relationships *as well as* (not instead of) formal roles.

This shift in emphasis can have significant implications for how a network functions. In training teams in AMBIT, we have discovered that the implications of such a shift have been potentially quite radical for some services. It has often led to new considerations of how to support a keyworker system across agencies. Such structural changes have sometimes been outside the remit of the changes that AMBIT was initially intended to bring about. The AMBIT approach does not have the authority to reorganize roles prescribed to staff either through professional trainings or through job descriptions. The changes proposed by AMBIT are intended to be shifts in principles and practice, rather than monolithic and universalist structural changes. In making sense of this different narrative of change, we have found that positioning theory (Watson et al., 2013; Harre et al., 2009) helps elucidate the changes that the AMBIT model is proposing; it is not so much about changes in roles, as changes in the way that staff become positioned in individual case work. The application of this theory will be more fully elaborated on in Chapter 7.

Conclusions

The AMBIT approach has four key general aspects, namely: (1) putting learning at the center of the team culture; (2) developing a whole-team approach that recognizes the interdependence of colleagues within a team, and using this team to support the development of strong individual keyworking relationships; (3) using a systems approach to emphasize interconnectedness and to explore and make more explicit the shared intentions that exist across the wider multi-agency network; and (4) using individual relationships with the client and their existing support network to build mentalizing capacity in a way that allows for more adaptive and sustainable coping, and thriving. These four aspects of the model will be further elaborated on in Chapters 4 to 7, which describe in more detail the knowledge and techniques behind each of the four quadrants of the AMBIT wheel.

AMBIT is not a revolutionary approach, but if there is a radical (perhaps radically obvious) message for potential "AMBITeers," it is that practitioners are not machines—they are people, and practitioners are not the systems within which they work, but are agents operating (and operated upon by) these systems. We need to purposefully create interconnections between systems that recognize the "agentiveness" of the individuals working within those systems. The system (whatever system) that delivers care and help is rational and benign, but it is also mindless. So the question is: how we can create a system that is mindful of the minds that comprise it? This is what this book is about.

Next, we need to look in more detail at the "engine" that not only provides a framework for making sense of all these ideas, but from which flows a series of practices that can be used to move through this challenging territory—and this is mentalizing.

References

Children and Young People's Health Outcomes Forum. (2012). *Report of The Children and Young People's Health Outcomes Forum—Mental Health Sub-Group* (London, UK: Children and Young People's Health Outcomes Forum), https://www.gov.uk/government/uploads/system/uploads/attachment_data/file/216853/CYP-Mental-Health.pdf, accessed 11 Jan. 2017.

Dallos, R., & Draper, R. (2010). *An Introduction to Family Therapy: Systemic theory and practice* (3rd edn, Maidenhead, UK: Open University Press).

Department of Health. (2004). *The Mental Health and Psychological Well-being of Children and Young People* (London, UK: Department of Health).

Department of Health. (2011). *No Health Without Mental Health: A cross-government mental health outcomes strategy for people of all ages* (London, UK: HM Government), https://www.gov.uk/government/uploads/system/uploads/attachment_data/file/135457/dh_124058.pdf, accessed 11 Jan. 2017.

Department of Health. (2013). *Better Health Outcomes for Children and Young People* (London, UK: Department of Health), https://www.gov.uk/government/uploads/system/uploads/attachment_data/file/207391/better_health_outcomes_children_young_people_pledge.pdf, accessed 11 Jan. 2017.

Department of Health, & NHS England. (2015). *Future in Mind: Promoting, protecting and improving our children and young people's mental health and wellbeing* (London, UK: Department of Health, & NHS England), https://www.gov.uk/government/uploads/system/uploads/attachment_data/file/414024/Childrens_Mental_Health.pdf, accessed 11 Jan. 2017.

Feigenbaum, J. (2007). Dialectical behavior therapy: An increasing evidence base. *Journal of Mental Health* 16: 51–68.

Fonagy, P., Butler, S., Goodyer, I., Cottrell, D., Scott, S., Pilling, S., … Haley, R. (2013). Evaluation of multisystemic therapy pilot services in the Systemic Therapy for At Risk

Teens (START) trial: study protocol for a randomised controlled trial. *Trials* **14**: 265. doi: 10.1186/1745-6215-14-265

Fonagy, P., Cottrell, D., Phillips, J., Bevington, D., Glaser, D., & Allison, E. (2015). *What Works for Whom? A Critical Review of Treatments for Children and Adolescents* (2nd edn, New York, NY: Guilford Press).

Harre, R., Moghaddam, F. M., Cairnie, T. P., Rothbart, D., & Sabat, S. R. (2009). Recent advances in positioning theory. *Theory & Psychology* **19**: 5–31. doi: 10.1177/0959354308101417

Lave, J., & Wenger, E. (1991). *Situated Learning: Legitimate Peripheral Participation* (Cambridge, UK: Cambridge University Press).

Liddle, H. A., Rowe, C. L., Dakof, G. A., Henderson, C. E., & Greenbaum, P. E. (2009). Multidimensional family therapy for young adolescent substance abuse: Twelve-month outcomes of a randomized controlled trial. *Journal of Consulting and Clinical Psychology* **77**: 12–25. doi: 10.1037/a0014160

Linehan, M. M., Comtois, K. A., Murray, A. M., Brown, M. Z., Gallop, R. J., Heard, H. L., ... Lindenboim, N. (2006). Two-year randomized controlled trial and follow-up of dialectical behavior therapy vs therapy by experts for suicidal behaviors and borderline personality disorder. *Archives of General Psychiatry* **63**: 757–66. doi: 10.1001/archpsyc.63.7.757

Main, T. (1957). The ailment. *British Journal of Medical Psychology* **30**: 129–45.

McManus, S., Bebbington, P., Jenkins, R., & Brugha, T. (2016). *Mental Health and Wellbeing in England: Adult Psychiatric Morbidity Survey 2014* (Leeds, UK: NHS Digital), http://content.digital.nhs.uk/catalogue/PUB21748/apms-2014-full-rpt.pdf, accessed 11 Jan. 2017.

National CAMHS Review. (2008). *Children and Young People in Mind: The Final Report of the National CAMHS Review* (London, UK: National CAMHS Review), http://webarchive.nationalarchives.gov.uk/20081230004520/publications.dcsf.gov.uk/eorderingdownload/camhs-review.pdf, accessed 11 Jan. 2017.

Rigter, H., Henderson, C. E., Pelc, I., Tossmann, P., Phan, O., Hendriks, V., ... Rowe, C. L. (2013). Multidimensional family therapy lowers the rate of cannabis dependence in adolescents: A randomised controlled trial in Western European outpatient settings. *Drug and Alcohol Dependence* **130**: 85–93. doi: 10.1016/j.drugalcdep.2012.10.013

Senge, P. (2006). *The Fifth Discipline: The Art and Practice of the Learning Organization* (rev. repr., New York, NY: Doubleday).

Tronick, E., & Beeghly, M. (2011). Infants' meaning-making and the development of mental health problems. *American Psychologist* **66**: 107–19. doi: 10.1037/a0021631

Ungar, M., Liebenberg, L., Dudding, P., Armstrong, M., & van de Vijver, F. J. R. (2013). Patterns of service use, individual and contextual risk factors, and resilience among adolescents using multiple psychosocial services. *Child Abuse and Neglect* **37**: 150–9. doi: 10.1016/j.chiabu.2012.05.007

Watson, D., Bayliss, P., & Pratchett, G. (2013). Pond life that 'know their place': exploring teaching and learning support assistants' experiences through positioning theory. *International Journal of Qualitative Studies in Education* **26**: 100–17. doi: 10.1080/09518398.2011.598195

Weisz, J. R., & Gray, J. S. (2008). Evidence-based psychotherapy for children and adolescents: Data from the present and a model for the future. *Child and Adolescent Mental Health* **13**: 54–65. doi: 10.1111/j.1475-3588.2007.00475.x

Weisz, J. R., Kuppens, S., Eckshtain, D., Ugueto, A. M., Hawley, K. M., & Jensen-Doss, A. (2013). Performance of evidence-based youth psychotherapies compared with usual clinical care: A multilevel meta-analysis. *JAMA Psychiatry* **70**: 750–61. doi: 10.1001/jamapsychiatry.2013.1176

World Health Organization. (2008). *Closing the Gap in a Generation: Health Equity Through Action on the Social Determinants of Health. Final report of the Commission on Social Determinants of Health* (Geneva, Switzerland: World Health Organization), http://www.who.int/social_determinants/thecommission/finalreport/en/, accessed 11 Jan. 2017.

Chapter 2

How the engine works: Trust and making sense of each other and ourselves

Introduction: The theory behind what makes help helpful

The AMBIT model in part simply formalizes ways of working that have naturally evolved between experienced clinicians responding both to the demands, traps, or pitfalls of this kind of work and to the intense difficulties and suffering experienced by the clients with whom we aim to work. Almost unknown to many of the people getting on with working in this way, it happens also to be closely informed by research and theory. In this chapter we shall try to explain some of the ideas and research findings behind AMBIT and point to the direction in which our current clinical and research thinking is taking us. Remember, AMBIT is a constantly evolving project whose essence is flexibility and adaptation. We hope it never achieves maturity. So the ideas sketched out here may be far better developed by the time you read this. The "live version" has always been, and remains, the online wiki-based manual (https://manuals.annafreud.org—follow the links to AMBIT).

Mentalizing

Mentalizing is central to AMBIT, and indeed it is the "M" at the center of our acronym. Mentalizing is defined as the ability to imaginatively try to make sense of people's actions in terms of what might be going on in their minds: what they might be feeling, and what they might need, desire, believe, or hope to achieve—to put it simply, understanding people in terms of mental states. The same process can apply to trying to make sense of one's own actions. An alternative to mentalizing is to interpret actions in mindless ways (i.e. in ways that do not take into account mental states), for example by using explanations based on social context or biology without reference to how both these drivers actually act by influencing how we think and feel. The capacity to understand both our own and others' actions in a mentalizing way is helpful for us to successfully navigate through our social world and whatever may be happening in it. It can also give us the resilience to withstand interpersonal challenges and stress, and it makes the world a kinder and less dangerous place by providing the empathy and compassion we need to collaborate and cooperate effectively.

Mentalizing is one of the most ordinary, and yet most defining, aspects of being human: the constant process of imagining other people's minds as we interact with them, of finding the thoughts that may explain their actions, and the simultaneous, equally challenging, process of making sense of one's own thoughts and feelings. By observing and interpreting someone else's state of mind we can fathom what they are doing and can judge their intentions; at the most simple level, we can make better judgments about whether they might turn out to be a threat to us.

This is just what mentalizing *other* people provides. Representing our *own* experiences as organized by mental states is, if anything, even more helpful. By understanding our emotions, we can regulate our feelings better; by thinking about our thoughts, we can link our actions to our thoughts and feelings; and by thinking about how people around us affect us, we can reflect on our needs, which can give clarity to our actions and our feelings. These are some of the invisible benefits of having a social mind—the kind of thing we do not notice until it jars, disrupting expectations or disturbing social norms. A simple example of this disruption might be when someone drunkenly misinterprets a jolted beer glass in a pub as an act of aggression, or when someone who is anxious about his or her body image interprets an acquaintance's breezy "You look well!" as insinuating that they have gained weight.

As these examples indicate, although we describe mentalizing as a natural part of being human, it is (as with all things human) something that can easily go wrong. Think how often parents of even typically developing adolescents exclaim: "You never think of others … you just don't think!" All adolescents experience mentalizing as a particular challenge because of the uneven sequence by which the brain matures. Troubled adolescents have these "normal" challenges to mentalizing in spades. The theory behind AMBIT is that consistent difficulties in mentalizing lie behind the interpersonal difficulties that troubled adolescents experience. Their poor mentalizing is often most conspicuously reflected in the kinds of social judgments they make that cause such concern and anxiety for those who are tasked with trying to help or protect them.

Development and mentalizing: How do infants learn to mentalize?

Learning to mentalize is probably best understood as being very similar to the way an infant learns language. The natural capacity to pick up the way people think and feel is something that babies are born with, just like the natural capacity to learn language. From birth, the infant brain is programmed to prefer interaction with humans over inanimate objects—they will, for example, look at faces in preference to other moving objects. But, just as which language a baby first learns depends on what is being spoken by those around them, the specific content of what the infant learns about other people's minds depends on the kind of social environment that surrounds them: parents, caregivers, siblings, and peers. There are differences between families, communities, and cultures in terms of what a person learns about minds, and even in the rate at which mentalizing abilities are acquired. Some less individualistic cultures, for example, may place less emphasis on the expectation that different people hold different beliefs, but they may teach greater awareness of how one's behavior might affect how other people think and feel. Across all cultures, however, learning to mentalize is likely to come more quickly and effectively in parent–child relationships characterized by greater sensitivity. And here is a little bit of magic that human natural selection has bequeathed to all of us.

A baby develops into an accomplished mentalizer through exposure to being mentalized by other people: the human mind is incubated by the minds around it. Long before a baby has learned to recognize or understand their own thought processes, or appreciate that other people have their own, entirely separate, minds, a caregiver interacts with their baby *as if* they already have a separate, independent mind. It is this constant process of interacting in a way that attributes valid and separate mental states to the baby that turns the infant into a fully fledged mentalizer. The mother or father (or grandparents, caregivers, or siblings), in their day-to-day actions, are performing an active task: they are making sense of the mental space inside the infant, for the infant. An example of this is the universal way that human caregivers mimic their babies. They respond to their infants with exaggerated facial displays of imitation and use of voice, which reflects how the infant may be feeling back to the infant, but they do this in a slightly pretend or "play-acting" manner. This is described as *marked mirroring*. By using marked mirroring, the adult is describing the child's emotional state as it is being felt by the child, in a manner that simultaneously makes it clear that it is the child's feelings that are being enacted and understood, not the adult's.

The parent who cannot (for many possible reasons) think about the child's mental state disrupts the child's capacity to mentalize. Trauma, maltreatment, and severe difficulties in the way that parents relate to their infants can all make it far harder for an infant to learn to mentalize themselves and others. This can sometimes show itself in the child's difficulties not only in identifying mental states but also, quite literally, in identifying someone else as being separate. They are more likely to be influenced by the mental states of others; they make fewer references to their own internal states; and they struggle to understand emotional expressions, particularly facial expressions. Children who have been neglected are more likely to muddle "me" and "you" both in conversation and in meaning itself, and even in adulthood they may continue to have problems in understanding other people's thoughts and feelings in an accurate and efficient manner.

Attachment and mentalizing

There is a strong link between attachment and mentalizing. Attachment relationships provide the ideal conditions for fostering mentalizing. Secure attachment relationships, where attachment figures are sensitive to the child's thoughts and feelings and the child feels safe to explore the mind of the attachment figure (Fonagy et al., 2014), encourage the infant to reach out and try to read the mind of others, and also to feel more confident of their own thoughts and feelings.

The theory of mentalizing developed in the context of clinical practice and the process of thinking about the mechanisms by which certain kinds of childhood experiences—such as abuse, extreme neglect, or highly insensitive styles of parenting—have such enduring and destructive effects on adult life. The first clinical application of the theory of mentalizing was in the treatment of borderline personality disorder (BPD), a chronic and highly disruptive condition that had traditionally been regarded as notoriously difficult to treat. According to the mentalizing approach, the frequent angry outbursts and self-harming behaviors of individuals diagnosed with BPD were attributed to limitations in the individual's capacity to mentalize others and to represent their mind as such (i.e. *as a mind*: partly understandable, partly opaque, prone to different moods and feelings that influence the way it thinks, and its tendency to freeze, prevaricate, or jump into action). The mentalization-based treatment (MBT) that was developed out of this work, and which has proved quite effective, involves helping individuals improve their capacity to mentalize interpersonal situations under conditions of emotional arousal. The clinical use of mentalizing is now being formulated as a central component of all effective therapeutic relationships (which we discuss later in this chapter). Its role across the spectrum of mental health disorders has been suggested (Bateman & Fonagy, 2012), and it is being considered in relation to disorders such as depression and eating disorders, which are not necessarily caused by a failure in mentalizing, but in which the absence of mentalizing can play a dangerous role in intensifying the sense of loss, isolation, and intractability, and in making the person harder to help.

The multidimensional nature of mentalizing

Mentalizing is not one simple thing. It is made up of four different kinds of mentalizing skills, or *dimensions*. To be able to mentalize effectively, we need to be able to master these four dimensions as circumstances demand. The four dimensions are: (a) *automatic* versus *controlled* mentalizing, (b) mentalizing the *self* versus *others*, (c) *internal* versus *external* mentalizing, and (d) *cognitive* versus *affective* mentalizing. Different types of psychological and behavioral difficulties tend to involve being "stuck" at one end of one or more of these dimensions.

Automatic versus controlled mentalizing

Controlled mentalizing is a relatively slow, steady process. It demands reflection, attention, awareness, intention, and effort. At the other end of the scale, *automatic* mentalizing involves much faster processing. It tends to be reactive and requires little or no attention, intention, awareness, and effort. Across day-to-day life and ordinary social interaction, most of our mentalizing tends to be automatic because most straightforward exchanges simply do not require more attention. Particularly in an environment where we feel secure, when things are running smoothly on an interpersonal level, more deliberate, controlled, or effortful mentalizing is not called for, and in fact the use of such a mentalizing style might hinder interactions, making them feel unduly intense or "heavy" (we refer to this as "hypermentalizing"). Both common sense and neuroscience tell us that we relax our controlled mentalizing and are less watchful or suspicious of social intentions in a secure attachment environment; a parent playing with their child or close old friends reminiscing will be using these automatic, intuitive processes. However, when necessary, someone with typical mentalizing abilities will be able to switch to controlled mentalizing if the situation demands it. For example, when a child starts crying during play, the parent will respond by trying to work out what is wrong, or the person in conversation may detect a change in tone and mood in their old friend, and wonder if the conversation has stumbled upon a difficult memory or association. In other words, well-functioning mentalizing involves the ability to switch flexibly and responsively from automatic to controlled mentalizing (and the other way).

Mentalizing difficulties often arise when an individual relies exclusively on automatic assumptions about the mental states of themself or others, which tend to be over-simplistic; they are impulsive, reach quick judgments about others' thoughts and feelings that are not reflected upon, and can give the impression of thoughtlessness or even cruelty, making interpersonal conflict almost inevitable. The person does not genuinely appear to appreciate the perspective of others, and when explicitly asked to do so becomes abstract, unconvincing, and shallow. In fact, it could be stated that any psychological intervention in essence involves challenging such automatic, distorted assumptions, and requires that the client make these assumptions conscious and attempt to reflect upon them in partnership with the therapist.

When we are in a state of stress, the use of automatic mentalizing naturally comes to the fore as part of the "fight or flight" response, and the brain systems that are associated with controlled mentalizing become disengaged. This has important implications for clinical work: any intervention that calls for reflection by asking for clarification or thought is, by its very nature, asking the client to engage in controlled mentalizing. Many clients may perform relatively well (in terms of mentalizing) under low-stress conditions. But under higher levels of stress, when automatic mentalizing naturally kicks in, the client may find it much more difficult to restore their controlled mentalizing processes and so to understand and reflect on what is going on in a stressful exchange. This can then lead the individual concerned to escalate the arousal and tension by responding in a highly emotive way. It is a rather bitter irony that for many of the clients on which AMBIT focuses, the settings and relationships provided in therapy services are alien and intense in a way that can trigger exactly this reaction, diminishing the clients' capacity to engage in the rudiments of the very skill that we are intending to build up.

Mentalizing the self versus others

The focus of mentalizing can be on the *self* (including one's physical sensations) or on *others*. The two things are closely connected: it is a central tenet of our attachment approach that a sense of self and the capacity to mentalize develop in the context of attachment relationships, and so the ability to mentalize the self and to mentalize others are closely intertwined. Neuroimaging studies suggest that the capacity to mentalize others is closely related to the ability to reflect on oneself because the two capacities rely on common neural systems. Therefore, it is not surprising that disorders that are characterized by severe impairments in feelings of self-identity—most notably, psychosis and BPD—are also characterized by severe deficits in the ability to reflect on others' mental states.

Some individuals, however, may suffer from less universal impairments in mentalizing in relation to the self and others, and have stronger skills at one end of this dimension of mentalizing. For example, individuals with antisocial personality disorder can often appear to be quite skilled in "reading the mind" of others but typically lack any real understanding of their own inner world. Clinically, we often see individuals who feel the need to assert themselves overly forcefully, controlling others' thoughts and feelings in the process, in order to limit the extent to which others impinge upon them.

Internal versus external mentalizing

Mentalizing can involve making inferences based on observable *external* features (e.g. facial expressions) or assumptions about "hidden" *internal* states.

This does not just refer to a process of focusing on the externally visible or internal mental state of others—it also includes thinking about oneself and one's own externally visible and internal states. A person with limited access to representations of their own ideas may continually seek external reassurance. In the worst case they may experience an overwhelming sense of emptiness from which only the most intense experiences provide relief. Lack of certainty about internal experience may leave such a person hypervigilant to others' reactions—but, unable to understand others by imagining them from the inside, they are limited to judging by appearance. What others do becomes excessively important, and making them prove their attitudes (of affection, commitment, or love) through action becomes the overriding goal.

From a clinical perspective, the internal–external distinction is particularly significant in helping us understand why some clients appear to be so seriously impaired in their capacity to "read the mind" of others, when they also appear to be highly attuned to other people's moods. They may, for instance, be hypersensitive to emotions resulting from what they read in other people's facial expressions or bodily posture. For example, people diagnosed with BPD often tend to hypermentalize emotions in others, including the therapist: if the therapist looks very fleetingly cross or upset, the client may believe that the therapist is furiously angry or disgusted with them. Mentalizing interventions often need to start by examining how the client's interpretations based on external features may indeed reveal part of the story in trying to make sense of other people. But, following on from this, the therapist may need to work at building plausible scenarios with the client about what various possible internal states of mind may correspond to those external features, and how those imaginary mental states may (or may not!) fit with what is currently happening. This process is called *contextualization*, and it involves increasingly taking into account the subtleties and complexities of people's internal worlds, as if peeling back the many layers of an onion.

Cognitive versus affective mentalizing

Finally, *cognitive* mentalizing involves the ability to name, recognize, and reason about mental states (again, in both oneself and others), whereas *affective* mentalizing involves the ability to understand the feelings that we experience, which is necessary for any genuine experience of emotional empathy. Individuals who give unbalanced weight to affective mentalizing can be overwhelmed by the emotions they encounter; they frequently catastrophize because the capacity to cognitively contextualize feelings is absent. They may be oversensitive to perceived emotional cues given by others, and vulnerable to overwhelming emotional contagion, making it hard for them to be able to separate someone else's feelings from their own. Such individuals may also attribute their own feelings to others in trying to imagine their state of mind, which can mean that despite their apparent emotionality, they have a limited capacity for genuine empathy, and instead show self-oriented distress when they are faced with someone else's sadness or pain.

Someone who is stuck at the other end of this particular mentalizing dimension can show good, rational, cognitive understanding of mental states, yet be unable to really access how they *feel*. This makes it difficult for them to show any genuine emotional empathy. This kind of mentalizing is often characteristic of someone with narcissistic or antisocial personality disorder traits.

The context-/relationship-specific nature of mentalizing

Mentalizing, then, is made up of different dimensions: we all have some strengths and weaknesses in these different kinds of mentalizing, but individuals with consistent interpersonal difficulties will tend to have pronounced impairments, resulting in an imbalance in mentalizing, and occasionally outright mentalizing failures. As we have seen, what becomes apparent is not so much what is not there (e.g. that there is an absence of cognitive mentalizing) but rather that the opposite end of the dimension is compensating for what is missing. To use an analogy that may be familiar to those suffering from a variety of back problems, it is not just the initial weakness that becomes the main problem, but rather the complications that arise out of the over-use of compensating muscles. In this section we will discuss the scenarios that are more likely to trigger mentalizing failures or difficulties, because as well as not being one single "thing," mentalizing changes over time, and certain situations and stimuli are more likely to trigger mentalizing difficulties.

Heightened psychological arousal tends to cause the capacity for controlled mentalizing to be increasingly lost, and automatic and often unreflective mentalizing starts to dominate. Up to a point this is a normal "fight or flight" response to stress, which has the evolutionary advantage of allowing us to respond to danger almost immediately. However, in many situations of social interpersonal stress, more cognitive and reflective functioning may be quite helpful, and an inability to use these more controlled and conscious skills may lead to real difficulties. Therefore, the degree to which an individual finds themselves affected by interpersonal stress may make a critical difference to their mentalizing skills across life experiences. It seems likely that individuals who have been exposed to early stress or trauma more easily switch into this automatic (fight or flight) style of mentalizing because trauma calls forth a general adaptation of increased readiness to respond to a biological emergency. There may also be a genetic influence on the sensitivity with which people are likely to switch to this fight or flight mode.

The emergence of imbalanced mentalizing modes

When mentalizing fails, individuals often fall back on imbalanced or *prementalizing* ways of thinking and behaving, which have some parallels with the ways in which young children think and behave before they have developed their full mentalizing capacities. These modes are important for the clinician to recognize and understand, as they can cause considerable interpersonal difficulties and can result in destructive behavior. The three modes are called *psychic equivalence, teleological mode*, and *pretend mode*. These modes of experiencing the self and others tend to re-emerge whenever we lose the ability to mentalize in a balanced manner (mostly typically in high-stress contexts).

In the *psychic equivalence* mode, thoughts and feelings become "too real" and it is extremely difficult for the individual to entertain possible alternative perspectives. When mentalizing gives way to psychic equivalence, what is thought or felt is experienced as completely real and true, leading to what therapists experience as a "concreteness of thought" in their clients. There is a suspension of doubt, and the individual increasingly believes that their own perspective is the only one possible. Psychic equivalence is normal in a child of around 20 months of age, who has not yet developed full mentalizing skills; it can appear as an overwhelming certainty about their subjective experience, whether it is that "there is a tiger under the bed" or "these Brussels sprouts are harming me." Such a state of mind can be extremely frightening, adding a powerful sense of drama and risk to life experiences. The sometimes exaggerated reactions of clients are justified by the "seriousness" with which they suddenly experience their own and others' thoughts and feelings. The black-and-white thinking of many individuals with mentalizing problems also derives from the re-emergence of a psychic equivalence mode of experiencing subjectivity.

The *teleological mode* refers to states of mind where mental attitudes are recognized only if they are "shown" as physically observable and lead to a definite outcome (hence the term "teleological"—which is derived from the Ancient Greek word *telos*, meaning "the final state of things"). The individual can recognize the existence and potential importance of states of mind, but this recognition is limited to very concrete, observable situations. For example, affection is accepted as genuine only if it is accompanied by a touch or caress, or a gift of an item or money. A client experiencing mentalizing failure and falling into a teleological mode may start "acting out": carrying out dramatic or inappropriate behaviors, as though thinking "the solution to my distress will be when I see blood/feel pain from cutting myself," or "things will be better if I have a spliff/ some whisky," or "the only solution to the threat this man poses is to hit him and break his nose." The teleological mode reflects an imbalance of the internal–external dimension toward the external polarity—the person is heavily biased toward understanding how people (and they themselves) behave and what their intentions are in terms of what they physically do.

In *pretend mode*, thoughts and feelings become severed from reality; in the extreme, this may lead to full dissociative experiences. A prementalizing young child creates mental models and pretend worlds, which can be maintained only for as long as they achieve complete separateness from the world of physical reality (as long as, for example, an adult does not interrupt or spoil the game by getting it "wrong"). Similarly, clients in pretend mode can discuss experiences in pseudo-psychological terms without relating them to any kind of physical or material reality, as if they were creating a pretend world. The client may *hypermentalize* or *pseudomentalize*, a state in which they might talk a lot about states of mind but what they are saying will have little meaning or connection with reality. Attempting talking therapy with clients who are in this mode can lead the worker into lengthy but inconsequential discussions of internal experience that have no link to genuine experience. A client who shows considerable cognitive understanding of mentalizing states but little affective understanding (as discussed earlier, in "Cognitive versus affective mentalizing") may often hypermentalize. This is a state that can often be difficult to distinguish from genuine mentalizing, but it tends to involve excessively lengthy narratives devoid of any real emotional core or even much connection to reality. On first impressions, the person may seem to have extraordinary mentalizing capacities, but they cannot resonate with the feelings underlying their mentalizing efforts (Allen et al., 2008). In addition, when there are no real feelings or emotional experiences that might constrain the individual, they may misuse their cognitive capacity in self-serving ways (e.g. to get others to care for or feel compassion toward them, or to control or coerce others).

The three prementalizing modes are particularly important to recognize as they are often accompanied by a pressure to externalize unmentalized aspects of social experiences such as trauma (so-called "alien-self" parts), which may be expressed in attempts to dominate the mind of others, self-harm, or other types of damaging behavior (Fonagy & Target, 2000).

Trust in communication

The concept of mentalizing is relatively well established within clinical work and research. Our thinking has now developed further, to try to explain how mentalizing difficulties become so deeply entrenched and how mentalizing might help us to think more broadly about the treatment of mental health difficulties. Our argument is that the path to all social learning, including learning about how one's own and others' minds function (i.e. learning to mentalize), is opened up by generating a particular form of trust in a person. This trust is normally first activated in infancy, in relation to the main caregivers. It is trust specifically in *the reliability of communications about the social world*. The term we have used to describe this particular form of trust is *epistemic trust*. This is to convey the sense that it represents trust in socially communicated knowledge about the world (*epistemology* is the theory of knowledge and how it comes to be known). For brevity's sake, we shall simply use the word *trust* here.

The idea of trust might sound rather vague, but we believe the concept is extremely important in understanding how children learn to think about, and interact with, other people. The theory is that one of the central advantages of the evolution of humanity's social mind has been the ability to pass on, from one generation to the next, complex social and cultural information that can help us survive and thrive in our environment. Having an inborn ability to teach and learn allows humans to adapt to very different and increasingly complex cultural situations, rather than having innate, fixed social instincts that would be helpful in only one particular environment. But this reliance on social communication creates a major challenge to the human learner. It would be dangerous to trust absolutely anything that anyone tells us, so how are we to know who to trust? We have evolved to trust those individuals whom we perceive to be invested in promoting the survival of our genes; with all others, particularly other humans, we had best be vigilant.

In short, the theory of epistemic trust emphasizes the social and emotional dimensions to the trust we have in the information about the world that we receive from people we are close to—the people who are "teaching" us. The extent to which we are able to treat the things communicated to us by those we are closest to as *true and personally relevant to us* has a fundamental impact on how much we are able to benefit from our interpersonal relationships. Two brilliant developmental scientists, Gergely Csibra and György Gergely (2006, 2009, 2011), have outlined a revolutionary theory about how humans evolved to teach and learn new and relevant cultural information from one another. They suggest that this human capacity for knowledge transfer is based on a particular sensitivity to signals that, as a learner, we look out for when trying to decide whether to trust, and that, as a teacher, we transmit in trying to encourage a learner to listen. We are using the terms "teacher" and "learner" broadly here; in evolutionary terms, the "teacher" would in most situations have been a genetically related elder seeking to convey useful information to a less experienced juvenile. But the same signals can be thought of as relevant in communication between a schoolteacher and pupil, a politician appealing to voters, or, of course, between a parent/caregiver and a child. The teacher must indicate to the learner that what they are conveying is relevant and should be stored in their mind as useful and valid cultural knowledge. They do this by giving what are termed *ostensive cues*—behavioral signals. Human infants are attuned to respond with particular attention to these ostensive cues, which include eye contact, contingent responding, turn-taking, and the use of a special tone of voice, as well as language as the infant develops, all of which appear to trigger a special mode of learning in the infant.

In brief, ostensive cues trigger *trust in communication*: they signal that what the caregiver is trying to convey is of interest and significance to the child. Ostensive cues appear to have in common a simple message: "I am here for you and I am interested in you," and this opens the child's capacity to listen. Broadly speaking, sensitivity to an infant's current mental state is an ostensive cue—it is likely to open the child's mind to the communicator's message. In a securely attached child, the caregiver, who has been generally sensitive to the infant, comes to be understood as a reliable source of knowledge (see Box 2.1). Good schoolteachers achieve the same thing by being interested in how their pupils

Box 2.1 Stimulating epistemic trust (trust in communication)

- **Attachment to a person who responds sensitively** in early development:
  - This attachment relationship is a **special condition** for generating trust.
  - There is a **cognitive advantage** to experiencing security.
- Generally, any communication marked by **recognition of the listener as an intentional agent** will increase trust and the likelihood of communication being coded as:
  - **Relevant**—the communicator understands this information as specifically applicable to the listener
  - **Generalizable**—it can be applied by the listener again in other situations, rather than just with the communicator
  - **Memorable**—it is retained in the listener's memory as relevant.
- **Ostensive cues trigger trust in communication**, which triggers a special kind of attention to knowledge relevant to the listener.

see the problem they are struggling to learn about. Politicians, too, open this channel of trust by showing (sometimes feigned!) interest in their audience.

But what happens with an individual whose social experiences have led them to a state of chronic mistrust? An individual who has been maltreated or neglected, for example, may learn that their caregiver is not reliable in what they communicate about the world; indeed, they may learn to regard their caregiver as outright ill-intentioned and malign in what they choose to communicate. In this context the individual will appear to be resistant to new information, and might come across as rigid or even bloody-minded, because they treat new knowledge from the communicator with deep suspicion: they will not consider it self-relevant and internalize it (i.e. they will not modify internal structures to accommodate it). They may hear what the communicator is saying, but they are not listening. Their trust in social knowledge and communication has been undermined. Everybody seeks social knowledge, but when such reassurance and input is sought, the content of this communication might then be rejected or its meanings confused, or it may be misinterpreted as having hostile intent.

Thinking about mental illness in terms of the propensity to generate trust or mistrust

To recap, creating trust in social communication is something that human beings evolved in order to be able to teach and learn the things that need to be passed on to assist the younger generation in understanding and surviving in their environment. The normal route by which a child develops this trust is via their relationship with a reliable and adequately mentalizing primary caregiver. In terms of thinking about mental health, the flipside of our complex sensitivity to social learning is that there is more potential for this learning to become disrupted or in some way disturbed; it is here that the theory's relevance to mental health difficulties comes in.

An individual who has been traumatized in childhood has little reason to trust, and will reject information that is inconsistent with their existing beliefs. We may end up describing these individuals as "hard to reach"; in fact, they are simply showing an adaptation to a social environment where information from most attachment figures was likely to be misleading.

We suggest that many forms of mental disorder that involve persistent difficulties with interpersonal functioning are connected to problems using this system for signaling the trustworthiness of social information. Individuals with complex, comorbid mental health difficulties, or who are often described as "hard to reach" because as professionals we find them so difficult to help, are, we suggest, often individuals who experience profound mistrust in relation to social communication. As clinicians working with them, we might try to give ostensive signals, showing that we recognize them and their individual agency, but this just does not seem to work. They understand what we say but they seem to refuse to change (see Box 2.2).

One of the factors that has motivated our thinking about trust is the fact that the traditional categories we use to diagnose and make sense of mental health disorders often feel unhelpfully far removed from the complexities of living with (or trying to help people with) mental health difficulties, particularly those at the more severe end of the spectrum. A serious challenge for anyone interested in mental illness (and its treatment) lies in the fact that many people's psychiatric history over their life course does not follow simple, symptom-defined, diagnosis-led categories. This is particularly true of clients with the kinds of complex needs often encountered in AMBIT work. A client may be referred on the basis of one particular difficulty, but other complications may well coexist, or emerge as more significant at a different stage. A frequently cited example might be conduct disorder in childhood and adolescence developing into depression in adulthood. In other words, as professionals working on the front line so often find, neatly defined psychiatric categories do not reflect the complicated reality of life experience and the overlapping difficulties often encountered by those with more severe levels of mental ill-health.

Box 2.2 Mistrust in social communication (or epistemic mistrust)

- Mistrust in social communication is the consequence of **high levels of vigilance** (the **over-interpretation** of motives and a possible consequence of **hypermentalizing**; Sharp et al., 2011).
- It is the result of a recipient of a communication assuming that the communicator's **intentions are other than those declared,** and therefore not treating the communication as coming from a reliable source.
- Mostly, it consists of **misattribution of intention** and seeing the reasons for someone's actions as malevolent and to be treated with **epistemic hypervigilance** or **excessive epistemic mistrust.**
- The most important consequence of epistemic mistrust is that the **regular process of adjusting beliefs** about the world (oneself in relation to others) remains closed.

Research on the way diagnoses overlap and shift across the life course suggests that it might be more meaningful to think about there being one general factor behind all mental ill-health, which has been labeled the "p factor" (Caspi et al., 2014). Different mental disorders may in part be distinct entities, but they also have features in common, so we should think of them in terms of a single dimension of persistence and severity. Some people (regardless of their specific diagnosis, such as anxiety or conduct problems) are simply more likely to continue to have this or other mental disorders, while others will recover from a single episode. The former group scores much higher on the p factor than the latter group. So we could think in terms of one overarching dimension of *vulnerability to psychological illness*, a vulnerability that can show itself with different symptoms at different times. As an analogy, some people are more likely to catch a cold than others. Why? Well, they have a weaker constitution. What do we mean by that?—perhaps something to do with the quality of functioning of their immune system? Is there a psychological equivalent of the immune system?—perhaps there is.

In addition to greater persistence, a higher p-factor score is associated with increased severity of impairment, more developmental adversity, and greater biological risk. The p-factor concept may help explain why, so far, it has proved so difficult to identify isolated causes, consequences, or biomarkers and to develop specific, tailored treatments for individual psychiatric diagnoses. However, what does the p factor, as described by several research groups, represent beyond a statistical concept? We propose that the p factor may signal vulnerability to psychiatric diagnoses because it reflects an individual's level of trust in social communication: an individual with a high p-factor score is one who, perhaps because of developmental adversity (whether biological or social), is in a state of *epistemic hypervigilance* and *epistemic mistrust*. They are "rigid" and inflexible in the way they respond to their social environment, leaving them unable to resist the assaults of further adversity (see Box 2.3). Their psychological "immune system" is not functioning well. We could say that they lack *resilience*.

This has major consequences for psychosocial interventions. It would mean, for instance, that people with relatively *low* p-factor scores will be most responsive to psychosocial interventions. A depressed person with a low p-factor score may, for instance, recover with the help of brief cognitive-behavioral therapy or psychodynamic therapy. These individuals are relatively "easy to reach" in terms of treatment because they are open to social learning in the form of therapeutic intervention. In contrast, a depressed person with a *high* p-factor score, who is burdened with high levels of comorbidity, longer-term difficulties, and greater impairment, is likely to show intense treatment resistance because

> **Box 2.3 Mistrust in social communication and the nature of psychopathology**
>
> - Social adversity (most deeply, **trauma following neglect**) leads to:
>   - The **destruction of trust in social knowledge** of all kinds
>   - **Rigidity**
>   - Being **hard to reach**.
> - The client cannot change because he/she **cannot accept new information as relevant** (to generalize it) to other social contexts.
> - **Personality disorder** is thus not "disorder of personality," but a condition of **inaccessibility to cultural communications** that are relevant to the self from the social context.
> - **Key relationships where this impacts:**
>   - Partner
>   - Therapist } **Epistemic mistrust** closes the client to learning from these
>   - Teacher

they cannot trust the interpersonal context of therapy; they hear but cannot listen. Their high level of epistemic mistrust, or outright epistemic freezing, creates an insurmountable block in the face of psychosocial intervention from a therapist, a putative attachment figure. We consider it likely that such clients will require more long-term therapy, which should (at least at the first stage of their treatment, and probably repeated throughout their intervention) mix whatever model of therapy it is with specific efforts to reopen trust in social communication.

Resilience

We have alluded to resilience already, but there is more that we can say about this complex concept. Psychological resilience and how to promote it has become a high-profile issue in policy discussions about adolescent mental health and what we can do to improve it. There have been many studies, which have produced myriad different findings about the possible factors that promote resilience, from biological and genetic explanations, to the family environment (attachment relationships and parenting style), to socioeconomic circumstances. This abundance of different possible explanations partly reflects the complicated reality of how our minds are affected both by the world around us and by our genes. However, it leaves us in a difficult position when it comes to dealing with the reality of what is likely to create more resilience in a vulnerable and troubled client.

To promote resilience, we need to understand not only what promotes resilience, but what the mechanism behind the development of resilience might be. Recreating the factors that promote resilience in one context may be totally irrelevant or even contraindicated in another. For example, high socioeconomic status (SES) normally predicts resilience, but one of the best studies of resilience, the Western Aboriginal Child Health Survey of over 5,000 Australian aboriginal children (Hopkins et al., 2012), found that high SES actually decreased resilience. This paradoxical finding could be readily interpreted in terms of the support aboriginal children get through a sense of belonging to their culture and being protected from prejudice. High-SES children had less knowledge of their culture, and as a consequence were heightened in their sensitivity to prejudice and oppression, which was also more common in the high-SES neighborhoods where they lived. It is not surprising, then, that the rates of depression and delinquency were highest in this group.

We argue that the mechanism of resilience is nested in social communication. This is because openness to social information and the potential to update social knowledge are essential ingredients of the ability to appraise the social world and optimize one's adaptation to social circumstances. In other words, without trust in communication, the individual may function well until such time that adjustment to changed social circumstances is required. If this adjustment depends on being able to benefit from the input of social communication from other people, then excessive epistemic vigilance will undermine resilience. Highly resilient people normally have strong trust in the social network on which they rely. The reopening of trust in communication—which can become closed down for many combinations of reasons (the myriad factors that undermine resilience, mentioned above)—is what can enable someone to become more resilient. Our understanding of resilience fits with the idea of a p factor for psychopathology: somebody who has a *high* score on the p-factor scale will have *low* levels of psychological resilience. Both the p-factor score and the level of resilience indicate individuals' likely difficulties in terms of their capacity to trust the social communication they receive (see Box 2.4).

So where does mentalizing come in? Mentalizing is, as we hinted above, the paradigmatic ostensive cue; we might even say it is the "royal road" to epistemic trust. Sensitivity of the caregiver to the child during the formation of the attachment bond also promotes trust in communication, which the child can then generalize to other relationships where appropriate. The way in which sensitive caregiving promotes this trust is via the caregiver's mentalizing. As

> **Box 2.4 The inverse relationship between the p factor and resilience (flip sides of the same process)**
>
> - **Low resilience** reflects an adaptation that results from persistent communication problems in development, combined with genetic vulnerability, resulting in epistemic hypervigilance, which prevents or undermines a reappraisal process and results in apparent rigidity (imperviousness to social influence).
> - **The failure to engage in meaningful reappraisal** creates a general vulnerability to psychosocial stress (low resilience), which yields to the high prediction of future psychopathology from the p factor.
> - **Improving mentalizing** increases trust in communication, which in turn generates resilience through the improved capacity for appraising and reappraising stressful events.

we have mentioned, mentalizing is generated in an attachment context, and its rapid development is linked to secure attachment. Good mentalizing develops the capacity to appropriately interpret the ostensive social cues from others. A good mentalizer trusts others more (research has shown this) and will accurately discern social cues from others showing genuine interest in their person—or, indeed, the cues that suggest it would be better to be more vigilant. The capacity to mentalize is the key that opens the psychological door to receive reliable social communication. It is also the lock that identifies when it is self-protective to be vigilant. An individual with appropriate openness to social communication is using their mentalizing capacity to good effect. Enhancing mentalizing in therapy improves this effective gatekeeping function in relation to social information—it rekindles the capacity to learn well and benefit from social experiences.

Trust as the common factor in therapies

"Psychotherapy" in all its many and varied forms might actually be best understood as simply a rather specialized modern variant of an activity that has naturally been a part of human communication for a very long time—turning to others in times of need to make sense of what is happening to us, particularly what is happening to our internal mental world. Using other people's perspectives and social knowledge—their minds—to gain reassurance and to help us find a balanced footing, while negotiating what is going on both in the social world and inside our own heads, is something we all do in different ways across life, albeit most conspicuously in infancy and childhood. But, for this to be meaningful, there needs to be a workable level of trust in social communication.

In saying that mistrust in the communication of social knowledge might underpin the p factor, we are also saying that the relearning or reopening of this trust may be an aspect, or a shared component, or may perhaps even be at the heart of all effective psychotherapeutic interventions. Put simply, we suggest that *effective interventions generate epistemic trust—trust in communication—in individuals who struggle to relax their vigilance in more ordinary social situations.*

The psychotherapeutic communication systems

Based on all the ideas we have discussed so far in the above section about mentalizing and trust, we have drawn some rather bold conclusions about what it is that makes any therapeutic mental health intervention effective. We want to do so not because we believe our model to be any more accurate than the hundreds of others that have preceded it; rather, we believe that the model offers a simple recipe for carrying out interventions of various kinds, including the multimodal and adaptive protocol proposed in this book. We propose that in most evidence-based effective therapies there are three distinct processes of communication at work at different stages that make an intervention effective.

Communication System 1: The teaching and learning of content

The first stage of any effective intervention involves the therapist using their practice model to explain to the client a way of thinking about their social situation and their physical and mental state in a way that seems sensible and believable to the client. The exact nature of the model explained by the therapist can vary massively from intervention to intervention: the point is that the model conveyed is experienced by the client as being personally relevant. The client has the experience of being understood through this therapeutic form of marked mirroring, which involves a subtle and rich process of ostensive cueing on the part of the therapist. It requires the therapist to be able to mentalize the client effectively; to be able to understand the client's state well enough to be able to respond with the right forms of ostensive cues; and to adapt their theoretical model of the mind, of pathology, and of change to the individual, so they can relate their model of intervention in a manner that fits with the client's own experiences of their own mental state. The actual content of the practice model can provide extremely valuable ways for the client to understand—to mentalize—themself and their reactions to others. But there is a much more generic advantage that comes from communicating this social knowledge: in this process, the client experiences being fully recognized as an agentive person with his/her own mind. This is what skillful, sensitive therapeutic mentalizing involves, and it results in the beginning of a relaxation of epistemic mistrust.

Communication System 2: The re-emergence of robust mentalizing

In describing how the intervention is relevant to the client's needs and experiences, the therapist has to work insightfully to recognize who the client really is and how they feel. By making the client feel recognized in this way, the therapist is in effect helping the client to reopen their trust in receiving social communication from attachment figures—a naturally occurring form of trust that has been damaged as a result of environmental adversity, genetic propensity, or both. By effectively mentalizing the client, the therapist is modeling how they mentalize in an open, trustworthy, and relatively low-arousal environment. As the client engages with the therapist's model and develops genuine curiosity about the model as it flexibly unfolds in relation to the client's own situation, the intersubjective processes that lie at the heart of creating a mentalized social environment come alive. This creates a virtuous cycle in which the client, in being sensitively responded to, gradually retreats from their epistemic isolation and may begin to exercise and develop their own mentalizing skills—skills that will help them discern ostensive cues outside the context of therapy. The process summarized here is a simplified version of what is often a complex, non-linear progression, but it is a process in which, ideally, the client experiences a shift in their levels of trust in communication and develops more balanced and robust mentalizing capacities.

Improvements in mentalizing or social cognition may thus be a common consequence of quite different interventions. However, we would like to suggest (in a way that may seem surprising for avowed supporters of mentalizing-based therapy!) that this improvement in mentalizing is not in itself the clinching objective of enduringly effective therapy. Mentalizing that just stays within the consulting room will not generalize into lasting improvement. The significance of improved mentalizing is that it enables the client to learn wisely, in a more discerning manner than hitherto, from their wider social world—which takes us to the final stage of the change process.

Communication System 3: The re-emergence of social learning

The improved mentalizing that results from a successful intervention ideally brings about improved social relations and experiences outside the consulting room. Improved levels of trust and the breaking down of rigid ways of interpreting and responding to social experiences pave the way for the client to accumulate experiences of social interaction that are benign, or at least manageable, in terms of maintaining resilient mentalizing. This creates another virtuous cycle in which more balanced and robust mentalizing generates and supports deeper, wider, and increasingly meaningful access to social information and social networks. This final critical stage of social learning *beyond* therapy is of course dependent on the individual's social environment being benign, or at least "benign enough." Therapeutic change can only be sustained, according to this thinking, if the client is able to use, and even to change (through the seeking out of more mentalizing relationships), their social environment in a way that allows them to continue to relax epistemic hypervigilance and foster their mentalizing strengths.

This concept of the three communication systems, and in particular the role of the client's social environment in determining how successful any intervention can ultimately be, redirects our attention to interventions that help to directly target the environmental factors that have the potential to support the individual's capacity to benefit from benign aspects of their environment. In the next section, we will discuss how culture and environment might relate to mental disorders, and how this emphasis on the environment lies behind the truly systemic nature of an intervention such as AMBIT.

The role of culture: Is mental illness a natural adaptation?

By definition, the kinds of clients we encounter in typical AMBIT work are often unable to manage within the norms and demands of certain aspects of mainstream life. This can express itself in very different ways depending upon the individual concerned: as extreme vulnerability, self-harm, aggressiveness and hostility, or substance misuse. However, as clinicians we are often also struck by the courage, endurance, and sharp intuition shown by these clients, who often have personal histories of considerable adversity, as they attempt to navigate their way through highly difficult circumstances.

The theory of epistemic mistrust incorporates the idea that despite the highly dysfunctional nature of some of the behaviors shown by the clients for whom AMBIT was designed, these kinds of behaviors do have underlying adaptive purposes. Although by normative social expectations they are dysfunctional, these behavioral responses are characteristic of a kind of fixed "emergency functioning" switched on by certain social and emotional conditions (and perhaps increased when combined with an individual's genetic propensity to function this way). Communicative mistrust and the mentalizing difficulties that go with it might more accurately be understood as a learned response to the social "lessons" to which they have been exposed (see Box 2.5). For example, lower levels of reflective and controlled mentalizing, greater aggressiveness, and higher

> **Box 2.5 Epistemic hypervigilance as a form of adaptation to the social environment**
>
> - **Lower** levels of **mentalizing**, greater **aggressiveness**, and higher **sensitivity** to perceived threats are all **adaptive** responses to certain **cultural environments** (hypersensitivity to issues of **shame and honor/lack of faith** in the support of external **authorities and institutions**) in which families are driven to psychologically enculturate their children.
> - **Social learning** from the immediate **family and culture** can help us account for the relationship between individual behaviors—adolescent male gun crime, for example—and the culture that engenders it.
> - **To succeed, mentalizing interventions** need to take place within the context of the family, and enhance the quality of **mentalizing within the family system.**

sensitivity to perceived threats are adaptive responses to certain very real and very threatening environments that families must psychologically enculturate their children into. These families are—for many possible reasons—operating at a level of stress/distress. What we are pointing out is that there is a close relationship between the wider social environment and the kind of social communication transmitted to the child by their family. If the wider environment is perceived as hostile, dangerous, or lacking in compassion—in essence, as non-mentalizing—it is only natural that certain non-mentalizing modes of operating within that environment are "caught" by the family and then "transmitted" within it. This is where our thinking about mentalizing social systems (discussed more fully in Chapter 6) is of fundamental importance to our understanding of how we can support mentalizing in families. If there is little or no faith in external authorities and institutions as safe, fair, and reliable adjudicators in the face of very real social conflict, then a mentalizing stance in relation to social relationships is likely only to leave the individual more vulnerable; for example, it may ultimately render the individual less able to make use of aggressive and violent social strategies, which might seem absolutely necessary for self-protection. In such an environment, more reactive, impulsive forms of mentalizing and non-mentalizing modes of behavior, which may most conspicuously take the form of aggression or risky sexual behavior, might be at one level an *adaptive* response to the mind's (not unfounded) understanding that it is functioning in a high-risk environment.

The theory behind the AMBIT model is, then, one that works at many different levels. We consider the impact of the most intimate interpersonal attachment relationships that infants first experience, and we also consider much wider cultural pressures and expectations that might impact upon young people's functioning and their resilience. We argue that it is via the concept of mentalizing and the related notion of trust in communication that these influences come to shape an individual's behavior and mental state.

This approach is fundamentally underpinned by the idea that we are all dependent on a mentalizing system around us to support our own capacity to mentalize. In the chapters that follow, we emphasize the importance of this concept in relation to the AMBIT worker as much as the client. We will argue that having a mentalizing team around the worker is essential for maintaining good practice. The clinical work with the clients we encounter involves constant exposure to non-mentalizing modes of thinking (the psychic equivalence, pretend mode, and teleological mode described earlier) and the behaviors they engender (self-harm, neglect, violence, etc.). We suggest that it is the impact of the creation of a non-mentalizing system of social communication, not the imperviousness of non-mentalizing per se, that makes such clients so clinically challenging.

One of the defining characteristics of "hard-to-reach" clients is that the patterns of social dysfunction they show are relatively enduring. Yet, our clinical experience points to a far more optimistic long-term outcome with these clients. The apparent inconsistency between these clients being labeled "hard to reach" yet in fact appearing quite responsive to therapy can be made sense of by thinking about the way the non-mentalizing actions of these clients can create non-mentalizing social systems that in turn sustain their condition; this includes the clinic settings where they are, often abortively, invited to attend. We suggest that it is unrealistic to expect a practitioner to maintain an effective mentalizing stance in the medium to long term if they are not adequately supported in maintaining their own capacity to mentalize, ideally by a surrounding team that is not directly exposed to—and thus protected from becoming part of—the client's (dysfunctional) social system.

To address this, a systemic intervention is needed. In the ideal imagined picture of a clinical encounter, the client and the practitioner are separated from external influences, almost splendidly isolated in their own clinical world within their specially designated space (a consulting room). The practitioner is then in a position to enhance the client's capacity to reflect, to question, and to focus simultaneously on both other and self, inside and outside. But the messier reality is that the practitioner becomes embedded within the client's social survival mechanism, and this survival mechanism tends to work to destroy balanced mentalizing, normally erring on the side of being unreflective, externally focused, emotional, and impulsive. It is unrealistic, and completely counter to our theoretical understanding of mentalizing as an interactive process, to expect the practitioner's compensatory mentalizing to be able to withstand such pressures. Practitioners require their own system of support relationships, primarily from other workers, in order to scaffold their capacity to mentalize, and in so doing, to be able to facilitate trust in social communication.

AMBIT is a systemic intervention in terms of its theoretical understanding of how low levels of trust in communication and subsequent mentalizing difficulties can be an adaptive response to an individual's environment. But AMBIT is also a systemic intervention in how it understands the keyworker's practice. Similarly, in using the keyworker as the main point of liaison with the various agencies involved with the client concerned, AMBIT tries to make sense of what often feels like a non-mentalizing, bureaucratically chaotic, and unsympathetic system. The AMBIT approach is at one level motivated by highly practical considerations, but it also reflects theoretical considerations about the importance of the social context as the unsung hero of successful therapy: the troubled client has learned—often for good reason—to distrust their social environment and to distrust communications about how best to navigate this environment. This is where the alienation of so-called "alienated youth" originates. AMBIT attempts to reopen clients' minds to a different kind of social knowledge—one that is more trustworthy—but it also seeks to support changes in the clients' social environment, to make it responsive and reinforcing of change.

References

Allen, J. G., Fonagy, P., & Bateman, A. W. (2008). *Mentalizing in Clinical Practice* (Washington, DC: American Psychiatric Press).

Bateman, A. W., & Fonagy, P. (eds.) (2012). *Handbook of Mentalizing in Mental Health Practice* (Washington, DC: American Psychiatric Publishing).

Caspi, A., Houts, R. M., Belsky, D. W., Goldman-Mellor, S. J., Harrington, H., Israel, S., … Moffitt, T. E. (2014). The p factor: One general psychopathology factor in the structure of psychiatric disorders? *Clinical Psychological Science* 2: 119–37. doi: 10.1177/2167702613497473

Csibra, G., & Gergely, G. (2006). Social learning and social cognition: the case for pedagogy. In: M. H. Johnson, & Y. Munakata (eds.), *Processes of Change in Brain and Cognitive Development. Attention and Performance XXI*, pp. 249–74. Oxford, UK: Oxford University Press.

Csibra, G., & Gergely, G. (2009). Natural pedagogy. *Trends in Cognitive Sciences* 13: 148–53. doi: 10.1016/j.tics.2009.01.005

Csibra, G., & Gergely, G. (2011). Natural pedagogy as evolutionary adaptation. *Philosophical Transactions of the Royal Society of London. Series B, Biological Sciences* 366: 1149–57. doi: 10.1098/rstb.2010.0319

Fonagy, P., Lorenzini, N., Campbell, C., & Luyten, P. (2014). Why are we interested in attachments? In: P. Holmes, & S. Farnfield (eds.), *The Routledge Handbook of Attachment: Theory*, pp. 38–51. Hove, UK: Routledge.

Fonagy, P., & Target, M. (2000). Playing with reality: III. The persistence of dual psychic reality in borderline patients. *International Journal of Psychoanalysis* **81**: 853–74.

Hopkins, K. D., Taylor, C. L., D'Antoine, H. A., & Zubrick, S. R. (2012). Predictors of resilient psychosocial functioning in Western Australian Aboriginal young people exposed to high family-level risk. In: M. Ungar (ed.), *The Social Ecology of Resilience: A Handbook of Theory and Practice*, pp. 425–40. New York, NY: Springer.

Sharp, C., Ha, C., & Fonagy, P. (2011). Get them before they get you: Trust, trustworthiness, and social cognition in boys with and without externalizing behavior problems. *Development and Psychopathology* **23**: 647–58. doi: 10.1017/S0954579410000003

Chapter 3

Active Planning: Mapping the territory and navigational skills for AMBIT-influenced work

Introduction: A map of the map

This chapter is the first of two that collectively cover the work that we do with our clients. This chapter tries to give an overview of the way teams and individual workers work toward creating structure and supporting progress in territory that is often experienced by clients and workers alike as extremely unstructured and directionless. It is really about how to create plans, and how our core theory of mentalizing contributes to this process, adding nuances and adaptations that are of value for our client group, in whom intentions and goals are often experienced as changing. The chapter has three sections:

1. **Having a plan is better than "winging it":** exploring the value of planning
2. **Map of the journey:** laying out a rather generic "map" or "treatment journey," and elaborating on some key tasks at each stage
3. **Active Planning:** describing the nuances and key adaptations to standard "case management" that mentalizing theory suggests, a process that we call "Active Planning."

In Chapter 4 we cover in more detail the way mentalizing theory supports a worker to conduct themself in face-to-face work, so this chapter is about *organizing* the work, and the next one is about *doing* it. Peppered throughout both chapters are references to other chapters, because, at the risk of repetition, AMBIT is as much about the activity that supports sustainable face-to-face work (working with your team and with your networks, and learning at work) as it is about the work itself.

SECTION 1. Having a plan is better than "winging it"

AMBIT has its own wheel (introduced in Chapter 1), but we do not claim to be reinventing the wheel. Working in an AMBIT-influenced way is not a practice designed out of disrespect for usual practice; many other already-existing approaches to working with clients have shown safety and effectiveness. Where differences from current practice do exist, we hope these are experienced as nuanced modifications, and where change is required we err in favor of incremental evolution rather than revolution. AMBIT seeks to make effective practices (often previously carried out implicitly by workers in teams) more explicit and intentionally chosen. In addition, it offers a learning framework both for understanding why such practices are helpful, and for continuing to develop more effective practices by learning from experience and evidence.

Establishing and conducting oneself in a therapeutic relationship may be likened to the circus trick of setting a number of plates spinning, then working to ensure you keep most of them going while more plates are added. This chapter aims to describe in simple terms the key spinning plates that are required, and the sequence in which to get them started, take them down, or pass them over to the care of others. In the second section of the chapter we offer a sequence of phases of work (the different spinning plates, as it were) that are required during the course of intervention.

An alternative (and marginally less daunting) analogy would be that of a journey through unfamiliar territory. We all know the basics of how to walk, and while some are more skilled than others at climbing or bushcraft, route-finding in any journey requires particular skills. AMBIT-influenced practice makes explicit attempts to balance and counterbalance the different elements of the AMBIT stance and core practices (see Chapter 1), and uses mentalizing and mentalization-based techniques as key "navigational aids," much as the hillwalker uses a compass. These techniques are habitually deployed in day-to-day AMBIT practice, just as the trekker on a cloud-scraped hillside must constantly use the discipline of referring back and forth between map, compass, and physical landmarks in order to steer a course through unfamiliar territory where the line of sight comes and goes.

> **Eric**
>
> Eric had agreed an initial plan directed at controlling his cannabis use and returning to college. On the "journey," his keyworker finds he is sometimes more preoccupied with his relationship with his father than he is with either of these two headline goals. The worker's challenge is to stay attuned to Eric's current worries while staying on track. Sometimes this requires "detours," and over time they agree that the map of Eric's progress requires some redrawing to include an additional destination that relates to family relationships. At times, as the worker and Eric swing back and forth between focusing on different goals and addressing occasional crises, it is helpful for the worker to have some means of reminding herself "where we are" in the overall journey.

Thus, an important part of the culture of any AMBIT-influenced team is a core and shared assumption that work should happen as part of an explicit and shared plan, assiduously avoiding the counter-position—that we simply work intuitively. If we are honest, the latter position suggests an underlying assumption that "what's good for my client is simply more of me." If they are like us, most workers will be able to put their hands up to having set forth on a session without a clear and explicit purpose in mind. Sometimes this will have worked out, but experience and evidence strongly suggest that it will have worked in spite of the lack of a plan, not because of it.

In the second section we lay out our "map" of the different phases of AMBIT-influenced work, which should orient the worker broadly to "what happens when," and offer a flexible timeline upon which the work described in Chapters 4 to 6 rests. We hope that most experienced practitioners will recognize the basic form described in this section—it would be unnecessary to veer dramatically from a core process that has evolved from practice over many years. Most teams will already have some version of this journey established, and we recognize that a radical restructuring dictated from elsewhere can cause as many problems as it seeks to solve. Our argument is that a range of refinements and adaptations to this "standard model" of a client journey is required to suit our particular client group.

Of course, the sequence of events that we lay out as "the map" is never straightforwardly linear in real life: face-to-face work is rarely, if ever, uncluttered by chaos, crises, and necessary revisions, and demands a much richer mix of iterative evaluation, trial intervention, re-evaluation, revised intervention, repeat evaluations, further revisions, and so on. To quote the systemic thinker Gregory Bateson (1972) and his philosophical predecessor, Alfred Korzybski (1941), "the map is not the territory." We reference this analogy throughout this chapter to emphasize the need to hold in mind that our plans (or maps) are always and only ever mental representations; an appropriately mentalized humility and tentativeness about their applicability is warranted, however crucial they are in the making of effective progress. Not only are the maps we have sometimes inaccurate, but the territory itself often changes. The faltering progress that we make alongside our clients is rarely without critical major diversions that characterize their vulnerability to circumstance: bereavements, legal crises, house moves, family break-ups, the impact of romantic attachments, drug or alcohol binges, bullying, exam results, and so on.

The third section of this chapter covers the principles and practices of this approach to planning, which we refer to as Active Planning, in more detail. We highlight a variety of nuances and adaptations, centered on mentalizing, that bring value when working with clients whose intentions and motivation—let alone their circumstances—frequently change. In addition, we highlight the requirement for a team culture that actively embraces these principles. Despite the difficulty of planning in these contexts, one of the axioms that AMBIT stands by is that having a plan is better than "winging it" without one.

So, this chapter intends to describe both a "map" and the required "map-work" (the two being quite different but of equal importance) that guide progress. The phases of work to which we now turn constitute the most basic outline of a prototypical map, while the map-work, which we call Active Planning, concludes this chapter.

SECTION 2. Map of the journey: The phases of AMBIT-influenced work

What we now try to sketch represents some of the key elements, milestones, or waymarks in the process of helping, but the precise details of how each team defines and operates in each of these phases will rightly vary as they adapt their practice to local ecologies.

Standard case management

There is, of course, no completely standard approach to the management of casework, but broadly speaking, most services apply some version of the process illustrated in Figure 3.1.

Standard models of case management involve linked processes of *engagement* and *assessment*, which together feed into the creation of shared understandings between worker and client, a process that is commonly framed as

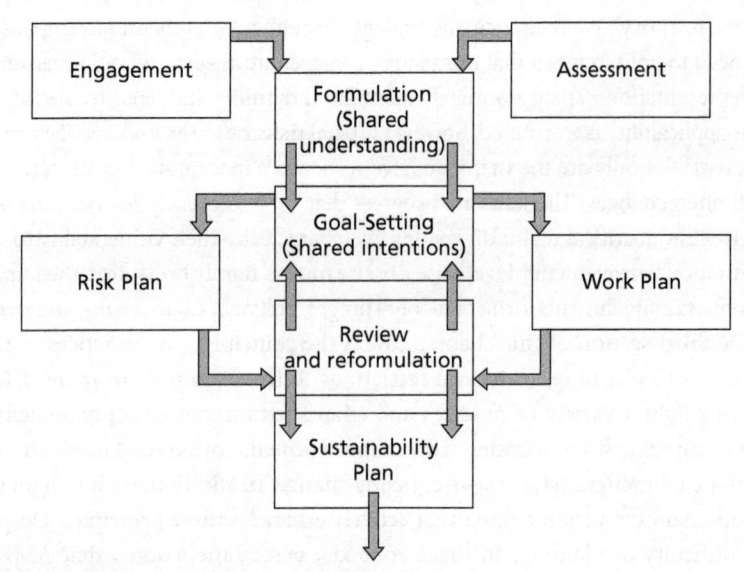

Figure 3.1 Standard model of case management.

formulation—explaining the nature of the difficulties, how they arose, and what maintains them. This may or may not include the more formal process of diagnosis, and may carry implications for the interventions that evidence suggests would be most appropriate to address the client's difficulties. Next, the process of clarifying shared intentions between worker and client allows for *goal-setting*, with a small number of overarching treatment aims (to feel better, to restore relationships with family, etc.) under which more specific goals are located (to improve scores on a specific depression measure, to reduce cannabis use by a specific amount or achieve abstinence, etc.). These goals will shape the *intervention (or work) plan*, with a range of specific activities required by the client, by the worker, or by other key individuals. Coupled to this, the *risk plan* takes account of likely (or less likely, but more serious) crises that present risks of harm to the client or others, and defines a series of contingencies that either mitigate these risks or provide the safest responses to predictable worst-case scenarios. Built into any such case management plan are regular *reviews*, which measure progress against predetermined goals and offer the opportunity for reformulating the difficulties in the light of this new evidence. In turn, these reviews may lead to adjustments to either the risk plan or the intervention plan. At a certain point the review leads to a final stage and, ultimately, an ending, and is therefore directed toward *sustainability planning* for the time after this process of facilitated and co-created change has run its course.

Table 3.1 outlines in the simplest terms the key phases of a "client journey." In the following sections, we describe each of these phases in detail, with practical pointers toward what happens when, and how. However, we deliberately do not lay out timescales for the phases of work; a mentalizing approach encourages us to keep in mind that this map is not the territory, and we must avoid creating a concrete or teleological program that risks being experienced as noncontingent (see Chapter 2) by clients or workers. Acceptance of local variability and the requirement for judicious adaptation is the rule here. Of course, for some teams that work over very short timescales, or within very tightly defined parameters of a very specialized task, this process might be significantly compressed or adapted. For others that work over much longer timescales, with a much broader remit, it will be different again, but the principles of knowing what you are trying to do, having plans that address positive change and risk, and having a system for reviewing how you are getting on, and plans about how to end well, are, we hope, fairly commonly accepted.

We cover the adaptive aspects of planning in the third and final section of this chapter under the heading of Active Planning, which seeks to capture the "map-reading" skills, including the adaptations required to use a map such as this helpfully in the territory where AMBIT seeks to exert its influence.

Table 3.1 The phases of AMBIT-influenced work

PHASE 1	Getting Started (Initial Phase)
1.	**Engagement:** The first task is engagement—to *create a relationship* with a client in their environment so that they would be prepared to meet again and to make steps on any kind of journey with their keyworker.
2.	**Assessment:** To *map the terrain* (emotional, economic, social, biological, educational, developmental, legal, etc.) where the client and their support network see themselves as being right now; where they need or want to get to (in other words, what effective help could hope to achieve); and how they might get there (in other words, what form such help might usefully take).
3.	**Risk assessment:** Safety and good governance requires that *crisis contingency plans* are drawn up to cover the most significant risks that have been identified.
4.	**Formulation:** To *develop shared understandings*, the ways in which key parties see the problem must be articulated and shared in ways that are both understandable and trusted. Differences between different viewpoints must be understood, and be experienced by each party as having been understood.
5.	**Goal-setting:** *Waymarks on the journey* (even if the final destinations that each has indicated may differ) must be agreed upon at least sufficiently to justify the beginning of purposeful work together. Then, it is important to *create some means of measuring progress* on the journey (so that not only the worker but also the client and others can determine whether the intended help is being helpful or not).
PHASE 2	**Working on Things Together (Intervention Phase)**
6.	**Working to plan:** At this point, what might be seen as *the work, proper* (i.e. more focused sessions and tasks) may begin, although of course much effort and planning will have already taken place.
7.	**Reviewing and reformulating:** *Regular reviews* of progress, and if necessary reformulation and the adaptation of goals in the light of new information and understandings, help to maintain and measure progress.
PHASE 3	**Sustaining Change (Maintenance Phase)**
8.	A *maintenance phase* may be required to support clients whose needs are so significant as to require lower-level monitoring and relapse prevention over a longer period of time.
PHASE 4	**Consolidating the Back-up Team (Ending Phase)**
9.	**Sustainability planning:** Finally (in fact, permeating the work from the very beginning) there is a separate stream, which evokes powerfully the AMBIT principle of "Scaffolding existing relationships." This is the *preparation for ending*, so as to leave the client at the appropriate point, with (hopefully) increased resilience, including ongoing plans and access to necessary resources—a back-up team of their own, just as their worker models how they are sustained by a team around them.

In Chapter 4 we will "zoom in" beyond this organization of care to address more directly how workers can apply theory to direct face-to-face work.

Initial phase

Initiating and creating a relationship (engagement)

Some of the practical skills and specific techniques that can be used to support the development of a therapeutic relationship with a client and his or her care network (i.e. engagement) are described in more detail in the third section of this chapter, and there is much more about this in Chapter 4. Attention to this task is the touchstone of most therapeutic work; of course, it is required at the very beginning of any planned treatment journey, but the activity of achieving attunement to the client's or carer's states of mind, and offering something of a fit between this and our interventions, should continue throughout the journey. This process of "finding a fit" describes well the activity and function of mentalizing.

(a) Introducing the worker and service

Careful consideration of how to introduce oneself (or the service) to the client and family is critical. Prior discussion with a referrer, a family member, or another professional who knows the client, so long as it does not break boundaries of confidentiality, may help a worker to predict the most effective approach to take when it comes to talking to them. Cultural aspects are critical; for instance, many families with a more traditional structure and hierarchy would object if a worker called and initially insisted on speaking to the young person, as this may implicitly undermine understandings of authority in that family. On calling a family, it is often helpful to ask, "Who would be the right person for me to speak to about …?" rather than assuming knowledge and asking for a specific family member.

(b) Team around the Worker

(i) *Context for a Team around the Worker.* In seeking to establish a helpful relationship with the client, the AMBIT-influenced worker is supported by their understanding of the "Team around the Worker" (see also Chapter 5). This phrase is used in AMBIT to highlight the critical importance of peer-to-peer supervisory relationships between workers, but it also invites a complementary mentalizing perspective on the client's predicament in a multi-professional environment.

In considering a new referral to the team, the Team around the Worker is an invitation to place the client's existing relationships of help centrally, rather than the organizational requirements to deliver help. We invite consideration from the very beginning of whether a worker *whom the client sees as trustworthy* is already engaged with this client, via whom the client might best be introduced either to the AMBIT worker or to the work that they do. In our view, it is too often the case that professional roles and responsibilities take priority over other relational aspects of help such as trust, understanding, and culture, so that helping systems are often organized in a rather "industrial" model that matches problems to (previously unknown to the client) expertise and authority (e.g. to perform cognitive-behavioral therapy (CBT), risk assessment, medication oversight, etc.) rather than prioritizing the likelihood that any help on offer is perceived as accessible, trustworthy, and acceptable. Where this "industrial" model works well, the procedures required to help tend to be clear, repeatable, and technically distinct (Porter, 2010), although we propose that it also requires a certain level of epistemic trust on the part of the clients (see Chapter 2). In the field where AMBIT is positioned, this is not so obviously the case. We do not in any way discount the value of expert interventions, but are here addressing the need for help to be accessible through working relationships.

From the client's perspective, we must acknowledge that a "Team around the Client" (or "Team around the Child," the conventional phrase used in the UK to summarize multi-professional input to a young person's needs) may be the last thing they actually want. Not uncommonly, while struggling to develop a single relationship of trust with one adult, young people in our target population experience the well-intentioned approach of additional workers or agencies (albeit with special skills and authority) as (a) overwhelming in relation to their fragile relationship-building skills, on account of the implicit demands for "serial intimacy"; (b) too demanding in terms of the number of appointments in their weekly diary, counteracting efforts to settle them into education, training, or work placements; and (c) offering a "tower of Babel" experience of differing professional jargon, advice, and (occasionally frankly contradictory) opinions.

The last of these points we see as inevitable in large complex networks, formed as they are from agencies with different remits, different targets, different assessment and treatment models, and different professional "languages." This "dis-integration" is discussed in more detail in Chapter 6. Redefining our expectations of multi-agency working in this way, however, does not mean that there are not practical and effective ways to counteract this "dis-integrating" influence, and these, too, are covered in more detail in Chapter 6. We must emphasize that we do not disagree with the notion that specialist skills, delivered by specialized agencies, are helpful. It is just that, in our experience, achieving this with multiple services in an integrated way is marginally more difficult than rocket science, and this seems to us to be a commonly overlooked fact, often leading to more heat than light.

Conversely, some clients (particularly those whose attachment style may be described as "disinhibited") appear to welcome the opportunity to engage multiple workers, but they may do so in ways that are not therapeutic. This might include making multiple superficial attachments, which have a "pretend mode" quality about them, lacking convincing emotional depth or frankness and instead allowing—even encouraging—the client to move back and forth between workers, often disclosing selective, alarming, stirring, or seductive elements of a worrying overall story to different workers. This response makes perfectly good sense if there is a fundamental epistemic mistrust (see Chapter 2) and expectations on the part of the client that full disclosure of the story to an individual helper would result in rejection or exploitation. However, such "helping" relationships do not make that help *helpful*. They increase fragmentation, often providing the context for a paralysis of the network's ability to understand or develop coherent strategies for risk management or change. This has been well described in the psychoanalytic literature over many years (Main, 1957).

(ii) *Taking the client's perspective: Who is the "key" worker?* Thus, in the initial stages at least, any worker or agency should first ask whether there is any requirement at all for a new direct relationship to be made with the client, and if so, whether now is the most appropriate time to do this. There might be a positive existing relationship (with a youth worker, social worker, or Youth Offending Team (YOT) officer, for instance) through which at least the earliest phases of a new workstream might be introduced or perhaps even delivered.

In such a case, this existing person would be the "keyworker" that a system of care should make itself aware of and consider how best to support. Critically, this keyworker is defined not by the *system* as an organizational role, in relation to their relative importance in the hierarchies of agency or task, but by the *client*, in their perception of "Who is key to me?", "Who seems most interesting/safe/helpful to me?", or "Who 'gets' me best?". Of course, we are not suggesting that statutory obligations are simply jettisoned (for instance, the YOT that must have weekly face-to-face contact with a client on the orders of the Court). Instead, alongside the inevitable demands and constraints of the system, the fostering of a complementary culture that explicitly considers the client's experience of care *and attempts to adapt the offer of help in the light of this understanding* is equally important.

We do not deny the challenges this approach may pose to systems inevitably constrained by finances and commissioning, regulatory, or organizational frameworks. It is our belief that there are reciprocal gains for the component parts of a care system, however, if the incremental strengthening of such a culture across a locality is encouraged. Support for increased role flexibility across agencies, based upon the needs of the client and within defined constraints, may improve the outcomes for clients who are otherwise prone to disengage from care, which may make things worse for everyone. We note that a well-functioning Team around the Client will often arrive at precisely the same position as this, functioning as a gatekeeper in sequencing and staging the approaches of additional workers into the clinical arena, avoiding the kind of unintentional overwhelming of the client that we have described.

Where there is no obvious existing keyworker identified in the client's life, then in some ways things are much simpler; the task is simply to find the most appropriate way to contact the client directly and engage them. We will cover this below.

Where it is possible to identify an existing keyworker from the client's point of view, the aims of the AMBIT-influenced worker are, first, to *do no harm to this relationship* (or, indeed, to strengthen it, following the AMBIT principle of "Scaffolding existing relationships" described in Chapter 1), and second, to consider in what ways that existing relationship might function as a portal to new help for the client. This may simply involve the AMBIT worker discussing with that trusted keyworker how best to plan a conversation with the client about the new (AMBIT) worker who is currently waiting "offstage"; a trusted keyworker may be able to use their own existing attachment relationship to increase the client's sense of safety, allowing them to explore the possibilities of a new relationship. For instance, it may be more helpful for an existing trusted worker to talk first about their *own* experience of being helped by the new worker, rather than opening the conversation by suggesting that the client should see that new worker or needs their help:

> "I talked to John to get some advice about working with a young person who's using a lot of cannabis. I didn't talk about you in particular. He helped me understand why the first thing for me to do is to really try to understand better why it 'makes sense' for you to be using cannabis at the moment. He helped me understand just how many different reasons there are for young people to get into cannabis. I found that helpful, and it made me curious to talk to you about that."

There are potential unwanted effects from any intervention; one of the risks of trying to establish a new relationship with a client is that, particularly if the new (AMBIT) worker engages very well with them, this may inadvertently undermine an existing professional (or informal) relationship that would actually be of longer-term value to the client—and perhaps of even greater value than the promise of work planned in the relationship with the new worker. If such a risk exists, the new worker may need to reach out to the existing keyworker in order to acknowledge how important the relationship they have already formed with the client is, and to emphasize the importance of preserving this existing relationship. What is absolutely critical is to avoid any unspoken competition for the engagement (or worse, the affection) of the client between different workers.

So, it is critical that the entry of a new worker into the clinical field is not seen as a threat to existing work, but as supportive of it. This may seem to be stating the obvious, but there are powerful forces at work, not always obvious to the main protagonists, that make this a task that is best conducted explicitly rather than relying on implicit expectations of "good behavior" among professionals. It may be necessary to explain the rationale for this new worker's (or team's) intervention—if an established keyworker accepts the sense of this additional worker's intended involvement, then they may be in a better position than the new worker to "translate" and hand on this thinking to the client. If the client hears positive things about the new worker from a trusted source, there is a higher chance of successful engagement. Moreover, if, prior to this, they have already heard how this new worker helped their existing worker (perhaps to help them, as in the case example above), the chances are further increased.

Sometimes it is helpful for the AMBIT worker to suggest that (regardless of each other's relative seniority) they are presented as having been in some sense summoned by, and working initially under the direction of, the existing keyworker. The existing keyworker is assumed to have not only a greater claim on the client's trust, but also much greater knowledge about how they function in relationships. Such a stance invites the AMBIT worker to demonstrate a certain amount of humility in relation to their role. This counters the risk that referrals to more specialist services may be seen in the eyes of the client (or by the family, or—worse—by practitioners themselves) as a kind of defeat on the part of the referrer (or existing local services); assuming that specialist skills are associated with greater seniority or higher ranking is a common and often destructive error. This is particularly the case if it implicitly demotes the existing worker(s), whose relationship(s) to the client may be of absolutely critical significance.

So, we highlight the fact that it is *not a given* that every worker who has already struggled to successfully engage a client will look upon the arrival of additional workers with unambiguous relief (even though, of course, in worrying cases this is often the case). The AMBIT principle of "Respect for local practice and expertise" is apparent here, as the AMBIT worker presents themself as actively supportive of the existing worker and sensitive to the fact that inviting them to try to talk to the client about this referral and to explore the client's questions about this might appear a "big ask" in the face of that existing worker's many other competing priorities.

(iii) *Taking the worker's perspective: Team around an existing keyworker.* If it is judged very likely that introducing a new worker will be met with outright resistance by the client, there may be scope for the AMBIT worker to adopt a supportive, quasi-, or actual supervisory role in relation to the existing keyworker, supporting them to deliver some of the early work that the new team might otherwise have been expected to deliver. In these situations the AMBIT worker may offer regular structured consultation to the existing keyworker, acting as part of the team around *this* worker. This may be only temporary, while the client considers the value of engaging with a new worker directly.

We do not underestimate the practical difficulties in developing a consultative "Team around the Worker" model such as this: some teams will have contracts that reward only face-to-face contacts, not liaison or consultation; workers whom an AMBIT-influenced team attempt to support in this way may feel that they are "being asked to do someone else's job" or to work outside their own role or competencies; and finally, to state the obvious, if an attempt to act as a team around another worker is not received by that worker as being actually helpful (i.e. as not addressing *their* perceived needs), it is unlikely to result in useful progress.

Nonetheless, faced with the alternative of no constructive work at all because of an unwillingness to engage, a client might in this way at least receive, for instance, basic psychoeducation about the risks of drug use, or harm minimization advice, with a hope that if this is received and found to be of some interest or help, then the door to engagement at a later stage may still be held open.

> **Summary example of Team around the Worker**
>
> Samira is a 20 year old whose family was previously unknown to services, but she has been temporarily excluded from her college after an unexpectedly violent incident with another student. In relation to this, she experiences great shame. She hides this from her family, pretending to attend college while privately self-injuring, acknowledging this only to her college counselor, Tilly, whom she trusts. Tilly refers Samira to an AMBIT-influenced adult crisis outreach service, as she is concerned that Samira's exclusion from college may isolate her further from support and increase the risk of more serious outcomes. Samira is strongly resistant to meeting with a worker from this mental health service, believing that her self-injury is an appropriate punishment for her behavior, and feeling more shameful than ever about her predicament.
>
> After Samira's rejection of their letter inviting her to meet, the AMBIT service talks to the college counseling service and clarifies the status of her counselor, Tilly, as the person who is most likely to be "key" in Samira's mind. Rather than approach Samira directly again, the team talks to Tilly, who made the referral, and to Tilly's manager, who supports the approach they now agree upon. Forming a "team around the counselor," the AMBIT service (represented by a worker called Frank) offers a face-to-face meeting and subsequent frequent telephone contacts with Tilly. Frank is at pains to acknowledge the worrying nature of Tilly's position, and to provide support to Tilly in making sense of Samira's predicament, as well as guidance about the next steps. They

talk about "red flag" warning signs for serious risk, and about the possible pathways to help that are open for Samira. Rather than simply invite Tilly to try to convince Samira to see him, Frank invites Tilly to talk first about the way that *she* has been helped by Frank and the AMBIT team. Tilly experiences Frank as attentive and available to her, and agrees to try this.

At her next meeting with Samira, Tilly shares Frank's attempt to mentalize the sense within Samira's withdrawal and self-injury (as "the 'best option' given the circumstances and resources available to Samira at the time"), as well as possible options for future help and contingency plans for possible crises they had discussed, and how helpful she had found this. Tilly talks with Samira about how seriously she takes her concerns about the self-injury and risk, and how Frank from the team is helping her to think about this. Frank checks in with Tilly several times over the next week by phone. For her part, Samira experiences Tilly as both responsive but also responsible, as she can see that in many ways her working directly with the adult crisis outreach team might be seen as the "proper" and professional response. Through hearing about Frank and his support of Tilly, she develops a more benign image of the crisis team, and also finds that her own distress is reducing. With regular contact with Tilly, who is supported by Frank and the AMBIT team, Samira begins to attend college again and things improve.

Had things not improved in this hypothetical scenario, it would have been appropriate for Frank and the crisis team to become more directly involved, and our hypothesis is that the likelihood of successfully engaging Samira would have been increased by the process of Tilly demonstrating trust in the crisis team.

(c) Communication channels

During the engagement phase, the use of text messaging or phone calls to initiate contact may offer low-impact ways of approaching a client, avoiding too much formality (like an official letter) or the suggestion that the service or worker may be adhesive, creating a claustrophobic experience if they do "get their foot in the door"—a negative expectation of such services that many young people describe. Teams using text messaging need to consider how they record these communications, and communicate to the client their commitment to safety and professionalism alongside their willingness to use less traditional modes of reaching out. For instance, an early text message might be along the lines of:

> Hope ur OK with me txtng u? We txt a lot of the young ppl we meet 2 keep in touch. This is my work phone—if u txt out of hours I'll rply ASAP when on duty. In emergency, pls call duty team on 12345678. Cheers! A.

(d) Deciding on the setting

Local teams must work within their own local constraints as regards risk management, but as a general rule, given appropriate risk assessment, *an invitation to the client to define the setting most conducive to being able to talk freely* (or as we might define it, to mentalize) is often a critical move in creating conditions for the formation of a relationship. Teams working under the influence of AMBIT have reported first meetings in cafés, burger bars, park benches, car parks, schools, youth clubs, local doctors' surgeries, or their own office base. Clearly, any meeting can be arranged only after an appropriate risk assessment has been conducted, and some teams will insist on two workers attending a first meeting, with one clearly taking the lead role.

Sensitivity to an individual's perspective, including the many possible cultural and historical influences upon their expectations (and those of their family) of a new helping agency, means that rigidly defined protocols are always likely to alienate some clients. The clients for whom AMBIT-influenced practice is particularly designed may have a particular tendency to experience alienation in this way. AMBIT seeks to provide a robust rationale for creating highly flexible and light-footed responses to individuals, but without allowing this adaptability to slip into unbounded chaos. Mentalizing is, after all, a supreme example of prioritizing the *specific* over more *general* attributes—but the experimental evidence is clear that, for mentalizing to be activated, a degree of stability and security is required (in other words, structure of some form or another). So, while AMBIT was initially designed as an approach to outreach working, this does not mean that, for some young people, coming to a reassuringly official "clinic" might not actually be the setting that feels safest, and many of the same principles have been adapted for use in services that are, by default, residential or clinic-based. Equally, the high degree of street-level flexibility suggested is only possible given the strong supervisory structures provided by AMBIT's emphasis on the need for its own keyworkers to be part of a well-connected team (see Chapter 5).

Assessment

Evidence (and common sense) points overwhelmingly to the fact that if help is to be helpful, then the nature of the problems being addressed must be understood, including sufficient attention paid to the context in which they have arisen. Working without any form of assessment is not justifiable. Following this information-gathering, there needs to be some process of formulation—that is, sharing and comparing the worker's and client's understandings of the problems, and their context and causes, and ideas about goal-setting (what we refer to as "comparing destinations" and "setting waymarks") in order to arrive at the kinds of shared intentions that form the basis of a plan. The process of assessment is always seen as a work in progress rather than a single operation; flexibility and the opportunity for learning and adaptation are intrinsic.

(a) Assessing across multiple domains

There are many ways to make an assessment. AMBIT makes no claim to startling originality in this field. Nor does it take a prescriptive approach about the nature or content of an assessment. The contexts in which assessment must occur vary widely—from clients formally referred into a highly specialist clinical service (say, for early-onset psychosis) to vulnerable young people being engaged via street-level outreach or in casual drop-in sessions at community venues. Inevitably, the depth, particular focus, and timescales over which some kind of systematic approach to information-gathering takes place will differ from service to service. However, although for these reasons AMBIT does not prescribe a single assessment process, it nonetheless takes a firm position that some systematic form of assessment according to an agreed and shared framework is essential for every team.

While flexibility is required and accepted in relation to the specific content and processes that shape local assessment frameworks, there is one important caveat. Assessment of the particular needs that a client (and their carers) present should always include exploration of the various resiliencies and resources that may support them. There is ample evidence for the value of strengths-based approaches. Understanding strengths and resiliencies allows work to be directed toward scaffolding these existing relationships (one of the core principles of AMBIT work introduced in Chapter 1).

The assessment needs to create some common and shared understandings—accessible to the client and, ideally, their carers, and to members of the team—that clarify and communicate the key risks and dilemmas currently being faced, as well as any resources or resiliencies that might be accessible in planning a way forward. To continue the analogy of a map, there needs to be sufficient agreement about where we find ourselves now, the nature of the terrain, and the direction in which a preferred destination lies; sufficient at least to allow the first steps to be taken. Following our understanding of mentalizing and the formation of epistemic trust (see Chapter 2), the key to this is an assessment process that offers the client a sense that *they are understood* in a way that is both accurate (and therefore seen as trustworthy) and compassionate.

(b) The AMBIT Integrative Measure (AIM) assessment
Having stressed the necessary flexibility and local adaptation of assessment frameworks, we do provide within the online AMBIT manual (available via the signposting site https://manuals.annafreud.org) one tool that can support this process: the AMBIT Integrative Measure (AIM). This is a 40-item measure that invites ratings from 0 (no problems) to 4 (very severe problems) in areas of functioning across a wide range of domains. It includes the option to mark some items as specifically being a strength or resilience factor. The questions are based on a much larger validated instrument, the Hampstead Child Adaptation Measure (Target & Fonagy, 1992), but this has been shortened to create the

AIM, providing a tool that is more clinically applicable. The AIM was recently used as a measure in the IMPACT study of adolescent depression (Goodyer et al., 2011) and a formal validation of this measure is now under way. Domains covered in the 40 questions include:

- The client's daily life, covering ordinary activities such as attendance at social activities and at school/work, attainment in these settings, physical health, disabilities, self-care, and social skills and interaction
- Socioeconomic circumstances, covering access to basic resources and housing
- Family, covering relationships, conflict, and discipline
- Social aspects, covering access to supportive adults outside the family, and peer group relationships (including whether or not these peers are seen as prosocial or antisocial)
- Mental health symptoms—covering a wide range of common mental health symptoms affecting children and young people, including use of substances, suicidality, self-injury, and aggression
- Response to the situation, covering the client's insight into the nature of their difficulties, and their response to the support that is available or on offer to them
- Complexity, covering both the chronic nature of any difficulties and their pervasiveness in affecting different areas of the client's life.

This measure is designed as a clinician-rated tool, to be completed by the worker after they have covered the relevant areas in the assessment. Teams using the AIM on a regular basis report that it provides a good "wide-angle" frame that ensures a systematic inquiry across a wide range of functional domains, even though it does not itself create any narrative for how a set of difficulties may have arisen. The scoring means that it can also be used as an outcome measure (i.e. by comparing scores at the beginning and end of any intervention).

In addition, an assessment tool that mirrors the basic framework of the AIM, but offers a *client-rated outcome measure*, has been produced. This tool is known as the "AIM Cards"; they are formatted as a set of playing cards with the same 40 questions "translated" into more youth-friendly language. Several AMBIT-influenced teams have gained valuable experience and developed high levels of client and worker satisfaction by using these cards. The playing cards can be laid out and sorted in different ways, facilitating exploration of how separate problems may be inter-related or may have arisen in a particular sequence, and how they may need to be addressed in a particular order. Clients report that having a broad set of possible problem areas printed out on playing cards makes it easier to see them all as common issues, and, correspondingly, thinking about and discussing them is less stigmatizing than having a worker look them in the eye and ask them if they have, for instance, any concerns in the area of sex and sexuality. As with anything else, they are not a universal solution, but compared with an "undiluted" face-to-face conversation, some clients find them significantly easier to get started with. Not infrequently, there may be significant variance between the client's rating of a particular item and the worker's own rating of the same item; this usefully highlights an area for further clarification and improved understanding.

Later in this chapter, we return to the AIM again, to discuss how these questions, combined with AMBIT's innovative approach to online ("wiki") manualization, can help address the questions of "what to do" and "where to start" when the problem areas are multiple. The browser-based version of the AIM (accessible via the online manual) allows a specific set of scores to be entered, and will sort and generate lists of potential interventions that can be ranked in different ways.

Risk assessment

Good governance and the principle of managing risk require that there is no ambiguity about the identification of, and appropriate responses to, risk, including safeguarding concerns. This is an example of how, at times, the non-mentalizing teleological mode, or "quick fix" thinking, carries the highest survival value by offering the most adaptive response to a hostile environment. Attempts to mentalize any of the parties when active or imminent abuse or violence has been identified could, in this context, look like pretend mode or prevarication. The young people for whom AMBIT is most specifically designed often present a range of risks. Failure to address these risks adequately places not only the client, but also other people, the worker, and the service in jeopardy—and it is of course this truth that underlies much of the anxiety for those who work in this field.

"Managing risk" is one of the eight key principles of the AMBIT stance—and holding the tricky balance between this and its paired but often contradictory principle, that of "Scaffolding existing relationships," is discussed in Chapter 1.

(a) Systematic approaches to risk assessment

Risk assessment can easily fall into either mechanical checklist ticking (an example of teleological or "quick fix" non-mentalizing) or, at the other end of the spectrum, into complacent abdication with an over-focus on engagement and relationship-building, based on the worker's implicit assumption that "I have a nose for danger." We acknowledge the range of different and often quite localized risks that geographically dispersed teams commonly face, and so, although we provide a standardized risk assessment as an example in the AMBIT manual, we do not stipulate the exact form that a local risk assessment should take. What is essential is that each local team involved in a young person's care has a shared understanding of the key risks that are present or may arise, and we strongly promote the systematic use of some form of standardized assessment in teams so that workers can provide evidence that risk has been considered, and are supported in "covering all bases" at times when anxiety might be running high, when areas of inquiry may temporarily be overlooked.

The use of a risk assessment inventory is useful only if it translates into:

- A clear *Crisis Contingency Plan* about how to minimize, mitigate, or manage risks that have been identified. In situations of high risk (where an individual worker's capacity to mentalize themselves or their client will be most challenged), this process is critically supported by two processes: first, strict adherence to local risk management protocols, and second, close mentalized consultation with other members of the team (see Chapter 5 for the theory and practice relating to this);
- An understanding of risk that is subsequently *communicated* clearly (with due regard to duties around confidentiality) to the other persons within a client's network that need to know. The extent to which it is appropriate and ethical to share information about risk across agencies and workers is often an area that requires reflection and consultation with senior colleagues; in this respect, Chapters 5 and 6 are also highly relevant.

Although the AMBIT manual includes a risk assessment inventory, it may be that teams are already using another risk assessment as part of existing local governance systems, or that their specific area of work includes specific risks not adequately covered in the basic risk assessment provided in the manual. We do *not* suggest that existing systems should be dismantled to be replaced with an AMBIT orthodoxy. The key points are that:

- All AMBIT-influenced teams should have an agreed risk assessment framework
- This risk assessment framework should be fit for purpose
- This framework should be used systematically by all members of the team.

(b) What to cover in risk assessment: A "three-legged stool"

Risk is perhaps best thought of as a three-legged stool, needing all three legs to be firmly grounded in order to stay upright. The three legs are:

1. Risk to the client
2. Risk to others
3. Risk to the worker.

The details and scope under these headings are, of course, myriad, and so we do not list these exhaustively here. A selection of some of the key areas for consideration under each heading includes:

1. Risk to the client
   - Self-injurious behavior or suicide
   - Abuse
   - Exploitation (sexual, economic, and criminal, including trafficking and gang involvement)
   - Physical health (from neglect of physical health needs and/or diet, smoking or substance use, accidents, violence, and sexually transmitted diseases)
   - Unwanted pregnancy
   - Mental health
   - Lack of educational/skills development
   - Homelessness

2. Risk to others
   - Violent, exploitative, or criminal acts by the client
   - Risks to the fetus in a pregnant client
   - Client acting as a vector in the spread of blood-borne viruses (e.g. HIV, hepatitis B or C)

3. Risk to workers
   - Violence specifically directed at professionals in helping roles
   - False allegations or vexatious complaints against workers
   - Rising thresholds for concern that lead to risk being overlooked ("therapeutic machismo" and the risk of reputational damage), or falling thresholds, leading to anxiety and burnout.

Formulation and goal-setting

The co-creation between worker and client of an account of the current difficulties and resiliencies, the explicit linkage of this understanding to a set of intentions for action, and the capacity to respond to fluctuations and diversions without losing headway are at the heart of what we call "Active Planning." This is an area in which AMBIT has some specific ideas, drawing on mentalizing theory; it is not limited to one of the sequential phases of work described here, so we cover this in more detail in the third section of this chapter.

Intervention phase

The previous sections will have clarified that work has really begun well before the intervention phase begins, when—following a process of assessment and collaborative planning—more focused sessions directed at making progress toward specified goals start to take place. We cover the details of how a mentalizing stance shapes face-to-face working in this phase in Chapter 4.

The nature of the different specific interventions deployed in this phase will vary widely according to the nature of the task for the specific team and the specific needs of the client. Of central importance, though, is that the interventions are drawn up to suit the needs of the client, rather than because they appeal to the worker for reasons of prior training, a team's orientation, or personal bias. The AMBIT manual includes a wide range of interventions, drawing on the evidence base that currently offers clues about which treatments work best for different types of patients and problems (Fonagy et al., 2015). However, we suggest that, whatever the specific problem focus or type of technique, the basic process of building mentalizing capacity in the client (and their carers if possible) lies at the core of most AMBIT-influenced work.

As an approach that seeks to create the conditions in which sustainable therapeutic change may become more possible, AMBIT's principled stance (see Chapter 1) requires workers to be determinedly systemic and wide-angled in their approach. This is what the AMBIT principle of "Working in multiple domains" refers to; this is explored in more depth in Chapter 6. Attending to basic needs—including living skills such as access to benefits, budgeting, or food preparation for a client living in semi-supported or bed-and-breakfast accommodation, or re-engagement in the social milieu of a local football club—may be of greater significance to the client than engaging in trauma-focused therapy at a particular point in time. However, the point of such "pre-therapy" is always to create the conditions in which deeper levels of therapeutic engagement and sustainable change become more possible.

On evidence and evidence-based interventions: Using the AIM to help choose relevant interventions

Many evidence-based practices have been developed in contexts and cultures that may be far distant from those in which the worker is trying to apply them. For a start, most effectiveness trials go to great lengths to select a group of patients that have relatively "pure" forms of the diagnosis under treatment, uncomplicated by co-occurring problems such as substance use, other concurrent diagnoses, or social problems. Likewise, most effectiveness trials are conducted in relatively well-controlled clinic-based settings, with the support of an enthusiastic research team and expert supervisors (who may have designed the treatment under scrutiny)—none of which may be the case for the clients of an AMBIT-influenced team.

This does not mean that such approaches are not worth trying, but the AMBIT principle of "Respect for evidence" also accepts a degree of skepticism about the immediate transportability of, for example, a clinic-based treatment developed in the USA, to outreach settings for the children of Bangladeshi parents living in a town in the north of the UK. Conversely, where there is a clear diagnosis and strongly evidenced interventions do exist, the worker would need to be able to justify why such an approach (even in a modified form) was overlooked in favor of an intervention for which there is little or no evidence of effectiveness in any setting. Following the work of Weisz et al. (2012), we are more convinced by the notion of evidence-based *components of practice* (e.g. the element of exposure to the feared stimulus in the CBT approach to anxiety) than by formalized packages that bundle a wide range of often quite disparate techniques, claiming that their effectiveness relies on a wholesale "all-or-nothing" adoption of the package.

The AMBIT AIM, as it is presented in the online manual, offers an opportunity to identify and sort possible evidence-based approaches to the difficulties with which a client may present. The questionnaire can be filled in online (note: entries are not saved because of the way the website functions), rating the problem-set with which a specific client presents. The online AIM contains within it a series of simple algorithms that generate lists of suggested interventions that are ranked in relation to the specific rating scores that have been entered for a specific client. These algorithms rank the likely helpfulness of specific interventions for identified problems (items that are rated as moderately severe or above are counted as relevant problems for possible interventions). These lists can be sorted using different algorithms to rank interventions in various ways—analogous to how a shopping website might rank items according to, for instance, their price, their consumer ratings, or their geographical proximity; this in itself is a reminder of the fact that there can be no mechanistic decision tree in cases with high levels of complexity.

First, there is a *global ranking*: this algorithm ranks interventions in order of how many of the client's identified problems each single intervention has shown some evidence of effectiveness in addressing. The greater the number of problems in a client's presentation for which a particular intervention shows promise, the higher in the ranking that intervention will appear. Family work tends to regularly score highly in this ranking, as it has been deployed, tested, and been found to have evidence of effectiveness in a great many different problems—substance use, eating disorders, and psychosis, to name but three. A global ranking is useful when thinking about creating an impact across the fullest spectrum of a client's difficulties, and perhaps trying to address some of the underlying and maintaining factors that are common to many or most of the client's problems.

In contrast, the *focal ranking* is more useful in helping the worker consider how to tackle the problems rated as most severe in a client's AIM scores—perhaps aiming for interventions that will be most likely to settle key symptoms and risks, before broader maintaining factors can be engaged. It ranks each intervention according to the severity ratings given for those problems for which it has been shown to demonstrate promise. The more severe the problems a client has revealed that, say, CBT is shown to be effective for, the higher in the rankings this intervention will appear.

Finally, either of the above modes of ranking can be applied while limiting the problem-set examined only to those that are labeled in the assessment as key problems (a maximum of six can be thus labeled).

Thus, the worker is offered a range of different ways in which to sift potential interventions without being limited to a single mechanistic list. If none of their currently chosen interventions appears in the top few entries of these lists, it does beg the question as to whether what is on offer is what the worker (or the team) simply *prefers* to offer, rather than what the actual problem-set might *require*.

Specific interventions in the AMBIT manual

It is important to reiterate that not all, and at times perhaps not even any, of the specific interventions manualized in the AMBIT manual are required ingredients for an AMBIT-influenced intervention. In keeping with the work of John Burnham (1992), who described a hierarchy of Approach, Method, and Technique, in which the higher levels provide the context for meaning in the lower levels, we see AMBIT as a mentalization-based *approach*. Many different *methods*, and still more specific *techniques*, may be deployed to create conditions in which clients can develop relationships of trust, social and economic stability, and symptom control, which in turn create conditions in which their mentalizing can begin to operate more effectively, both implicitly and explicitly, allowing in turn more accurate communication and successful relationships, affect regulation, self-agency, and a more adaptive relationship to help.

The specific interventions listed below are provided in simple manualized form in the AMBIT manual. They are not all equally "evidence-based," and in this context (and in keeping with Burnham's definition) they constitute methods and techniques that may be deployed within AMBIT's mentalization-based approach.

As described in Chapter 7, local teams are encouraged to add to this list if appropriate, or to record their local adaptations or improvements—preferably alongside evidence. As the evidence base moves forward, so this manualized content is expected to be refined.

- **Cognitive-behavioral work**—A simple guide to cognitive-behavioral principles and techniques is provided.
- **Crisis contingency planning**—Referred to earlier in this chapter, this category of intervention does not easily fall under the rubric of evidence-based practice; by their nature, contingencies are situation-specific and responses to them are likely to be highly local, but there is ample evidence to suggest that the lack of robust and rehearsed crisis contingency plans tends to exacerbate risk.
- **Educational-vocational training**—This refers to work directed toward reintegration into school, training, or employment. Here, basic principles and techniques are described, without claiming that these specifically represent an evidence-based approach; a lack of meaningful activity and structure in a young person's life, however, alongside lack of qualifications, is strongly associated with poorer outcomes.
- **Emergency procedures**—Material is offered on managing violence, safeguarding crises, suicidality, and the use of mental health legislation.
- **Family work**—In AMBIT, we offer the model of mentalization-based treatment for families (MBT-F), a systemically oriented approach that is augmented by a focus on mentalizing, and which was used as the family intervention in an encouraging randomized trial for adolescents with self-injurious behaviors (Rossouw & Fonagy, 2012).
- **Giving advice**—This is hardly an evidence-based practice, but links to evidence-based advice are provided, as well as general guidance on advice-giving.
- **Group work**—This offers manualized material on how to run basic groups, drawing on existing models of practice including the mentalization-based group work that has shown promise in complex treatment-rejecting hospitalized youth (Malberg, 2013).
- **Living skills**—There is limited formal evidence for providing training in living skills, and yet this is a very commonly identified need in young people, especially those who may be forced into independent or semi-independent living rather early in their development.
- **Mentalization-based treatment for adolescents (MBT-A)**—This is one of a very limited pool of evidence-based approaches to working with

self-injurious adolescents (Rossouw & Fonagy, 2012), especially those with emerging borderline traits in their developing personalities.

- **Motivational work**—This has a relatively strong evidence base for effectiveness in substance use work, and some evidence for effectiveness in eating disorders, as well as being used extensively in other areas, especially where client buy-in to treatment is low.
- **Multi-family work**—There is some evidence to support this as an effective intervention in families with severe behavioral disturbance, where neglect and abuse are concerns. Clearly in the latter situation, the resolution of safeguarding issues constitutes the first-line response.
- **Pharmacological interventions**—The AMBIT manual describes how workers might support the prescribing interventions that are primarily the responsibility of a doctor.
- **Physical health matters**—This includes advice on basic screening for physical illness, sexual health, and identifying and responding to common side effects of medication.
- **Relapse prevention**—This has an evidence base in work done with psychosis, but the principles are equally applicable to other chronic relapsing and remitting problems.
- **Social-ecological work**—This refers to interventions directed at improving access to positive elements of the social environment around a client (peer group relationships and access to prosocial meaningful activity, etc.).
- **Subsistence support**—There are strong evidential links between poverty and depression, as well as a range of other disorders. Effective action to ensure basic provision of housing and nutrition is not an uncommon requirement.
- **Substance use disorder**—A manualized treatment is presented that draws on the best-evidenced techniques and principles, including motivational work and family work.
- **Work with other professionals**—Liaison work where there is a high level of case complexity has a strong evidence base as well as high face validity given the high numbers of workers and teams that may become involved with young people fitting the criteria for an AMBIT-influenced intervention.

In Chapter 4, we focus in more detail on the interaction between worker and client, and how mentalizing informs, shapes, and directs this interaction through a "mentalizing stance."

Maintenance phase

Some, but not all, AMBIT-influenced teams work with young people whose problems are very long-standing. These teams have a remit to provide much longer-term interventions, continuing to support clients at a lower level of intensity after more intensive interventions have created positive change that is nonetheless vulnerable to relapse.

Here, relapse prevention plans (discussed in the section Ending Phase, below) will be in place, and the emphasis is on creating a sustainable network around the client (a "well-connected team" for the client—analogous to the team that should support the AMBIT keyworker in their work, but consisting not only of professionals but also including, and ideally led by, family members or trusted friends). In this sense, the AMBIT stance principle of "Scaffolding existing relationships" is to the fore in this phase of work, as the AMBIT team works, ultimately, to make itself redundant. Such a network must be able to maintain vigilance for previously identified signs of relapse (sometimes referred to as the "relapse signature") with readiness to call into action a previously agreed relapse "drill" (a specific form of crisis contingency plan, with graded responses and interventions according to the degree of seriousness of the signs of relapse).

Family work, basic living skills training and support for basic subsistence needs, and efforts to promote social engagement in education, employment, or training, would all constitute appropriate activities in this phase of work, as the effort is geared toward strengthening other relationships in being able to support the client.

Ending phase

Why introducing the end at the beginning makes sense

In ancient Greece, the code of conduct for how islanders should respond to shipwrecked sailors was "Welcome the coming, speed the going guest" (Homer, *Odyssey*, Book xv.1.83). This was a cultural code that made eminently good sense; shipwrecks were as common as car crashes, and we may assume that in those days sailors were forever getting washed up on one another's alien shores. Despite all the cultural, linguistic, economic, and political differences and rivalries that existed between different islands and coastal towns, a basic common code was maintained that allowed shipwrecked sailors to hold secure basic expectancies about the care they would receive: food would be offered, wounds tended, and boats patched up and stocked for the return journey. Come the day, though, they would be pushed off back to sea, to return to their own kith and kin. It is important to emphasize here that the *temporary* nature of the contract between shipwrecked and rescuer was both a critical and an *explicit* part of the contract of hospitality. Guests could be confident that they would not be held against their will, but neither could they expect to outstay their welcome.

Now, in the case of clients coming to the strange shores of an AMBIT-influenced team, such an explicit code is almost certainly lacking in the first instance. A second motto, promoting the importance of broadcasting the *temporary* nature of the relationship the AMBIT worker is offering, could be T. S. Eliot's words from his great poem *East Coker*: "In my beginning is my end."

The objective of AMBIT-influenced work is to re-establish the client in a social network that is as independent from professional input as possible, and which, as much as possible, is in keeping with that individual's understanding or cultural expectations of family and social relationships. Identifying and scaffolding a client's existing relationships (some, or even most, of which may require strengthening or changing to create more safety) constitute one of the principles of the AMBIT stance, discussed in Chapter 1. The point of doing so is to create the conditions into which it is safe and possible to "speed the going guest." In setting about such work within an AMBIT framework, though, the worker must make enthusiastic efforts to create conditions for as secure an attachment as possible between worker and client. To continue with our ancient Greek analogy, this attachment is what allows the shipwrecked sailor to accept and trust the quality of the rope, canvas, and food supplied, so as to justify loading them aboard, ready for the onward journey. In our therapeutic version, security of attachment creates the conditions for epistemic trust (trust in communication; described in Chapter 2) that, in turn, facilitate learning. This attachment-building is carried out in a context in which subsequent separation is not only inevitable, but intended—and is actively broadcast as such.

How can these two apparently contradictory elements—attachment and separation—be reconciled? First, research is clear in demonstrating that securely attached children manage separations better than insecurely attached ones (Ainsworth, 1993). Second, in the case of clients whose expectations in relation to helping relationships are often highly insecure or distorted, it is not a given that they will wish to cling to any help-giver; on the contrary, in many instances it is the fearful expectation that they will meet something adhesive, invasive, or claustrophobic in such a relationship that makes sense of their efforts to push away or avoid well-intentioned offers of help. Alternatively, their expectation may be for a sudden and unannounced abandonment that would inevitably be experienced as (perhaps yet another) betrayal, and this may make sense of their resistance to engaging in the first place.

In response to these challenges, the worker broadcasts their true ambit (sphere of influence) from the very first contact. Of course, this ambit is necessarily limited, not least in terms of time availability. However, the worker can also broadcast the fact that, for what it is, and while it does last, this relationship is dedicated toward creating more security in the client's independent life and relationships. This confronts and challenges implicit assumptions that what is on offer may be either a life sentence or, alternatively, an invitation to uncertainty (waiting for the day when, unannounced, suddenly nobody is there to answer the call).

Acknowledging that one's ambit extends only so far, so that an ending is broadcast as inevitable from the very beginning of working together, signals something else, too, that is quite particular to the therapist's mentalizing stance. This is the open acceptance and unflinching honesty from the worker about their limitations and fallibility more generally. Mentalizing theory is absolutely clear that failures in accurate mentalizing are a common part of the human condition (misunderstanding is the recurring joke in the "comedy of errors" that people play out between each other). Correspondingly, modeling confidence in our belief that good-enough mentalizing or, for that matter, good-enough time availability is indeed *good enough* (Winnicott, 1953) is an important part of the stance. Of course, in promoting this stance we also make clear that this is not a green light for the slapdash or lazy therapist: we are always interested in doing better work, especially when we discover we have got something wrong. But the question of "What do we think is the *right* time availability or length of treatment?", when asked in this context, becomes a much more mentalizing exercise that might profitably be shared with a client:

> "So OK, I can hear that you are saying, 'What's the point of seeing this worker at all, because she'll only leave after a few months', and that makes good sense to me—or at least it would make *very* good sense if you knew I would suddenly just 'up and leave' without any warning—but I hope you can see that I'm talking to you now because one of the things I really don't want ever to do is spring surprises on you, or mislead you.
>
> But what if you and I could 'book' exactly how long I should stay in touch with you? If we could just decide how long would be exactly the right length of time for you and I to be meeting up, making plans, and getting stuff done together—then how long do we think that would be? I'm assuming you wouldn't be too happy to have me traipsing round after you when you're, say, in your early thirties!"

In such circumstances, the worker, by broadcasting the time-limited nature of what is on offer, has created conditions for a discussion about "how much time" that is no longer teleological ("Unless you stay for X months, it means you don't care and you will be no help") but is now a conversation about coming to understand what the client needs, and what the worker might be able to offer.

The therapeutic bargain

It is the perceived *authenticity* of what is broadcast in this offer from the worker that will influence the likelihood that claustrophobic or anxious concerns on the part of the client are reduced. Ideally, this reduction of anxiety will be sufficient to allow further exploration of possibilities in this temporary attachment on offer; at least the prospectus is clear enough. Of course, this is no easy task: keyworkers must not only say what they mean, but mean what they say, and although life circumstances are never entirely predictable, the therapeutic relationship does depend on sufficient predictability in the worker's behavior to justify the enormous leap of faith asked of the client, something that has been described as the "therapeutic bargain" (Allen et al., 2003).

The client who comes into a therapeutic relationship is "putting a lot on the table," and the worker must be sure to acknowledge this and act accordingly, showing the greatest respect for details such as making the effort to be on time (even when it seems inevitable that the client will be late again, or will fail to show up at all) and to broadcast well ahead of time any planned breaks. In short, the worker makes every effort to make themselves as predictable as possible, acknowledging their human fallibility all the while, and being quick to acknowledge and take responsibility for errors, omissions, and other behaviors that (whether the worker is "guilty" or not) have created conditions for the client to experience the worker as unpredictable or unsafe.

This is why the initial relationship-building and assessment phase can and must focus on agreed aims and goals—defining the point of the relationship and measures of success in reaching toward goals that highlight recognition of the *client's* aims, rather than the worker's. As attention is directed first at clarifying where the client wishes to get to, and the worker broadcasts their intention to help, preoccupations may surface such as whether or not the "taxi driver" (the worker) will ever drop the client off after they have arrived at their destination, or whether they might abandon them in some unknown street on the way. Having created an opportunity for the client to experience their needs and wishes as having been authentically understood, it is easier for the limitations and constraints of the therapeutic relationship (or the client's fears about these) to be explored, acknowledged, and then (hopefully) tolerated.

Predicting turbulence

Workers will be alert to the fact that, not uncommonly, some of the original disturbance that brought the client into contact with the team, or new crises, will arise in the lead-up to discharge. This can be dispiriting for the worker as well as for the client; it is as though nothing has really changed. In many cases it represents anxiety and perhaps mixed feelings about ending, which in turn signals powerfully the fact that an attachment has been made.

Some clients find endings especially hard—particularly if their personal histories include sudden, inexplicable, or hurtful separations that have been left unresolved. In such circumstances it is not at all uncommon for major difficulties to arise and for the worker to find themselves rejected or even actively condemned as being the cause of these. One way to make sense of a behavior that could mistakenly be interpreted as ingratitude (which might, in turn, prompt less than helpful interactions from a wounded worker) is that for some clients it is quite impossible for them to think of leaving a positive, supportive, and helpful figure (why would they ever choose to do that, when there has been so little of this around in their lives beforehand, and there may be so little promise of it in the future?). Instead, it becomes possible to leave only by first identifying some (or many) unacceptable shortcomings in the worker/team to be left. This is not unlike the manner of leaving that some adolescents achieve from quite settled homes—rebelling and confronting what is (perhaps suddenly and quite surprisingly) seen as the intransigence, unfairness, or insufferable dullness of home; it is these complaints that allow the adolescent to attain "escape velocity" from the comforting gravitational pull of home. Accepting this while ensuring that the grounds for complaint are not reflective of what is actually being offered is hard. Of course we do not do this work for expressions of gratitude—a sentence that is easier to type than it is to live with.

Relapse prevention planning

As the end of treatment approaches, the worker will again need to broadcast this fact clearly, well ahead of time, leaving space for acknowledgment and exploration of the possible pain of loss. Here, there is a focus on a more specific form of planning that tries to create proactive strategies and contingency plans to avoid the most likely (or risky) crises; these are similar to, but more focused than, the crisis contingency plan described earlier in this chapter. Following work that was mostly carried out in the field of early intervention in psychosis (Jackson & McGorry, 2009), we call this *relapse prevention*. This involves a number of key stages. First, there is the identification of any specific markers of deterioration that might be gleaned from the history of the most recent episode of difficulty. The theory (and some evidence) suggests that for many people (although not all), future deteriorations in their mental state follow quite similar courses to past episodes; this is often referred to as the work of establishing the "relapse signature." Workers may use sets of cards recording a wide range of symptoms and social circumstances to help map out this signature for a particular client (the AMBIT AIM assessment cards described above can be used in this way, for instance); the relevant cards can be selected and then laid out as a timeline (e.g. by placing them on the floor), mapping events and the arrival of symptoms for a particular client.

"Does this card say anything about what it was like for you back then: 'Experiencing paranoid thoughts?'... OK, and what about this card—'Feeling I had to injure myself in order to cope'—Is that something you experienced in those early weeks? OK, and when did that come in? Was that *before* or *after* this one you picked out just earlier: 'Feeling numb in public places'?"

Card sorts such as these often demonstrate how, although a small number of events and symptoms triggered the deterioration, these then amplified, drawing in increasing multiples of other difficulties, symptoms, or signs, so that on the timeline a thin line of cards marking early symptoms evolves into more of a cascade as the passage of time is marked out. Being able to walk around and observe these cards on the floor can be a helpful exercise in developing insight, but it also allows the worker and client to try to divide the "relapse signature" into early, middle, and late phases of the relapse/crisis. These can be shown to family members or other professionals to gain other perspectives and make specific contingency plans for each phase. Producing a credit card-sized document that records both the key indicators for these different phases and the most helpful interventions at each stage, which can be shared with key family members or other professionals, is the final stage of this exercise.

Team around the Client

As an ending nears, attention is increasingly focused on who will be in the client's ongoing support network (professional and/or informal), which will be in place once the AMBIT worker has withdrawn. The notion of the "Team around the Worker" in AMBIT allows the worker to model what help-seeking looks like (see Chapter 5) and in some senses to normalize that process. The invitation (implicit or explicit) is for the client to try to construct their own "back-up team" around themself; some of the members may be other professionals in their network who will remain in contact, while others may comprise informal relationships—family, friends, tutors, bosses, etc. By now, after scaffolding and any necessary repairs to these relationships have been applied, it is hoped that they will be more available and sustainable as a resource for the client than was the case at the beginning of the work.

Arranging and supporting handovers

It is helpful for an AMBIT-influenced keyworker at this stage to think strategically about how best they might support those relationships that will continue after discharge. If there is a handover to another team or another worker, then rehearsing the journey to and from clinic appointments, accompanying the client to early meetings, and marking support for this new worker by "standing beside them" in the company of the client may be key maneuvers in helping new relationships of trust to develop.

The option of a "long tail" of gradually diminishing contact

In some teams there will need to be a clear break in contact, and handover or discharge will be a single event in time. For some teams and in some instances, however, it may be possible and desirable to design a "long tail" of gradually diminishing contact with a client, so that meetings are reduced from several times a week, down to weekly, fortnightly, or monthly "check-ins" or just booked telephone calls. In these meetings the focus would need to shift from more active therapeutic work toward something more akin to coaching—offering a perspective on progress against plans that had earlier been agreed, with encouragement, advice, and redrafting of plans as required.

Marking endings, making memories

When discharge does come, the worker should mark this ending in some way that is appropriate and that gives a final opportunity to create a memory—or an *aide memoire*—that might prompt revision of the work done and of the advances made during this work. In some cases this might be a letter or a card noting the distance traveled and reminding (literally "re-minding") the client of the fact that although this relationship, as planned, is now coming to an end, on a personal level they will be remembered in the months and years ahead. The fear that, on ending, a client will be automatically discarded from their worker's mind is often a powerful one, despite the fact that in reality this is never the case. In other cases some kind of small ceremony—such as going out for a cup of tea together, or sharing a cake with other family members—may be more appropriate.

Summary

We have now mapped, in the simplest terms, the kind of "treatment journey" that an AMBIT-influenced team might offer for clients, stressing the fact that in many settings this might need considerable modification (for instance in residential settings, or with much briefer outreach interventions). We hope that this map is not confused with the "territory" that is the actual work, for which the map is a merely a guide. Much of what we have covered lays no claim to originality. In the last section of this chapter, we turn to the skill of "map-reading" in a territory that is subject to fairly constant change. How do we make plans, and follow them, when intentions and circumstances shift like sand?

SECTION 3. Active Planning: Working with clients whose intentions change

Active Planning is the habitual culture that AMBIT teams promote, alongside a variety of specific adaptations to quite standard processes and techniques that support collaborative co-production of a "map" with the client and its use in effective route-finding toward desired outcomes. Earlier in this chapter we referred to this as the activity of "map-reading," as opposed to the map itself. If we were to stretch that analogy to breaking point, mentalizing might be the flickering compass needle that helps us orient the map, even if the peaks and valleys ahead of us are shrouded in mist, or are themselves moving, like sandbanks in an estuary. Active Planning is specifically designed to address situations in which clients quite frequently demonstrate *changing* intentions. It is an attempt to create and hold the delicate balance between having a plan and implementing that plan, while also remaining responsive to rapidly changing circumstances and states of mind so as to maintain engagement.

Active Planning is, in an important sense, simply the application of the therapist's mentalizing stance (see Chapter 4) to the broader field of the collaborative planning and management of therapeutic interventions. This might just as well be called "being practically, safely, and effectively helpful over a period of time," and in that sense AMBIT has been described as a type of "pre-therapy," creating the conditions most likely to allow therapeutic work to take root.

The client group for AMBIT-influenced teams

In Chapter 1 we outlined some of the particular, although varied, features of the client group for which AMBIT has been designed. The complexity of these clients' presentations, their non-standard (if not actively rejecting) stance toward help-seeking, and the high levels of risk they present all point to the fact that the relatively simple and linear map we have laid out in the section above will require modifications if it is to be applicable and helpful in the process of organizing help.

Active Planning is an attempt both to capture this process of modifying, and to describe some specific modifications. It brings together the processes of engagement, assessment, and planning into something that, through the application of mentalizing, may be experienced as more flexible, responsive, relational, and client-centered, but which retains the purpose of maximizing the likelihood of positive and sustainable change in a dysfunctional system. It is important to emphasize that in spite of these modifications, the intent underlying Active Planning is essentially no different from the standard model of case management that has already been presented in this chapter.

The problems of planned work: Holding the balance between planning, broadcasting, and attunement

Without wishing to introduce too much of a spoiler, in Chapter 4 we will describe the therapist's mentalizing stance. One of the four key principles of this stance is "Holding the balance" between a range of different (and often competing) potential elements of therapeutic work that require attention. Directly in parallel to this, Active Planning similarly involves a critical effort to hold in balance often competing aspects of the process of navigating toward treatment goals.

Evidence-based approaches to practice have emphasized repeatedly that the establishment of clear, and ideally measurable, goals and plans is critical to success in delivering positive and effective change. However, engaging a client in any form of planning (and implementing those plans) requires two other components to be active. The first of these is achieving and sustaining sensitive *attunement* to the demands the client is experiencing in their current state of mind; this will largely dictate the extent to which any suggested plan offers sufficient contingency (its "fit" with the demands of the moment) so that the client maintains a trusting relationship toward this help. Second, sufficiently clear *broadcasting* of the worker's intentions is required to elicit support for the plan, allowing the client to opt in to (collaborate and co-produce) a plan rather than to experience it as something being "done to them." Individually, each of these three elements—planning, sensitive attunement, and broadcasting—carries risks if it becomes too dominant and squeezes out the other elements (see Figure 3.2).

For instance, slavish adherence to an overly rigid plan risks delivering, at best, the right help at the wrong time—although it is much more likely to be received by the client as simply the wrong help. While sometimes it will be necessary to hold one's nerve and encourage persistence with a plan, the risk is always that this might offer an experience of overwhelming non-contingency (a lack of fit

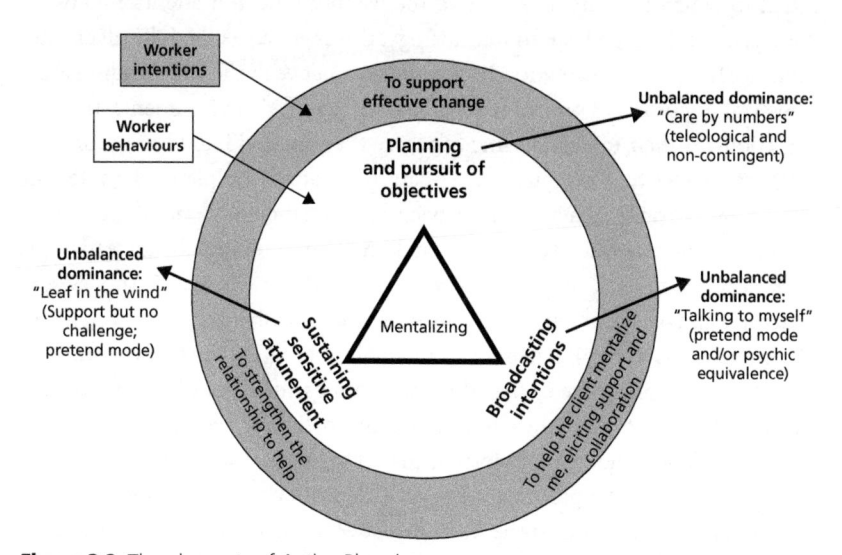

Figure 3.2 The elements of Active Planning.

between what is on offer and the predicament being experienced in the "here and now" of the client's mind). This powerfully undermines the client's trust in communication (see Chapter 2) and reduces the likelihood of them learning from the experience, risking the therapeutic relationship. This would be a good example of the impact of teleological (quick-fix) thinking on the part of the worker ("Just stick to the plan and it will be OK").

Similarly, overemphasizing the broadcasting of the worker's own intentions, without maintaining sensitive attunement to whether these intentions actually indicate a direction in which the client is ready or willing to go, risks the worker falling into a "conversation with themself"—an example of pretend mode ("elephant in the room" thinking). Worse still, too much certainty that "my thoughts about this are the way it is, the only way it could be, and how it must be" are an example of psychic equivalence (inside-out thinking) on the part of the worker, which may quickly alienate a client by being experienced as intrusive or oppositional.

Finally, sensitive attunement to the client's predicament is critical in creating contingency between what is on offer and the client's dilemma, but an overemphasis on attunement to the client's experience risks losing hold of the worker's (and their team's) separate perspective on other realities (e.g. real risks that need addressing, real timescales such as the beginning of an academic year, or the end of a housing contract that will impact on future plans if ignored) so that the conversation takes on a "make-believe" quality (another example of pretend mode thinking) that serves only to sustain a chaotic drift.

The worker's capacity to mentalize themself and their client will influence the extent to which they are able to hold the balance and shift attention between these priorities. To go back to our analogy, this is much as the hillwalker must continually shift their attention back and forth between the surrounding landscape (taking bearings on real objects in their physical environment), the map that confirms their understanding of where they are and intend to go, and the compass needle that orientates the map, translating the planned route into a direction of travel. Leaving out or becoming fixed on any one of these three actions will inevitably lead to navigational problems; holding a balance between them is what the task requires. As we will explain in Chapter 5, supervisory structures and trusted relationships between team members are critical elements (the compass, as it were) in helping to maintain this balance in the worker.

Shifts in the landscape—what the client brings in terms of intentions and motivation, or ruptures in the environment in which they are coping (the breakdown of a relationship, new disclosures that raise safeguarding concerns, emerging post-traumatic symptoms, etc.)—will almost inevitably arise and will most likely require adaptations to the plan. Sensitive attunement to emerging resistances or barriers to progress should pick up on this, and the worker (supported by supervisory structures in their team) will need to model adaptability in considering new avenues. At the same time as we are battered and thrown off course by crises and events, keeping a steady aim toward more distant goals is critical if the work is to be more than just the temporary provision of company.

Active Planning as a team culture

In Chapter 5 we discuss working with the team as one of the four main quadrants of the AMBIT wheel, without which progress will falter. Applying mentalizing in purposeful and explicit ways between members of a team is as important as it is in direct work with clients. An AMBIT-influenced team must find ways to foster and sustain an explicit culture that will best support mentalizing in its members, and this includes a strong culture of planning.

As mentalizing is chiefly concerned with the link between intentions and actions, emphasizing the centrality of planning is quite a logical step; plans are a pure example of the open broadcasting of intentions. Where plans are co-created they broadcast *shared* intentions, and this territory is, quite literally, a worker's ambit (their sphere of influence). We expand further on the value of "broadcasting intentions" at numerous points throughout this chapter.

Where such a culture is in evidence in a team, all members share an understanding that time is an extremely valuable resource and should be spent as wisely as possible, and that planning offers a greater return on this investment. Thus, team members assume as a core part of their role the need to support each other with the constant process of identifying aims and goals that fit with the present formulation of a client's difficulties, and ensuring that these shape the plans they develop with their clients.

A culture of planning is visible not just in relation to the long-term "treatment aims" that a worker develops with their client, but also across much shorter timescales. At team meetings, workers are encouraged to become explicit in marking plans for their work in the week ahead, identifying intermediate goals that could represent progress toward more meaningful outcomes. Even in brief professional discussions about work, we encourage a discipline called "Thinking Together" (described in depth in Chapter 5) in which there is an explicit marking of the task for that specific conversation, which is, in effect, a collaborative planning process about how to conduct a conversation.

Active Planning: Adaptive responses to barriers in a common process

So, while there is no argument with the standard case management approach to planning, AMBIT does mark a difference by choosing to refer to the process of "Active Planning." What is the difference? Our experience is that, while for many clients a standard collaborative planning process is extremely helpful, the clients for whom AMBIT is designed often struggle, as do AMBIT workers, with a range of barriers to its use in this context.

Table 3.2 shows a small selection of some of the most common barriers that arise at different stages. These barriers are set beside a range of some of the specific adaptations that AMBIT promotes to overcome such barriers, building in sufficient adaptability without losing the underlying structure and purposefulness that have been shown to be of value for less complex and more conventionally help-seeking populations.

Here, we expand on some of the key elements mentioned in Table 3.2 that characterize the process of Active Planning.

Engagement

Engagement is also covered in depth in Chapter 4, as it is a theme that runs through all direct client work. Earlier, we mentioned two activities that support engagement and need to be held in balance with planning: *Attunement* and *Broadcasting Intentions*.

(a) The systematic application of sensitive attunement: Checking "what's here"

In Chapter 4 we describe a "mentalizing stance," which is a "way-of-being-with" that offers the best odds for rekindling or developing mentalizing in a relationship. Without wishing to spoil the surprise, one of the four key pillars of this stance is the quality of *curiosity* or *inquisitiveness*. At every face-to-face contact, the worker needs to engage regularly and persistently in answering the question of "What's here, now?" in relation to their self and their client.

These kinds of status updates require the application of sensitive attunement: attending and listening in order to understand rather than to respond, and demonstrating a willingness to change one's own mind (to accommodate a truer understanding of the client's predicament) well before considering what changes, if any, your client's mind or life may benefit from. Sensitive attunement is about "here and now" interactions, a presence of mind attending first to the inventory of "What's here?" in terms of the other person's (or one's own) feelings, thoughts, beliefs, intentions, hopes, and fears at this point in time. Ultimately, when we get to the higher levels of mentalizing, understanding these things and how they influence each other is how we come to make sense of how and why the person is behaving the way they are, but before this "mentalizing proper" can begin to take place, first there must be more grounded attention.

Insofar as it is dependent on immediate contingencies (what your client is bringing in that moment), this kind of episodic status update or "check-in" is, of course, not particularly amenable to being systematized or turned into a

Table 3.2 Common barriers to effective help and AMBIT adaptations to overcome these barriers

Stage of case management	Problem/barrier to effective help	AMBIT adaptations
Engagement	Poor relationship to help (low trust)	Emphasis on predictability (attachment security—Chapters 2, 3, 4); Mentalizing and the creation of trust in communication (Chapters 2, 4); Broadcasting intentions (Chapters 3, 4); Reassurance of the ordinary (use of ordinary language, choice of venue (cafés, home visits, etc; "Where do you think you would feel most relaxed talking about this?")—Chapters 3, 4); Use of existing professional relationships (Team around the Worker—Chapters 3, 5); Use of social media and text messages, and use of humour (Chapters 3, 4).
	Worker over-identifies with client, or is unbalanced by rejection	Use of Team around the Worker (Chapter 5); Mentalizing of worker by members of well-connected team using strong supervisory structures and disciplines (e.g. Thinking Together—Chapter 5); Culture of insistence on mentalized explanations for behaviors (Chapters 1, 5); Culture of help-seeking in the team (Chapters 5, 7).
Assessment	Low client tolerance of multiple questions and "scrutiny"	Acceptance of partial information and staged assessments over time (Chapters 3, 4); Use of card sorts (AIM cards) and other adapted materials (Chapters 3, 4, 7); Preparedness to shift focus to other quick wins or "low-hanging fruit" (Chapter 4).
	Low worker confidence in relation to complex multi-domain assessments	Structured tools supporting assessment across multiple domains (e.g. AIM assessments—Chapter 3, Dis-integration grids—Chapter 6); Team-based support via peer-to-peer supervisory structures (Chapter 5).
Risk assessment	High risks	Strong emphasis on risk and crisis contingency planning (Chapter 3); Mentalizing with clients (Chapter 4) and team-based supervisions (Chapter 5) address risk planning collectively and collaboratively.
	Impact of risk on worker (burnout, or risky "therapeutic machismo")	Emphasis on a well-connected team, with mentalizing colleagues forming a Team around the Worker (Chapters 1, 3, 4, 5); Explicit culture of help-seeking within the team (Chapters 5, 7).

(continued)

Table 3.2 Continued

Stage of case management	Problem/barrier to effective help	AMBIT adaptations
Formulation (developing shared understandings)	General mistrust, poor previous experiences of help	Theory of epistemic trust (trust in communication) (Chapter 2); Tentativeness of mentalizing stance (Chapter 4); Broadcasting intentions (Chapter 3) and explicit marking of the link between understanding and actions (tools such as the "Egg and Triangle"—Chapter 3); Use of text messages/videos/letters (Chapter 3).
	Multi-agency contradictions	Emphasis on mentalizing across networks, including use of "Dis-Integration Grids" and "Pro-Grams" as part of network assessment (Chapter 6).
Goal-setting (developing shared intentions)	Sudden changes to life circumstances (crises) that derail previous plans by rendering them "non-contingent"	Use of mentalizing (Chapters 2, 4) and tools to foster broadcasting of intentions and clarification of overlaps with client's intentions, such as the "Egg and Triangle" (Chapter 3); Judicious avoidance of non-mentalized teleological responses (Use of team—Chapter 5); Offering sufficient contingency in responses ("firefighting" and flexible adaptations to the plan, such as switching to pursue a quick win—Chapter 4).
	Changing intentions and motivations toward previously planned change	Worker attention to attunement (Chapter 3); Co-created, clearly shared written care plans with effort to map areas of overlap in worker's and client's intention (e.g. use of "Egg and Triangle"—Chapter 3); Capacity to re-evaluate and adapt these plans, but also to hold to the value of core outcomes (Chapter 4); Use of a well-connected team to help the worker find the balance between scaffolding existing commitments and relationships and managing the risk of disengagement (Chapter 5).
Intervention	High drop-out rate	Assertive outreach approach where required (Chapter 5); Seeing clients in non-standard settings, with flexibility to provide contingent care; Worker less constrained to work exclusively within rigid professional role boundaries (quick wins, and "hospitality" as core elements of the method—Chapters 1, 4, 10).
	Ineffective or uncoordinated multi-domain interventions	Purposeful attention to the use of the worker's ambit (sphere of influence) and time to address "dis-integration" across networks (Chapter 6); Broader range of interventions, including social-ecological interventions, e.g. engaging with local sporting/educational/cultural resources (Chapter 4).

Table 3.2 Continued

Stage of case management	Problem/barrier to effective help	AMBIT adaptations
Review system	Changing client priorities mean we don't "measure what matters"	Explicit adaptation of shorter-term goals is expected, but framed by a mentalizing stance that contextualizes the intentions underlying such activity (Chapter 3)—for example, the "Egg and Triangle" tool invites consideration of immediate ("Now") and intermediate ("Next") goals under overarching intentions ("Why?"); Careful attention to developing or choosing appropriate and meaningful measures of progress (Chapters 3, 4, 7).
	Variable attendance and disengagements lead to missed review sessions	The mentalizing stance and "Mentalizing Loop" embed intensive checking back and adaptation as core to the working method (Chapter 4); Emphasis on session-by-session reviewing (Chapters 3, 7) rather than depending solely on scheduled formal review episodes.

protocol, beyond the not-knowing, curiosity, or inquisitiveness suggested by the mentalizing stance. It is a broad orientation toward better understanding of states of mind.

To return to our map-reading analogy, this activity of sensitive attunement equates to taking compass bearings on real elements that are visible in the landscape and matching these to what is depicted on the map; it is the use of a compass to reorient the map so that it aligns properly with the real territory it represents. So, it is impractical and probably unwise to try to create rigid protocols, procedures, or checklists for this kind of activity, which is in fact quite spontaneous. Creating conditions of calm to allow "implicit," everyday, automatic mentalizing to come "online" may be enough. Despite this, there may be value in contemplating a rational sequence for considering which core concerns to check in on in a stepwise manner, starting with consideration of immediate orientation and physical safety, and moving on to the immediate relational context, then the immediate cognitive and behavioral circumstances, and finally into a consideration of present intentions and future planning. This can be summarized in the simple sequence: *Where? Who? What? Why?* (see Figure 3.3).

Where? Consideration of the physical context (e.g. immediate surroundings, bodily sensations) as a first step is essentially a grounding technique, common in many mindfulness exercises and forms of meditation. For confused elderly patients in hospital who may have become distressed or aggressive on

Where next?

Why? — What **underlying intentions** might have led to this present state of affairs? Why are we here and doing/saying this?

What? — Focus on the **cognitive and behavioral** content: what's happening here and now? What thoughts are presently occupying the mind; what else is going on around me, or between us?

Who? — Focus on the **relational context**: who is in relationship to whom—right here and now? Alone or in company, how do I (or you) feel connected to others, or to other parts of my/yourself? What positions do we occupy in relation to each other (helper/helped, victim/bully, master/servant, etc.)?

Where? — Focus on **what is physically present** in the self and surroundings, and on establishing physical safety; what are the physical surroundings? Am I (or are we) oriented to them? ("Is my office OK?") What bodily sensations are present just now—signs of stress, or relative calm? Consider this a "grounding" excercise, such as many "mindfulness" exercises contain.

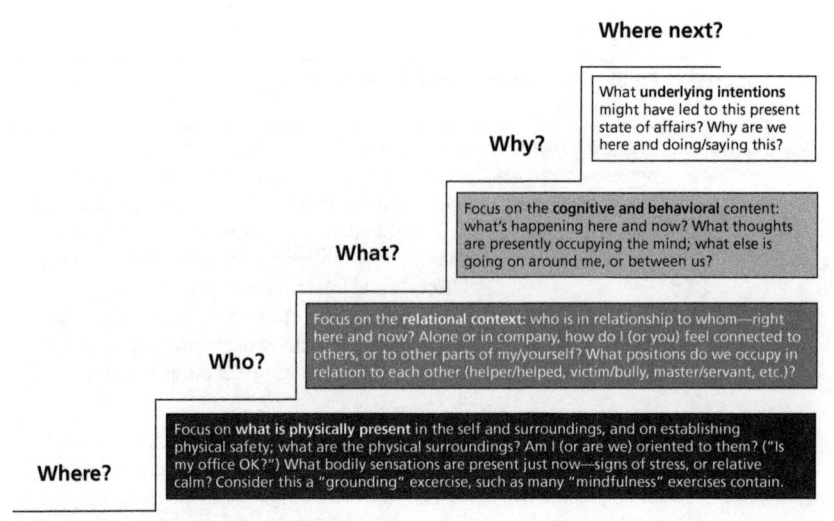

Figure 3.3 Sustaining sensitive attunement: a model for a "status update."

the ward, turning on all the lights, and telling them where they are, can literally "re-mind" them; in therapeutic work with clients, focusing (however briefly) on this kind of physical orientation is not so distant from the same process. At its heart is the question of safety. One cannot consider one's physical surroundings and bodily sensations in the here and now without answering the question of basic safety—essentially, "Are you or I in any immediate physical risk right here, right now?"

> "How's my office? Is it OK for us to work here?" may help break the ice in a session—even if the "office" is in fact a table at a local café, or a park bench, in which case the question may bring a bit of humor. "Before we go anywhere, let's just check in here and now; to me it looks as though you are quite relaxed/stressed—but have I got that wrong?"

Who? After physical safety and orientation is established, the next step is to find a simple way to remind the client of the *relational context*; at its most basic, this requires establishing who is present, and the safety that may or may not exist in that relationship.

> "This may seem a bit stupid, because in ways it's so obvious, but can we just remind ourselves who's here, and who isn't, right now?"

This not actually as simple a question as it might appear. For some clients, asking a question like this may feel too intimate, intrusive, or just strange (if the client and worker are sitting in front of each other!). The point of suggesting such an inquiry is just to establish that "we are paying attention to each other" and that there is enough safety in the relationship.

> "You know me a bit now, and you know a bit about my job, too, I guess. I'm reminding you about this because I think that my first job is to help you get to know me enough to decide that I'm safe, that I understand enough, or am professional enough to put some trust in."

It may be more appropriate to remark much more simply:

> "Well, here we are, busy in this office/on this bench again!"

This is also an opportunity for the worker to broadcast their own intentions in the relationship:

> "It may sound as though I'm stating the obvious, but I always want to be sure the work I do with you feels helpful to you."

Relationships are influenced by the positions held by (or pressed upon) each party in the relationship—helper and helped, persecutor and victim, seducer and seduced, master and servant, etc. Grounding the worker and client in a re-statement of the nature and purpose of the helping relationship is critical if thinking is to be activated about what is happening, here and now, within this context: "Are we OK right now?"

In thinking about the relational context, it is also helpful to hold a balance by acknowledging who is *not* present physically, but who might anyway be powerfully present in the mind of one or other of us. Even in solitude I am in some kind of relationship with myself, and the world around me, and there may be several other people in my mind who, although they are not physically present, I am still in some relationship with (e.g. if I am brooding over a recent misunderstanding with a colleague):

> "Is anyone else on your mind at the moment? They may not actually be here, but if your mind is full of thoughts about them, it might be helpful for me to know, so I don't ignore that fact."

What? This is where the *content* of the task, thoughts, memories, or feelings that are present is considered. Perhaps too often we tend to move into this phase of conversation or inquiry before first establishing the safety that "Where?" or "Who?" questions help to clarify.

> "So we're here talking about what happened when you went to college the other day, when you had an argument with one of the teachers. Can you help get clear in my mind what you remember about that? Who was saying what just before you started arguing?"
>
> "I can see and hear that this is a horrible situation you feel you're stuck in—but help me understand a bit more about the kinds of thoughts you have going through your head about this, will you?"

> "I'm probably being slow here, but I remember we've talked before about you being someone who has learned to be good at keeping your feelings quite well hidden. I just want to check that you think I've properly understood what you're feeling about this plan for you to move out from your mum's flat? It seems to me that you're talking about a mixture of feelings—part of you is quite excited or relieved, but part of you is a bit nervous about how it will work. Is that right? Does it feel like there is a sort of tug of war going on?"

"What?" questions encourage accuracy in detail and an attempt to be objective: they show respect for the facts of the matter in the here and now, before embarking on the less transparent task of clarifying the motivations and reasons behind why these things may be happening. Again, it is not uncommonly the case that conversation escalates beyond the "What?" questions to the "Why?" questions rather prematurely; this carries the risk that explicit mentalizing starts to take place based on faulty understandings of present states of mind.

Why? Here, what we think of as "explicit mentalizing" takes place—that is, considering how we make sense of what is happening, or has just happened, on the basis of the states of mind of the person or people involved. If "Why?" questions are explored using a mentalizing stance, there is a tentativeness and curiosity in the inquiry, rather than a high degree of certainty in the conclusions. The emphasis here is on the process of inquiry, the "making sense of," rather than any concrete conclusions that are drawn from this (which may be accurately or inaccurately mentalized). In the kind of sensitively attuned "checking in" that we are referring to, this is also a reflective process in the here and now. It may start with the worker reminding themselves aloud about the original intent that lay behind this process of checking in.

> "So, first of all I'm reminding myself about the reason I really wanted to check in and get a kind of 'status update' from you just now, because if you feel I really don't 'get it,' the chances of me being any real help to you are small!"
>
> "But I'm also wondering about how you make sense of why these very real worries have particularly come up today? This is probably way too simple, but I was wondering if there's a connection between you being so short on sleep recently, as though that has worn down the strength you usually have to keep these worries away?"
>
> "Now I've got a better understanding of what happened between you and this teacher, I'm really interested to hear how you make sense of what might have been going on to make him behave in the way he did."

Now that we have drawn out these ideas about sensitive attunement, there is a risk that they might be interpreted as a step-by-step guide to talking with a client, but this is not the case; what we are trying to offer is just a broad understanding of the approach—style tips, as it were—about pacing the conversation and ensuring safety, so as to hear what is there. Above all else, the worker must show authenticity in how they manage themself, adapting and learning from the client.

(b) Broadcasting intentions

In our enthusiasm to arrive at an understanding of a client's predicament we should not assume that our intentions are as transparent to the client as they may be to ourselves. Most workers are clear that they do this work to be helpful. For many of our clients, the experience of being scrutinized—which any form of assessment or help-seeking must involve—is excruciating, perhaps conjuring shame and expectations of rejection, or claustrophobic anxiety about the risk of a breach in carefully constructed defenses against a world of abusers, bullies, and exploiters. This may even lead to violent defense of their privacy. Under the scrutiny of the most well-intentioned assessment, our clients' fragile capacity to mentalize may easily collapse; their curiosity about us may be replaced by certainty about our "true" intentions (psychic equivalence) or the need for immediate action (walking out, or other teleological solutions). A mentalized explanation of such responses justifies significant additional preliminary effort on the part of the worker to broadcast as explicitly as possible their intentions. This is a moderated form of self-exposure, allowing—encouraging, even—the client to "inspect the goods," as it were. In the earliest stages this might take the form of stating what, to the worker, may seem blindingly obvious:

> "I want to be helpful, so when you and I go our separate ways you might remember me like, 'He was OK, he made a difference.'"
>
> "I want to make sure that the picture I get in my head about you is one you could say, 'Yeah, you've just about got it, that's how it is.'"
>
> "I may know about some of the things other young people have told me, and what other young people have found helpful, but I know very little at all about how it is to be *you*; so I'm trying to get that right in my head—to make sure I'm properly accurate—and I'll need your help with that, to tell me if I'm getting something the wrong way round."

Supplying an account of one's intentions as a worker gives the client the opportunity to propose a different view, for example, "You've only come because you are paid to" or "You only want to take me away from my home." The purpose of broadcasting is not to get into an argument, but to make sense of a client's behavior by bringing implicit beliefs and constructs into a more explicit form, which renders them amenable to thinking about ("If that really was my intention, it would make very good sense to avoid contact with me!"). Implicitly, and perhaps increasingly explicitly, the conversation moves toward the issue of trust:

> "So, am I right that one of the things I absolutely must understand about you is that you've got good reasons for *not* trusting people like me?"

"So if I'm to be of any use or interest to you, it seems like I've got to make sure I keep putting my cards on the table—really explaining why I'm doing whatever I'm doing, and letting you really question those reasons. Is that right? No surprises, then?"

Earlier in this chapter we described a key area in which broadcasting intentions plays a major role—in discussion about the end of the treatment journey—a discussion that starts at its very beginning.

Formulation and goal-setting

As the process of drawing out the client's story progresses, the broadcasting of the worker's intentions will include what is commonly described as "reflecting back." This is a kind of re-telling of the client's story—in the worker's own words—that attempts to capture key themes and preoccupations in such a way that the client can recognize their dilemma, but, crucially, offering this alongside the worker's intentions (to help). The word "re-cognition" is a helpful prompt to what is being described here—the client seeing and (re)thinking about their predicament as it has been seen and understood by the worker. This reflecting back needs to be offered tentatively, so that the client feels not only empowered but encouraged to correct, expand upon, or deepen the worker's understanding where necessary. The therapist's mentalizing stance, described in depth in Chapter 4, is designed to facilitate this process. This enthusiasm of the worker to enrich their own mind with better understandings of their client's mind could be explained thus:

"It is not my business to try to change your mind here, but to show you how I can change my own mind about you! To let go of ideas I might have got wrong about you, and put the right ones, the helpful ones, in their place."

"It suits me much better to get an understanding of you that you can understand and recognize. I suspect that this will be more helpful for you too."

"I am guessing that before we go anywhere together you'll need to know if I've got the imagination or the ears to really hear what it is you're trying to deal with in your life … that's why I keep asking these nosy questions."

(a) Direct linking of formulation to goal-setting ("comparing destinations" and "agreeing waymarks")

As assessment and understanding deepens, broadcasting takes the form of laying out our understanding of the client's predicament and starting to outline the kinds of destinations that, given *my* understanding as a worker, would make sense to me. This direct linkage between mentalizing and planned behavior makes sense in relation to the direct connection between mentalizing and intentionality. Mentalizing can easily be misinterpreted as being something rather airy and disconnected from action, but at its heart is something quite concrete—the making sense of behavior on the basis of intentional mental states. This requires careful consideration because, of course, much remains unknown about our own intentions, let alone other people's, but accurate mentalizing usually leads inexorably to purposeful changes in behavior.

In most cases there will be at least some areas where differences in understanding and interpretation remain, despite best efforts. In these scenarios, it is important to find ways to make these differences explicit and to agree to differ. Mentalizing each other is not the same as agreeing with each other. We seek as a minimum some explicit understanding of the difference of views, so that they do not inhibit experiments directed at helpful change. The development of a worker's ambit (sphere of influence) is really the task of mapping a set of understandings and intentions in the worker and client that overlap sufficiently to get started on some kind of agreed work.

Efforts to broadcast—particularly in relation to possible "destinations" (aims) and "waymarks" (goals)—are always made with an acute sensitivity to the possibility (or even probability) that the worker is mistaken, and with invitations to help them correct these errors. This is very close to the themes of "curiosity" (Cecchin, 1987) and "safe uncertainty" (Mason, 1993) that systemic thinkers have written about previously. The worker is showing their map to the client, with a best estimation of "where we are" and "where we could usefully go," and inviting the client to show theirs.

We hope that by now it will be clear why making explicit our current formulation of a client's difficulties, and our ideas about what might help with these, is useful. There are many different ways to communicate ideas about how difficulties might have arisen and why they persist, and many existing and well-evidenced therapeutic approaches have already demonstrated the benefits of this kind of explicit broadcasting. For instance, cognitive analytic therapy (Clarke et al., 2013) and MBT-A (Fonagy et al., 2014) both use letters addressed to the patient. Many versions of CBT use (more visual, less literary) flow diagrams to illustrate the ways that thoughts, feelings, and behaviors interact to maintain or amplify problems, and multisystemic treatment (Henggeler et al., 1998) uses "fit circles" that highlight the many contributory factors to a single problem. Most formulations, however they are constructed and displayed, will have something to say about predisposing "upstream" factors (to do with disposition and pre-existing vulnerabilities, e.g. prior exposure to trauma), precipitating "triggering" factors (current stressors, which may be in the realms of biology, psychology, relationships, or economics), and what factors or mechanisms might perpetuate the cycle (this is usually based on some notion of the most important feedback loops that are in operation). Thus, well-made formulations usually carry implications or include explicit statements about what might help *given this particular way of understanding the situation.*

AMBIT does not take a position that there is a single right way to communicate a formulation, but only that explicit efforts to communicate it effectively are essential—especially efforts that assume that formulation is constantly a work in progress, building in opportunities for ongoing modification, collaboration, and co-construction with the client. Later formulations will be rich and detailed, earlier ones more sketchy and partial.

Here we provide two examples of techniques that might assist in the task of broadcasting: first a "mentalizing letter," and second an example of a simple tool, the Active Planning Map, which has come to be known colloquially as the "Egg and Triangle."

A mentalizing (formulation) letter

This is an attempt to communicate the beginnings of a formulation, quite early in an intervention. In this example it is assumed that the (fictional) client is able to digest the text of a letter. For clients with poorer literacy skills who would struggle to use such a format, consideration could be given to supplying, for instance, short video clips or audio recordings of the worker trying to explain their thinking. What seems to us to be important is the way that the formulation is presented as some externally created thing, rather than the worker simply "telling" the client. We theorize that in externalizing the content, it becomes less personalized and more accessible as something that can be improved upon or corrected. Aside from the worker's success or otherwise in creating resonances and recognition in the client with their account, perhaps what is equally important is the communication of effort and a certain amount of humility on the part the worker.

> *Dear Jen,*
> *Thanks for spending the time with me over the last week or so, and helping me try to understand the many difficult things weighing you down at the moment. There's a lot, which is why this is quite a long letter. In this letter I have tried to show you how I imagine it might be to be in your shoes. It makes sense to me that you might be feeling pretty hopeless about things changing. However, I'm hopeful that we can improve things, and I'm writing to try to show you where I've got to in my understanding and ideas, so you can be clear whether the plans we might now agree on together are the best we can do (and help make them better!).*
> *At times it must have been frustrating to have me struggle to understand things the way you see them, and I'm sure that I am not there yet. Just like when we meet, what I really like is when you correct my mistakes, so please feel free to use a red pen to correct things in this letter! I'm not being deliberately slow, by the way, but I've learned that when I get too certain that I've got all the answers, it's usually unhelpful. Anyway, here goes.*
> *You've told me how often you have this horrible feeling of worry and "numbness," and I imagine on top of just feeling this way you might also worry whether this will ever stop; from what I've understood it seems getting rid of this feeling is the most important thing. As well as that, you've suggested that you're probably smoking too much weed, even though you*

ACTIVE PLANNING | 113

are mostly doing this because it's the only thing that takes away the feelings in the short term, and it's only when you are stoned that you can feel OK. We've talked about my understanding of how cannabis can actually increase anxiety, even though it may relieve it in the short term, but at the moment we've agreed that we have different ideas about this. I think you've had a lot of people telling you about cannabis, and you don't want more of the same from me right now.

As well as this, you've shown me some other things about yourself that might be easy to forget when everything feels so difficult. The one that stands out for me is your love and talent for art. I was very moved when you talked about your grandfather, who is also very artistic, and your wish that you could find ways to make a living from this skill, because you know this would make him incredibly proud.

You've explained that, apart from your grandfather, you feel the rest of your family don't really "get" you at the moment, and in many ways it is hard for you to "get" them too, as they seem to "blow hot and cold"; sometimes they seem kind and understanding, while at other times (often just when you need support) you can feel terribly rejected by them. You are hoping to move out in the months ahead, but at present it is really frustrating to know that there isn't any alternative place for you to go. However, you also describe some very important and supportive friends (even though they are also the group that you tend to smoke weed with). It seemed important for me to know that you know that these friends really care about you. It was easy for me to see how you could be someone who makes strong friendships.

Outside home, you talked about how boring and irritating you find school. We spent a bit of time thinking about what it is about school that really gets under your skin; one of the things we noticed was how easy it is for you to feel patronized and treated as if you were still a young child. We talked about how you'd be able to let me know if I ever fell into that—I'm hoping that isn't the case, but it seems important for me to check in with you about that occasionally. You've also shown me how you feel very hassled by the Youth Offending Team, who need to meet with you regularly—it's easy for them to seem patronizing and bossy because of this, too, and you are worried that you might snap at times as it makes you so stressed and angry. We thought a bit about this—how, when you get that sense that people are patronizing you, it gets right under your skin, and that when you are upset you tend to become more certain about your beliefs about these people (that they are doing this on purpose to wind you up). We discussed how, when we are calmer, it is easier to think about people in lots of different ways, and to understand how complicated and difficult they are to make sense of. I don't know if you remember, but at that point you seemed to get a bit calmer, and I was impressed at how you were able to see that these teachers and YOT workers "have a job to do" and are probably trying to help you stay on track, even if the way their words come out aren't very effective for you.

I am sure that there are many other things that are also important, maybe from difficult times earlier on, but I have wondered if, quite sensibly, you want to take your time about deciding whether to talk about them to me. That makes sense to me—you don't yet know me very well, and I am sure I would want to check someone out for a while if I had difficult and complicated things to sort out. You agreed that perhaps I could check in occasionally to see if there were other things that would be useful to think about, and if that's OK with you, I will do that every so often.

I have tried to show you how I understand what you've told me so far. Do let me know if I've missed important things out or explained things the wrong way. So what might we do *together from here? Here are my thoughts—but remember, they are just my thoughts, and between the two of us I am sure we can improve on them.*

1. *It seems to me that the most important thing for you right now is to find ways to stop feeling so worried and numb all of the time. If we don't do something about that quickly, anything else I do to try to help might seem a bit pointless. At the moment that makes sense to me as our first priority.*
2. *As well as that, though, helping you to get through your Court Order and not lose your temper with the YOT and school seems like a key priority to me.*
3. *After that, I am less sure what you think we should work on next. Some of the things I've wondered about are listed here:*
   - *Helping you find out whether there is a way to change things around at school so you are doing more work that you are interested in.*
   - *Finding ways for you to talk with your family—can we help them make better sense of you, and you to make better sense of them? Can we find a way for you to talk with them about your ideas for future living arrangements?*
   - *We have already talked about your cannabis use, and it seems to me that at present you are balanced between wanting to continue using and wanting to cut down or stop, rather than being firmly decided about what you want to do. You understand that I have some ideas about cannabis making anxiety symptoms worse, and perhaps we could think further about this over the coming weeks?*

Finally, how could we prevent or respond to crises that might happen, that could make things even more difficult? You helped me understand that the biggest risk at the moment would be the times when you are already feeling numb or worried, and a teacher or YOT worker then tries to encourage you to do something that feels too much. If you get a strong feeling at that time that you are being talked down to (which is often when these feelings arise), you worry that you could get aggressive in ways that could get you into trouble, or get somebody hurt. We agreed that this is definitely something we want to avoid. That is why I will make contact quickly with your school and the YOT, and we will try to create a plan so that you could use a kind of code word, or show a card, which would mean you could "take time out" quickly to calm things down. You thought that a plan like this might help, but you weren't sure, so we agreed we should keep checking to see whether it is working, and whether there are more things that could be done. Of course, if we can help reduce your anxiety in the meantime, this is likely to reduce the number of times when you feel overwhelmed in this way.

I do hope these thoughts make sense, and I look forward to the chance to improve them with you—this is just a place to start from.
Best wishes,

The Active Planning Map ("Egg and Triangle")

The Active Planning Map, or "Egg and Triangle" tool (see Figures 3.4 and 3.5), offers another way for workers to broadcast their intentions and invite collaboration with a client in developing a plan. It is also used in trainings as part of a role-play to support the practice of an inquisitive and not-knowing stance (this is very close to what systemic therapists have also referred to as the "one-down" stance). It requires the worker to "place their cards on the table": a series of brief

Figure 3.4 The "Egg and Triangle" tool.

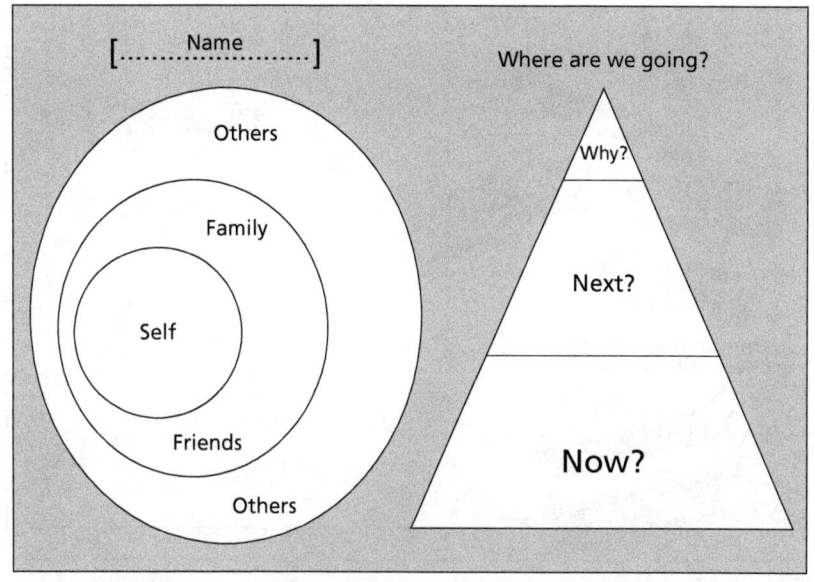

Suggestion: Worker fills this in after initial discussion, *then* asks the client to help correct it

statements—that, in the worker's mind, best capture their current understanding of the client's dilemmas and strengths—are recorded on the "egg," focusing on statements about self, family/carers, friends, and others (agencies such as school, social care, YOT, etc.). The "triangle" is a simplified version of Maslow's "hierarchy of needs" (Maslow, 1943), which offers a place to record suggestions about what seems to need attending to *now* (in the worker's mind, this is likely to be dominated by questions of safety in the first instance, while the client may have rather different ideas about their priorities), and what might be lined up for attention *next* (these might be more specific therapeutic goals, such as improvement in anxiety, reintegration into college, or feeling less paranoid in public, etc.). The top of the triangle is where "the point" of these goals/interventions is recorded; this represents the most general intentions or aims, and—if the worker has understood the client to a degree—this might be where more general agreement between worker and client can be anticipated. Are we both heading for the same overall aims?

Compared with the other ways of developing shared formulations mentioned earlier, the "egg" offers a very simple level of formulation that is not much more than a demonstration of active listening, with opportunities for the client to see how much the worker has gleaned about their life and circumstances. The purpose of the diagram is to link this understanding explicitly to a

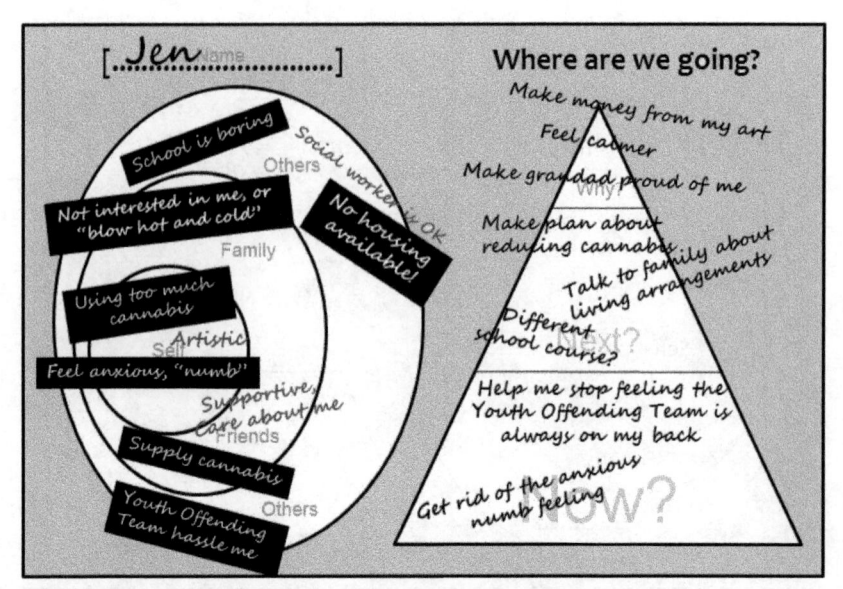

Figure 3.5 Example of a completed "Egg and Triangle."

process of purposeful change or help (represented by the "triangle"). Our experience is that many young clients find this near-impossible in the early stages, as they have such limited internalized models of processes of help and learning through relationships with adults. Questions about how they would like their life to be different or better are often met with derision or sheer incomprehension. In some ways the Active Planning Map is an exceptionally hard task in the early stages, but the intention is that it represents a model of help that is not just about getting to know each other but creates a context for exploring shared intentions and possible activities. This can be very hard to sustain, as the early contacts with many clients may be characterized by highly fluctuating preoccupations on the part of the client in which there is little continuity from one contact to the next as to what the client's needs are.

So, the most important use for the Active Planning Map is in its presentation to the client, and the invitation to talk together about what is written in it; the worker's intention in doing this is to improve the accuracy of the statements so that these first attempts to capture something of the client's dilemmas can be improved upon.

(b) Co-constructing the plan (agreeing waymarks)
Presenting this material after perhaps one or two initial meetings offers an opportunity for the worker to demonstrate their mentalizing stance (see Chapter 4). If a client is particularly wary of engaging, and information is shared at a much slower pace, this might take significantly longer. The client may have different ideas and

priorities, and almost inevitably there will need to be some balancing of what, for either party, may be seen as non-negotiables. The effort is to make as explicit as possible the reasons for making the suggestions that are on offer, reducing the likelihood that unspoken assumptions will foster reasons for disengagement.

At this point it may be helpful to distinguish between *aims, goals*, and *plans*. The aim of work is its point, the "longest-range" intention that motivates any planned activity that follows—it is the direction of travel toward a point on (or beyond) the horizon, as it were (e.g. "to get on better with my mum and not drive her to start drinking again"). Goals represent the stepping stones or waymarks on this journey ("to reduce my cannabis use so I don't have to steal so much money from my mum"), whereas the plan is a much more practical set of actions that lays out in more detail the immediate steps ahead ("this week, to only have a spliff at the weekend"). Through collaborative negotiation of the kind that we have outlined above, a plan for the work with a client comes to represent the map of a journey.

Example plan
Aims:

1. For Jen to feel happier and less anxious or "numb"
2. To improve family relationships
3. To support Jen toward some kind of arts training or employment

Goals:

1. Reduce anxiety symptoms until they fall within the normal range (by [date]).
2. Explore and create possible adjustments to Jen's weekly timetable in order to minimize conflict over attendance/appointments at school and with the YOT (by [date]).
3. Reduce family conflict (fewer arguments, more laughter) by improving communication/understanding and conflict resolution strategies with family work (by [date]).
4. Address the possible contribution of cannabis use to anxiety (and consider a reduction plan) (by [date]).

Plan:

1. Arrange for a psychoeducation session about panic and anxiety symptoms. Develop and practice using measures of anxiety symptoms. Collect baseline measures.
2. Arrange for basic CBT and relaxation exercises.
3. Consult with the Child and Adolescent Mental Health team about the possible need for more specialist assessment and treatment, or guidance to support the CBT we are delivering.

4. Contact the YOT and school, clarify perspectives on the problem (non-negotiables and negotiables), and create a plan for possible adjustments to Jen's timetable.
5. Embark on motivational/mentalization-based work to help clarify Jen's intentions and motivation in relation to work with her family and in relation to her use of cannabis. Draw up new plans as required in relation to this.
6. Check in with Jen, as agreed, about whether there are additional issues that would add to our understanding or could be helped by other interventions.

Considerations/protocols in relation to crisis contingencies:

1. The main risk is of aggression when Jen is already anxious and misinterprets communication from teaching or YOT staff.
2. Jen is aware that she is responsible for her actions.
3. Set up a system of "start of the day check-ins" at school and with the YOT, with a shared "code word" (or "Get me out of here" card) for her to use with staff at points of escalation.
4. Review this in two weeks' time.
5. If aggression does occur, use existing emergency/crisis protocols in place at school or in the YOT.

Review by: [date]

Review system: Creating measures of progress

Once a map of "where I am and where I want to get to" has been created, AMBIT's principle of "Respect for evidence" requires that the worker, together with the client and, ideally, his or her carers and other professionals (perhaps teachers or a social worker), create some means of measuring the extent to which the goals have been achieved. Progress against these goals can then be mapped, offering more tangible measures of improvement, or markers for areas where innovation and renewed effort are justified.

Why this emphasis on measurement? There is a risk that, by creating specific outcome measures, the essential flexibility that this work requires could be reduced to a rather mechanistic (teleological) set of exercises in pursuit of better scores that soundly fail to "measure what matters." In spite of this, we forcefully maintain that the risks of not measuring progress are even greater. We have already stressed the complexity of the problems and systems in which workers become immersed with their clients. In such situations, there is often an overwhelming experience of chaos; some things go according to plan, but new crises or unsettling pieces of information emerge, some things steadfastly do not change, and others deteriorate, necessitating unplanned changes of direction. In these situations the worker and client are subject to a barrage of "data" (feedback from many different people and perspectives, exam results, assessment reports, hearsay and rumors, the immediate reactions of individuals to news without access to their more measured reflections that may follow later in the day, etc.); in these circumstances it is difficult to hold any degree of certainty about the direction in which the work is going.

In setting some key measures of progress, the worker and client will have to balance therapeutic optimism with a realism that avoids setting unattainable targets, which themselves might reinforce despair. But if measures of what matters can be derived and applied in something approaching a systematic way, they are invaluable.

There are a wide range of standardized and well-validated outcome measures available, and a number of these are included in the AMBIT manual. While these are of great value, they are seldom sufficiently specific to a client's personal dilemmas. Moreover, measures that rate severity across a wide range of symptoms or functional areas (the AIM or The Current View (Jones et al., 2013), for instance) will rarely offer large-scale changes in total scores, and changes in total scores on such broad measures may appear to gloss over very significant improvements in one or two critical domains. Shifting scores on standardized measures can, in any case, appear rather meaningless (which client will feel their spirits lift when told that they have risen from a score of 45 to 54 on the Children's Global Assessment Scale?) For this reason, other goal-based outcomes (Law, 2013) may be selected that will have more meaning for the client and the worker. For instance, individually defined goal-based measures might include:

- Being able to stay in college for a week without incident
- Feeling calmer in myself (perhaps using a personalized scale, where "totally calm" is scored 10 and "totally agitated" is scored 0, and a shift of 3 or more points is seen as personally significant)
- Not getting so stressed by my parents
- Avoiding all use of MDMA and other illicit powders or "legal highs" for a month
- Scoring my mood as at least 5/10 each day for a fortnight
- Contacting my friends more and not thinking that they don't want to see me
- Not self-injuring for a month.

Alternatively, the AMBIT AIM assessment described earlier in this chapter allows up to six items to be selected, through collaborative discussion between the worker and client, as "key problems"; the items that are selected can be allocated as goal-based measures, with the target being to reduce scores in these particular items to 2 or less (out of the maximum severity score of 4).

Care needs to be taken to set goals that are safe (a client with calorie-restricting anorexia might wish to set a goal of losing 5 kg in weight, but this would clearly be far from helpful or safe from the perspective of the worker) and that are sufficiently challenging to represent real benefit, but without being so challenging as to be an example of "setting you up to fail." Conversely, goals that are very limited in ambition may represent a genuine desire on the part of the worker to allow the client an experience of success, but may equally be driven by a less honorable desire for the worker's or the team's outcomes to look better.

The use of session-by-session measures is increasingly gaining traction. These may be simple scales of progress toward (or away from) predefined goals (scaled from −5 to +5, for instance), or questions rating the client's experience of the session ("Did we talk about what was important to you?", "Was it easy to talk?", "Was what we spoke about understandable?", "Did it help in ways that could make a difference after this session?", etc.). In the UK, the work of the Children and Young People's Improving Access to Psychological Therapies (CYP IAPT) initiative brought such measures to the fore in many services for young people, and this is a development that AMBIT strongly supports. Such measures, when used repeatedly over time, can plot subtle changes in a client's trajectory through the process of help or therapy. They also invite innovation in a therapeutic journey ("The progress we made in the early weeks of working together seems to have stalled. What do we need to do differently to move forwards again?"). They also provide an immediate and concrete example of the worker's genuine curiosity to understand the client's perspective and to make a difference that is of value to the client, providing a regular platform for the worker to model a mentalizing stance, reflecting on "whether the help that I'm trying to put together with you is as helpful as we can make it."

Conclusions

This chapter has tried to provide a sense of the phases of AMBIT-influenced working—a style of working that attempts to square a tricky circle: to *remain attuned* to the personal experience of a client and their predicament, while also maintaining shape and boundaries so as to *exert effective action*.

Key to this puzzle is Active Planning, which could be seen as an attempt to nuance the pragmatic operations involved in planning and working to plans by incorporating the understandings of mentalizing theory. This chapter seeks to support workers in moving from implicit practice ("I always do it like this") toward an explicit style of practice that encourages the worker and client to map "where we are" and "where we are heading" and to develop the disciplines required of any good navigator: a culture of constant checking between observations in the external world, representations of intention, and measures of the fit between these two—just like a landscape, map, and compass.

References

Ainsworth, M. D. S. (1993). Attachments and other affectional bonds across the life cycle. In: C. Murray-Parkes, J. Stevenson-Hinde, & P. Marris (eds.), *Attachment Across the Life Cycle*, pp. 33–51. London, UK: Routledge.

Allen, J. G., Bleiberg, E., & Haslam-Hopwood, T. (2003). *Understanding mentalizing: Mentalizing as a compass for treatment* (Houston, TX: The Menninger Clinic).

Bateson, G. (1972). *Steps to an Ecology of Mind: Collected essays in anthropology, psychiatry, evolution, and epistemology* (Chicago, IL: University of Chicago Press).

Burnham, J. (1992). Approach - method - technique: making distinctions and creating connections. *Human Systems: Journal of Systemic Consultation and Management* 3: 3–26.

Cecchin, G. (1987). Hypothesising, circularity and neutrality revisited: An invitation to curiosity. *Family Process* 26: 405–13.

Clarke, S., Thomas, P., & James, K. (2013). Cognitive analytic therapy for personality disorder: Randomised controlled trial. *British Journal of Psychiatry* 202: 129–34. doi: 10.1192/bjp.bp.112.108670

Fonagy, P., Cottrell, D., Phillips, J., Bevington, D., Glaser, D., & Allison, E. (2015). *What Works for Whom? A Critical Review of Treatments for Children and Adolescents* (2nd edn, New York, NY: Guilford Press).

Fonagy, P., Rossouw, T., Sharp, C., Bateman, A., Allison, L., & Farrar, C. (2014). Mentalization-based treatment for adolescents with borderline traits. In: C. Sharp, & J. L. Tackett (eds.), *Handbook of Borderline Personality Disorder in Children and Adolescents*, pp. 313–32. New York, NY: Springer.

Goodyer, I. M., Tsancheva, S., Byford, S., Dubicka, B., Hill, J., Kelvin, R., … Fonagy, P. (2011). Improving mood with psychoanalytic and cognitive therapies (IMPACT): A pragmatic effectiveness superiority trial to investigate whether specialised psychological treatment reduces the risk for relapse in adolescents with moderate to severe unipolar depression: study protocol for a randomised controlled trial. *Trials* 12: 175. doi: 10.1186/1745-6215-12-175

Henggeler, S. W., Schoenwald, S. K., Borduin, C. M., Rowland, M. D., & Cunningham, P. B. (1998). *Multisystemic Treatment of Antisocial Behavior in Children and Adolescents* (New York, NY: Guilford Press).

Jackson, J. H., & McGorry, P. D. (eds.) (2009). *The Recognition and Management of Early Psychosis: A preventive approach*. 2nd edn (Cambridge, UK: Cambridge University Press).

Jones, M., Hopkins, K., Kyrke-Smith, R., Davies, R., Vostanis, P., & Wolpert, M. (2013). *Current View Tool Completion Guide* (London, UK: CAMHS Press), https://www.ucl.ac.uk/ebpu/docs/publication_files/current_view, accessed 27 Jan. 2017.

Korzybski, A. (1941). *Science and Sanity* (New York, NY: Science Press).

Law, D. (2013). *Goals and Goal Based Outcomes (GBOs): Some useful information* (London, UK: CAMHS Press), https://www.ucl.ac.uk/ebpu/docs/publication_files/GBOs_Booklet, accessed 16 Jan. 2017.

Main, T. (1957). The ailment. *British Journal of Medical Psychology* 30: 129–45.

Malberg, N. T. (2013). Mentalization based group interventions with chronically ill adolescents: An example of assimilative psychodynamic integration? *Journal of Psychotherapy Integration* 23: 5–13. doi: 10.1037/a0030268

Maslow, A. H. (1943). A theory of human motivation. *Psychological Review* **50**: 370–96.

Mason, B. (1993). Towards positions of safe uncertainty. *Human Systems* **4**: 189–200.

Porter, M. E. (2010). What is value in health care? *New England Journal of Medicine* **363**: 2477–81. doi: 10.1056/NEJMp1011024

Rossouw, T. I., & Fonagy, P. (2012). Mentalization-based treatment for self-harm in adolescents: A randomized controlled trial. *Journal of the American Academy of Child and Adolescent Psychiatry* **51**: 1304–13. doi: 10.1016/j.jaac.2012.09.018

Target, M., & Fonagy, P. (1992). *Raters' Manual for the Hampstead Child Adaptation Measure (HCAM)* (London, UK: University College London).

Weisz, J. R., Chorpita, B. F., Palinkas, L. A., Schoenwald, S. K., Miranda, J., Bearman, S. K., ... Research Network on Youth Mental Health. (2012). Testing standard and modular designs for psychotherapy treating depression, anxiety, and conduct problems in youth: a randomized effectiveness trial. *Archives of General Psychiatry* **69**: 274–82. doi: 10.1001/archgenpsychiatry.2011.147

Winnicott, D. W. (1953). Transitional objects and transitional phenomena; A study of the first not-me possession. *International Journal of Psycho-Analysis* **34**: 89–97.

Chapter 4

Working with your client

Introduction: What to do face to face is only a quarter of the job

This chapter covers what might well conventionally be seen as the main course, or indeed the whole meal, if AMBIT were simply the menu for another brand of therapy; what to do when face to face with clients and their families? Perhaps differing from the manuals for some other types of intervention, this element of the work is squeezed into just one chapter. We argue throughout this book that setting up the right context (emotional, relational, organizational, and systemic) for effective help to take root is absolutely central to its success, and that perhaps holding this balance is more critical than the technical details of specific therapeutic maneuvers. If we were to use a mountaineering metaphor, in which the goals of therapy are the summit, then the technical skills of the mountaineer with axe and crampons out in front, breaking the trail, are of course crucial, but they are far from all that is required to get there. As we know, the relationships and communication between the team members further back, who are holding the rope or engaged in the logistics of route-planning and the expedition supply chain, are just as critical.

This chapter will focus in particular on the range of methods, techniques, and skills that are required on the front line. Specifically, we will describe how mentalizing requires a relationship, and informs a *stance*—a general "way-of-being-with"—for the worker in relation to their client. This stance is designed to create a relational context that supports the development or recovery of mentalizing. This happens in the therapeutic moment, but must also involve wider learning if it is to be helpful in more than simply that moment; we want our clients to go on to use this more balanced form of mentalizing in the rest of their life, in other relationships, and across time. We also need to consider our own capacity as practitioners in teams to sustain our work, adapt, and improve over time. Consequently, in this chapter we will regularly refer to other chapters that cover the various "mountaineering aids" that a worker in the field will rely on to organize this challenging work. For the reader who may be "dipping in," we particularly refer you back to Chapter 3, where we describe the phases of

AMBIT work and the process of Active Planning—this chapter is particularly closely connected to Chapter 3.

This chapter, then, will begin by outlining the basic approach of mentalization-based interventions, namely the *mentalizing stance* and the *mentalizing loop*. These have been described elsewhere (Bateman & Fonagy, 2016; Asen & Fonagy, 2012) but are briefly restated here. We will then focus on some familiar ways in which workers may be led off track in trying to do this work, or "lose their balance," as we prefer to call this. Remember that AMBIT is designed for a world of work in which temporarily losing one's balance is the norm rather than signaling professional failure. Modifications to these basic working methods in relation to the AMBIT approach, which take account of working in a community context and with clients who have very poor relationships to help, will then be highlighted. We will finish with a discussion of some of the ongoing limitations of these methods and some of the dilemmas and challenges that these present for workers in the field.

The mentalizing stance

The theory of mentalizing was covered in Chapter 2. We believe that better practice arises when workers really understand the theory as well as the practice. Like good jazz musicians who know their music, they can improvise better. The basic techniques underlying mentalization-based practice have been thoroughly described in other texts (Bateman & Fonagy, 2016, 2012; Fonagy et al., 2014) and will be described briefly here. The mentalizing stance is a "way-of-being-with" our clients. It is important to say that, in relation to AMBIT, this stance is not something that we invite workers to use only in neatly delineated sessions, but in *any* contact with clients: on the phone, via text messages, over a game of pool, or during a more formal session. The stance is intended:

- To model mentalizing (it is more about "showing" than it is about "telling")
- To create as many opportunities as possible in the here and now to foster and mark instances of mentalizing in the client (learning through experience)
- To build up a bank of experience and learning about mentalizing (whether or not it is called by this technical name, or referred to in other ways such as "careful thinking," "front-brain thinking," or "puzzling out people") that our clients can take away and try out in the rest of their lives.

The mentalizing stance consists of four easily remembered prompts for workers that have been likened to the four legs of a table—ideally, all should be in contact with the ground:

1. Not-knowing, curiosity, or inquisitiveness
2. Punctuating or terminating non-mentalizing

3. Reinforcing positive mentalizing
4. Holding the balance.

Not-knowing, curiosity, or inquisitiveness

This is often also referred to as the "inquisitive stance," but it should certainly not be confused with behaving as though you are part of a constantly interrogating inquisition! Instead, the worker tries to hold in mind the truth that *all minds are opaque to one another*, accepting the fact that there is much about this other person's mind (and indeed, only to a slightly lesser extent, about their own) that they do not, and cannot, ever fully know. The very opposite of mentalizing is "mind-reading," in which we simply assume to "know" the experiences, hopes, fears, and beliefs that explain someone else's behaviors at a point in time. Behaving in a way that suggests we are mind-reading risks being intensely and infuriatingly or terrifyingly intrusive, or (if we are lucky enough to get something right) shuts down our client's efforts to mentalize, as they "outsource" their own mentalizing to this "outboard brain." Instead, the not-knowing and curious stance acts respectfully and always very tentatively—ideas about the client's mind are put forward as possibilities that have come into our mind, offering plenty of opportunities for rebuttal, or more accurate refinements, by the client, and perhaps lightened with a bit of gentle self-deprecating humor:

> "What you're saying has really got me thinking. Now, I may be way off target here, and you already know I can definitely get things wrong when I try to figure these kinds of things out ... but in my head I've got this idea now—that when I say the words 'social services,' some pictures come into *your* head that might be very different from the pictures that I have in *my* head. Does that make any sense to you at all?"
>
> "... because when I was talking about social services just then, I had this picture in *my* head of a social worker who's a bit knackered from being overworked, maybe a bit stressed, a bit frustrated because there's not enough time, not enough money to pay for the things that are needed, and so on, but basically someone wanting to try and do the best they can ... but then I saw you were frowning, and you sounded really irritated, and I was thinking, 'Doh! I've managed to annoy you,' which wasn't what I wanted at all! So first of all, I'm sorry if I did that, but second, I'm wondering if perhaps in your head when you heard me say 'social services,' you might have been thinking of someone very different—I don't know, someone with the power to take your mum away from you, someone quite powerful in a sort of threatening way. Do you think that's where I tripped up, or was it just me being a bit annoying in another way?"

Another aspect of this not-knowing and inquisitive stance is the extent to which it is something that is *open and shared* by the worker, rather than held covertly (as though not-knowing were something to be professionally ashamed of). In the past, the TV detective Columbo (played by the actor Peter Falk) was often held up as an example of this. Younger readers may not remember this shabbily dressed character, who would pace around the room scratching his head and wondering (hypothesizing) aloud, quite comfortable about sharing his puzzlement and the process by which his many errors—each corrected one by one—inexorably led to the truth.

A more modern analogy might be between this open acknowledgment of the limits of the worker's knowing as they grope toward more powerful understandings of their client, and the way that "open-source" computer programming works. Open-source projects start from the principle that collaboration is always preferable to secretive efforts to launch a perfect finished product. From the very beginning, the bones of computer code are shared on the internet, and this invites two things: first, awareness of its many imperfections, which spurs the originator on to greater efforts to make good the most embarrassing of its shortcomings, and second, access to real-world feedback as other people try out these "thoughts," identifying bugs and incompatibilities, and offering improvements and fixes, so that slowly (actually, often quite nimbly) the project advances. Well-known web browsers such as Firefox or Chrome are built using this methodology. In many ways the curious, inquisitive stance is the psychological equivalent: "open-source thinking." AMBIT itself draws much inspiration from open-source programming, describing itself as an open-source approach to treatment development.

Punctuating or terminating non-mentalizing

If the goal of much of our work is to stimulate, reawaken, or sustain mentalizing in our clients, then passively allowing non-mentalizing states of mind to fill too much of a session makes little sense. We can assume that the client (or the family as a whole) is already spending quite long periods of their waking hours in non-mentalizing states of mind, so leaving them to do more of the same, unchallenged, is unlikely to prove helpful. Thus, in relation to the broad range of ways that workers from different therapeutic traditions interact with their clients, on a scale of "assertiveness" or "worker activity" the mentalizing stance would rate relatively high. Workers using the mentalizing stance are active and engaged, and will almost certainly at times interrupt their clients, although ideally with sensitivity, appropriate apologies, and in awareness, with explicit purpose (and, ideally, having forewarned the client that this is part of how we work):

> "It's important I don't keep nodding and saying 'Aha, OK, I see …' if actually I haven't properly understood what you're saying. Sometimes we actually find that interrupting a bit helps to slow things down enough for both of us to see things in new ways. I guess what I'm saying is that this isn't really an 'ordinary' kind of conversation—I hope that makes sense to you?"

What this means needs to be teased out a little carefully, though. It would be very easy to take the advice to "punctuate" or "terminate" non-mentalizing in a (paradoxically) rather non-mentalizing and concrete or teleological way, as though our noticing the first inkling of non-mentalizing in a client should trigger an automatic reflex action to stamp it out. This is not the case!

Workers should first try to engender a stance of constant "behind the scenes" monitoring; we are constantly asking ourselves whether what we observe in our clients at any particular point in time suggests that they are mentalizing, or are not mentalizing. This skill can be practiced at any time (watching a movie, discreetly observing other people in conversation on buses and trains, etc.). In Chapter 2 we described some of the key features that would help workers decide whether what they see in their client is likely to indicate mentalizing or not. It is important to remember that mentalizing is an activity that all of our minds become engaged in doing for a period, but will then be replaced with some other (non-mentalizing, but contextually perhaps more useful) mental activity. These two states often switch quite rapidly back and forth, influenced by the rising and falling of emotional arousal, anxiety, and other passions.

Noticing that non-mentalizing is taking place is the first step. The second step is for the worker to reach the explicit decision in their mind that in order to return to a mentalizing frame of reference, something needs to be done (this is where the act of therapy can, in one sense, be seen as teleological!). After this, there is a fairly high degree of creative freedom for the worker—because the way to "kick-start" somebody's mentalizing when it has stalled will depend very much on individual circumstances and the context. So long as the primary intention is clear, the possible means to that end are more likely to emerge:

> "In order to help John (back) into a mode of thinking that is curious, not-knowing, exploratory, and imaginative about the minds involved, to (re-)engage his mentalizing [to be even more concrete, I could say "to activate his prefrontal cortex"], what could I do?"

Punctuating non-mentalizing might therefore be quite a gentle invitation to the client; can they momentarily step aside from the dialogue they are busily engaged in, to think about that dialogue and place it in context?

Client: "Of course my dad's always going to take my sister's side, isn't he, that's what he's always done. He hates me."

Worker: "You said that with real feeling, real passion; I can imagine that's a horrible place to be. Look, I don't want to interrupt you unhelpfully, but I do really want to ask you just now if you think I'm right in noticing the change in temperature since you started talking about your dad. Do you notice the way your mood changed over the last minute or so?"

Client: "Mmm, yeah. I get really mad when I think about him."

In this example the worker manages to shift the client's dialogue along from one about the father "hating" (the degree of certainty about the father's inner world, and why he behaved in the way he did, suggests this is psychic equivalence) to a more reflective dialogue about the client's own mood and how it changes in relation to thinking about these things. The client has—momentarily, at least—started to mentalize himself again (even if not yet his father). Potentially, this could lead on to a discussion about how, when he is in a calmer state of mind, he is able to think about or explain his father's behavior in other ways.

Another technique, frequently used to punctuate non-mentalizing and invite this kind of perspective-taking, is "Pause, reflect." This can be supported by an analogy with video recording:

Client: "I don't know why I bother talking to you at all! You don't know anything about me. I know you're only doing this for the money or something."

Worker: "Can I just press the pause button here? It feels like I've got us into something really unhelpful just now, and I absolutely get that you've every right to feel annoyed about that. Look, just say you had a remote control and we'd videoed this session; where would you need to wind it back to, to show me where I started to get lost and unhelpful?"

Client: "I dunno."

Worker: "You see, I thought that when we were talking about your money worries a few minutes ago, we seemed pretty much on the same page … I don't know if you see it that way at all, but that was how it felt to me. So I wonder if you scrolled forwards from there and pressed pause when we started talking about whether you could approach your dad for a loan … do you think that's where I started to get things a bit upside down?"

Client: "Probably—you just don't get it at all."

Worker: "That's helpful … what did you think was in my mind when I made that suggestion? It sounds like you kind of knew it was a daft suggestion, but what do you think was going on up here [taps head] that made me blurt it out?"

Client: "I dunno, I suppose you think my dad's rich, or kind—but he isn't."

Here, the worker takes responsibility for "getting into something unhelpful" and validates the client's anger and frustration, but also takes some control of the conversation by inviting a pause. By turning the conversation into a "video" the worker invites the client to think about it again, about the way it has gone (and why), rather than simply being in the conversation and being overwhelmed by it.

Other techniques to invite a pause, and kick-start mentalizing, include the invitation to consider how a third party might have understood and felt about a situation. Family/systemic therapists will recognize this as a form of circular questioning; the intent of the practitioner who does this in a situation where non-mentalizing has erupted is, as ever, to invite a change in the style of thinking, and to try to create a position to think from that is less "hot" with emotion:

Client: "My teacher's just a stupid cow."

Worker: "So if I've got it right, your teacher said these things at the meeting with you and your mum that you just found really really unhelpful. Look, this might sound stupid, but imagine we could just magically 'beam' your mother out of that moment, and put her somewhere where she was feeling really calm and safe—with a cup of tea, and a nice view, you know. Imagine then we asked her just to think very calmly for a while about why that teacher said those things; what do you think she'd be saying? . . . Say she was really trying to make sense of this in a way that you and I could understand?"

Yet another version of the same technique is to apply it to a pet—for instance, with a young man who owns a dog and is very attached to it. This technique may not be commonly used, but is offered here to emphasize the range of creative possibilities. The invitation is simultaneously playful and serious:

Client: "I just don't give a toss. Everyone would be glad if I was dead anyway—they all hate me; none of them want to know me."

Worker: "What you're describing sounds awful. Look, I want to try to understand more so we can think how to cope, and it feels as though I need help here. What I'm going to suggest might sound crazy, but I'm serious, so can you just go with me on this? I want you to imagine your dog—who you've often said is the only one you can really trust—imagine your dog could talk for a moment; you and I know that dogs can sometimes have a kind of 'sixth sense' about the people they love—so what do you think he'd say to explain to me about what's really going on for his owner right now?"

Client: "That is a mad question, but ... I guess he'd say I'm hurting. Maybe lonely. I dunno."

When emotion is running extremely high, and engaging in any kind of mentalizing dialogue is proving impossible, a more dramatic approach may be required. This is referred to as the "Therapist's use of self" or the "Stop! Stop!" technique. Here, there is a much clearer (and in one sense purposefully "teleological"—see Chapter 2) effort on the part of the worker to interrupt something (an argument between a parent and child, for instance, as in the example below) that is escalating and has proven unstoppable by other, gentler, interventions.

Here the worker tries to be open about the effect that this high emotion is having on their own ability to mentalize, inviting a change of tempo in order to support their mentalizing. Thus, it is not a "surrender" or admission of failure, but more a way of modeling how, even in these high-impact moments, it is at least possible to be aware of the impact of powerful emotions:

> "Stop! Stop! [Holds up hands] Please stop shouting! Look, I really want to be helpful here … I'm not telling anyone that you don't have the right to feel as furious or hurt as you seem to be … It's just that when the temperature and the volume are this high I find I can't think so clearly, or come up with useful ways to make sense of what I'm witnessing. That's how it is for me, and I think I'm less useful to you like that … I just wonder if that's the same for you, too?"
>
> "It's funny how just at the time we most need that front bit of our brains to be working hardest (you remember, the bit that I said only ever reaches a kind of whispering volume? [saying this in a "stage whisper" can often introduce a dramatic and playful shift in the tempo of the session]), it gets knocked out by the really loud bits that are full of passion and certainty … Can we start again but take it in turns—what if I act as a kind of referee here, and give each of you a couple of minutes to talk as calmly as you can to try to explain what's going on for you? What if the other one really tries to listen in order to understand, not in order to respond. Can we try that?"

Reinforcing positive mentalizing

If the intention of the worker is to help the client (or family as a whole) to build, regain, or sustain their capacity to mentalize, it is important to reinforce instances of positive mentalizing. Basic behavioral science and learning theory explain why this is so. Being noticed by someone else whose opinion seems to matter when you are performing in a certain way, and having the nature of what you are doing described and positively affirmed, makes learning and repetition of what you are doing more likely.

First, pointing out examples of when the client is mentalizing gives a good opportunity to describe and enrich understandings of what this state of mind is, and why it might matter:

> "Sorry to interrupt you again, but I just have to point out that I noticed you got really thoughtful and curious just then; did you notice that too?"
>
> "I have a hunch that you were thinking in quite a different way just then—probably using different parts of your brain to do it, even. Compared to just earlier, when you seemed pretty angry and very certain about why your teacher had said what she did, you seemed to be kind of busy puzzling her out, trying to put yourself in her shoes—that's what it looked like to me. Does that make sense to you?"
>
> "It's hard work, that, but I guess if you can come up with better understandings of what was going in her mind, then you're in with a better chance of patching things up in ways that are better for you—and for her. I think this is that 'whispering' part of your brain at work that I've mentioned before. We have a word for that particular kind

of thinking: 'mentalizing.' Other ways of thinking are useful at times, of course. For instance, deciding stuff really quickly, being very certain, and so on, are very helpful if your life's in danger because a tiger's standing in front of you; you don't want to spend too much time puzzling him out! But that slower, quieter kind of thinking that I think you were busy doing just then is probably the most useful thing we've got when we fall out with people, or just misunderstand them, or if we find ourselves doing things that don't make much sense."

Second, it emphasizes the fact that this is not a totally new skill that needs to be learned from scratch, but something that is already possible, and frequently used.

> "You see! You're at it again, aren't you?! From here it looks to me as though you've just got straight back into that quiet 'wondering-about-what's-in-minds' kind of thinking again: can you see that I'm not teaching you anything you don't already know? Perhaps I'm just pointing out how often you already use it without noticing!"

The difference is that in marking and defining mentalizing clearly, bringing it into explicit awareness, there is an intention of creating familiarity with what mentalizing feels like, and a sense that this is a valuable skill that can be aimed at—particularly when emotions are running high and the natural tendency may be to shut it down.

Finally, it is often crucial that even the briefest attempts at mentalizing do not get overlooked or taken for granted; if we miss this special kind of effort, it makes it all the less likely that it will be tried again. Many young people and family members whose backgrounds include hardship, neglect, or abuse find this kind of thinking particularly hard to do, or to sustain. Accordingly, the worker in this field needs to calibrate their expectations about what mentalizing might "look" like in these circumstances. They may need to be prepared to "give the benefit of the doubt" when, in the midst of an angry ten-minute non-mentalizing tirade, there is a brief lull, the client suddenly goes quiet, briefly looks down, shakes their head, and says, "I don't know what's going on," before picking up where they left off and raging again. That brief lull—the fleeting admission of being lost—might be the closest thing on offer to mentalizing during a whole session (here, it is the client mentalizing their self), and it is crucial it is not allowed to pass unnoticed.

> "Do you know, as you were talking over the last ten minutes I was sitting here and really wanting to try to understand and to find a useful way to sum up how angry and frustrated you're feeling. I wasn't doing a great job. But just now—when you suddenly went a bit quiet, looked so thoughtful, and said how you 'don't know what's going on' ... that felt to me like a very genuine, very thoughtful reflection of what it's really like to be you. It reminded me how just not knowing what's going on can feel really awful; you're quite right. Do you remember doing that just now?"
>
> "Anyway, I just wanted to say that, for me, the way you changed gear in your thinking just then, and what you came up with, that really helped make proper sense to me of

how hard it is for you at the moment. Can I ask, when you stopped and drew breath just then, do you think you did manage to capture something quite real about what it's like to be you, underneath all the anger you feel?"

"You may think I'm making too much of this, but you see I think the way you managed to change gear and slow your thinking down just then is really important. I don't know what you think, but I think it could be really helpful if we built on that skill you showed just then—of being able to slow down suddenly, and getting to look behind how furious and hurt you feel—to see other feelings that get lost at other times. I wonder if that makes any sense at all to you?"

Holding the balance

Mentalizing is in itself a balancing act that the prefrontal areas of the brain are specifically evolved to manage. To work effectively, a mentalizing worker holds a series of balances:

- Between the three therapeutic activities of *planning and working toward goals*, *broadcasting intentions*, and *sustaining sensitive attunement*, as described in Chapter 3;
- Between *achieving states of calm* (which requires efforts at soothing, which risk the worker operating exclusively as a support to the client, without any challenge—almost as a kind of "fan club"—and thus allowing the "pretend mode" (see Chapter 2) to take hold, as if there is nothing that needs mentalizing, or making sense of at all) and *offering challenge* (that risks creating or allowing states of such high arousal and anxiety that mentalizing is overwhelmed). Mentalizing work might be characterized as working harder than some other approaches to take responsibility for moderating the level of affect (emotion) in the room; mostly this is about reducing the level of arousal, but at times (if the client is firmly in pretend mode, so that there is an "elephant in the room" that is being ignored) the worker will have to act in ways that gently raise the affect (this is discussed in more detail below);
- Between *mentalizing the self*, and *mentalizing the other person* (or people) they are working with;
- Between *mentalizing the thoughts and beliefs* (cognitions) that might be influencing behaviors, and *mentalizing the feeling states* (affect) that influence these (and are influenced by them);
- Between *mentalizing the here and now* (what is happening here, in this one-to-one session with this particular client, for instance) and *mentalizing the wider context* of that client's life (whether what is happening between us here has any relevance, or echoes with the struggles that the client faces at home, or at school).

The principle of holding the balance is thus an invitation for workers to consider not just what is happening in the here and now, but also to consider what is *not* happening because of the present focus, and whether they need to plan to achieve some kind of counterbalancing as this, or the next, session plays out.

Holding the balance does not imply that nothing can ever be allowed to "play itself out," that any moment of (non-mentalizing) passion needs instantly to be squashed or balanced out—far from it; a helpful balance needs to be struck between allowing enough passion and heat to ensure that we are in contact with something real and authentic, but not so much that the affect (the emotion in the here and now) rises to the point where mentalizing becomes impossible. As stated above, mentalizing work involves a conscious effort to "moderate the affect," and most commonly the effort is to soothe levels of arousal. However, in situations where the client is engaged in pretend mode (words that may be coherent, even clever, but fail to address the reality in the here and now; see Chapter 2), balancing may require maneuvers that gently increase the temperature (finding ways to challenge the client with emotional realities that they may have sidestepped, glossed over, or denied). Raising the level of affect in such situations ("You say that alcohol's no problem in your life, but what about the driving ban, and the fact that your parents have thrown you out?") risks unbalancing in a different direction, tipping the client into psychic equivalence, an unhelpful certainty about what is in the worker's mind: "You're just like all the rest of them! You just want to pull me down, and rub my face in it! You're all so holier-than-thou!" A better tactic in these situations is sometimes to take responsibility for the "temperature rise" by offering your not-understanding, and inviting help:

> "Look, I'm hoping you can help me out a bit here, and that this won't just be annoying. I don't think I'm getting the story straight in my mind quite yet. I'm trying to put together the positive things you feel about drinking—the fun, the excitement, the feeling of release ... with some of the other things we've talked about that in my head seem like a very heavy price to pay. You see, in my head the price you're paying seems too high, but I'm not sure if I'm getting it right, because that's not what I'm hearing from you. Help me see it the way you see it, will you?"

Returning to the four "legs" of the mentalizing stance, holding the balance is therefore something more akin to the worker consciously trying to hold a "helicopter perspective" (technically, a *meta-perspective*) on the session and on the series of sessions as they unfold over time, and trying to balance things out across this expanse of hours. For instance, it may be that in recognizing that we spent most of the last session thinking about events outside the room, I plan a bit more focus on what is happening within the session (between the client and me) at our next session. Alternatively, if an argument breaks out in the first section of a family session, this might lead me to start inquiring about whether what the family members have shown me in the room is a good example of how things can go wrong back at home. Inviting a family to reflect in this way is, incidentally, a good way to punctuate non-mentalizing without it becoming an additional confrontation. If the relationship is sufficiently strong, some humor can be injected to defuse very high emotions and "ground" participants back in the room with our shared intentions to be helpful. So, for example, from a heated family argument in a session, a worker might offer the following:

> "It feels like you've given me a taste of some of the passion and intense feelings you all have about what's going on in this family; but if you don't mind, I just want to check whether you think what you've shown me is anything like what I'd see if I was a fly on the wall at your home? If it is, then this seems really important for me to 'get.' But if this sort of thing only happens here, and you're serious about wanting these painful arguments to stop, then the treatment is simple: keep well away from me! What do you think? Is what you were able to show me here just now anything like how trouble breaks out at home?"

It is tempting in our work to concentrate all our effort on mentalizing our clients, but in doing so we may lose balance in mentalizing ourselves as workers. Noting the impact that high levels of anxiety, anger, or despair in the room have on one's own capacity to mentalize is critical for two reasons. First, it avoids the pitfall of falling into a non-mentalizing state of mind about one's client—becoming increasingly certain that my theories about their intentions and attributes are simply the way it is (i.e. psychic equivalence), rather than what they really are—just my current hypotheses. Second, it models mentalizing for the client—as an activity that is generally satisfying to be on the receiving end of, and which also evokes trust in the mentalizer from those who are being mentalized.

The Mentalizing Loop

We have covered the mentalizing stance and (in Chapter 3) the necessity of checking in with sensitive attunement to the client's mental states in the here and now. Both of these aspects of face-to-face work are "ways-of-being-with," but there is also some comfort and containment in having degrees of structure to a session. The structure promoted in mentalizing therapies is referred to as the "Mentalizing Loop" (see Figure 4.1). Again, this is not presented as a checklist to be followed in strict sequential order, but more as a map of the different territories or tasks that a worker may be engaged in at any time during a session. In that sense, the emphasis is on moving from implicit to explicit practice—being able to hold an awareness of "where I am and what I am doing" at any time

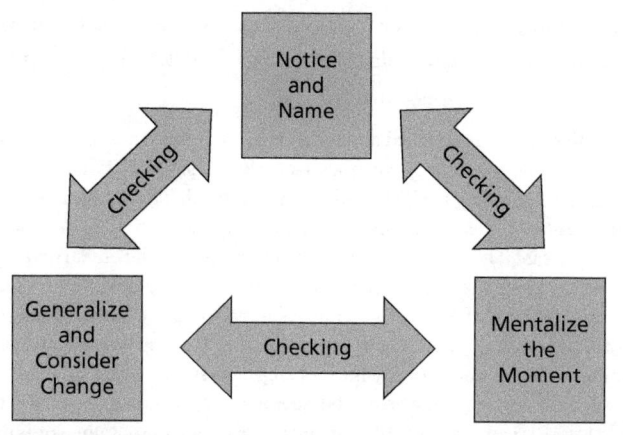

Figure 4.1 The Mentalizing Loop: structure inside a session.

in a session. Understanding these different steps or "regions" in a session gives a sense of the forward momentum that a worker is trying to achieve in:

- Mapping the most common "pitfalls" where mentalizing is lost
- Making sense of these misunderstandings, misattributions, and failures in mentalizing
- Practicing the recovery of mentalizing in such situations
- Creating new arrangements that might reduce repetition when the identified pitfall recurs.

In particular, the worker does this through engaging with specific experiences that have real salience for a particular client (or family).

The Loop covers the following areas of activity:

- Checking
- Noticing and Naming
- Mentalizing the Moment
- Generalizing and Considering Change.

Checking

The common thread that runs between all three areas of activity in the Loop is *checking*. This is really the inquisitive, not-knowing, tentative element of the mentalizing stance in action. The worker never assumes that they know where the right place to be is, or that an idea or suggestion is exactly how the client sees it. Instead, the worker demonstrates a genuine enthusiasm to find out, to correct errors, to build a picture in their own mind that, step by step, becomes less inaccurate and more closely attuned and responsive to the way the client experiences it, and to orient their collaboration toward addressing the reality of the client's life.

> "I noticed that, after I mentioned about preparing for your Court case, you seemed to start talking about other things, and then you went rather quiet. It made me think that I'd brought up something that you really didn't feel much like talking about just now—and I just wanted to check whether I was right about that."
>
> "When you said it felt as though I was deliberately provoking or patronizing you just then by asking about the Court case, I wanted first of all to apologize, as that must have felt horrible. It wasn't at all what I had in my mind to do—actually, I think I was just feeling a bit ignorant about the Court case, something that you've explained is a big deal in your life. So I hope you'll forgive me for being clumsy ...It would be helpful to check whether I'm the only person who can blunder in like that and make you feel provoked or patronized—if I am, then the solution might be for me to shut up!—or is this something that can happen at other times in your life, with other people, too?"

Noticing and Naming

In this section of a session, the worker is primarily attentive and responding to what comes up, but is also "scanning the airwaves" for evidence of whether there is active mentalizing going on, or whether some other non-mentalizing forms of thought have taken precedence. The worker may well have a pre-existing plan to explore a specific area, and we have previously (in Chapter 3) discussed the "dance" that requires holding a balance between having a plan and its associated objectives, broadcasting one's own intentions, and retaining sensitive attunement to what is in the client's mind. Critically, in Noticing and Naming the worker is looking for in-the-moment instances of a collapse into non-mentalizing, although occasionally the client may bring an example from the past that is still present in their mind (a recent argument, for example).

Clues that mentalizing has been overwhelmed would include high levels of certainty about the minds of other people (psychic equivalence) or a large volume of words that, however coherent and "reasonable" they may sound, fail to address the immediate emotional context in which they are spoken (pretend mode). Teleological modes of non-mentalizing are easier to spot—as action-based language ("I'm gonna hit him if he does that again!"), or actual physical acting out, that sees the solution of any form of unease in some measurable physical outcome.

Where it is noticed that mentalizing is being overwhelmed by more primitive forms of thinking, then (in accordance with the mentalizing stance described at the start of this chapter) the worker should try to punctuate or stop the non-mentalizing and reintroduce reflection and thoughtfulness about what is happening, and why. At this point, the session will have shifted to the next step, which is "Mentalizing the Moment"—of which more below. Ultimately, what the worker is trying to do is to help identify and name a small number of the most typical ways in which this particular client (this could apply to a young person, or a whole family) tends to lose the ability to mentalize the people around them, or themselves. As one of these "pitfalls" becomes clearer, it is helpful to find ways to label or name it—an analogy would be the placing of marker buoys in the sea around an area of treacherous rocks, to warn shipping of a known risk, and perhaps to mark these on a map for future reference by navigators in the same waters. The most effective "names" are those that spontaneously arise in the client's discussion rather than those imposed by the worker. It would be rare for a name to arise the first time around the Loop, but in general the worker's aim is to identify the few (perhaps two or three) most salient ways that this particular client is liable to lose their mentalizing capacity, to help them recognize such moments, and then to develop the skill of holding on to or recovering their mentalizing at such times. In the example below, a name begins to emerge from the discussion about what has been noticed:

Worker: "So these kinds of moments seem to happen particularly when you're talking to an adult who sees themselves as having some kind of responsibility for you, having some kind of authority. Is that how you see it?"

Client: "Yeah, I guess so—I just hate it when people talk to me like I'm stupid."

Worker: "So it could be your parents, or a teacher, or very easily me! It seems to me—and I may have this wrong ... tell me!—that it's when they start to talk to you about organizing stuff, making suggestions, you know, that this is when you can start feeling like you just said—as though they think you are just stupid. Is that right?"

Client: "Yeah. I know they probably mean well and all, but they always seem to switch into a kind of creepy patronizing way of talking, like they're gonna win whether I like it or not, and I feel like ... like I've got to be some kind of freedom fighter. I know that sounds stupid, but it's like it feels like it's them or me at that point—it drives me mad; I have to fight back, and I just say 'No.'"

Worker: "I really like that phrase you used—it's quite a neat way of marking these kinds of 'freedom fighter' moments. I'm not sure I've understood them completely yet, but I just want to check that you think we're talking about moments that seem *important* to you—and does your phrase 'freedom fighter moment' make any sense as a way of describing them—so we know what we're talking about?"

Client: "Yeah—I like that. It doesn't make me sound like I've just lost it—there's a reason why I lose it at times like that."

Of course, it may require a number of times around the Loop before the similarities in circumstances that trigger a loss of mentalizing start to become clear, and before a name for such a scenario comes to light. It is easy to describe this work as though it all falls into place first time around, and that would be an error on our part.

Mentalizing the Moment

To reach any understanding of how specific situations or relationships tend to overwhelm a client's mentalizing capacity, and what (including what form of non-mentalizing) tends to happen then, the work of mentalizing is required.

If the worker can show an ability (perhaps just an authentic willingness to try, and in so doing, get some of the way there) to make sense of the client's mind at these critical "breakpoints," this is likely to reduce agitation, build the client's trust in communication (see Chapter 2), and in itself help rekindle the client's own mentalizing capacity. In this phase of a session the worker's efforts are directed (using the mentalizing stance) first at punctuating or terminating non-mentalizing, and then at trying to find ways to adjust the emotional intensity in the session to allow mentalizing to return. Once mentalizing is back "online," the worker can collaborate with the client, sharing that curious, not-knowing, exploratory, inquisitive state of mind in which imagination is applied, in order to develop a more coherent narrative that might explain the momentary loss of mentalizing that is under examination.

How to do this is open to almost any amount of creativity on the part of the worker—sensitive attunement might guide one into straightforward dialogue in one case, while another instance might be better helped through the use of some form of creative art. (Talking about a drawing, and how it might make sense that some object or person has been portrayed, and in some particular way, is nothing if not mentalizing; externalizing the emotional "charge" in a piece of artwork might help to create sufficient emotional distance to allow mentalizing to begin again, where direct face-to-face discussion about the same subject would have been too arousing.) The use of the video analogy (or, indeed, watching and repeatedly freeze-framing some real video shot in-session) is a helpful technique.

Worker: "OK, just then, when we had that 'freedom fighter moment' between us ... can we just imagine that we caught that on a DVD, and we had the remote control here? Where should we rewind back to in this session where you could say 'Everything was fine until you said that?'"

Client: "Um ... I reckon it was when you gave me that look after I told you about the weed I was smoking with Kevin. I just didn't want to talk about Court,

I wanted to talk about something fun. And I could tell you were all 'Oh dear, oh dear, now I've got to tell him how dangerous weed is, and then we need to talk about the Court case' before you even started going on about it."

Worker: "I like the way you're straight in there! . . . thinking about what happened, and the thoughts that were going through your head about the thoughts that might be going through *my* head [*positively reinforcing some mentalizing by the client*]—but if we could freeze-frame our heads just at that moment, can we just think a bit more about what was happening? I think you're right that a lot was happening very quickly. If we were looking at you on that DVD for a moment, just then, what do we think it felt like to be you just as you thought you recognized that expression on my face?"

Client: "Dunno ... I was just having a bit of a laugh. Then I was thinking, 'Here we go again,' and then I just felt pissed off, like I had to bloody argue it all out again, and that's so boring."

Worker: "And looking at the film of me back then ... I'm trying to remember what I might have been feeling—what do you reckon about that?"

Client: "You were probably going, 'Oh god, here we go again, too!"

Worker: "Go on, this is good work ... You're good at this! I do think I remember feeling a bit like there were things I'd rather be talking about than cannabis. But you said you saw something in my face—like 'I knew I had to give you a talk about cannabis' ... can you say some more about that?"

In this way, through mentalizing, the worker painstakingly peels "onion layers" away from a moment in time that the client has identified as significant, and which had led directly to some kind of rupture—not just in their own mentalizing, but in the relationship itself. Crucially, this is done with exquisite respect for the fact that behaviors stem from experiences in people's minds—some of which may be hidden not only from the worker but from the client themself as they enact the behavior—so that coming to understand these experiences allows a misunderstanding to be better understood, without there having to be "winners" or "losers."

Later in this chapter we describe a selection of more explicit "games" that have been found useful for similar reasons. By creating a playful (remember the connection between play, imagination, learning, and mentalizing) set of "rules," emotion that might otherwise be overwhelming may be sufficiently contained to allow the work of mentalizing to take place. The online AMBIT manual (https://manuals.annafreud.org—follow the links to AMBIT) contains a selection of videos showing workers role-playing these games as prompts for possible adaptations in real clinical work.

The aim in mentalizing any moment is twofold. First, it gives first-hand experience of what it is to mentalize—that very particular activity of the mind that very often deserts us when we most need it. What the worker wants is opportunities to mark and positively connote this action as it happens—distinguishing it from other forms of (non-mentalizing) thinking, which, as we know, may have their place, but are often uninvited guests. Second, and ultimately, the aim is to arrive at that point where the client (and perhaps the worker, too) experiences their actions, and the actions of others, as being understood, or understandable, rather than feeling blamed, shamed, or otherwise overwhelmed.

Generalizing and Considering Change

When a particular instance of a break in mentalizing has been noticed, marked as relevant, and then worked through so that the circumstances are better understood, it may also be possible to place such an episode in a wider context—to see that it represents just one iteration of a repeated pattern of similar misunderstandings and poorly adapted reactions. This is the first stage of generalization—seeing that the material covered here has relevance outside the therapeutic session, and that learning in this session might also be transportable and applicable to the wider world.

In generalizing, the worker invites the client to identify other instances in their life where the same dynamic might be at work: where the client finds themselves positioned in the same particular way, loses their capacity to mentalize because of the emotions that rear up in such situations, and then behaves in ways that are poorly adapted to the task of moving toward longer-term intentions ("to get into fewer fights," "to feel calmer," "to have a steady relationship," etc.). If the idea of finding ways to avoid or repair these breaks in mentalizing gains sufficient traction (if it seems valuable enough to the client), then the door may be open to move into a more problem-solving phase of the session.

Here, the worker may invite the client to brainstorm different alternative outcomes and new approaches that might direct things in more positive ways. Role-playing these approaches in low-key, spontaneous, and playful ways might help in building the client's confidence to try them out after the session has finished. Producing simple written aims or diagrammatic formulations (see Chapter 3) offers something to take home that may provide a prompt. Remembering our previous descriptions of trust in communication (*epistemic trust*), the extent to which the client feels understood by the worker will strongly influence the extent to which the client develops trust in the value and applicability of the ideas developed in the session to their life overall. Above all, in considering change, it is helpful to bear in mind what many years of research in other fields of therapy have shown: it is much better to agree on small, practical, achievable steps that can subsequently be built upon ("I will try to notice myself getting angry and excuse myself and leave the room *twice* in the next week—and I'll try to write down or remember those two occasions") than to set unattainable, idealized targets such as "I will have fewer arguments."

Mentalizing in different contexts: Places, games, and techniques

There are a wide range of games and techniques that can be drawn upon to provide a calmer context that might facilitate Mentalizing the Moment. In fact, because mentalization-based approaches privilege the bolstering of the practice and skill of mentalizing under pressure, there is a huge freedom in what practical techniques can be deployed to support this overarching aim.

Not a prescription

For some clients, the idea of any kind of game-playing would be unhelpful; they might feel patronized or trivialized, and for them face-to-face talk would be more appropriate, perhaps with pens and paper available to draw out a record of the thinking and formulating that takes place (see the Active Planning Map/ "Egg and Triangle" tool in Chapter 3 for a simple example). For others, face-to-face discussion would be too intense, too intimate, or too intimidating, and the provision of structured activity, sometimes with intentionally playful "gamification," may be more supportive of mentalizing.

Examples

Location It is not necessarily a given that conducting a session in a clinic or consulting room will promote the best atmosphere for calm reflection. For many clients, a room (that for the worker may come to feel like a "home from home") with book-lined shelves, tidy institutional artwork on the walls, two upright chairs, and a sign somewhere outside that reads "Mental Health Clinic" is about as far from their idea of normal as imaginable. Thus, in some situations, meeting a client in a café, or going for a walk in the park together, may create conditions much more conducive to mentalizing. (Note: we address the vulnerability for the worker in these situations in Chapter 5. It is *not* helpful for the worker to create conditions that, in pursuit of satisfying their client's need for the reassurance of the ordinary, are so isolating or distracting for the worker that their own mentalizing is threatened! The "well-connected team" is used to protect against this.)

Creative arts There is a long tradition of using the creative arts in therapy, and some evidence of effectiveness (Uttley et al., 2015). Allowing or encouraging a client to doodle, or to create some piece of artwork to represent their experience of some interaction, or to offer a piece of music from their phone or MP3 player that they feel best expresses what it's like to be them, may avoid the persecuting sensation of intense scrutiny that face-to-face conversation may evoke. In the discussion that might follow about that work, the distancing (talking about *the work* that is about the client, rather than talking *about* the client) may allow for more mentalizing to occur.

> "I like the way you have made those really strong scribbles there. OK, now this is me being a not very good art critic … You see, in my mind they seem to be about how *strongly* you feel about this stuff, and how those incredibly strong feelings can almost cover up all the detail that is underneath. I don't know if that makes any sense to you though—what do you think about why you needed to make those powerful marks?"

Playful modeling of mentalizing Having a particular object or toy available that can offer a physical "metaphor" for the process of mentalizing can be very helpful. The following example, involving a doctor's stethoscope, is taken with gratitude from Dr Eia Asen's practice, and is commonly taught in the training for mentalization-based treatment for families.

Few people, given the chance, will turn down the opportunity to play with a stethoscope—the opportunity to listen to one's own heartbeat or breathing is almost too tempting to resist. Introducing a stethoscope in a session (maybe just leaving it out in plain view on a desk) and allowing a client to listen to their heart can be a powerful way of modeling the kind of quietening that is required to mentalize oneself, and the grounding in reality that comes with this. This can be built on by inviting the client to imagine what they might hear if that stethoscope could hear not just their heart beating, but their heart talking to them about "how it feels" at a particular moment in time. They might also imagine what they might hear if they placed it on some other protagonist's heart:

> "Just imagine you had this rather magical stethoscope and we had freeze-framed your father, just at the point when you'd told him about your arrest the other day. If you could hear his heart telling you how he felt at that moment, what do you think it would be saying? Now, say this stethoscope was even cleverer, and you could put it to the side of your father's head and hear the kinds of thoughts that were going through his head just then—what do you think we might hear?"

A stethoscope can be an effective ice-breaker in work with families—particularly with younger children, who may enjoy actually placing the stethoscope on other family members and telling people what they "hear" in response to these kinds of mentalizing questions about a specific moment. Using this playful technique allows for physical proximity and touch between participants, and through its playfulness may allow emotions to settle sufficiently for serious reflections to be articulated. For older adolescents this might be less appropriate, but talking about it in abstract, "as if" terms can still be effective.

There are many more games and techniques, several of which are described, and for which there are video role-plays, in the AMBIT manual. These give a taste of the range of possibilities available if the compass bearing is set toward the core intention of stimulating or helping to sustain mentalizing, particularly during interactions where this is most likely to fail.

Balance and unbalance: Scaffolding existing relationships versus managing risk

It is no help to a client if we create a powerful, contingently responsive, and trusting relationship with them, only for this to be broken off some months later at treatment end without any sustaining changes in the rest of their life being in place. Identifying and strengthening resiliencies in a client's existing relationships mean that work is not simply negatively focused on problems, but also scaffolds and strengthens existing relationships that might contribute to the sustainability of changes in the client's life, addressing the realities of their wider situation. By "existing relationships" we refer not only to family, carers, and friends, but also to other professionals who may have longer-term commitments with the client (social workers, youth workers, general medical practitioners, etc.). Even more important, of course, is the relationship that a client has with themself.

The tension that this stance immediately awakens is that for many of the young people we target with this help, their existing relationships may be far from ideal and there are real risks. A client may tend to hold their self in contempt, expressing this through self-injurious behaviors, fighting, or vulnerability to exploitation. Family members may have limited resources for expressing care and interest in their child or sibling on account of their own problems with addiction, mental health, poverty, or criminality. Friends and acquaintances may offer support and safety, but only in relation to shared gang membership, while at the same time providing invitations and access to drugs, alcohol, offending, and other high-risk activities.

Returning to the case of Dan, described in Chapter 1, we can see the potential effect of unbalancing this emphasis on engaging and working with the realities of his social milieu in this example:

> Dan has begun to make a connection with his AMBIT keyworker, Steve, after first hearing positive things about him from one of the only school staff members that he got

on with—his teaching support worker in the workshops. Although Dan had initially refused to meet with Steve, the teaching support worker had told Dan about his own meetings with Steve, who had dropped into the school several times anyway; he told Dan about Steve's efforts to hear in some detail about the many times that Dan had showed real promise in the workshops. After Dan heard about Steve's efforts to persuade the school to make some allowances for his behavior, and to keep his temporary exclusion as short as possible, he had agreed to meet him, and found that this man—rather like his teaching support worker—seemed to like him, and seemed genuinely interested in getting to understand him (all the while joking that he was "a total beginner when it comes to Dan!").

They had tended to meet at school at first, but Steve had begun to think out loud about Dan's friendship group outside the school, and now they were talking quite openly about this. Dan liked the fact that Steve was not judgmental about his friends, particularly the older group of men whom he had enjoyed hanging around with recently. Steve seemed genuinely interested to understand how important this group had become for Dan, rather than just telling him they were dangerous and to stop seeing them. Dan found himself explaining things in ways that surprised him, such as how being around these men meant that he didn't feel worried about getting attacked by some of the other youths in the neighborhood who had a grudge against him.

Meanwhile, Steve found himself in a dilemma. He felt pleased that he had managed to engage Dan and had identified some resiliencies in this tough youngster who cared (worried) about his family and who was quite handy in the workshop. He felt the time was coming when he could start to do some work with Dan at home, to look at how to scaffold those existing relationships (that seemed fragile at best, though he had little first-hand information to go on at this point). Nevertheless, he was increasingly worried that his stance toward the older gang members (who Dan seemed to admire and want to join even more closely) might be seen as accepting or even condoning the criminality and exploitation that he felt sure was a part of the picture. He was aware of the fact that these men were constantly available to Dan, in ways that he himself was not, and that they offered (at least in the immediate present) a sort of physical security that he could not; however, further enmeshment in this local gang seemed to present the greatest risk to Dan.

A critical tension in working with clients and the reality of their relationships is finding the right balance between engagement and repair work on the one hand—that is, following the AMBIT stance principle of "Scaffolding existing relationships"—and managing real risks on the other (see Figure 4.2). The latter may at times require action rather than deliberation and further efforts to understand the client's perspective. It would be easy to go several steps too far in the work of engaging Dan and building his self-esteem by emphasizing the fact that his wish to join with this gang is not entirely foolish (scaffolding Dan's relationship with his own self, as it were) without inviting a more critical stance toward these men, or "whistle-blowing" on what might be outright and dangerous exploitation. Conversely, to move into action (attempting to separate Dan from these men) too quickly risks breaking a new therapeutic relationship that

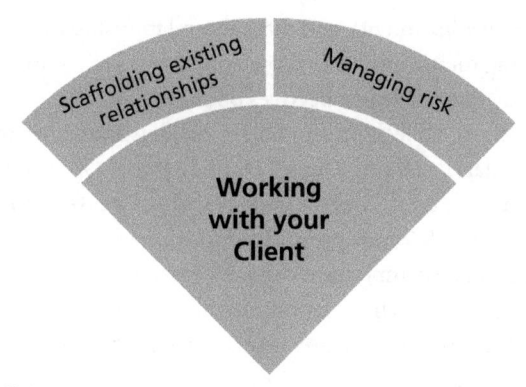

Figure 4.2 Scaffolding existing relationships versus managing risk.

might offer the first chance to create real change in Dan's predicament and, assuming there is no relational or legislative framework immediately available to enforce his abstinence from the gang, might paradoxically push Dan further into its grasp.

These kinds of situations are incredibly common in AMBIT work; indeed, it is very rare in such situations for a worker to feel anything other than somewhat out of balance—although hopefully without this resulting in them actually "falling." Much like a tightrope walker who is never in fixed equilibrium but makes constant, small, rebalancing adjustments to their center of gravity, what is required is great sensitivity to when balance is being lost and the direction required for corrective action. The tension between the principles of scaffolding existing relationships and managing risk offers a language for marking out some of these unbalanced sensations, so that attention can be brought to thinking about the details. What is the available evidence that Dan is in imminent risk of significant harm from these men? What are the risks of Steve signaling these concerns to colleagues in social services, and what are Steve's professional obligations in this regard? Is there merit in exploring further what Dan meant by the statement that he feels safe around these men, and is the creation of safety perhaps a good start for a treatment aim? Was Dan's reflection about his sense of safety (or lack of safety) a good example of him starting to mentalize himself, which should be acknowledged in some way and built upon?

Mountaineers traversing a precipitous knife-edge ridge will generally hold in mind the fact that, at any stage, one side is the "more lethal" so that, if they had to fall, it would be better done on the opposite side to that one—and so they adjust their route accordingly, walking just a few steps nearer to the "less lethal" side. AMBIT's approach to the worker's stance is that they should be constantly alert to these small adjustments, and that their relationship to their team-mates (who are "holding their rope") will allow both parties to communicate important information about their perspectives on these risks.

Overall, as Professor Eileen Munro (2011) emphasized in her review of child protection in England, echoing Turnell and Edwards' (1997) approach to safeguarding known as Signs of Safety, it is likely that poor case-management decisions will arise if we seek (or are pressurized to "guarantee") too much certainty. In our view, this can be compounded by worker isolation and quite predictable anxiety. Such conditions do not support mentalizing, and the AMBIT approach is to recognize these risks and create a team approach that aims to mitigate them (as discussed in Chapter 5).

Adapting the basic mentalizing stance to AMBIT work

In this section of the chapter we offer a range of suggestions about how to adapt a mentalizing approach to the challenging conditions of working with highly troubled young people and other clients. The perceptive reader will notice that some of these adaptations may appear to be contradictory and that we are asking workers to do several things at once—for example, to create trust and to emphasize that our role is only temporary; to be helpful but, in fostering self-efficacy, not too helpful! We do not apologize for this as, for us, it resonates with what we do, and we do not pretend to have reconciled these apparent contradictions. Our aim is to create a description of the work, and what makes it hard, that workers recognize; this directly parallels how we see our task with clients as starting with the articulation of their specific dilemmas in ways that they can recognize as authentic.

Not offering to listen when I need a place to sleep: The welcome, and contingent care

In Chapter 3 we described under the heading of "Active Planning" the critical balance required between planning and maintaining engagement. The best plans are worth nothing if the client does not have the trust required to follow them. In keeping with our understanding of human communication and how trust develops, the earliest phase of contact with the client or family member should offer an experience of contingency—that is, a fit between their experience of an immediate predicament and what is on offer. Sensitive attunement to what is to the fore of the client's mind, also described in Chapter 3, is what enables this to happen. This may present a challenge to a worker who feels that they have trained to do specialist work but finds themself taking a client around the corner to buy a sandwich, giving them a lift to the gym, helping them look through a benefits claim form, or negotiating some leniency from a teacher wanting overdue homework handed in. The research described in Chapter 2 supports common sense in suggesting that it is via these rather menial acts that the conditions are created for an experience of being understood to arise; when the client feels understood in their individual predicament by the worker, the client's trust in the social value of the worker's communications and knowledge grows. The walk to the sandwich shop, or the car journey, may also provide a context in which more intimate relationship-building and information-sharing becomes possible. What the therapist might assume to be a comforting security and confidentiality in their well-boundaried consulting room may, for many young clients, in fact be experienced as claustrophobic and dangerously isolated. Car journeys give a paradoxical assurance to a young person that they will be spared the experience of a powerful adult's penetrating gaze—giving them the opportunity to look, without being looked at too closely in return.

A focus on trajectories

There are plenty of pithy sayings that get wheeled out to ram home the point that everything is always on the move: "change is the only certainty," "the journey is the destination," or "in my beginning is my end" (T. S. Eliot). Nowhere is this more apparent than in adolescence—this blurry, loosely defined, transitional stage straddling childhood and adulthood—but younger children, too, are careering into adolescence, and young adults are careering out of adolescence (some more slowly and falteringly than others).

The notion of various developmental trajectories is an important frame of reference in thinking about introducing helpful change into our clients' lives. Trajectories are curves if you draw them on paper—for instance, the curve that an airplane describes as it takes off, accelerating and climbing at just the right rate so as to clear the buildings or trees that lie just beyond the end of the runway. The airplane at take-off is not a bad analogy for adolescence—the young person is loaded with fuel (albeit these are sex hormones and adrenaline, rather than jet fuel), with his/her engines on full power, and is trying to make the subtle adjustments required to avoid climbing too steeply (risking a stall) while yet achieving sufficient lift to clear real obstacles that lie ahead—things such as the need to master basic literacy, numeracy, emotional self-regulation and resilience, and communication skills. If these basic competencies are not achieved by the end of the teenage years, there is a significant chance that a trajectory of lifelong disadvantage will follow. Still more worrying, at the same time, is the fact that the familiar supports on which younger children can rely (family, statutory educational, and social care services) are steadily falling away from the adolescent (certainly in developed westernized communities); expectations of independence and of financial and emotional self-reliance increasingly come into play, shaped as they are by culture, politics, and economic necessity.

The time-critical nature of so much of adolescent development means that there is less time to spare in marshaling the right help and making changes than there is for an adult who has already achieved the basic skills and capacities. It is important to remember that the child or adolescent who is standing still in developmental terms is going backwards relative to his/her peers, who are all forging ahead.

Adolescent turbulence tends to settle down as prefrontal brain structures reach maturity. If all goes well, a narrative of failure and rebellion in the education system may be replaced by one of success in entrepreneurial business activity, artistic creativity, becoming a parent, and so on. The comings and goings of key friendships or teachers in a young person's life will each have their own trajectories, too—sometimes operating over even shorter timescales—and so, of course, will the course of any helping intervention. Earlier, and in Chapter 3, we discussed the fact that the temporary trajectory of any helping intervention may be used as a tool to help engagement and stimulate a focus on defining achievable outcomes, as much as it may trigger avoidance ("There's no point in getting to know you, you'll be gone soon") or anxiety ("How do you expect me to cope when you walk away?").

Why do we place such an emphasis on trajectories? Quite apart from the fact that to ignore all of this flux would be to miss the nature of the beast (an example of "pretend mode" thinking), we return to the nature of mentalizing itself. One of the hallmarks of active mentalizing is that it confers the capacity to step aside from thinking and behaving, and to think *about* these activities *in their contexts*—to create more or less coherent narratives about "how you (or I) came to be in this situation, behaving in these ways, here, now." This narrative-making is close to the heart of what mentalizing is about: describing a past trajectory and possible future ones that help one to predict behaviors and suggest adaptive responses to make life more livable.

In my beginning is my end: Avoiding traps like the "adhesive worker" and the "honeytrap"

This emphasis on the trajectory of the helping relationship makes space for interventions that may help in engagement. In Chapter 3 we referred to the importance of early broadcasting about the temporary nature of the relationship that is on offer, in relation to the process of engagement, as well as for the exploration of shared intentions in developing plans.

> "I am thinking and hoping that if we can work together over the next few months then—when you wave me goodbye—you might think to yourself, 'S/he was OK, s/he actually helped me with problems X and Y ... I feel like I am more in control of my life than I was when we first met.' What I don't want you to worry about is questions like 'Will this person ever leave me alone?'!"

This confronts the risk that a client may fear that inviting this worker into their life will result in them never leaving (the "adhesive worker trap"), or indeed a fear that this worker is trying in some way to seduce and exploit them rather than to help them (the worker as "honeytrap"). These are just particular instances that illustrate the importance of the worker broadcasting their intentions clearly and simply, offering a strong sense of trajectory.

Learning about help: The client's relationship to help

As we have frequently emphasized, many of the young people approached by AMBIT-influenced teams do not have a positive relationship to "help." Their past histories may well have set up expectations about what follows offers of "help" from powerful authority figures (parents, teachers, therapists, social workers); far from bringing relief, in the past such offers may have resulted in abuse, humiliation, manipulation, or hurt. These kinds of expectations are what, in attachment theory, are described as *internal working models*—maps of how certain kinds of relationships tend to work. One of the underlying suggestions in AMBIT is that alterations, shifts, and corrections made to these models of the "relationship to help" can be achieved during the course of the work—that an improved relationship to help (with somewhat more secure expectations for helping relationships in the future) is likely to make sense as a desired outcome from therapy. This, like most of AMBIT, is not a new idea—indeed, the father of attachment theory, John Bowlby, was saying the same thing about therapy over a quarter of a century ago (Bowlby, 1988). In their efforts to form trust and relatedness, the AMBIT-influenced worker strives to reignite the fading embers of a *secure* internal working model of helping relationships—one that, in many cases, is likely to have been painfully frail from the start (perhaps built on some early, fleeting positive experiences with a grandparent, or a nursery school teacher) and which repeated knocks and exclusions have now all but extinguished in favor of a map that instead predicts viciousness, manipulation, or cold disregard.

Coupled to their own discouraging internal working models of helping relationships, many young people have families who powerfully reinforce their avoidance or outright rejection of care. Parents may encourage their child to disengage rather than supporting them to attend—especially if their own experience of "help" was of being forcibly removed from their own parents only to be placed in abusive institutional care, or if they fear that their own current misdeeds will be exposed and punished if the authorities start to "poke their noses" into the family's business, or if there is a "strong family" story that proudly rejects dependency on others.

So, while as a keyworker I might innocently think that I have been clear, polite, respectful, and helpful toward a client, their robust rejection of my offers of help may be quite conscious and purposeful, making perfectly good sense in *their* mind. As a worker, forgetting that I am a beginner in the work of understanding *this particular client* is a recipe for misunderstandings, misconceptions, and mistakes:

- I may approach with an intention in my mind to reach out actively to a client with compassion, warmth, and commitment. The client might see a dangerous seducer, somebody insulting them by telling them they can't cope, or intruding, and react with denial or withdrawal.
- I may approach with an intention to present authentically and truthfully the capacity that I see in them, so as not to "pathologize" them by assuming they need treatment, instead encouraging them to use existing mainstream and family resources to cope. The client might see someone who is uncaring and rejecting toward them, and react with anger or by clinging.
- I may reach out with an intention to acknowledge the limitations of what I am able to offer right now, all the while holding a hope that, with what is still possible, we might see things improve in the future. The client might see someone who is helpless and defeated, and react with despair.
- I may approach with the intention of offering straight talking that does not shy away from naming the nature of the problems I see. The client might see someone bent on deliberately stigmatizing or shaming them, and react with fear or shame.

This is represented diagrammatically in Figure 4.3.

Another way to make sense of this is with an alternative version of the AMBIT wheel, written not to make sense of the worker's role and behaviors, but to support the client's effort to make sense of (and make use of) their worker's role (see Figure 4.4). This alternative wheel is a new development in the AMBIT model, and although it has received positive feedback from AMBIT practitioners, its deployment in the field has not yet been tested. In that sense, the brief section that follows is an example of how the AMBIT model continues to grow and develop over time, rather than a report on existing or evidence-based practice.

ADAPTING THE BASIC MENTALIZING STANCE | 151

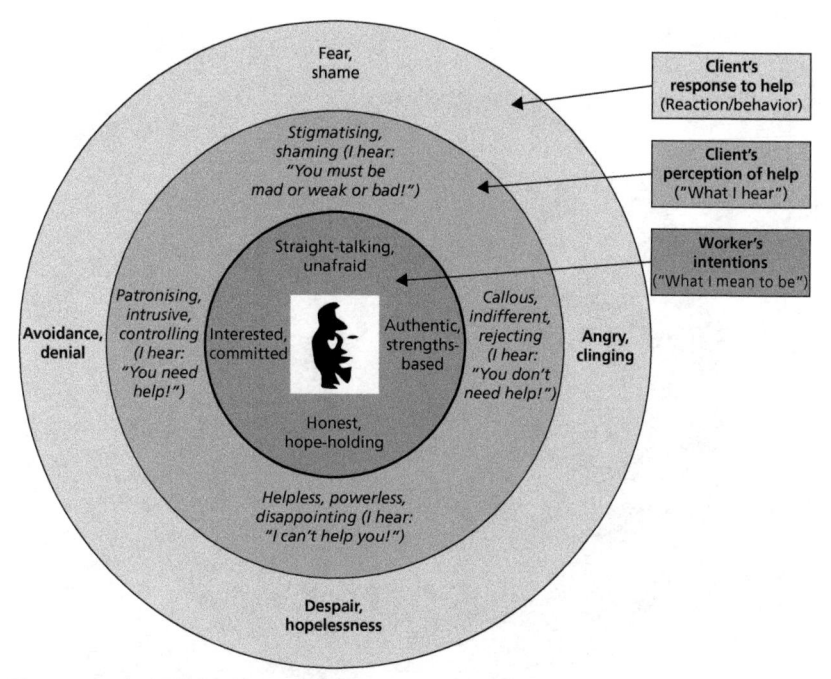

Figure 4.3 The different faces of help.

The client's wheel: Parallel processes

The client's version of the AMBIT wheel simply emphasizes the parallel processes that the worker and client must be engaged in if help is to become helpful and sustainable.

The client first needs to engage in a helping relationship (the "Working with Help" quadrant, on the left of the wheel, which parallels "Working with your Team" for the worker), so where the worker's stance is directed at the formation of an *individual keyworker relationship* with the client, in reciprocation, the client's first task is to develop *trust* in the worker and in the helping relationship. The worker counteracts the risks associated with forming such intense keyworking relationships by placing equal emphasis on remaining *well connected to their team*, who help the worker to keep their balance in this work (discussed in Chapter 5). In turn, as the client witnesses the helping relationships modeled by their keyworker, they may develop *understanding* of the nature of the help on offer (that their worker is not an omnipotent "lone ranger," that there are responsible layers of supervision, and that receiving help is less a sign of weakness or failure and more one of professionalism).

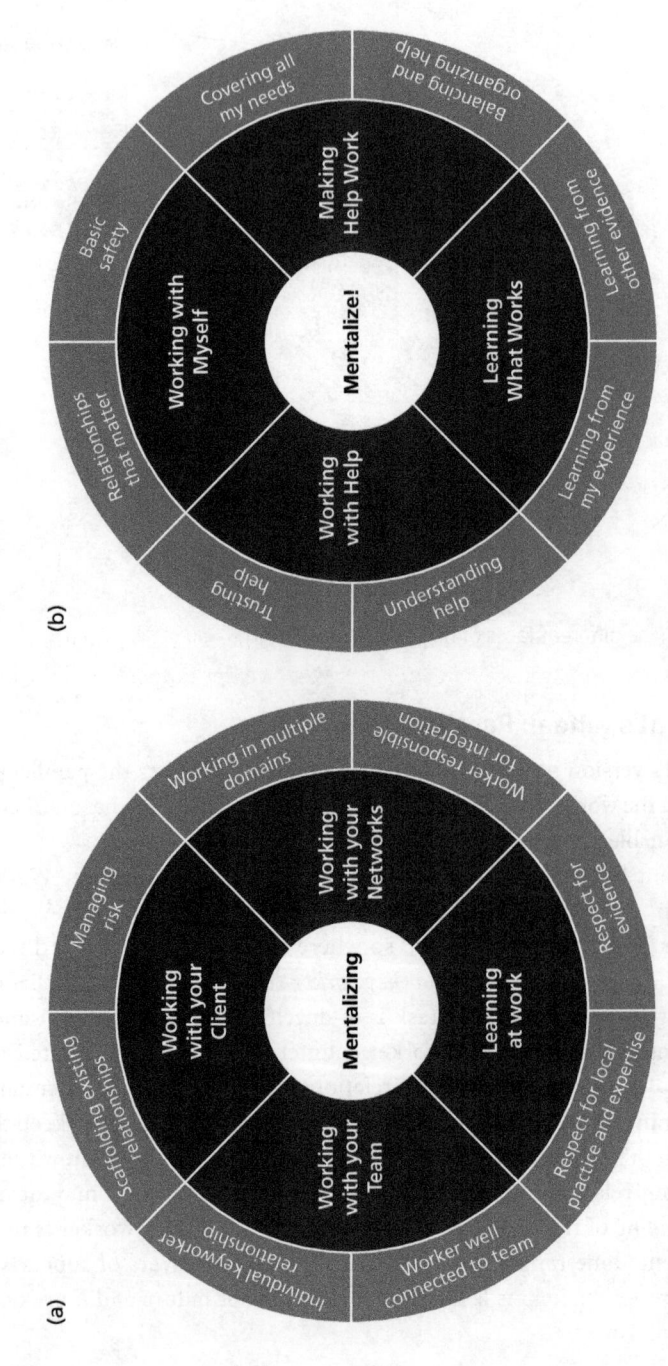

Figure 4.4 (a) The standard (worker's) AMBIT wheel; (b) the client's AMBIT wheel.

Next, the task involves "Making Help Work" (the right-hand quadrant, paralleling "Working with your Networks" for the worker). The worker's efforts to ensure that this is directed across *working in multiple domains* (individual, family, education/employment, etc.) are echoed by the invitation for the client to ensure that *all their needs are covered*. As a rich multi-domain and multi-modal package of interventions is developed, almost inevitably involving other workers and other agencies, the client witnesses the efforts of their worker to take whatever responsibility they can for *integrating* these workstreams (see Chapter 6). In turn, the client witnesses and ultimately shares or takes responsibility for the work of *balancing and organizing* the various forms of help that they are receiving, which will include making sense of (mentalizing) the actions of the different players, and if necessary—helped by their worker—helping the different players to make sense of and accommodate each other's roles.

With the foundations for "help that is likely to be helpful" in place, the client may be better placed to take more responsibility for work on the self (the "Working with Myself" quadrant at the top of the wheel)—and, obviously, the worker's corresponding responsibility is "Working with your Client." Here, the effort of the worker to identify significant existing *relationships that may require scaffolding* (starting with the client's relationship to their own self, extending to family or carers, key friends, and other workers) invites the client to consider in parallel the *relationships that matter* to them, and the kinds of work that repair and strengthening these relationships might require. As worker and client engage in this work, the worker's counterbalancing focus on *managing risk*, aside from simply averting disasters, evokes a similar focus by the client on what is required to assure *basic safety* in their life.

There is a more future-facing focus in the bottom quadrant for the client ("Learning What Works"), which parallels "Learning at Work" for the worker and their team (see Chapter 7). Here, the task for the client is to begin to distil not just the lessons of what has helped and why, but also the "how" of learning itself—the fine balance between *learning from experience* and *learning from other evidence*. The worker's role here is—if they are successful—to allow themself to become positioned as part of the "other evidence." If they can model their own balancing of *respect for local practice and expertise* with *respect for evidence* alongside the epistemic trust (essentially, trust in communication; discussed in Chapter 2) that has already been built, then there are grounds for hope that a more lasting shift in the client's relationship to help might begin to take effect.

The two wheels can be printed on opposite sides of a single card, to show how the paired, equivalent sections form "two sides of the same coin." However, whether a version of the "client's wheel" presented alongside or on the back of the standard AMBIT wheel might provide a helpful field tool for workers struggling to help their clients make sense of the work remains to be seen.

Partial-sightedness: The case for moving from implicit to explicit intentions

So, we can see that it is easy for the worker to assume that their own intentions are clear to the client: "it's self-evident that I'm one of the good guys!" However, this often could not be further from the truth—partly because of the harsh past history that the client may well have, but also because of the stress involved in the very nature of the therapeutic encounter. We have already referred to this paradox: the more authentic, truthful, and intimate the psychological contact between a client and their worker becomes, the more anxiety-provoking this can be, so the harder it becomes for them to sustain or practice their mentalizing—the very function that the worker is so keen to encourage. This is particularly likely to happen if the worker acts in ways that are perceived as "unnatural" or "weird"—long silences, inscrutable gazes, the use of jargon or "therapese." For example, therapists often speak of the requirement for "engagement" in therapy (as, indeed, we have done in this book): it is not inconceivable that in using such language when speaking to a client we might be misunderstood as implying that we are inviting a client into some kind of marriage.

The worker coming face-to-face with a client or their family/carers is thus, at best, "partially sighted" when it comes to conjuring the kinds of pictures required to understand what their client wants, and the same is certainly true for the client as they look at the worker. Inevitably, there will be a range of implicit (hidden, not clearly broadcast) ideas, hopes, fears, and intentions about this new relationship: what are the other person's desired outcomes from coming together in this way? Or, to put it more plainly, what is the point of us spending time together?

It is not unreasonable to assume that *some* of the implicit aims and intentions in the worker are likely to overlap or coincide with some of the implicit aims and intentions held by the client, but there is no way of knowing at the start which ones do, and which do not. One of the assumptions that we make in AMBIT is that the process of engagement and the forming of a therapeutic alliance are closely related to efforts to shift these intentions from being held *implicitly* (like the cards in a poker game) to being shared *explicitly* (thus, "putting my cards on the table" is a phrase not uncommonly used by a worker, describing their efforts to broadcast their own understandings and intentions as clearly as possible). In Chapter 3 we talked about "broadcasting intentions," and we expand further on this theme below, but the theoretical assumption is that a worker's ambit (their sphere of influence) is really limited to those areas where their own explicitly stated intentions are explicitly noted as overlapping and shared with those of the client.

This emphasis on the relationship to help is important, too, as we consider the desired outcomes for an intervention that a worker might be broadcasting. AMBIT, as we have noted before, is not a single rigid and monolithic therapeutic method, but instead is designed to support a wide range of AMBIT-influenced services—whose therapeutic goals and "primary outcomes" may be quite different from each other's. If there was to be a universal "primary outcome" for AMBIT-influenced work with our clients, then, as we have explored above, it would perhaps be in relation to adaptive changes to the client's "relationship to help": creating more secure expectations from help, and a higher likelihood of epistemic trust opening up the client to learning in these kinds of relationships. Evidence increasingly points toward the value of improving the relationship to help in these ways as an important factor contributing to resilience in future years (Fonagy & Allison, 2014). The measurement of this in clinical fieldwork, however, is of course a challenge.

Broadcasting intentions

When we described broadcasting intentions in Chapter 3, this was primarily in relation to engagement and the development of shared intentions in relation to the planning of care. Here we discuss the same basic principle in relation to the helping relationship and engagement. If we are to extend our ambit (our sphere of influence) with a client, then first we have to work hard to make explicit, or broadcast, our intentions.

One of the first assumptions of any mentalizing practitioner is the understanding that *minds are opaque* and cannot simply be "read" (indeed, behaving as if this is so is one of the markers of active mentalizing). When I initially approach a client, I may put into words or use other non-verbal means to communicate some of my intentions, but in the normal course of events many of them are actually held implicitly (unspoken) by me. This is often particularly the case with the most obvious of our intentions—such as: "I want to be genuinely helpful to you."

Correspondingly, the client I meet may articulate a selection of their intentions behind the investment of their time in meeting me, but many others will likewise remain implicit ("to prove to my mum that I'm not faking it," "to expose what my dad is doing to mum," "to get a flat of my own," "to get the Court off my back," etc.).

Of course, some of the worker's intentions in the work (e.g. "to persuade and help you to stop smoking cannabis") may hold absolutely no attraction for the client; some more deeply hidden intentions (the worker who is driven in their work "to make reparation for hurts that I suffered in my own childhood" or "to reduce the sense of guilt I carry"), besides requiring deeper mentalizing of their own self (our own minds are partly opaque to ourselves), are much more appropriately thought about in the privacy of individual therapy—and might, if the worker stopped to mentalize the client for a moment, be actively unhelpful to share. Equally, it is very likely that some of the client's intentions may appear unsafe, unhealthy, or unreasonable. Despite this, where there is an overlap between a worker's explicitly broadcast intentions and those of the client, *there lies the worker's ambit*; these are the areas where they can legitimately expect to have some influence. Without this systematic attempt to map out areas of shared (and of non-shared) intention, the worker may underestimate or miss the opportunity to operate effectively within their ambit, just as easily as they may wrongly assume that they have influence where in fact they have little or none.

By making their own intentions as explicit as possible, even to the point of stating the obvious ("If I possibly can, I want to be helpful here"), the worker communicates the fact that they do not take it as a given that these are shared understandings, in addition to opening the way for conversation about the client's doubts or fears about their true intentions. Another way of framing this is as an invitation by the worker to the client, normalizing the process of "checking me out" before they invest time, effort, and emotional energy in working together; this is an entirely appropriate stance to take in any new transaction with another person who is previously unknown, and is thus to be applauded.

Boundaries and intelligent membranes

If such a large part of the work in an AMBIT-influenced team is directed toward the creation of secure trusted expectancies in the relationships between workers and young clients or their carers, then it is important to state the obvious: that this depends upon making conditions as safe and predictable as possible—in worlds where these qualities might often seem like startling anomalies.

Boundaries help to create conditions of safety, but only so long as they are well marked out and signposted, and do not operate as hidden tripwires. In Chapter 5 we will discuss working with the team, but the reader will by now understand that AMBIT, above all, emphasizes that local teams are invited to empower themselves through setting about the business of deciding, defining, and delivering their own explicit and purposefully shared culture. In Chapter 5 we describe more about the development of a set of "social disciplines" and "rituals"—many of which will have already been adopted and adapted by local teams (whether they know it or not, and whether or not they see themselves as influenced by AMBIT). Such disciplines and rituals collectively mark out "our ways of working" and the boundaries that form part of these. Examples that are particularly relevant here include:

- **Punctuality and timekeeping**—workers being where they are when they say they will be
- **Confidentiality and its limits**—clarity about the rules protecting client confidentiality, and about the rules protecting clients, staff, and others from significant harm that might trump these demands for confidentiality
- **Client–worker relationships**—boundaries that support the development of authentic intimacy but protect clients and workers from harm in cases where the professional helping/therapeutic nature of the relationship may become less clear—for instance, in relation to personal disclosures, favors, finances, friendship, attraction, and physical contact. Likewise, and to state what should be the blindingly obvious, sexualized contact of any form between client and worker is always unacceptable.

There is another paradox when we come to think about boundaries and the subject of "contingent care"; what if the "help" that is called forth by a client's predicament falls outside a boundary? We have spent much time arguing about the great value of highly contingent responses—that is, responses from the carer (or worker) that appear to offer a close fit to the young person's immediate context and mental state, and what their current state appears to "call out for." The mother who simply smiles beatifically and coos at her baby in the cot as it howls in terror is not offering quite so much contingency as the one who gathers it up in her arms, whose eyes mimic wide-eyed fear while her mouth pouts and smiles, and whose voice expresses a sing-song (what has been termed "motherese") caricature of breathless fear, all the while offering reassurance that this frightened baby of hers is understood, and is going to be just fine. In the case of adolescents or young adults, what they might require in order to feel understood and accepted will often be more complicated.

Some services, for instance, have strict "no-touch" boundaries in place between workers and clients. For the sake of argument, let us assume there are understandable reasons for this (even though in many settings this might be quite impossible to maintain, such as youth work, where games of football or dance might be part of the work). Despite this boundary, however, a young person who is desperately distressed might still understandably reach out to a trusted worker, seeking "a shoulder to cry on" or a hug. Under such a regime, a worker may conceivably recoil from physical contact—not because the client is repugnant, but because they are fearful about holding on to their job. The client is likely to struggle to mentalize that behavior, though. In fact, there is a high risk that in those circumstances the client would assume that the worker *did* find them repugnant—and the precious relationship could be damaged. So, the imposition of a boundary that is too rigid (*teleological*, to put it in mentalizing terminology) can inadvertently lead workers into offering non-contingent responses, which hurts the therapeutic relationship. This is another example of the difficulty in finding the right balance between the two AMBIT principles of "Scaffolding existing relationships" and "Managing risk."

In addressing this paradox we invite comparison between two kinds of boundaries: impermeable walls and "intelligent membranes." The latter, which are structures that are common in nature, can still stand as explicit markers (things are on either one side of a membrane or the other), but unlike walls, membranes have some constrained capacity to be more or less permeable according to the circumstances and context. To continue this analogy, an organic membrane adapts its permeability not as a disconnected or "secret" action, but in relation to receptors and gated channels that are in communication with other parts of the wider biological system. Translating this back into the world of working in AMBIT-influenced ways, we think that practice boundaries are better conceived of as "membranes" rather than "walls"; marking the territories on either side of them as "safe" or "less than safe," but allowing a certain amount of therapeutic risk-taking across these boundaries, *so long as this is done in open communication with the wider system or team*. What would be of the greatest concern would be situations in which there were boundary violations in secret that could not be mentalized with help from a colleague.

Low-hanging fruit

In the earliest stages of engagement and planning, it is helpful to identify a range of shared goals and intended destinations. This is covered in more detail in Chapter 3, under the heading of Active Planning. In the process of coming to shared understandings of where we are, and where we agree we want to get to, a number of simpler, often quite practical, tasks or achievements may reveal themselves; these may seem somewhat "off target" in the larger scheme of our therapeutic work (for the client to clear a bedroom, sort out their benefits, open a bank account, etc.) but may serve as "low-hanging fruit." Keeping a list of these simple achievements can be helpful. The list can be pulled out at points when the work seems to stall; they offer an opportunity to offer contingency (that sense of "fit" between the client's dilemma here and now, and what is on offer) and to do what experts in motivational interviewing have in the past referred to as "rolling with resistance" (Miller & Rollnick, 1991).

Specific manualized interventions in AMBIT

There is evidence that certain approaches and techniques are effective for certain conditions. Respect for this evidence is one of the core features of the AMBIT stance, and is covered in more depth in Chapter 7. It is certainly disrespectful to our clients to apply completely non-evidenced approaches where evidence does exist. However, in keeping with the work of John Weisz and Bruce Chorpita (Weisz et al., 2012), and particularly with this client group, we are more impressed with the notion that this points us toward evidence-based components of practice, rather than the adoption of specific manualized packages. The latter are often carefully branded, may be persuasively marketed, and sometimes involve a rather zealous approach to the protection of copyright and materials, despite the fact that in most cases the intellectual property of these approaches is built on the cumulative work of generations of theorists and researchers, and that the costs associated with such an approach risk reducing the dissemination of effective practice. AMBIT's "open-source" approach to developing and sharing best practice is a direct challenge to this: all of our teaching materials are openly available online, so that, theoretically, it would be possible for a team to train itself entirely independently.

The bold claim of mentalizing theorists (along with the fact that there is nothing new about mentalizing) is that, although they may name it differently, most evidence-based treatment methods have found very effective ways to promote mentalizing; that mentalizing is, as it were, the "final common pathway" of most, if not all, effective therapies. Following this logic, a wide range of specific and evidence-based interventions are included in the AMBIT manual (those present in the manual at the time of writing are listed in Box 4.1). In future years there may be further additions to this list, and certainly there is room for expansion and refinements to the specific evidence-based components of practice that are currently included. Each specific intervention is manualized so as to supply the *basic theory, key session structure*, and *practice steps* required to deliver this work. The intention in providing these is twofold:

- First, this may allow a less experienced practitioner to have an understanding of the kind of work that their client may be doing with, or receiving from, another worker or team in the network, so that at the very least they can support this work from a reasonably informed perspective;
- Second, with appropriate supervisory support a keyworker may be able to deliver basic elements of evidence-based practice to address specific needs

> **Box 4.1 Specific interventions currently manualized in AMBIT**
>
> - Cognitive-behavioral work
> - Crisis contingency planning
> - Educational-vocational training
> - Emergency procedures
> - Giving advice
> - Living skills work
> - Mentalization-based work
>   - Individual
>   - Family
>   - Multi-family
>   - Group
> - Motivational work
> - Supporting pharmacological interventions
> - Supporting physical health interventions
> - Relapse prevention
> - Social-ecological work
> - Subsistence support
> - Substance use disorder work
> - Working with other professionals (liaison)

in the field contingently, operating as what we term a "barefoot practitioner" who has the advantage of trust and a working alliance, as well as light-footed flexibility and access to significant other areas of the client's life.

At the very beginning of this book, we emphasized that there is "no such thing as AMBIT"—that is, there is no all-encompassing set of working instructions. There is certainly enough in the AMBIT manual to provide that, but to use it so would be to miss something of the point about AMBIT being an *adaptive* approach. AMBIT is designed so that, as required, it can wrap around existing evidence-based practices, supporting the creation of (and sustaining) contexts that enhance their effectiveness.

Some examples of the relationship of AMBIT to evidence-based approaches may be helpful here; there are more accounts of real-world applications in Chapter 9.

The Cambridgeshire Child and Adolescent Substance Use Service has adopted an AMBIT approach to its work and makes full use of evidence-based methods of working with young people with substance use problems. In this way, the team is, for instance, fully conversant with motivational interviewing techniques, which are used as a routine part of the team's practice. Similarly, the Adolescent Multi-Agency Support Service in Islington, north London, has used evidence-based techniques, set within an AMBIT-influenced framework, in working with parents of young people at risk of family breakdown. In both of these examples, the AMBIT approach to establishing the basic processes of engaging young people and families in processes of help, and sustaining purposeful activity in often chaotic situations, is not in opposition to a range of more focused evidence-based practices.

We acknowledge that there may be strong arguments supporting the referral of a young person or a family for specialist expert service provision rather than the kind of "barefoot" provision that this might imply. However, a number of factors support the development of flexible, multi-skilled "barefoot" practitioners. First, this is not a binary "either/or" option; in most cases, it can and should be "both/and," with the keyworker's "barefoot" interventions forming part of a "shepherding" function—bringing a previously non-engaged young person into mainstream specialist services if this is ultimately what is required to help them. Second, there may be significant delays before specialist expert help is available, so that the family that required one kind of help some months ago is found to have broken apart and reconfigured by the time the appointment comes through, and now has a different set of needs. Third, such specialist care, while desirable and justifiable, may simply not be available or affordable. Fourth, the multiplication of workers, teams, and different kinds of expertise in a "Team around the Client" is not always a solution that is experienced as most helpful by the client (and family); we cover this "dis-integration" in more depth in Chapter 6. What a single, well-supported keyworker may lose in terms of specific expertise in a particular intervention may be more than counterbalanced by the flexible and highly contingent care that they are able to offer, leading to engagement and alliance, trust, and improved integration.

The process of deciding which of these interventions to use, and when, requires careful assessment, which may include use of the AIM assessment in the online AMBIT manual (discussed in Chapter 3). Acknowledging the complexity and risk involved in this work, the worker who is faced with collaboratively planning a path forwards will also need to be reminded of the imperative to remain well connected to their team. As Chapter 5 emphasizes, the supervisory structures in the team are directed at helping to support the mentalizing of the worker who may be unbalanced by the competing demands for solutions to multiple problems and risks.

Risk management

The principles and process of risk assessment and crisis contingency planning have been covered in Chapter 3. At the risk of repetition, but unapologetically so, "Managing risk" is the second of the two elements of AMBIT's principled stance that stand over "Working with your Client," alongside (and sometimes in apparent opposition to) "Scaffolding existing relationships."

While finding the attunement to engage and understand a client and other key relationships in their existing support network (family, carers, friends, other professionals) requires the "softer" mentalizing skills of flexibility, imagination, empathy, and some degree of therapeutic risk-taking, in a much more hard-edged sense there is no room for a lack of clarity in managing risks when they are identified. In many ways the management of risk can be seen as a positive use of teleological thinking ("Things will not be sufficiently safe until X and Y protocols or procedures have been put in place"). Teleology is often seen in pejorative terms, as one of the non-mentalizing modes of thinking, and therefore "wrong," but this is not the case. Just as spending time and mental effort in mentalizing an approaching tiger offers very low survival value, so in this work there are times (for instance, the disclosure of active abuse) when the appropriate response is clear, timely, and decisive action. Nevertheless, when action is completely unmentalized and precipitate, there is a high risk that the carefully nurtured relationships of trust and understanding that the worker is busy scaffolding can be damaged (which, in the longer term, if the client disengages, may paradoxically increase risk). We are always at risk of losing our balance in this work, and this accounts for the stress we quite appropriately experience, which in turn subdues our mentalizing just when we most need it. Coping with this is covered in Chapter 5, which focuses on working with the team, because it is in being accurately mentalized by a trusted other that we can most reliably regain our own capacity in this regard.

The formation of robust crisis contingency plans in individual case management, and the existence within a team of explicit, shared protocols and procedures for predictable crises, which are subject to regular discussion and adaptation in light of that team's experience, are critical elements of any well-functioning team. AMBIT does not claim any originality in espousing this. If there is an AMBIT "slant," then it is our emphasis on how a team should take responsibility for making explicit, regularly rehearsing, and continually adapting their approach to risk, and standing under this shared understanding by broadcasting it online in their local version of a wiki-manual (see Chapter 7).

Challenge and support—persecutor, fan club, abdicator …

Among the many ways in which this kind of face-to-face work can leave a worker feeling out of balance, the tension between scaffolding existing relationships and managing risk could be seen as describing a common dilemma: at times it is important to *challenge* (e.g. when a behavior presents significant risk that cannot be ignored), but at times it is equally important to provide contingent care and support to *scaffold* what is already there. Very often, the worker finds (or perceives) themselves to be slightly too far in one direction or the other.

Many teachers and therapists have described the dilemma of finding the balance between knowing when to challenge and when to offer support in helping to bring about change (Sanford, 1966). All challenge and no support turns the worker into a "persecutor," while all support and no challenge provides only a "fan club" with no reasons or encouragement to change. The worker who fails to offer either support or challenge is effectively abdicating from any active role in relation to their client's struggles. The journey toward creating a really effective therapeutic relationship is thus rather like a sailing boat that has to tack back and forth in order to make progress into a headwind. There are likely to be times at which the worker's estimations of what is the right level of challenge turn out to be wrong; at these times the client may well experience being pushed too hard or being misunderstood, or may react dramatically in ways that suggest they feel rejected or that they have been deliberately humiliated. The capacity of the worker to take responsibility for these episodes, to consider the possibility that they were mistaken in their assumptions when they introduced a particular challenge, to apologize appropriately, and to show genuine enthusiasm to understand better for next time, is critical to success (see Figure 4.5).

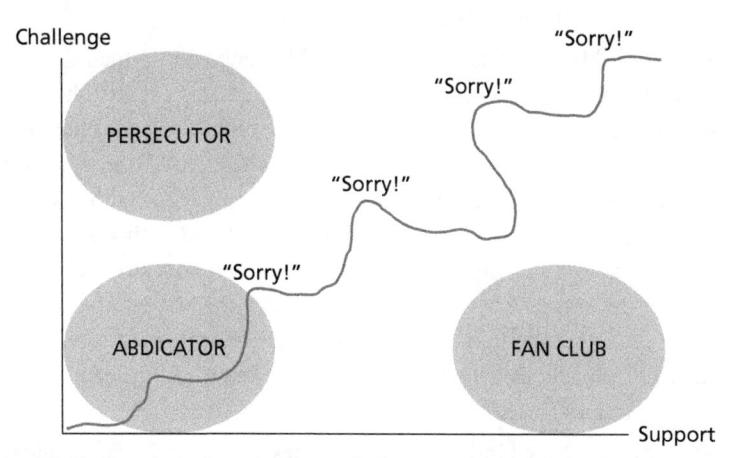

Figure 4.5 Finding the balance between challenge and support
Adapted from N. Sanford, *Self and society: Social change and individual development*
© 1996, The Authors.

The use of forewarnings, offered early on in the work, can help to mitigate against harms done to the therapeutic relationship in this way:

> "One of the things I want to be clear about as we get to know each other is that I'm very likely to get things a bit wrong occasionally—not because I want to, but because I'm human! It's hard for me to know just when you might be needing support rather than for me to be pushing you a bit, like a football coach pushes his players. If I never help you face any challenges, I probably won't actually help you make the changes you want to make, but I really want you to feel able to say if you think I'm being too pushy. Do you think you'd be able to show me when I haven't read you quite right?"

Limitations and challenges

It is one thing to think about what to do or say, and why, and another to know what to do and get on with doing or saying it. The pressure on the worker to "get it right" is not inconsiderable, especially where the worker is keen to be helpful and effective. The distress or anger of a client only adds to this pressure. This kind of pressure, as we now understand, is the enemy of our own capacity as workers to mentalize in the moment. Mentalizing failures on the part of the worker are thus inevitable.

Non-mentalizing in the worker

The non-mentalizing worker is at risk of becoming unhelpful in a number of ways:

1. They may develop unhelpful levels of certainty in their ideas about the client (psychic equivalence), leading them to speak with a sense that they know a client's experience, beliefs, motivations, or intentions, so that they are experienced as disturbingly intrusive, or arrogant;

2. They may fall into over-activity or controlling behavior in their enthusiasm to achieve concrete outcomes (teleology) where this activity shows no fit with the client's sense of what they need or want. Thus, the client experiences the work as being done *to* them rather than *with* them, even still less *by* them. Sometimes the management of risk simply requires this (especially with children and the obligation to safeguard them, although even then there may be ways to explain the rationale for an intrusion that somewhat mitigates the aversive nature of such an experience), but, in other situations, overly precipitate action risks eroding trust and the therapeutic relationship, which in the longer term may paradoxically promote disengagement, reduce learning, and increase risk;

3. They may slip into a kind of clever wordiness (a pretend mode, which may capture the complexity of the issues accurately and coherently enough but

still miss the immediate emotional context). Pretend mode may be characterized by a kind of "analysis paralysis" in which clever formulations are promoted that are experienced by the client as meaningless and missing the point, leaving them feeling as though their individual predicament has been completely overlooked; they may feel they are invisible as an individual to this worker, who is lost in their own thoughts and is treating their *ideas* about a problem rather than *them* (the client) as a person. Worse still, the worker may become "lost in thought" at those critical moments when it is action that is in fact required.

These are risks common to all therapeutic work. If there is any difference in the mentalizing "school," it is that the worker is explicitly attuned to the inevitability of, and is expecting, such failures in their own mentalizing. Perhaps because of this they may avoid becoming too self-punishing when these failures do occur. This is certainly not to say that failures in our own mentalizing are desired, or engineered, but rather a statement of fact: they happen. In response, the mentalizing worker tries to use these misunderstandings as a way of broadcasting to the client the inevitability that they will happen (as part of the "comedy of errors" that it is to be human), of modeling the necessity of being able to recover from them, and of using these episodes as opportunities to develop deeper understanding: "How did I come to get that wrong in that way ...?"

No magic in mentalizing

There is a risk, too, that the very activity of mentalizing gets turned into some quasi-magical activity that simply needs to be "done" with (or, worse, *to*) the client. Usually this stems from a rather concrete understanding of what mentalizing is or looks like. It is easy in such cases for a certain amount of blame to be shifted to the client: "I've tried mentalizing him, but he just doesn't seem to get it. He's really resistant to it." Another way of looking at this is that the worker may have tried in good faith to mentalize their client, but what they came up with still did not fit the client's actual inner experience—the worker's mentalizing efforts failed to produce any recognition in the client that their immediate predicament had been understood, or was understandable. This highlights the difference between the *activity* of mentalizing and the *product* of such activity; mentalizing may still be inaccurate, mistaken, and perceived as unhelpful, however well-intentioned the effort of the worker. Reminding oneself of the need for an inquisitive, tentative, and humble stance for this work may help here: mentalizing is never mind-reading. We cannot know, but only imagine, check, correct, and try again. Sometimes the best mentalizing results in a change of subject, the offer of something concrete like a cup of tea, or an apology. Mentalizing is not the same as helping, but accurate mentalizing is probably a (if not *the*) prerequisite for help being helpful.

In thinking about the question of which intervention(s) are most likely to work best for which client(s), it is important to acknowledge that the evidence base for mentalization-based approaches as a unimodal treatment in a number of specific mental health problems (e.g. anxiety disorders, depression) is lacking, while other approaches that have a relatively strong evidence base exist for these conditions. In keeping with AMBIT's principled stance of "Respect for evidence," it is important *not* to read this chapter as a suggestion that mentalizing work is a universal panacea: it is not. As mentioned above, the AMBIT manual provides pointers to the most evidence-based approaches (and, in many cases, simple manualized versions of these approaches) for a range of the more common mental health diagnoses. Where appropriate, and if the expertise and supervisory structures exist to support it, these should be applied as the primary intervention. However, mentalizing is, by its nature, an integrative theory and practice (it draws quite explicitly on social-cognitive, systemic, psychodynamic, and neurobiological models), and it is the authors' contention that the application of a mentalizing framework should augment and support the application of other approaches, such as cognitive-behavioral, systemic, or motivational therapy. It would be powerfully non-mentalizing to use "mentalization-based treatment" as a kind of stick with which to beat another evidence-based practice. Nor is mentalization-based treatment without risk of unwanted (iatrogenic) effects. Even though it is, of all the therapeutic approaches, perhaps the most explicit in "grasping the nettle" of the therapist's potential to do harm as well as to help, and the need to take explicit steps to avoid this risk, there are potential pitfalls in relation to particular client groups.

Perhaps the most obvious potential pitfall is in the context of working with a client with callous-unemotional traits in their temperament, and behaviors that suggest they may be developing a severe antisocial personality disorder (things such as deliberate cruelty to animals, serious premeditated aggression with a complete lack of any apparent remorse, or lack of empathy). In teaching skills about using imagination to think about the perspectives and feelings of others, there is a potential risk that we simply train such clients to be more effective at causing pain and distress. In such (rare) circumstances, the need for careful supervision is even more important, and as a general rule it is advised that the focus is more on teaching the mentalizing of self than of others—helping the client to notice and name different feeling states in themselves, or to identify some of their own core beliefs and common triggers that might drive particular antisocial behaviors, from which negative consequences (legal, relational, etc.) may follow.

The overwhelmed and burned-out worker

The worker who is engaging highly complex and risky clients who are not help-seeking in any conventional sense will not uncommonly experience a sense of feeling lost, overwhelmed, wrong, or stuck. Aside from the pitfalls described above, the accumulation of such experiences will feed the likelihood of burn-out. The capacity to mentalize the self in such circumstances is essential, and this is where strong supervisory structures, including the presence of a "well-connected team," is critical (for more on this, see Chapter 5). We regain our own capacity to mentalize fastest when we have the experience of being accurately and sensitively mentalized by a trusted other. The AMBIT approach involves holding a balance between a focus on forming strong individual keyworking relationships in which epistemic trust may be built, while also being closely connected to the team; this is exemplified by the fact that there is no individual training in AMBIT, as it cannot be conducted alone. As stated at the beginning of this chapter, in addition to the work of relationship-building with our clients, we place equal stress on strengthening mentalizing between team members as a counterbalance to the entropy and chaos that this work so often entails (again, see Chapter 5 for more detail). The colleague or supervisor who is further removed from the emotional impact of this work may, like the mountaineer's partner who stays back, paying out the rope, have a view of approaching overhangs and other risks that is denied to their colleague who is engaged on the cliff-face. Correspondingly, the worker who never seems to discuss their own loss of balance, sense of frustration, or concern, but acts as a "lone ranger" in the field, should be the one who most activates a team's concern.

The potential tyranny of outcomes

Finally, we return to our earlier emphasis on the need for the systematic evaluation of outcomes in the face-to-face work conducted with clients. The online AMBIT manual gives many suggestions about which measures may be of use to assess outcomes; AMBIT also has a measure of its own (the AIM, described in Chapter 3). There is always a risk, however, that the measurement of outcomes becomes a primary outcome in itself, and a persecuting force rather than a support for learning at work. In other words, organizational pressure to record outcomes may end up making the submission of measures of outcome more important than making sense of, and adapting practice in the light of, what the outcomes tell us. This is the very antithesis of learning at work. It is a powerful argument, among others, for the use of session-by-session outcome monitoring, as the worker is granted immediate feedback in terms of progress toward goals and the client's own experience of the session that has just taken place.

A recent study of clients in psychotherapy (Falkenstrom et al., 2013) showed that the *therapeutic alliance*—how positive the relationship with a worker was perceived to be—in a given session was the most powerful predictor of symptom improvement as measured in the subsequent session. We argue that this study provides some evidence that the establishment of epistemic trust is what stimulates the client to generalize what is learned in a session, and to try out new ways of interacting with their social world, in the time period before their next session of therapy. We might add that systematic session-by-session inquiry by the worker about "How am I doing here?" (avoiding an implicit assumption that what I am doing, and how I am doing it, is simply the best that can be done) is likely to add a helpful focus on improving the client's experience of the work. Session-by-session outcomes certainly model, in a fairly concrete way, the not-knowing curiosity about the client's experience that mentalizing holds at its core.

Conclusions

Mentalizing is "just a theory," but it is one that is built on an increasingly firm evidence base from developmental psychology, neuroscience, and clinical trials. In many senses it is not a new theory, either, but a reframing of many existing understandings in a way that increases coherence and offers practical applications that are relatively easy to grasp, even if it still takes a lifetime to refine our use of these tools. Its effectiveness in face-to-face work with clients has been proven in a number of specific clinical groups, particularly adults with borderline personality disorder (for whom mentalization-based treatment is approved in the UK by the National Institute for Health and Care Excellence as a treatment that can be provided by the National Health Service), and self-injurious adolescents. There is high face validity in the assumption that it can be applied to people with a wider range of difficulties, for whom other, more specific, evidence-based treatments may also be indicated, but who are at high risk of treatment drop-out, as well as of developing more chronic personality-based difficulties in the future.

If increasing the capacity to sustain mentalizing is the core aim in mentalizing work, then it allows for a wide range of creative possibilities as to how that end is sought. Equally, what we understand about epistemic trust suggests that in many ways our own accurate mentalizing of our clients is, at least in part, only a means to another end—the establishment of some trust in the value of our various ideas about "how to live a more adapted, happy life" as they might be applied and generalized in other areas of our clients' lives. The real therapy is what happens when the worker is nowhere to be seen, but a situation arises in which the client tries out a new (more mentalized) response. If we (or, more particularly, our clients) are lucky, the social environment might, on some of these occasions, be benign enough for such clients to taste success and gain positive feedback, sowing the seeds for repetition, and thereby long-term change.

References

Asen, E., & Fonagy, P. (2012). Mentalization-based therapeutic interventions for families. *Journal of Family Therapy* 34: 347–70. doi: 10.1111/j.1467-6427.2011.00552.x

Bateman, A. W., & Fonagy, P. (eds.) (2012). *Handbook of Mentalizing in Mental Health Practice* (Washington, DC: American Psychiatric Publishing).

Bateman, A. W., & Fonagy, P. (2016). *Mentalization-Based Treatment for Personality Disorders: A Practical Guide* (Oxford, UK: Oxford University Press).

Bowlby, J. (1988). *A Secure Base: Clinical applications of attachment theory* (London, UK: Routledge).

Falkenstrom, F., Granstrom, F., & Holmqvist, R. (2013). Therapeutic alliance predicts symptomatic improvement session by session. *Journal of Counseling Psychology* 60: 317–28. doi: 10.1037/a0032258

Fonagy, P., & Allison, E. (2014). The role of mentalizing and epistemic trust in the therapeutic relationship. *Psychotherapy* 51: 372–80. doi: 10.1037/a0036505

Fonagy, P., Rossouw, T., Sharp, C., Bateman, A., Allison, L., & Farrar, C. (2014). Mentalization-based treatment for adolescents with borderline traits. In: C. Sharp, & J. L. Tackett (eds.), *Handbook of Borderline Personality Disorder in Children and Adolescents*, pp. 313–32. New York, NY: Springer.

Miller, W. R., & Rollnick, S. (1991). *Motivational Interviewing: Preparing people to change addictive behavior* (New York, NY: Guilford Press).

Munro, E. (2011). *The Munro Review of Child Protection: Final report. A child-centred system* (London, UK: The Stationery Office), https://www.gov.uk/government/uploads/system/uploads/attachment_data/file/175391/Munro-Review.pdf, accessed 24 Jan. 2017.

Sanford, N. (1966). *Self and Society: Social change and individual development* (New York, NY: Atherton).

Turnell, A., & Edwards, S. (1997). Aspiring to partnership. The Signs of Safety approach to child protection. *Child Abuse Review* 6: 179–90.

Uttley, L., Scope, A., Stevenson, M., Rawdin, A., Buck, E. T., Sutton, A., ... Wood, C. (2015). Systematic review and economic modelling of the clinical effectiveness and cost-effectiveness of art therapy among people with non-psychotic mental health disorders. *Health Technology Assessment* 19: 1–120. doi: 10.3310/hta19180

Weisz, J. R., Chorpita, B. F., Palinkas, L. A., Schoenwald, S. K., Miranda, J., Bearman, S. K., ... Research Network on Youth Mental Health (2012). Testing standard and modular designs for psychotherapy treating depression, anxiety, and conduct problems in youth: a randomized effectiveness trial. *Archives of General Psychiatry* 69: 274–82. doi: 10.1001/archgenpsychiatry.2011.147

Chapter 5
Working with your team

Introduction: This is not work for lone rangers

AMBIT is exclusively and explicitly a *team* approach to working with hard-to-reach clients, even though the main means of delivering this work is via individual keyworking relationships. The rationale for this approach has been outlined in the first two chapters of this book: essentially, this is worrying work, and if a worker never gets worried that is all the more worrying, suggestive of a lack of mentalizing (possibly "pretend mode" thinking) and disengagement from the realities of how risky this work can be. So, feeling occasionally worried or unbalanced in this work is quite normal, we argue—something that, far from warranting professional shame (as if worry were a mark of one's failure as a worker), instead requires professional plans and professional responses. As we now also know, too much worry overwhelms our mentalizing, leaving us at risk of becoming overly certain about our ideas (psychic equivalence thinking) and prone to knee-jerk actions (teleological thinking), or, conversely, to needless prevarication (the pretend mode again) where, in actual fact, timely action is called for. We also know that mentalizing is a process that originally develops, and is most easily recovered, in relationships of trust. So the purpose of this chapter is to flesh out what we mean in emphasizing that AMBIT is a whole-team approach, and how specific aspects of team functioning can address the dilemmas we have outlined and are crucial to the team's effectiveness and outcomes.

Nearly all health and welfare services are delivered by teams of staff working together around shared tasks and objectives. These groups vary greatly, ranging, for example, from teams of health visitors, social workers, or youth workers, through multidisciplinary youth offending teams or mental health professionals in Child and Adolescent Mental Health Services (CAMHS), to a tightly knit hospital surgical team. All of these groups of workers would probably see team functioning as a more or less critical part of their working practice. There is a very large literature about how such teams function, what makes them function better, and what are some of the obstacles to effective team functioning (e.g. Carpenter, 2003). This general literature is as relevant to AMBIT as to any health care team (and, equally, as it is to a car sales team or a group of mountaineers).

One aspect that differentiates these teams is the degree of interdependence that may exist between its members. For example, individuals in a surgical team in a hospital are completely reliant on each other to conduct a successful operation. If the anesthetist is not there, the operation cannot take place. If the anesthetist makes a mistake, the rest of the team are directly affected by the anesthetist's actions. Other teams may not be so interdependent, involving more independent and autonomous working, and team processes may involve ensuring coordination rather than active co-working around a specific task. For example, health visitors, social workers, and community CAMHS staff often work with a high degree of autonomy in their day-to-day work, so that their interaction with clients may be largely independent for much of the time. This variability in levels of interdependence will be explored more fully below.

Balancing autonomy and dependence

For many teams, there is often a strong culture of autonomous working, whereby workers may spend the day visiting clients in their homes, or meeting them in other community settings to create strong therapeutic relationships, and assertively trying to engage other agencies, often by visiting schools and other important parts of the wider network. However, AMBIT's principled stance includes the "Keyworker well connected to the Team," explicitly emphasizing the necessity of a high degree of mutual interdependence within the team (see Figure 5.1). The basic assumption is that in order to help, the worker's capacity to make sense of the complex and distressed lives of their clients requires them to have *not only* a strong keyworking relationship with the client (remember that we use the word "keyworking" to denote the client's sense that "this person is key

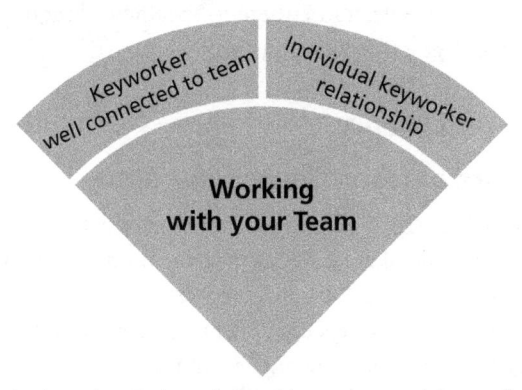

Figure 5.1 Developing a keyworker relationship versus remaining well connected to the team.

to helping me" rather than as an organizational role, and that it emerges when the worker has shown their ability to mentalize the client's mental state) *but also* close relationships with colleagues who can support them in mentalizing not just their clients, but also themselves. Perhaps surprisingly, we would describe an AMBIT team as being as closely interdependent as a hospital surgical team.

There is no doubt that an AMBIT-trained team will function better if general features of good team practice are in place (e.g. effective leadership, feeling supported, having clear roles and responsibilities); in this chapter we will briefly refer to these features and highlight their importance for team working. However, we will pay greater attention to outlining team practices that directly support aspects of team working that are at the heart of AMBIT, namely: supporting mentalizing in the team; the need to recognize the impact of anxiety and other aroused states of mind on one another's capacity to mentalize states of mind in oneself and others; and the need to make sense of helping processes in systemic terms (see Chapter 6 for more details of this). The AMBIT approach places high demands on teams, in relation not only to their general functioning, but also to one of the core features of the AMBIT approach, which is the requirement for systematic effort toward creating, developing, and sustaining an explicit and specific local team culture. This may start with the adoption and encouragement of the eight principles that together make up the AMBIT stance (the "outer ring" of the AMBIT wheel, presented in Chapter 1) but, crucially, it requires teams to embark on a sustained course of developing further local adaptations, through the gradual addition of detail about "how we do what we do." Of course, this process overlaps with another core feature of AMBIT—Learning at Work, which we cover in Chapter 7.

The purpose of this chapter is therefore to focus on the knowledge and theory relating to general and specific aspects of team functioning related to the AMBIT approach. It will then link these to specific techniques and practices that support AMBIT practice within a team.

Knowledge and theory

The importance of team climate and culture

As a team approach, AMBIT relies on a team being relatively well functioning in order to deliver some of the core parts of the model. There is an extensive research literature about what the core components of a well-functioning team are, and, because AMBIT is dependent on these components being in place, they will be briefly summarized here. The aim is to recognize a number of key features of team functioning that are likely to facilitate and support AMBIT practice.

The characteristics of a well-functioning team have been defined and summarized by a wide range of authors (e.g. Mickan & Rodger, 2000) and, although their different models vary in detail, there is a broad consensus about the key components. Teams need to have a shared purpose, with team members having clear roles and responsibilities led by authoritative leadership and supported with adequate resources for the task. Effective teams tend to be well coordinated, have good internal communication and cohesion, and demonstrate effective decision-making and the capacity to manage conflict where it arises. Last, but crucially, teams—and those in leadership roles—need to be responsive to feedback from both staff and clients (Mickan & Rodger, 2000).

Teams in which there is persistent conflict between team members, rivalries between different sub-groups, repudiation of agreed power structures, and lack of clarity about roles and responsibilities will find the AMBIT approach extremely challenging. Perhaps more than in other approaches, the AMBIT method of working depends on staff having sufficiently trusting and supportive relationships with each other in order to do the work. The AMBIT model does not prescribe a specific team structure to achieve these positive team conditions. It is clear through our work with a broad range of teams that the core requirements of the approach can be achieved across highly varied team structures. For example, some teams have very flat, democratic decision-making cultures, whereas others have more traditional management and supervisory systems. What matters is the achievement of a positive team culture that can provide the foundation on which specific AMBIT functions and tasks can be built.

There is an extensive literature on the importance of a positive "culture" within organizations, much of which is descriptive and anecdotal (Martins & Terblanche, 2003). However, more rigorous research on organizational culture has found measuring the concept of "culture" to be elusive, and that establishing the relationship between a positive culture and successful organizational outcomes is less clear than perhaps was anticipated (Stanford, 2010).

Within the field of mental health services for young people, the effect of organizational culture has been most extensively researched by Charles Glisson and his team over a period of almost 20 years. Out of this impressive program of research, Glisson and his colleagues developed a model of organizational functioning known as the Availability, Responsiveness, and Continuity (ARC) model (Williams & Glisson, 2014). This model has two distinct components: *organizational culture* and *organizational climate*.

Organizational culture "describes the shared behavioral expectations and norms that characterize and direct behavior in a work environment" (Williams & Glisson, 2014, p.758). Organizational culture has three dimensions that increase the likelihood of poor decision-making: (i) rigidity (a culture of a high degree of centralized control and rule-following by staff); (ii) resistance (a culture of rejecting innovation and change); and (iii) lack of proficiency (where staff do not have up-to-date knowledge and do not place the wellbeing of clients as a priority).

Organizational climate focuses on how the work impacts on the wellbeing of staff; it, similarly, has three factors that reduce the effectiveness of team functioning: (i) lack of engagement (workers do not feel that they achieve personally meaningful outcomes for their clients); (ii) lack of functionality (workers experience their team as not supportive, and lacking role clarity and adequate resources); and (iii) high levels of stress (driven by conflicting demands and emotional exhaustion).

A number of studies by this research group have indicated that improved client outcomes are achieved by teams that have a positive organizational culture and climate. In a recent study of over 70 teams in the USA working with children coming into the care system, Williams and Glisson (2014) examined the particular mechanisms by which climate and culture affect outcome. This study suggested that organizational climate has a direct impact on the clinical outcomes of clients, whereas factors of organizational culture only indirectly impacted on outcomes, through their impact on climate factors.

These findings are extremely valuable for AMBIT, as they indicate key themes around team functioning that are needed to improve both team culture and climate:

- Reducing rule-following that is rigid or "blind" (or poorly mentalized)
- Increasing openness to innovation
- Increasing knowledge and skills around new forms of practice.

These themes are all highly consistent with the AMBIT training model. The suggestion is that, if this type of culture can be achieved, it may well reduce stress for workers, increase a sense of engagement with the client group, increase role clarity, and support realistic expectations around client change.

AMBIT aims to develop a specific team culture in which team members are comfortable in supporting a mentalizing model of working, and are familiar with the whole AMBIT approach to balancing work with their clients with attention to team processes, relationships across the wider network, and ongoing learning from experience. As such, team members should be able to rely on each other in an explicit way that is expected and accepted, and have the knowledge and skills to use systems thinking to improve team effectiveness. There is a clear need to establish a team culture that is safe, non-blaming, and supportive of staff. Two specific features of functioning needed for an AMBIT team will be highlighted below: AMBIT's *capacity to support mentalizing* and its *commitment to facilitating learning*.

Developing mentalizing within a team

AMBIT aims to enable workers, supervisors, and managers to develop a more mentalizing approach to team functioning. This requires all team members to have a basic knowledge of mentalizing and to have the confidence to use mentalizing techniques for team processes where these are endorsed as being part of team practice. For example, the four components of the mentalizing stance (curiosity, holding the balance, terminating non-mentalizing, and highlighting mentalizing) may be equally useful in interactions between team members as it is in those with clients and their families. In our experience, this presents a number of subtle but important challenges for a team.

First, mentalizing does not replace other aspects of team functioning. We have known teams that, in their enthusiasm for adopting a mentalizing stance as part of the team function, have tried to use explicit mentalizing as a response to all types of team processes and functions. This would be the equivalent of a family in which every aspect of daily routine became explicitly mentalized (a seriously dysfunctional state). For example, decision-making about a team member's annual leave does not, in general, require explicit mentalizing; implicit, automatic forms of "background" mentalizing are perfectly adequate for this task. Similarly, when there are disagreements in a team, these cannot necessarily be resolved by explicit mentalizing (unless the disagreement is based on a misunderstanding of a team member's state of mind). The majority of disagreements can be addressed in the usual way through negotiation and, where necessary, by the exercise of authority. Where an activity labeled explicitly as "mentalizing" is found to be undermining the basic team functions described above (e.g. challenging appropriate hierarchies of authority and responsibility in a way that is unhelpful), we would suggest that this may not in fact be a very mentalizing stance! Thus, what takes place in most "ordinary business" within a team will be implicit mentalizing, as is the case in most adaptive interactions. In many ways, a healthily functioning team (as with a family) will be characterized by its high levels of *implicit* mentalizing that is reasonably accurate. Frequent *explicit* mentalizing is probably a sign of trouble.

To address this dilemma for AMBIT-trained teams, we encourage team members to use explicit mentalizing in a *marked* way. This means that it is preceded by communications between team members in which agreement is sought as to whether it would be helpful to try to mentalize the states of mind of those involved in the issue that is being considered.

> "We're looking for solutions here, so would it be helpful for a moment to look at this from the point of view of the states of mind of those involved?"
>
> "I wonder whether we should look at this more from a mentalizing point of view? It seems we are getting very drawn into who did what, and maybe we are missing something here."

This clearly demarcates implicit from explicit mentalizing and enables team members to make conscious judgments about whether or not the specific context would make this useful. This may seem somewhat over-deliberate, but there is a risk that introducing a mentalizing culture into a team may lead to some team members feeling more vulnerable and exposed, as though forced into making disclosures about their own states of mind in ways that increase their anxiety rather than promoting a sense of safety. Any sense that explicit mentalizing is being imposed on team members is likely to reduce the capacity of the team members to engage in it.

That said, there are likely to be a number of processes in which explicit mentalizing may prove valuable, such as team meetings and supervision. Wherever possible, we invite teams to make use of such forums to explore the value of adding explicit mentalizing in a marked way, and evaluating its benefit or otherwise. In general, it is rarely productive for teams to set up additional forums "to practice AMBIT skills." Given the usual work pressures experienced by outreach teams, such forums usually fall away as being unsustainable. As stated previously, the test for AMBIT is whether it reduces the burden on services and team members—influencing the ways existing tasks and allocated time-slots are conducted, rather than adding new demands and complexity to already-complex team processes.

Developing methods of team learning within a team

Helping AMBIT clients with complex, diverse, and often long-standing needs is difficult. It is difficult for many reasons, among them the fact that there is a dearth of highly effective, evidence-based interventions for this group of people. This does not mean that what the team is already doing is not helpful, but rather, it is useful to recognize the fact that the success that is achieved will vary between different clients, and we sometimes don't know why this is. In this way we are suggesting that the "evidence bottle" may be only half full, but it is not empty.

The ambition of AMBIT is to enable teams to add some more evidence to the bottle over time—drawing not only on evidence from peer-reviewed research, but also on local evidence based on learning, thinking, and reflecting on what has worked (and what has *not* worked), and why, for individual clients in a specific local setting. This may require some courage to recognize mistakes and occasions when a team loses engagement with a client (if this is a mistake) or when a risk assessment proves inaccurate. Our assertion (which we are unusually confident about) is that every team we have ever worked with shares these difficulties.

With respect to team processes, the capacity of a team to learn from feedback, by looking at its outcomes and reflecting on specific events, is similar to what air traffic control systems call accident investigation (or looking at near misses). Similarly, all the literature on basic team processes advocates the importance of looking at mistakes or unintended variations in outcomes. This requires a team climate that balances an explicit expectation of difficulties (and the safety to acknowledge them openly when they occur) with the robustness to call these out and respond appropriately when they do come to light. AMBIT is not a concrete rule book, but is set up as an open system in which teams are encouraged to elaborate from a basic set of principles and practices. This function will be more fully covered in Chapter 7, which covers the process of ongoing learning at work, and the team's manualization (achieved by mentalizing) of its own practices. Here, we simply need to highlight that what is proposed is an active process of developing and promoting a culture in which the team works collectively to create shared knowledge. This is very different from the most common way in which individual practitioners learn about their work, which is simply by doing it.

The challenge here is for teams to create enough space in their work to engage in an explicit process of working out what may be best for all team members in particular situations, or in response to particular needs. For example, what is the best way of working with a young client in this particular locality, within this particular ecology of services, who is being cared for by a single parent with a significant alcohol problem? Based on previous experiences and local knowledge, can the team come up with a method of working that would be helpful for a worker faced with this situation in the future? Such learning requires teams to discuss, reflect, and invest in this process so that some "institutional memory" is laid down, and pre-existing wheels do not have to be completely reinvented. Again, we contend that investment in such processes may reduce the burden on staff in the longer term, by improving outcomes, instilling curiosity and hope (in the workers, that they will "get better" at this work), and reducing the repetitive "re-learning" that often characterizes many health and social care teams. Perhaps even more than mentalizing, this represents a major shift in culture for many teams.

Balance and unbalance: Developing a keyworker relationship versus remaining well connected to the team

At the heart of the AMBIT approach is the challenge of trying to establish a helping relationship with a client who is often deeply distrustful of professional (or, at its most simple, "adult") help. This approach is highly influenced by attachment theory, and the aim is to create a relationship that offers a degree of safety and trust for the client. The purpose is to stimulate in the client's mind what is described in attachment studies as a secure "internal working model." A person's internal working model provides them with a mental model of what (in this context) a helping relationship might promise. Of course, many of the clients targeted by an AMBIT-trained service will have had unsatisfactory, brutalizing, or humiliating past experiences of authority and help—experiences that have left them with, at best, only the vestiges of a secure internal working model (perhaps from one or two more peripheral figures in their early life—a grandparent or teacher, for instance). Their internal working model more likely promotes the expectation of impending abuse, exploitation, or neglect and abandonment than of help. However, there is some evidence that even if such negative expectancies form the predominant part of a client's internal working model, so long as there have been *some* instances of "good enough" care, there may still be a less prominent, but more positive, internal working model existing in parallel; it is on the embers of this that an AMBIT-influenced worker can hope to blow, in the hope of rekindling something more hopeful in the client's expectation of, and relationship to, help.

As we pointed out earlier in this book, it is not assumed that this "key" relationship will necessarily initially be with a worker in the AMBIT-trained team. In a situation where a pre-existing relationship can be identified in which there is evidence of the client having some positive trust in another professional (e.g. a youth worker or teacher), the AMBIT worker may wish, in the first instance, to act to scaffold that professional relationship; in time, that relationship may support the formation of a stronger keyworking relationship with the AMBIT worker (or may, of course, allow the identified problem to be overcome without the intrusion of additional professionals at all). This is an approach that we have referred to as the "Team around the Worker," and is described in Chapter 3. In brief, our approach to relationship-building is to invest in relationships that already exist and to remember that, in terms of the number of different face-to-face contacts with a client, less is often more.

So, in the early engagement stages of work, an AMBIT worker may be more effective in working via a pre-existing positive professional relationship, rather than immediately requiring new face-to-face contact that might be experienced by the client as intrusive or overwhelming. By the worker tactfully coming alongside this other professional, and modeling helpfulness *to that professional* (ideally in ways that the client can witness or hear about from this trusted worker), it may be that a direct face-to-face relationship can later be fostered. Care is always taken to scaffold and strengthen existing (positive) relationships, avoiding the risk that if the AMBIT worker is seen as "better" than an existing worker (outreaching to the client, acting in more flexible and contingent ways), the pre-existing relationship—which might offer greater longevity, or more systemic influence, than the one with the AMBIT worker—could potentially be disrupted or diminished.

Let us assume, however, that a key face-to-face relationship is now developing directly between the AMBIT worker and the client. Why might this still present a dilemma for effective practice? Keyworker relationships almost inevitably expose workers to relationships with clients that engender strong feelings in the worker. The worker may feel intensely gratified that the working relationship with the client is being experienced by the client in a positive way. The worker may thus become rather identified with the client and their perspective and experience of the world; from this position, though, the worker is vulnerable to being drawn into tacit collusion with quite pathological or risky behaviors. Beliefs communicated by the client about the relative value (or lack of value) of other workers may be implicitly adopted by the worker as an unintended consequence of their effort to engage and mentalize the client. For example, the client may convey their distrust of a social worker, or hostility to the police; the worker may then be implicitly influenced by this, concluding that they are now perhaps uniquely able to understand the client's point of view on things and thus provide effective help. This state of mind would be consistent with an attachment framework in which the worker develops a level of trust and intimacy with the client by validating their unique experience of themself and the world. However, it is well recognized that such processes of rather idealized relationship-building are prone to later episodes of hostility, denigration, and subsequent distrust by clients (consistent with the poor "relationship to help" described above, attributable to earlier negative experiences of being cared for).

So, although the successful engagement of the client by the AMBIT worker is one of the cornerstones of effective work, the ensuing relationship may expose the worker to states of mind that make it more difficult to maintain their mentalizing stance (in relation to both their client and themself). Perhaps the most pervasive of these is the exposure of the worker to high levels of anxiety or other powerful feelings owing to the immediacy of the client's predicament and the risks involved. AMBIT workers may experience the degree of threat or despair that the client feels in such a way that it becomes hard to retain a capacity to assess risks, threats, and opportunities in a dispassionate way. Workers are at risk of burnout because of the stress, or, conversely, they are at risk of a subtle readjustment of their thresholds for concern that may be justified in rather "macho" terms—as if (and we caricature here) "only a naive newcomer would allow a bit of self-mutilation or intravenous injecting to get to them."

It is in order to counteract these unwanted effects of close keyworking relationships that AMBIT emphasizes the need for the worker to maintain a high level of connectedness with the other members of the team. Indeed, we suggest that as much effort should be directed at maintaining these peer-to-peer relationships as at creating and sustaining the key relationship with the client: relationships with team members are seen as directly resisting the "entropy" (things tending toward collapse and chaos) that working with such clients can cause. The mechanics of intra-team relationships involve formal supervisory processes within the team as well as more direct and formalized ways of conducting purposeful dialogue between colleagues (sometimes via mobile phones in the field—and even while in direct contact with the client), conducting case consultations with colleagues with the phone on loudspeaker mode so that the client can be a part of the thinking process and can observe the phenomenon of someone asking for, and getting, help. This latter use of the team parallels how systemic therapists use a "reflecting team," although with a specific structure, which we cover later in this chapter.

The purpose of this connectedness is not just to provide "support" for the frontline worker, or to provide an alternative (meta-)perspective on the current dilemmas presented by the client. In an AMBIT-influenced team the function of this connection is explicitly to enable the frontline worker to retain or regain their own capacity to mentalize the predicament of the client, and also their own predicament as a worker. As we have described already, the loss of effective mentalizing on the part of the worker may well be associated with an increase in risk in the system. Mentalizing theory suggests that contact with a trusted team member who is able to mentalize the worker's predicament is the most effective mechanism for reawakening the worker's own mentalizing. The AMBIT stance of the "worker well connected to the team" proposes that workers need to pay specific attention to regulating the "distance" between themselves and both the team that they work in and the clients they engage with. In a typical intervention, it is likely that the worker will sway between becoming overly close to the client and a bit disconnected from the team, to being very much on task from the team's point of view but perhaps a bit out of tune with the client. These are common oscillations, which a well-connected team can readily address.

Techniques and skills

AMBIT is a team approach and not an individual therapy provided by an individual therapist to a single client. The aim is therefore quite explicitly to try to create a team culture that explicitly recognizes and amplifies the interdependence of team members in going about their work with clients. As we explained at the start of the chapter, team culture is not easy to define, but if one were to observe an AMBIT-trained team from the outside, we would hope that some of the behaviors described below would be evident.

Team members asking each other for help in making sense of their clients' behavior and their own experience

We believe that in all teams individual workers will have ways of discussing with colleagues the dilemmas they face in their work: we are not claiming in any way that this is a unique feature of the AMBIT approach. In many ways, perhaps, AMBIT is just a conscious attempt to explain and to make explicit what best practice in highly effective teams already is. However, in AMBIT, the process of mentalizing oneself and one's client is at the heart of the therapeutic endeavor.

So, within an AMBIT-trained team, we would hope to see team members asking each other for help not just around practical tasks (e.g. "Can you put these outcomes into the spreadsheet for me?") or instructional ones ("Can you help me put together an agenda for the team meeting?"), but also around what might be described as emotional or thinking tasks, for instance about how to make sense of a client, a worker's current plans for working with that client, and the worker's reaction to the client.

The cultural expectation in AMBIT is that the behavior of clients is often hard to make sense of, and that *not understanding them* is a routine and familiar part of the work, which requires routine input from others. Here are some examples of starting points for conversations between colleagues that we would expect to see in an AMBIT-trained team:

Worker 1: "Can you give me a hand for a few minutes? I really can't understand this client. One day she is really engaged in trying to improve her relationship with her mum and then for a couple of weeks she will completely avoid me. Could you help me try to make better sense of this?"

Colleague: "Sure, I've got a few minutes. Tell me what you think is going on for her at the moment, but don't worry too much about telling me about what she does. What's it like to be her?"

Worker 2: "John, I'm feeling so stressed by one of my clients. It feels as though I can't get Social Care to take the risks seriously and I don't know if I am seeing this right. Something about this case is winding me up. Could you just help me make sense of why I'm getting so stressed?"

Colleague: "OK, can I just make a call and then we can talk. Maybe we should just put our heads together about having a fresh look at the risks and the risk plan. Happy to do that."

Worker 3: "Sometimes I think we are just fooling ourselves. Some of our clients are never going to change much and we run around anyway trying to make small changes happen, but as soon as we stop they will go back to their old ways. Sometimes I don't know why we do this stuff. It feels pointless."

Colleague: "That doesn't sound like you. I worry that you might be getting a bit isolated with this stuff, and I wonder what's happened to produce this kind of feeling for you? How about we have a sandwich together at lunchtime and you tell me more about what's been going on for some of the clients you have been seeing?"

Using mobile phones to obtain live input to case situations

AMBIT-trained workers are encouraged to connect with team members as much as they wish; linking back to the team is likely to help in restoring a sense of balance and supporting a mentalizing stance. With outreach working, the use of a mobile phone to allow workers to make such connections, even if geography is working against them, is strongly encouraged. The worker who very rarely seems to consult with colleagues would in this sense be the one to raise concern, insofar as they do not seem to be "well connected" to the team. Obviously, though, team practice needs to accommodate the variation between individual workers in how helpful and necessary this is, and there is no intention of creating a somewhat rule-bound orthodoxy.

For example, an AMBIT worker may have just completed a meeting with a client in a café and come away feeling particularly hopeless and despairing about how things are going. In an AMBIT-trained team we would encourage the team member to call a colleague and just share this feeling and try to make sense of it before moving on to their next contact or meeting. Such "Thinking Together" (see below) may not be particularly problem-solving in an explicit way, but our experience is that new angles on the case often emerge from such conversations. We think of this not so much as workers being supportive to each other (although hopefully it is), but as having the more precise function of helping a worker get their own mentalizing back online so that they are not excessively unbalanced by the strength of feeling that has arisen in the course of the previous contact. Mentalizing theory asserts that it is the contact with another person, who is experienced as trusted, available, and reasonably understanding, that facilitates this. Such co-consulting is promoted as a core part of the work, certainly not as a "luxury extra" or a special favor.

Explicitly referring to the team, and team members, in working with clients

Although the AMBIT approach promotes the development of a degree of attachment and trust between the worker and the client, the approach also encourages workers to refer in conversation explicitly to their position as part of a team; a worker's relationships to other team members should be reasonably transparent to the client. For example, we would encourage workers to refer to conversations that they have had with (named) colleagues about the client: a worker might say, "When I was thinking about your situation with my supervisor, Janet, she helped me wonder whether I had quite understood properly the impact on you after you discovered that your sister had been abused by your uncle. It made me wonder if I had under-reacted to how awful that might have been for you." This comment could easily have been made without reference to the supervisor, but the intention here is to model the way the worker develops ideas and understandings about things through talking—and thinking—with others; it models the worker as someone who seeks, and receives, help from trusted others. The aim is to enable the client and the worker together to be able to regulate distances in their relationship by developing a degree of transparency about this. Of course, such a process needs to be balanced with a need for respect and privacy, and so clients will also need to be clear in their understanding of who the worker is *not* going to speak to about them. "Take-home messages" from other team members are generally always framed in affirming, strength-focused terms, modeling the example of benign external relationships that make reasonable efforts to be helpful.

There are many other ways in which AMBIT-trained workers can regulate the distance between themselves and their clients and model their own relationship to help from colleagues. The main purpose here is to illustrate the way that the dilemmas of relationship-building with clients (whose previous experience of helping relationships may be very troubled, volatile, or distant), and retaining balance in such work, require a high level of team input.

Case example

Janine is a 15 year old who had been exposed to a high degree of family violence. She had dropped out of school and was frequently not at home, staying overnight with various friends, or her exact whereabouts were often unknown. Janine engaged very well with her AMBIT worker, Tony, and disclosed a large amount of highly pertinent, emotionally laden information relatively quickly. Tony felt that he was doing really well with Janine and felt good about the work he was doing with her. Janine emphasized that she found it impossible to talk to her parents and with other workers, and that she found Tony's input very helpful. She was unhappy when Tony indicated that he worked as part of a wider team, who discussed each other's work. At that point, Tony felt compromised about whether or not he should share some of the case material with others in the team. He explained to Janine why he needed to do this, but following that conversation she avoided contact over a two-week period, overdosed on painkillers, and was seen in the emergency department. Tony then re-engaged more closely with colleagues in his team and they reviewed the risk management plan for the case. Tony was able to recognize that he had become very organized around Janine's powerful disclosures to him, so that he had not recognized and monitored indications of risk of self-harm in his work with her, and had missed opportunities for engaging with her family support network. He built a new plan to work much harder at explaining to Janine how helpful he found regular contact with his team, emphasizing that the overarching intention of this was to be helpful in his work with her, and offering to conduct some of these conversations by phone so that she could listen via speakerphone and get a better sense of how respectful and serious they were when they discussed their work with Janine.

Thinking Together

In AMBIT we have developed a technique of discussing client work, anxieties, and more general issues in a more disciplined way than happens in usual practice. We have named this technique "Thinking Together." At its core, a Thinking Together conversation is a highly disciplined and pragmatic method of trying to make sense of the worker's, and then the client's, current state of mind in a relatively brief period of time (5–10 minutes), in order that these conversations can take place in the immediacy of outreach work. Such a disciplined form of interaction does *not* replace the many other ways of communicating that already take place within a team, but the Thinking Together format can also shape longer case discussions, as well as these "real-time" exchanges. It is designed to provide a method of explicitly supporting mentalizing in a colleague. Thinking Together is a label that teams can use to mark out clearly (as an *ostensive cue*, described in Chapter 2) what is about to happen. As a signaling mechanism, the crucial quality of any name is that there should be a shared understanding of what it refers to, hence the importance of training as a team.

All teams that complete the AMBIT basic four-day training program are taught the Thinking Together technique. It is important that everyone in the team has a chance to practice the technique and to learn the basic steps together, so that each team member knows the core skills involved and what to expect. Having someone use a Thinking Together framework in a conversation with a colleague without any prior knowledge of this would probably feel a little odd; this is a good example of why AMBIT is exclusively a team training, emphasizing as it does the creation of a shared culture between workers.

Many teams who have undertaken the AMBIT training have commented on how useful this technique has proved to be.

Why do we need the process of Thinking Together?

Case discussion is an ordinary part of any team's work, and even individual therapists will have supervision sessions to explore thoughts, feelings, and plans for their work. Much case discussion (both formal and informal) between colleagues can be well intentioned, but may not be as productive as it might be with respect to meeting the needs of the person with the problem. Our observations about this are not new or original; indeed, from working with large numbers of teams we have found this view to be quite widely shared. A number of difficulties can easily arise in discussions between colleagues about cases. We give some examples here:

Others do not know the case as well as oneself. In discussing a case, colleagues may make suggestions about the case, which make sense on the basis of what has been shared in the conversation but are not persuasive in relation to what else the worker already knows (and has thought) about the case in general. In this way, a lot of suggestions are made that are discounted by the worker for good reasons, and the exchange is not helpful.

Others answer the wrong questions. Case discussion may become focused on one element of the dilemma that, although potentially important and offering valuable future directions for the worker, somehow does not quite "hit the spot" for them. Not uncommonly, this is not just because the team has "followed the wrong lead," but because the worker themself may not have been entirely clear what they wanted from the team (or colleague) when they started to present the case.

Others have very good ideas that make one feel worse. In some discussions colleagues may come up with a list of very good ideas, but these may not be easily applicable to the state of the casework at the time of the discussion, or may not necessarily address the worker's underlying (perhaps unspoken) feelings about the work. The fact that they did not come up with any of these ideas themself can lead to the worker feeling that they are just managing the case badly, or do not have the knowledge and skills required (as their colleagues seem to); at worst, the worker may feel even worse than they did at the beginning of the conversation.

Colleagues demand a lot more information before they can offer any suggestions. Some case discussion, particularly team discussions, may invite lots of questions asking for more and more information about the case. The curiosity of the team has been aroused and the discussion focuses on gaining a comprehensive picture of the case. Relatively little time is then left to focus on the specific dilemma of the worker, and this is only dealt with rather cursorily at the end of the discussion.

The worker engages in storytelling. This is similar to the previous pattern, but reversed. It may start with a worker requesting to have some space to think about a case and then continue with the worker presenting very detailed descriptions of recent sessions or conversations with a worker from another agency, and so on. The information shared is nearly entirely descriptive and often lacks a formulation, goals, or ongoing outcomes. We may assume that this reflects rather a (teleological) non-mentalizing response on the part of the worker—driven by a strong (maybe even rather obsessional) sense that things will be better once the full complexity, in all its detail, has been presented. Such presentations of case material may become memory tests rather than giving much sense of reflective thinking other than emphasizing that the worker feels "stuck" and that this is vaguely linked to the impact of the client's complexity on the worker's state of mind.

Case discussions can be very long. It is often extremely hard to describe the key details of a case succinctly. If not carefully structured and chaired, case discussions may easily go on for 30–60 minutes. Most teams have limited time, and so only a few cases can be considered in this way. While there is much to be said for a longer, more detailed case discussion, in most clinical meetings there is a major need for conversations to be succinct enough to allow a wide range of cases to be addressed effectively.

This is not intended to be an exhaustive list of the pitfalls of case discussion within teams. The aim here is simply to recognize that there is a clear need for team meetings to enable workers to access thinking and feeling by their colleagues about serious cases in a succinct way *that is experienced as helpful by the worker* who is managing the case. It is these considerations that prompted the development of the Thinking Together method.

Thinking Together can take place between any team members in an AMBIT-trained team; it is not confined to supervisee–supervisor conversations, although it can be used in these settings, as well as in team meetings. It can be carried out over the phone or in face-to-face meetings, and relies on both people in the conversation having an awareness of the process in which they are engaged. Thinking Together is a bit like a dance in which it helps if both people know the steps and can understand what each person is trying to do. The technique aims to foster a team culture of mutual interdependence and an insistence on mentalized understandings; it advocates that all colleagues can be helpful and responsive to each other when they are approached to "think together" about a case. Helping one's colleagues in this way becomes a core team task, rather than being seen as an act of special generosity or, worse, as having no particular importance in the work of the team.

Thinking Together is a set of socially interactive and explicitly ritualized steps in which all participants are expected to be active. These steps are designed to maximize the amount of useful information (context, states of mind) that can be "passed outwards" from places of greater disturbance toward calmer places or people, where attuned and more mentalized thinking may be more possible. The aim is to enable more accurate information to be passed outwards from a very chaotic and overwhelming situation so that it can be digested and acted upon in a timely, effective, and therapeutic way.

Before we describe each of the steps involved in Thinking Together, we will offer an analogy to explain the theory. In trainings, this has been used for some time to clarify a key point that we are making about anxiety; in particular, we are interested in the relation between its proximity and our mentalizing capacity, especially as it relates to dialogue about a case.

Ripples analogy: The view from the edge of the pond

When a stone hits still water, at the exact point of impact there is (mathematically speaking) chaos. There is no predictable pattern to the mass of ripples that are generated, and no amount of science could predict where each one might be and where it might be heading. This is not so different from the situation that a worker experiences when they are close to a client in crisis. Further out, however (and this is not a bad example of chaos theory), the jumble and energy of the impact reliably resolve into concentric ripples, each one of a reasonably predictable size, traveling in predictable directions, and at predictable speeds (see Figure 5.2). For the worker "in the middle" with a client, hit by any number of worries or other powerful emotions, it is always hard (and perhaps impossible) to make complete sense of things (i.e. to mentalize). However, for a colleague or supervisor "on the bank", although they inevitably miss out on crucial details of the visceral reality that their colleague is experiencing, the larger patterns emerging from the chaos may be much more visible; less troubled by anxiety, they are more able to mentalize. These two perspectives—from the turbulent and chaotic point of impact, and from the more tranquil riverbank—are together much more informative than either one is alone.

Figure 5.2 Ripples in a pond: the view from the edge of the pond.
Photo by Dickon Bevington.

The point of supervisory structures is to create a discourse that combines these perspectives so that some purposeful course can be set by, for, or with the worker in the middle. How can information be most reliably transferred from where the turbulence is greatest to where perspective-taking is more possible, so that useful new information can be returned to where it is most needed? What follows is a disciplined four-step approach to conducting these kinds of conversations that we suggest offers the best odds of achieving this.

The four steps of Thinking Together

1. **Marking the Task**—marking this out as a Thinking Together discussion and inviting the worker to mentalize themselves in defining the desired outcomes.
2. **Stating the Case**—conveying the key information that needs to be communicated.
3. **Mentalizing the Moment**—describing "what this is like for me, here, now"; "what might be going on for X and Y . . ."
4. **Returning to Purpose**—bringing the discussion back to the task set out at the beginning and what needs doing now.

Marking the Task

An air traffic controller told a story about noticing, when he was working in the control tower one day, that a plane just taking off had flames pouring out of one of its engines. He recounted how his training "came to life" and he calmly spoke to the pilot thus: "Be advised, there are flames coming from your starboard engine. *What are your intentions?*"

Why would he phrase his intervention like this? We would like to suggest that this is not far from Marking the Task. In that simple phrase, "What are your intentions?" he packed a lot in: he assumed that the pilot, although presumably afraid and weighed down by responsibility and technical challenges, still had a mind, and had personal agency. By inviting the pilot first to consider his/her own intentions, he was kick-starting the pilot's own mentalizing, which in the circumstances would likely be under great stress. Without overdoing it, he was also insisting that what was to follow would be a thoughtful, professional, and boundaried relationship in which the pilot was still the pilot. He was also clarifying the ways in which he, as an observer with a different set of skills and authorities, might be called upon to help through their relationship in the crucial minutes ahead.

Thinking Together in AMBIT work generally begins with a request from one worker to a colleague (or colleagues) for help with a particular situation or case. This request needs to be explicit and differentiated from other general requests for help about practical or organizational matters (where there is less clouding of the matter in hand by worry). The request here is for help in understanding something more fully, such as a worker's feelings about a client, or the client's puzzling behavior or statements, or the degree of risk that is being presented and the reasonableness of the plans in place. So the process starts with a marked request—by asking someone "Can we think together?"—which indicates that this particular collaborative exercise is what is requested. Some shared "marker" that all team members will recognize is therefore required. We happen to have called this "Thinking Together"; any other phrase, so long as its meaning is shared between all members of the team, could signal that a specific kind of communicating is being requested. Teams may wish to agree on their own name to mark the introduction of this disciplined way of communicating, a simple form of words that carry a shared meaning as part of the team culture (one team agreed to call this process "Professional Conversations"). What is important is that these rituals or social disciplines are explicitly agreed, rather than just being implicitly assumed to be in place. For example, a team member may say, "Can we think together about a current case that is bothering me?" Some staff who have been trained in AMBIT have found this initially awkward and artificial, replacing something that apparently happened naturally with additional and unnecessary rules and formality. We recognize that this may be the experience of some team members, and can only suggest that this is explored further by practicing it a few times and then reflecting together as a team about how this is experienced.

As practitioners, we talk about our clients in all kinds of ways and in all kinds of places. Sometimes we talk simply because the work is fascinating and intellectually intriguing, sometimes because we need to clarify how we feel about something, sometimes because we have quite a specific sense that something is not quite right, and so on. In our experience, conversations in this territory very commonly take place *without any such marking*. When one worker simply starts to talk, their colleague may quite gradually begin to pick up that this person seems a bit "out of balance" in their experience of the situation, perhaps a little uncertain or worried, and might then begin to wonder precisely what it is (about what is often a complex story) that is worrying them, and what kind of help they may be asking for. While this mentalizing on the part of the listener is going on, simultaneously they need to attend to the content of what they are hearing. That is a lot to ask.

Marking the Task is about highlighting that this conversation is important and that the worker really wants some help, and to ensure that collectively the worker and their colleague(s) make best use of the time required for conversation. There is always a risk that one worker's capacity to mentalize what their colleague is actually requesting, and why, may not be accurate. A colleague may view the conversation as just "having a chat" while the worker is actually requesting a very serious discussion about important clinical material that they are worried about. So, the process of marking helps to ensure that both workers clearly recognize the task in which they are engaging.

What do we mean by *marking*? The use of the term "marking" draws on the theory of marked mirroring and ostensive communication that explains how mentalizing develops through interactions with caregivers across infancy (see Chapter 2). In Marking the Task, the worker takes responsibility for (or is quite firmly invited into) mentalizing, just as the pilot in the scenario outlined above was, from the very beginning, invited into clarifying their intentions as the person in the hot seat; it has been described as "kick-starting the worker's mentalizing." By this we mean that Thinking Together has a fairly tough "outer shell"—a gentle but firm insistence that this conversation is, as far as possible, going to use mentalized understandings of the minds involved, starting with the worker. Hence, the worker is first helped in the task of establishing with clarity their communicative intentions: "What am I asking for help with, and why?"

This could be seen as turning the conversation upside down and starting with the ending, defining the intentions or goals of this interaction ("What would it look like at the end of this conversation if it had achieved its purpose?"), and thus minimizing the likelihood of misunderstandings about what is being asked for. In practice, this can sometimes be achieved very quickly (if teams use this approach consistently, their members will know that in order to get going they need to do this basic mentalizing, and will more likely come prepared), but sometimes it can be surprisingly hard. By Marking the Task for a discussion we mean saying something that explicitly delineates what is wanted out of the conversation. Simple marking statements range from the general to the specific, and we encourage specificity:

> "This is important. I'd really value your help with this case for the next ten minutes."
> "I would really appreciate your help here. A few minutes of Thinking Together might help me work this out better."
> "I'd like to think together, and the task is to check whether my risk assessment is still reasonable after what happened over the weekend."

Marking the Task is a collaborative process Marking the Task is not something that one person can do on their own—it requires the active collaboration of the worker and their colleague. Nor, as we have mentioned, is it easy to do if either party does not have a basic understanding of the steps involved and the point of using them. Although the worker will generally initiate the process, as described above, this is a joint task between the worker and their colleague, in which both parties actively need to clarify what this conversation is for.

Managing resistance to Marking the Task For the colleague approached by a worker, this can often feel like trying to stop a train in its tracks, as the worker may well convey a preoccupied or stressed state of mind and may start by narrating all sorts of recent events—who said what to whom, the risks, and the complexities—before it has been established why the colleague needs to know this. Of all the four steps in the Thinking Together "dance," Marking the Task is the most challenging. For the colleague who is being consulted, it may be necessary to be very active and explicit, even firm, in requesting that the worker really stops for a moment and thinks about what they want (this is the most forceful example of "kick-starting mentalizing"). For a worried worker, being asked to "mark the task" can easily feel like an obstructive interruption just as they are getting into their flow, and the consulting colleague may need to rise to this, mirroring the intensity of their feelings by reminding them that they want to be helpful, and they need this clarity in order to be helpful. Thus, Marking the Task is almost the opposite of just listening, as it involves actively collaborating with the worker to establish very clear boundaries (of task and of time) before they can begin to engage in the more reflective and less event-focused mentalizing that comes later in the sequence. The sort of things a colleague might say are:

> "Can we just stop a minute? I can see that this is important, and I want to be clear so I can help—are you asking me to think together with you? You see, I'm not quite sure if I've grasped the task for me quite yet—what it is you're asking me to do with what you are trying to tell me?"
>
> "This sounds very important but what are you hoping to get from the next ten minutes of us talking this over? How would I know if I'd really helped with this issue? Take a breath and try to help me understand this first!"
>
> "I do get it that what you're talking about is stressing you. Let's put the client aside for a moment and just think what would be helpful for you right here, right now. I want to be helpful but I need a clearer understanding of the task for me. Help me mark the task."

Defining other boundaries of the task Thinking Together is an attempt to recreate—for workers in high-pressure, quick-fire, and mobile jobs—some of the safety that the boundaries of a fixed appointment time, a consistent consulting room, and a clearly defined patient–therapist relationship are designed to provide in formal therapy. That is why the conversation "front-loads" the boundaries; of course, unless a worker knows that further into the process there will be an explicit attempt to create space for thinking and feeling, it can feel quite tough (or "clunky," as one trainee put it.) Once the conversation has become more balanced, both the worker and the colleague may need to agree other boundaries of time, space, and authority. For instance, once the outcome that the worker seeks is clear, they may need to clarify how long they both have (Thinking Together could shape a ten-minute conversation in a corridor, or a one-hour group or individual supervision), whether their physical location is good enough for the job (it can be conducted by phone with a worker in a park, in a car, in a corridor, or in more formal settings), or whether they have the authority to make the decision that they have agreed needs to be made. Together, the two parties should work to address some of the following points:

- What would a satisfactory outcome of this discussion look like?

  - Is there a key issue that needs a decision (and do we have the authority to make this, or are we deciding whether to take this up to a manager, etc.)?
  - Is there an area of confusion that needs a better framework for understanding it?
  - Is there a crisis that needs an emergency management plan to ensure safety (even if only for the next few hours)?
  - Is there a wish for some "venting" of feelings (with the intention that these feelings can be better "named" and understood)?

- Do we have enough time (now? later?) to do this?
- Is our physical location suited to letting us get on with this?
- Are we "quorate" (do we, together, have the authority) to make the decisions that we agree need to be made?

Once these things have been established, it is possible to proceed to the next step. However, this may take more than a few minutes; it can easily feel that this is time not being well spent, and that "we should be getting on with talking about the case." Our view, however, is that time spent actively planning (see Chapter 3 for in-depth description of this) in this way is a crucial investment; if successful, it helps to punctuate a worker's (let us assume, rather non-mentalizing) flow of thoughts, set the minutes that follow in a more mentalized context, and put the colleague who is being asked for help in the strongest possible position to deliver on this request. When the colleague has more clarity about what they are being asked for help with, they can listen with much more focused attention to what follows.

Stating the Case

It is important for the worker and their colleague to clarify what the simple "bones" of the story or problem are. They need to focus on delineating what needs to be covered in order to be able to address the issue agreed in Marking the Task. The worker needs to consider "What information does my colleague need in order to help me with the task we have agreed?"

There is never time to tell the whole story, so the worker must act as an editor, trying to represent to the best of their ability the situation in question, but in an abbreviated form. Over-long "storytelling" in the context of a task-focused and time-limited conversation such as this may easily reveal a form of pretend mode thinking. There is a need to provide sufficient information to convey the richness and complexity of the story, but without coming out with an overwhelming "sea" of facts. At times, in speaking about a case, we may be drawn into adding detail that connects facts and adds to the overall coherence of the narrative. This is tempting, and almost inevitable if we are to help our colleague form a three-dimensional picture of the client being described. However, it is important that, if we do find ourselves doing this, we mark the fact that this is our interpretation or hypothesis quite explicitly:

> "Now, this is my assumption, rather than anything Jane has directly said to me, but it seems that after her difficult experience with her father she went on to get into a series of other difficult relationships with older men."

The colleague who has agreed to join the worker in Thinking Together should broadly "allow them the floor" for this phase. However, this is not the same as sitting back passively. The colleague has effectively contracted to hold the speaker to the agreed boundaries of task and time, so they have a duty to interrupt if the worker is simply not clear on details, or if they feel the worker (perhaps driven by anxiety) is drifting into over-inclusivity. This is common, and it may be necessary to point out: "Hey, do we need to keep to the simple bones here... is this getting into storytelling?" Equally, the worker giving the account needs to hold on to this shared understanding of the task, so that such prompts are not taken as criticisms.

Thinking Together requires a degree of trust, and allows for conversations that might be seen in other environments as blunt or accelerated. In the team that, following AMBIT's principled stance, is "well connected," workers should hope, over time, to develop sufficient knowledge of each other so as to understand the individual variations in how each member works best within these broad constraints. By establishing these quite tough boundaries around the task, the time, and the content, the worker and colleague seek to create security. What makes this business-like start to the conversation more possible is the knowledge that there is an explicitly delineated step ahead, which is markedly different in pace and tone. We call this next step "Mentalizing the Moment."

Mentalizing the Moment

In a powerful sense, the first two and the final (fourth) step in the Thinking Together process are designed deliberately to hold open between them the space that this third step attempts to create. In Mentalizing the Moment the aim is for the worker who has just stated the case to be steadied enough by the mentalizing presence of their partner to allow them to mentalize more accurately. This step is also sometimes known as "Mentalizing the Affect," as it is here that engagement with the *emotional* content is encouraged. This primary focus on the mind of the *worker* is key to the value in Thinking Together: the task is to restore the mentalizing of the worker, rather than to leap straight into mentalizing and working out a plan for the client or family. Thus, first of all, the colleague's attention is directed toward mentalizing the worker rather than the client (to state the obvious, the client is not present, but the worker is—mentalizing the client can come later). It is like the advice in the safety message before a flight: "In the event of a sudden loss of air pressure, oxygen masks will drop automatically from above your head. If you are responsible for a child be sure to place your own mask on first, before attending to the child." Here, mentalizing is a good substitute for oxygen—without it, the worker is very unlikely to be able to help their client.

This is not about selfishness; it is about ensuring that our best intentions to help are supported by intact thinking. The ritualized, marked, and boundaried "dance" that these steps describe gives the worker permission to discuss their own emotional reactions, and reflections upon their thinking, alongside those reported by the client or family. The intention is to purposefully create a temporary hiatus of calmer musing, acting "as if" there were no strict time constraints (although of course there are), allowing for the play of ideas, and fostering a more curious and exploratory kind of thinking that moves from the worker and extends out to the client. For an external observer, one might hope to see a noticeable "change of gear" in the atmosphere, so that this section of the conversation does not compulsively shut down real thinking on the grounds that the professionals should "already know the answer," or that further thinking would somehow be indulgent when "it is action that is now required" (this last version would be a good example of teleological thinking).

So here, the colleague who is offering help may first try to briefly summarize and offer back their perspective and reflections upon the worker's dilemma as they have perceived it. To return to our analogy of ripples in a pond, it is as though in "Stating the Case" the story of a client and their worker's dilemma has been passed outwards from the chaotic and turbulent point of impact to the colleague, who is less exposed ("on the bank," so to speak); being somewhat protected from the immediate impact of affect, this helping colleague is likely to be more able to mentalize and make sense of the difficult experience in context. In this "reflecting back," the helper's aim is to try voluntarily and temporarily to place themself in the middle of the "pond" (where the worker actually is). In doing so, the helper offers the worker a temporary seat "on the bank," watching them try to capture the dilemma in words and expressions that (if successful) will give the worker the sense that their specific (and perhaps until now rather isolating) dilemma has been recognized. The helper's intention, of course, is to generate (or add to existing) epistemic trust (i.e. trust in communication; see Chapter 2) in the worker toward them. As the helping colleague shows them that their dilemma may be understandable, the worker is invited to join in acknowledging, clarifying, and naming their own feeling states, which may or may not be a direct reaction to the client's dilemma. The worker is encouraged to mark these feelings as their own.

Colleague: "OK, let's just change gear for a moment. Let's take a breath, mentalize a bit! I've been listening to you and although I probably only get a fraction of the reality, I can really see this is exhausting, and frustrating—it seems to me that you really want to help X, but it feels as though you're being pushed away at every opportunity. Wow, this is tough stuff, I'd imagine feeling pretty bruised in this position."

Worker: "My own emotional reaction is despair; on hearing myself tell this story I find myself thinking that giving up is the only option . . . and that makes me feel horrible, like I'm not just a failure but not a very caring person."

Mentalizing the affect means being able to feel a feeling and simultaneously to mentalize this experience. So, although the feeling in the here and now is a potential barrier to thinking, an *awareness* of it may also provide crucial information for the worker—even if only to acknowledge the likely impact that this strength of feeling may have on their evaluation of risk, planning, and other tasks. Remember that one of the features of accurate, active, successful mentalizing is contemplation and reflection—the desire to reflect on how others (or oneself) are thinking in a relaxed rather than a compulsive manner.

After this initial focus on the worker's state of mind, it may be helpful for both helper and worker to spend some time mentalizing the client's behavior, looking for new perspectives that might have been missed in the chaos and pressure of the moment.

The interval provided by "Mentalizing the Moment" is thus an important space to allow current states of mind to be acknowledged, in order to allow more accurate assessments of the changing levels and nature of risk, as well as therapeutic opportunities, to emerge. Our hypothesis is that with more accurate mentalizing at work in the system, risks are reduced.

It should be noted that there are strong similarities between this process and Mentalizing the Moment in the Mentalizing Loop (see Chapter 4), which we use in mentalizing approaches to therapy/exploration with clients and their families. Effectively, this is exactly the same process, but applied to case discussions with colleagues.

Returning to Purpose

At the end of the Thinking Together exercise, there needs be a return to the overarching task, and it is again part of the consulting colleague's "contracted" responsibility to ensure that this is delivered in a timely way. How this "Returning to Purpose" is played out will depend largely on the nature of the task that was marked at the beginning of the exercise; in many cases this may involve facilitation of the worker's own thinking and planning about their next steps, while in others it may result in some form of delegation, or a straightforward instruction if the consulting colleague is also a senior team member whose responsibility and authority include this role. Alternatively, there may be an agreement about an interim plan ("You'll call the parents, and get these extra bits of information in the next couple of hours …") with a more comprehensive mechanism for resolution set in motion ("… then we'll meet with the team leader at 4 pm to make a final decision about informing the police or not").

In this respect it is helpful to remember the "START" criteria around any piece of work, so that it is protected by boundaries of:

- **Space** (Where are we doing this? Is it appropriately safe and private?)
- **Time** (How long have we got?)
- **Authority** (Do I have it for this piece of work?)
- **Responsibility** (Should it be me doing this, or someone else?)
- **Task** (What am I doing, and how would I know when I had been successful?).

All Thinking Together conversations have a task that relates back to the search for some kind of "product" (a decision, an intervention, an understanding, a different state of mind, etc.) that ultimately offers promise as help for the client/family. The previous stage is a deliberate suspension of this task-focus, to enable what we refer to as "the curious exploratory play of ideas." So, to end the exercise, there must be a return to purpose. If no progress is made—if a decision cannot be made, or an understanding is not reached—then the workers may decide they need to resort to formal supervisory structures and/or emergency procedures, or they may be able to agree a process to carry forward their thinking to, say, one of the next team meetings.

In feedback from AMBIT-trained teams, the exercise of Thinking Together is consistently rated as one of the most useful techniques in the AMBIT model. Teams have consistently commented that Thinking Together has enabled teams to reduce time spent on case discussions and reduce repetitive themes, and for discussions to take place that enable workers to recognize states of mind and shift their thinking in response to this.

For some teams, the Thinking Together method has been adopted in team meetings to discuss cases; for others it is a method employed when phoning a colleague in the course of a home visit intervention. However, it is also important to recognize that the technique involves a significant shift of practice for many teams; the explicit recognition of workers' own states of mind may prove to be a new and potentially exposing aspect of good practice. There is little doubt that some workers are more comfortable with this level of intimacy in work than others (the same could be said of the AMBIT principle of the "well-connected team" as a whole) and that there is a need for routine team practices (team meetings, supervision) to provide opportunities to practice such techniques. Otherwise, the tendency to revert to previous habitual practices remains high. The AMBIT web-based manual (available via https://manuals.annafreud.org/—follow the links to AMBIT) contains considerable information and numerous video examples of this practice, which can be viewed alongside the accounts given in this book.

Graded assertiveness: Intervening when a colleague is *not* asking for help, but concerns arise

Thinking Together is all very well if a colleague asks explicitly for help with a problem, or is obviously upset about an issue (in which case, even though they may not have volunteered to use Thinking Together to clarify a way forward, they may agree to the process once their discomfort has been sympathetically acknowledged). However, what about the scenario in which a worker becomes concerned for a colleague or about aspects of their practice, but there is no acknowledgement of any problem on that person's part? In this situation, there is a different task—to find a way to stop and reflect—which involves assertiveness. The problem is all the more acute if there is a difference in seniority or power between the worker and the colleague they are concerned about. How do you challenge your boss? How does an administrator or youth worker challenge a clinical psychologist or doctor, whose specialist skills may be intimidating? Of course, it should almost go without saying that the capacity for a team to allow for transparent inquiry and challenge across all levels and grades is critical to safety.

There are ample examples of exactly the same issues arising within the airline industry (an industry that, above any other, has led the way in the creation of learning organizations, and from which AMBIT draws much inspiration). Matthew Syed (2016) has recently published a very readable book on this, drawing out the similarities and differences between how the airline industry learns from mistakes, and how the worlds of medicine and social care frequently do not—for example, cabin crew who could not find it in themselves to tell the pilot he had shut down the wrong engine (the working one, rather than the burning one) despite the fact that they could see both engines, while the pilot could not; a junior navigator who could not convince the pilot and co-pilot that their lengthy efforts to check whether or not the landing gear had correctly deployed, while admirable and understandable, were less critical than the fact that the plane was running out of fuel. Thanks to the existence of "black boxes" in airplanes, the conversations leading up to these (and other) disasters could be analyzed, demonstrating two things: in the language of AMBIT, there was a failure to mentalize (what could also be described as "perceptual narrowing") on the part of the pilots, but it was also the case that the crew's deference to seniority and expertise, fear of embarrassment if wrong, and fear of recrimination from their seniors were significant barriers to their raising a concern that could have saved lives.

As a result, and in keeping with the way in which a learning organization works (see Chapter 7 for AMBIT's take on this), the airline industry developed social rituals or disciplines to support staff to make such challenges, known as Crew Resource Management. A number of models of "graded assertive communication" drawn from this model are now being taught in a variety of medical settings, such as in intensive care units and during surgery (Sutcliffe et al., 2004), of which two are referred to by the acronyms PACE and CUSS (reflecting the name of each level of intervention in the model—see Table 5.1). Both of these models consist of four escalating levels of intervention by one team member to another worker in the event of concerns arising about their practice. Each stage is marked by the use of different language as the level of assertiveness increases, with an expectation that (barring obvious and critical threats) a worker would usually start at the lowest level and build up to the highest. As in Thinking Together, a team that has collectively accepted, adopted, and rehearsed these four steps is at an advantage, as the keywords used can act as helpful triggers, reminding the recipient of the essentially benign purpose of the intervention. Table 5.1 maps the four levels of assertive intervention across both systems, which are very similar.

Translating this into the context of AMBIT's principled stance, which focuses on the necessity of a "well-connected team," we would want to emphasize our team's cultural presumption of human fallibility that is at the heart of our understanding of mentalizing—which itself is fragile. The assumption in AMBIT is that in doing this work with our clients we are all placing ourselves in a field of immense complexity and, potentially, high risk. It is well documented that serious untoward incidents are rarely attributable to single acts of monumental carelessness, but are much more commonly the result of an accumulation of small errors that were allowed to go unchecked. In such a situation, it is risky to think anything other than that, in this work, we are all constantly losing—or at imminent risk of losing—our balance. So it is the feedback from our colleagues of their "on the bank" perspectives, given via clear and non-punitive communication, that enables us to make the multiple (and small, if we get there in time) adjustments and rebalancing movements in order to avoid a calamitous fall. These graded assertive interventions, as in Thinking Together, are no less important than the ropes holding mountaineers safely together in treacherous settings, and it is important for team members to remind each other of their benign intentions in using them.

For the lower levels of assertiveness described in Table 5.1, if the worker whose practice is causing concern is able to step back and reflect on their intervening colleague's perspective, then Thinking Together to clarify an appropriate alternative response might be the most appropriate vehicle for this thinking.

Table 5.1 Graded assertiveness: the PACE and CUSS systems

Level	PACE	CUSS	Notes
1	Probe	Concern	This is the lowest level of assertiveness. Here, the worker offers a question (probe) that models a tentative, not-knowing mentalizing stance but also offers their own mentalized sense of being concerned to know the answer: "I may have misunderstood this, but I'm **concerned** that you might be taking a lot of calls from X out of hours" or "I just wanted to **probe** a bit to check things are OK in how you and X are working together?"
2	Alert	Uncertainty	Raising their assertiveness, the worker shares (alerts the colleague to) their own uncertainty about whether what is happening is OK: "I want to **alert** us to the fact that the relationship between you and X seems to be getting very intense, which we know is risky" or "I'm feeling **uncertain** about whether you might be becoming quite seriously isolated with this."
3	Challenge	Safety	At this stage, the worker is clear that in their mind there is a real threat, and the intervention is more explicitly challenging, making reference to the lack of safety in the situation as it is perceived: "I think we need to **challenge** the assumption that only you can help X, as to me this relationship is now clearly outside normal professional boundaries" or "The way this relationship is working seems **unsafe** to me; at the very least it puts you at risk of being accused of professional misconduct, and it may be harmful for X."
4	Emergency	Stop	This is the highest level of assertiveness, calling for very clear and blunt communication: "I am calling this as an **emergency** now, until we can get clarification on what is going on and how best to support X and you safely" or "You need to **stop** taking calls from X, and we need to talk to a manager."

Supervision

Supervision is a component of good practice, although the degree and structure of supervision may vary radically across teams. In our view, unless supervisory systems within teams adopt and support at least some key parts of the AMBIT approach, the approach will not be sustained by worker initiatives alone. This can prove complicated if existing formal supervision arrangements are with professionals working in separate teams with very specific and different models of practice, but in that case the team may offer a local training session to their supervisors, which may actually create a powerful learning opportunity for team members themselves (based on the principle that there is no better way to learn about something than to explain it to someone else).

In this section we suggest a number of ways in which supervision could be adapted to include explicit AMBIT principles and practice. However, we wish to recognize that supervision prior to AMBIT training is likely to already include components of mentalizing. It would be odd if it were otherwise, as probably all forms of supervision include some element of aiming to recognize the states of mind of the worker and the client in any case discussion. In this way, we do not wish to suggest that mentalizing is particularly new or should be seen as some additional burden; rather, it may be helpful to make sense of what works in existing supervision through the lens of mentalizing, as well as sharing some common language and practices within the team. Similarly, we recognize that most methods of supervision involve creating a relationship of trust between the supervisee and supervisor, which would be entirely consistent with our understanding of the role of kindling epistemic trust—trust in communication—in processes of help-seeking. It is abundantly clear that these features of effective practice are already widely recognized and delivered without the necessity of having to read academic papers on the developmental science underlying this form of trust.

For AMBIT, a realistic aim is to build on existing structures and processes rather than insist on wholesale reorganization. Are there any specific AMBIT "slants" to the supervisory process? Wherever possible, the intention is to try explicitly to ensure that the needs of the supervisee are being effectively met (because they are in the room with the supervisor, and the client is not) and to make these processes as productive, concise, transparent, and focused as can be achieved. One obvious application of AMBIT techniques is the use of the Thinking Together process in supervision. Most supervision practice involves reviewing a number of cases that the supervisee may be concerned about; compared with other models, the Thinking Together approach may reduce unnecessary descriptions and focus more on the worker's states of mind in such a way that this links to clarifying actions.

A second approach is the AMBIT Practice Audit Tool (APrAT), which is designed to be used as a way of systematically reviewing cases (see the AMBIT manual for more details). This tool, which makes use of a short set of questions, simply invites workers to consider whether they have been mindful of all four quadrants of the AMBIT approach in their work with a client. In our experience, it is very easy for workers to become preoccupied with one area of work (such as engaging with one of the client's parents) at the expense of considering other domains (helping the client to make sense of traumatic memories, or maintaining positive links with social services), which may have equal value in addressing the client's life difficulties. There may be good face-to-face work with clients, and evidence of a well-connected team, but a significant and unaddressed problem in the functioning of the wider service network. The value of the APrAT is in enabling the supervisor and supervisee to hold a "wide-angle" lens to the work—in particular, to become aware of areas that may not be currently highlighted as a result of the usual reactive dramas of the client's life, but are nonetheless crucial to the progress of the work. In general, one of the functions of supervision for workers engaged with this client group is to be able to step back temporarily from immediate preoccupations about risk and unpredictability, which may dominate the worker's experience of trying to help a client, to allow them to think about the wider trajectory of the intervention.

A third way of reassessing the client's progress and development would be to review the AMBIT Pro-Gram (described in detail in Chapter 6) if this was completed by the client at some point in the early stages of the work. The Pro-Gram is a simple graphical way of representing a client's helping network that highlights their perception of the quality and extent of helpfulness in each relationship. Reviewing this "map" of a client's professional and informal relationships may indicate the degree to which the position of the client with respect to helping agencies has shifted in any particular way, and how such change (or lack of change) can be understood. Assuming that the longer-term aim is to try to establish a helping ecology that is sustainable after the AMBIT worker's involvement has finished (in line with the AMBIT principle of "Scaffolding existing relationships"), it may be very useful to review who may be being experienced by the client as increasingly helpful through the joint agency work that is ongoing.

A fourth tool that may be useful in supervision when discussing joint agency or multi-professional work is the Dis-Integration Grid (described in detail in Chapter 6), which essentially offers a tool to support systematic mentalizing across the professional and informal network around a client.

Jack is a young client who is beginning to establish a more trusting relationship with his older sister, who lives in the same neighborhood and who has provided a place for Jack to stay occasionally when he has had a row with his father, with whom he lives. These rows happen periodically, usually related to alcohol use by either Jack or his father. Before the AMBIT-trained team became involved, these rows tended to result in a chaotic pattern of Jack being on the streets for a few nights and getting involved with gang-related peers, resulting in sustained alcoholic binges and sometimes attendance at the hospital emergency department. More recently, Jack's sister has agreed to him staying overnight at her place when their father has been drinking, on the condition that Jack does not drink at her flat. Over the past two months, this had worked sufficiently well to reduce Jack's emergency hospital attendance to zero.

In supervision, a new focus arose on whether there might be other family or educational staff who could also be engaged, further extending Jack's "back-up team."

Lastly, supervision may be enhanced through consideration of the AMBIT Integrative Measure (AIM) assessment (described in Chapter 3). This comprehensive overview of a client's circumstances and difficulties may benefit from being jointly reviewed by the worker with their supervisor. A common challenge for a supervisor is to enable a worker to pick out small positive changes (that could be built upon) amid the client's chaotic life conditions, which threaten to blind workers to potential strengths and resilience factors. For example, it is not uncommon to hear in supervision about a client's self-harming behavior, and for this to take up a considerable amount of supervision time, but then to be reported, toward the end of the conversation, that the client had attended college for two days during the same week. The client may not have been attending college at all before the AMBIT team became involved. The potential for the college attendance to be lost from sight amid the more emotionally salient (and understandably preoccupying) issues around the client's self-harm is high. The value of reviewing the client's progress against the AIM is that this may well highlight areas of change in the client's life that have not been focused on in the direct work. This also includes recognizing where things may have deteriorated—for example, an unrecognized but worsening sleep problem.

What characterizes these different aspects of supervision is the effort to move thinking from events to patterns, to draw workers away from the frontline battles in order to reflect on what is driving the war. The assumption is that this process may also involve reducing exaggerated feelings of responsibility in the worker and developing realistic expectations of change, based on the client's previous history. These processes are intended to create conditions that enable the supervisee to mentalize their own state of mind in relation to the case in a more dispassionate (or less self-critical) way than may be possible without the connection with a trusted colleague.

Limitations and challenges

There is no doubt that the AMBIT approach presents many major challenges for a newly trained team. We will highlight three such challenges here.

AMBIT can be seen as an external model imposed on the team

AMBIT is a whole-team approach. The aim is to create an explicit shared team culture in which a number of key aspects of practice are agreed, understood, and supported. However, in practice, the team coming to AMBIT training may easily feel that their existing methods of work are being replaced by some externally imposed model of working or, worse, that there is some implied criticism of their existing practice and expertise. The degree to which such team training implies criticism of current ways of working is a particularly sensitive point. Although the training narrative can be based around improvement and investment in improving workers' skills, team members may easily feel disinclined to adopt new methods of working that have not arisen out of their own valued expertise. Although AMBIT aims to validate the expertise of team members and local services, the experience of training can easily be off-putting for workers who may feel that the trainers do not really understand the environment in which the team operates.

In regard to the principled AMBIT stance of showing "respect for local practice and expertise," there is clearly a parallel between how the team does this in relation to their work, and how the AMBIT training team does it in relation to the trainees.

Acknowledging variability in enthusiasm about AMBIT within the team

A second aspect of whole-team training is that there will inevitably be a mixture of enthusiasts and skeptics in the group. For it to be otherwise would be unnatural. In our training of teams we explicitly mark and recognize this, making efforts to reposition the skeptics into positions that allow them to have a valid voice, testing the ideas and practices espoused by AMBIT against the reality of work in this setting. In some ways, the trainers model skepticism of the AMBIT approach as a way of mirroring this inevitable aspect of team functioning. Apart from varying levels of enthusiasm for (or irritation with) mentalizing theory, we know from positioning theory that, within any group, there will be an adaptive process across which team members position themselves in relation to each other and the trainers in a variety of ways. The varying positions taken up by different workers may in some ways mirror the stance of the client group with which the team works; some workers will extol their belief in other frameworks and the value of their own independent knowledge and individual experience (mirroring the adolescent striving to find their own mind), while others may wish to be positioned as wanting to be part of a group process (mirroring the desire for absorption and socialization as part of a gang). Although these aspects of training a whole team can be anticipated and named, the actual experience of the training will vary: these differing positions can result in a team moving forward (particularly if space is made for reflection, and emphasis given to the value for teams of being able to tolerate thinking across differences), or the initiative for change may be subtly but effectively paralyzed.

Some team members are occasionally found to be rather influential and powerful critics of this group effort at change, and it is easy to view such individuals in rather definite and teleological terms ("If only X would just stop criticizing and challenging the trainers and get with the program!"). This non-mentalizing stance is unlikely to be helpful or successful, and may overlook an important warning about the need for local adaptations to be made, or the need to recognize and respect local expertise. Powerful individuals who take a more critical position in relation to the team process of training may in fact be helpfully included by inviting them to deliver or design some aspect of training in which they may be recognized as having particular expertise.

An often-quoted phrase is that "there is no such thing as an AMBIT team," by which we mean to emphasize the fact that AMBIT offers only a framework of some evidence-based practice and principles, some evidence-oriented practice and principles, and the invitation for teams to make explicitly marked adaptations to these practices and principles to fit their own practice-based evidence, guided wherever possible by learning from local outcomes.

Team culture and mentalizing

Mentalizing is a tricky concept that can stimulate a range of reactions, from the positively enthusiastic to "this is something we do already" (true) to "this is something that's a bit weird to make such a big deal about" (which might also be true). For some teams, the language of "mentalizing" exacerbates this, as the word feels alien and unnatural to many frontline workers. Even those who like the ideas can find the use of the word "mentalizing" somewhat uncomfortable. In AMBIT, the aim is to put the process (but not necessarily the name) at the center of our efforts to be helpful to our clients. As part of this, a team does need to find a language by which the process can be named, nurtured, and developed. This problem resulted in the naming of the technique of Thinking Together as trying to clearly mark a definite process while at the same time using ordinary language.

At the center of this rests a quandary. It can be too easy to avoid the problem by being overly casual and informal, so that mentalizing comes to mean little more than inviting people to say how they feel—which is wildly inadequate, diminishing the concept to the extent that the whole framework lacks definition. Chapter 2 will, we hope, have made clear that mentalizing involves a lot more meaning-making, or narrative-creating, than simply understanding the feelings involved. However, too rigid an application of alien words and outside knowledge can result in the process becoming a matter of compliance with something applied externally rather than a psychologically salient function. We justify using the word "mentalizing" because there is no other word that quite captures the activity of mind that it defines; because it "does what it says" (it is about attributing a *mentality* as the driver of behaviors); and because we are all mental (to be otherwise is to be *mindless*), and in so reminding us, the use of the verb "to mentalize" may play a tiny role in reducing the damaging stigma attached to mental health.

Maintaining momentum

In our experience, despite extremely positive feedback from the trainees we have been working with over the years, teams navigate between these rocks with varying degrees of success; our experience of training approaching 200 teams suggests it is unlikely that a team will reach a comfortable equilibrium quickly. For many teams this process may take anything up to a year following the initial training. Achieving cultural change in a team is hard work, and it is easy to return to old habits or lose the momentum for change. If a team is likened to the crew of a small boat, there are very often powerful organizational and political gales blowing that can leave our relatively subtle "navigational skills" training with little room to maneuver.

The AMBIT training involves recognition that some members of a team are more suited than others (by virtue of personality, role, and authority, among other factors) to becoming purposeful "culture carriers" for a team. With this in mind, we have created the role of *AMBIT Leads* for such people (in other trainings, we have developed this role further to create *Local AMBIT Trainers*). These are a small number (perhaps two or three) of people in a team who are given some additional training in:

- Navigating and using the online AMBIT manual, so that they can help other team members to find and use the wealth of resources there
- Setting up and facilitating brief local practice/training sessions for the team

- Recording local adaptations and learning in the team's local version of the online manual (see Chapter 7)
- A range of approaches to provide gentle reminders of AMBIT principles and prompts for AMBIT-influenced practice.

Often, the last of these points involves very simple practical actions, such as placing a few posters showing the AMBIT wheel or the four steps of Thinking Together on strategic walls in the workplace, or helping team members to save the online AMBIT manual as a bookmark in their web browser so that it is easy to find. Some teams have created a set of cards with the eight AMBIT principles (the "outer ring" of the AMBIT wheel, outlined in Chapter 1) printed on them, and they "deal these out" at the beginning of team meetings so that the holder of each card becomes a temporary monitor for that element of the AMBIT stance during the ensuing discussions. This acts as a regular reminder of the principles the team shares, as well as adding to the sense of containment that the group may offer to its members—that, even if they are temporarily subject to blind spots in the work they present, the team as a whole may be systematically oriented to picking these up. Other teams have a set of cards with the "usual suspects" of a typical extended multi-agency network, which they can use to quickly "sculpt" a specific client's network in a case discussion (mirroring with cards one of the training exercises used to think about working with networks, described in Chapter 6).

Finally, regular sessions of team manualizing (see Chapter 7), in which the team sets aside brief periods of time to discuss work and their practice, making small incremental local additions and edits to pre-existing content in their own local version of the online AMBIT manual, encourage the team to develop its own specific (and increasingly explicit) culture. Local versions of the online AMBIT manual avoid any "branding," encouraging teams to create their own logo and title, for instance; the idea is for the local version to become a "work in progress" that documents a team's increasingly explicit and shared understanding of "who we are, what we do, and why" that can act as a powerful aid to the induction of new team members and a reminder to workers about their collective learning. Our hypothesis, backed up by some research (Wilson, 2007; Najavits et al., 2000; Addis et al., 1999), suggests that workers show more inclination to sustain manualized practice if it is seen as representing local expertise as much as it does remotely generated (and potentially locally inapplicable) evidence.

Conclusions

AMBIT is a whole-team approach for teams working with hard-to-reach clients—predominantly designed for adolescents, but increasingly used with younger and older populations too. Its aim is to support the creation of a team culture that enhances mentalizing, reduces staff isolation, reduces work burden, and fundamentally increases team effectiveness with respect to outcomes for clients.

However, teams comprise individuals with very different approaches to their work and for whom a "team approach" may evoke mixed feelings and reactions. One key aspect of adopting a whole-team approach is to ensure that those who are less enthusiastic about the approach are enabled to mentalize their experience of the model itself. AMBIT and mentalizing cannot simply be a compliance-led approach: the individuality of frontline workers will not allow this. The challenge is to avoid creating a new team orthodoxy, and for all team members to retain a stance of curiosity with respect to each other's authentic experiences, but with sufficient structure and shared understandings to promote safe and effective work. The healthy paradox of this is that it includes accommodating individuals who do not experience mentalizing as a particularly helpful approach; a well-functioning team should be able to allow this opinion to be voiced as well as (we hope) finding small, incremental ways of deepening understanding between workers and enhancing support for better practice. The chief coach of the highly successful British Olympic cycling team in the London 2012 Olympics, Dave Brailsford, came up with a pithy phrase to explain the method that led to the startling success of his team: "The accumulation of marginal gains"—if there was to be a motto for AMBIT, we would probably have to steal this one.

References

Addis, M. E., Wade, W. A., & Hatgis, C. (1999). Barriers to dissemination of evidence-based practices: Addressing practitioners' concerns about manual-based psychotherapies. *Clinical Psychology: Science and Practice* 6: 430–41. doi: 10.1093/clipsy/6.4.430

Carpenter, J. (2003). Working in multidisciplinary community mental health teams: The impact on social workers and health professionals of integrated mental health care. *British Journal of Social Work* 33: 1081–103. doi: 10.1093/bjsw/33.8.1081

Martins, E. C., & Terblanche, F. (2003). Building organisational culture that stimulates creativity and innovation. *European Journal of Innovation Management* 6: 64–74. doi: 10.1108/14601060310456337

Mickan, S., & Rodger, S. (2000). Characteristics of effective teams: A literature review. *Australian Health Review* 23: 201–8.

Najavits, L. M., Weiss, R. D., Shaw, S. R., & Dierberger, A. E. (2000). Psychotherapists' views of treatment manuals. *Professional Psychology: Research and Practice* 31: 404–8. doi: 10.1037/0735-7028.31.4.404

Stanford, N. (2010). *Organisation Culture: Getting it right* (London, UK: The Economist/Profile Books).

Sutcliffe, K. M., Lewton, E., & **Rosenthal**, M. M. (2004). Communication failures: An insidious contributor to medical mishaps. *Academic Medicine* **79**: 186–94.

Syed, M. (2016). *Black Box Thinking* (London, UK: John Murray).

Williams, N. J., & Glisson, C. (2014). Testing a theory of organizational culture, climate and youth outcomes in child welfare systems: A United States national study. *Child Abuse and Neglect* **38**: 757–67. doi: 10.1016/j.chiabu.2013.09.003

Wilson, T. (2007). Manual based treatment: evolution and evaluation. In: T. A. Treat, R. R. Bootzin, & T. B. Baker (eds.), *Psychological Clinical Science: Papers in honor of Richard M. McFall*, pp. 105–132. New York, NY: Psychology Press.

Chapter 6
Working with your networks

Introduction: Whole systems, positions, perspectives, and practice

Working with the network around a client is one of the key aspects of the AMBIT approach. This chapter will begin by presenting the different strands of thinking that provide the platform for a number of specific, practical techniques to enhance network functioning. Our starting point is a recognition that the professional networks around our clients (particularly young people) are often experienced as complicated by the clients, their relatives, and the professionals themselves. It is hard to mentalize the different minds that make up these networks. Complications do not just arise from the fact that many people may be involved in some way with the client, with different models for making sense of their difficulties, but also from the diversity of responsibilities, which can make collaboration a tricky "dance" for everyone. Much of this complexity cannot be completely captured by linear, rational descriptions of how a network *should* function. A broader systems approach that acknowledges the extent and nature of complexity in this territory is essential if we are to make sense of the experience of frontline workers in their efforts to make networks function well (Sloper, 2004).

Let us begin with an example in order to be clear what we mean by a "network." The intention of this example is to show a network that is quite well coordinated and makes clear efforts to work together. Many networks are less coherent than this, but even in this example there are still many challenges.

Jo

Jo was 14 years old and was attending a local mainstream secondary school. He had a previous history of frequent school exclusions that had started in nursery. These exclusions were because of his aggressive behavior toward peers. He would attack other pupils apparently without warning and the attacks had sometimes resulted in serious injuries to the pupil concerned. His parents had refused to agree to Jo attending a Pupil Referral Unit and had successfully challenged this with legal support. The family believed that many of the exclusions were an indication of systematic discrimination against African pupils in the school. Partly because the case created a lot of anxiety for the school and for other agencies, a large number of workers were involved. Jo had a learning support worker and had been referred to a voluntary sector mentoring program and also to an after-school homework club for African youths, also run by a voluntary sector organization. He was discussed at Year 9 Pastoral Care meetings, and the Special Educational Needs Coordinator (SENCO) applied a behavioral management approach in order to provide positive incentives for prosocial behavior. There was intense pressure for Child and Adolescent Mental Health Services (CAMHS) to be involved, and Jo was referred for help with his anger. However, Jo did not believe he had a problem with anger as, in his view, his aggressive behavior resulted from his being "disrespected" by other pupils. The frequency of the problem fluctuated over time but did not systematically improve. The school felt that it was trying to manage very real risks over which it had little real control.

The professional network was well organized, and a meeting was convened by the school each half-term to coordinate the work of the different agencies. This meeting lasted about an hour and was relatively well attended. Each agency would feed back what they had been doing, and at the end there was agreement about when the network would meet next. One member of the group would feed back to the parents, and another would feed back to Jo. What was striking was how little discussion took place in these meetings as to why Jo was behaving like this. Informally, outside of the meetings, this was discussed sporadically, and very different beliefs were expressed—about whether his behavior was due to excessive parental chastisement at home, the influence of his father (who had a criminal record), his difficulties with reading, and also whether he might have a high-functioning autistic spectrum disorder with specific social communication problems.

The lack of a shared formulation across agencies resulted in very different beliefs about what kind of intervention might really be most helpful. For the school, the belief was that Jo should be in a more specialist educational setting, whereas some of the support agencies believed that the problem would lessen if the school could manage Jo in a more flexible way. The involvement of CAMHS (Jo actively engaged in individual sessions following a cognitive-behavioral model) was highly valued by the school, as it supported their view that Jo had exceptional psychological needs. However, staff at the school rarely expressed much curiosity as to how the CAMHS therapist understood Jo's difficulties, and conversely there was little detailed discussion with CAMHS about Jo's work with a learning support teacher or his mentor. The overall impression was that the seriousness of Jo's difficulties required a high amount of different agency input, and that the main task of the network was to coordinate this.

We hope that this represents some themes of complicated network functioning that the reader will find familiar. We know that many networks work less cohesively, and pressures on time may mean that some never meet at all. In this example, the network shared a belief in the need to work together and took a high level of responsibility for the problem. The main network activity was around information-sharing to coordinate each agency's contribution to helping Jo. There was perhaps a collective unstated assumption that "more help" automatically meant "more effective help," and there were repeated calls for more specialist help. The direct work with Jo involved four different workers developing helping relationships with him, and although the explicit purpose of their contact was defined by their respective roles and contexts (such as homework, school behavior, or anger), what was striking was that there was little discussion about what Jo made of all this.

In this chapter, we will describe techniques and methods of practice that can be applied to a range of professional networks to help such networks operate in a different way with more effective interventions, perhaps even requiring fewer resources. Our focus explicitly aims to challenge what we see as an overly dominant narrative in working across networks, namely one of responsibility, accountability, and, implicitly, blame. We believe that, although many networks around a client may be experienced by individual workers as frustrating and disappointing, and that professional rivalries or poor professional relationships and limited resources may be real problems, a dominant narrative of blame focused on individual agency workers (e.g. "That social worker is abdicating his responsibility"; "This psychiatrist is never available") is neither justified nor useful. Our view is that these narratives are usually symptoms of severe and complex underlying systemic problems, and high levels of professional anxiety, with consequent failures in mentalizing.

By the end of this chapter we intend to have reframed expectations about multi-professional and multi-agency networks by applying a mentalizing approach. We will suggest that, from a mentalizing perspective, the natural resting state of these networks is in fact one of "dis-integration," rather than an idealized integration from which workers may be seen as having fallen, owing to poor practice or personal failures. We would want to emphasize that this is very far from being a counsel of despair, but, rather, that a mentalizing approach to networks may lead to more adaptive behavior by workers; adapting to dis-integrated systems in ways that sustain rather than suppress mentalizing may lower these natural barriers to success. As discussed at the beginning of this book, we think that rocket scientists have unfairly cornered the market in definitions of complex work; the work of participants in multi-agency and multi-professional networks more than gives them a run for their money, and perhaps there is more at stake, too.

We adopt this stance as we have not come across a local ecology of inter-agency practice that does not experience these kinds of difficulties, so it makes little sense to see this entirely in terms of individual practice and failings. In this way, the general approach of AMBIT is unambiguous in adopting a non-blaming approach to such difficulties. We do, of course, recognize that there are occasions in which professional competency, or malpractice, is a factor in network difficulties, and certainly do not want to deny this possibility. Despite this uncomfortable reality, in general experience suggests that professional competency (or lack thereof) or malign intentions are used too readily to explain matters that have much more complex, multiple, and systemic causes. Our approach is to focus on the quality of relationships within the network, on the (often very different) ways people make sense and mentalize the problems of the client and each other's states of mind, and on how professionals, family members, and peers become "positioned" in a helping system. As with other parts of the AMBIT model, this approach is underpinned by making particular use of mentalizing and systems theory as a framework for a number of core techniques and practices for more adaptive network functioning.

Knowledge and theory

What are networks?

Although detailed consideration of the nature of social networks is outside the scope of this book, it may be helpful to understand a little more about their general characteristics. Social networks have been defined as a social structure made up of a set of social actors (such as individuals or organizations) and a set of the dyadic ties between these actors (Wasserman & Faust, 1994). Prompted by the success of the internet, there is now a major area of study known as *network science*, which bridges mathematics, computing, biological and social sciences, and psychology (Lewis, 2009). Networks, as we are referring to them here, can be conceived as a form of social organization in which physical proximity has been replaced by other ways in which individuals become linked together. Traditional communities can perhaps be described as social networks organized around geographical locations, kinship, and economic ties, whereas information technology and professional specialization have further extended the development of social networks in which people are brought together around shared interests, expertise, identities, and roles.

The World Wide Web in general, epitomized by the phenomenon of social networking sites such as Facebook, indicates the scale and dynamism of this process, although the expectation that this technological evolution would lead to people simply having larger and more densely connected social networks may be misplaced. For example, work on mobile phone use (Holme & Saramäki, 2013) suggests that, for many individuals, social networks remain relatively stable and small, despite the opportunities for widening them that modern technologies seem to offer. Indeed, the idea that a specific network in which every member (or "node") is in close communication with every other member is somehow "functioning better" has been definitely shown not to be the case (Scott, 2013). Networks tend to self-organize into non-random patterns, with a limited number of well-connected "hubs" and larger numbers of less-well-connected (more specialist) individual "spokes." It is the "degrees of separation" between different actors in a network that allow specialization and, ideally, rapid transfer of the right information or resources to the right parts.

The intention here is, first, to recognize that networks of all sorts (whether professional, family, or peer) have a critical role in supporting—or hindering— processes of repair and recovery around the social and emotional difficulties of young people, as well as supporting (or hindering) their ability to thrive in the longer term. Second, we want to emphasize that many pre-existing relationships in a client's network will of course continue long after the AMBIT worker's involvement has run its course, so *scaffolding these existing relationships*, allowing for repairs or strengthening in readiness for that time, is, as we know, one of the core principles of AMBIT's stance (see Chapter 1).

Multi-agency and multi-professional networks: Working with dis-integration

The system as it is

For AMBIT, the specific focus on networks has two parts. The first is the *non-professional* social network around the client, which includes their immediate family or carers, their wider family and long-term acquaintances, and their friendships and peer group. Essentially, this network includes everyone who is linked to the client without having a formal (whether paid or unpaid) role. There is no prescribed definite endpoint in time to their involvement. The second, *professional*, network includes all those who have a paid or unpaid but formal role in relation to the client, and includes teachers, primary care doctors (in the UK, the general practitioner (GP)), social workers, youth workers, sports coaches, therapists, counselors, specialist doctors, residential care staff, learning support workers, and so on. The involvement of these professionals is often time-limited and is determined by the roles and responsibilities that they carry.

Professional networks for an individual client are fluid and specific to that person, so they need to be worked out on a case-by-case basis. Agencies will make separate autonomous decisions as to whether the case is open to them or not, and such decisions may be consistent (or not) with the beliefs of other agencies. A great deal of guidance has been provided by government—e.g. in the UK, *Future in Mind* (Department of Health, & NHS England, 2015) and *Working Together to Safeguard Children* (HM Government, 2013)—and by professional bodies—e.g. *New Ways of Working for Psychiatrists* (Royal College of Psychiatrists, National Institute for Mental Health in England, & Changing Workforce Programme, 2005)—advocating the importance of different agencies working together. This guidance has often been quite strident in trying to challenge agencies to increase collaboration between each other. The production of such guidance has sometimes been fueled by a child protection tragedy in which insufficient communication and collaboration between agencies was a significant factor in increasing the risks for the young person concerned—e.g. *The Protection of Children in England: A progress report* (Lord Laming, 2009).

There is an existing and extensive literature on the way agencies should collaborate around such work, including the idea of a "Team around the Child" (TAC) (in AMBIT, we also refer to this as the "Team around the Client" in respect of the fact that our clients may be adolescents or adults), the need for a lead professional (Children's Workforce Development Council, 2009), and the importance of integrated provision (in the UK, the government report *Every Child Matters* (HM Government, 2003) is a particularly good example). "Integration" may include having a shared budget (although this may first be shared and then subtly divided up into the components that the "integrated" organization has historically always been split into). Moreover, it should be more than just a common/single point of referral (because placing children and young people into a single assessment system by no means guarantees that outputs will be individualized), and it should include a committee that represents all the stakeholders in children's and young people's mental health services (although education, social care, physical and mental health, youth justice, and the voluntary sector do not lose their historic value systems just by following unified terms of reference). On the whole, as will become clear, at least one reason why workers from all agencies are at their least integrated around (and, indeed, are worst at reaching) those at highest risk is because each "intervention failure" generates overwhelming inter-agency blame, helplessness, and subsequent demotivation, hammering another nail into the coffin of integration, be it as policy or ideal. As we will see, while implementation science provides some guidance, integration is *not* primarily an organizational construct; it implies the transformation of human relationships rather than of organizations. At its core, the integration of organizations or agencies means human beings helping each other to achieve each other's aims. For this there can be no simple pro forma or recipe.

Existing guidance has tended to suggest that the lack of collaboration in networks lies in the mind-sets of managers and frontline workers "working in silos," and that this is what needs to be changed. This has resulted in two sorts of initiatives—namely, cross-professional training initiatives and more structural developments such as creating integrated service structures such as Children's Trusts (Department for Children, Schools and Families, 2008). Structural solutions also exist at a team level—for example, the development of joint agency teams such as Youth Offending Services with staff from youth justice, social care, education, and health agencies all working together under a single management structure. As well as these more structural developments, there have also been valiant efforts to clarify specific roles within a network such as the development of guidance around a "lead professional," "Teams around the Child," and so on.

The key components of integration, as these guidance documents describe them (although they have rarely been tested and perhaps even less often met), are:

1. An alignment of governance and oversight structures to define a single framework
2. Active cross-training as part of a process of integrating
3. Joint teams with shared roles (e.g. having fully integrated health and social care teams for children "at the edge of care" reduces the likelihood of them being taken into care)
4. Comprehensive sharing of information, supported by information-sharing agreements (consent from families for information-sharing is routinely requested on first contact or soon after)
5. Support for modes of care within adjacent specialties that offer a close fit with one's own, epitomized by, for instance, Professor Eileen Munro's work (Munro, 2011) and the "Signs of Safety" approach (Turnell & Edwards, 1997) to safeguarding practice, which advocate relational as opposed to procedural social work practice.

As we shall see, these specifications are far from arbitrary but reflect an underlying principle of enhancing the interpersonal trust that must be the background or underpinning of any systemic integration. It is in the conversation about enhancing interpersonal trust across networks that AMBIT, via the theory of mentalizing and the associated theory of epistemic trust (see Chapter 2), has more to say.

AMBIT and multi-domain working

AMBIT accepts the proposition that agencies need to work together and that isolated (or, in our terminology, *dis-integrated*) agency practice is likely to be unhelpful for young clients and their carers. That much may seem obvious; after all, it is hard to imagine finding an advocate for dis-integrated working! However, let us first go back to remind ourselves of first principles—why an intentional stance toward achieving integrated working makes sense—before saying more about what makes achieving this so hard, and how the relational stance and practices of AMBIT may provide crucial lubrication for the various cogs in the complicated machinery of multi-agency help.

One of the core principles of the AMBIT stance (see Chapter 1) is the imperative to ensure there is "Working in multiple domains" for the clients we work with. We have already stressed the complex array of difficulties in these clients' lives, with their deeply intertwined origins, and the destructive reciprocal synergies at work *between* these different problems. Our clients are characterized almost above all else by the extent of their comorbidities, or co-occurring problems; one problem opens vulnerability to, or amplifies, another, or undermines the helping processes directed at another. It makes sense that an AMBIT-trained worker should deliberately ensure that efforts are targeted at creating change across multiple domains—using a "wide-angle lens," as it were. Without this, any amount of excellent work in the realm of, say, psychological motivation or insight would simply be undermined by the entrenched and unhelpful attempts at problem-solving in the family (e.g. substance use or violence), or by continued lack of opportunity in the arena of employment or training.

Moreover, our clients want to know that their "problem" is being addressed, and they are not characterized by their tolerance of delay. Their perception, too, of what constitutes "the problem" may not only fluctuate from day to day, but may differ from the focus currently on offer by a worker with a prescribed role and specialist skills. They may receive the right help but at the wrong time, and easily experience this as the wrong help. However, because some of their problems may be quite specific, requiring high levels of specialist training or particular authority to address them (access to specialist housing, compliance with a Court order, specific mental health problems, etc.), an expanding network of professionals or agencies will almost inevitably be required. This is a difficult circle to square, and inevitably a worker intent upon addressing difficulties in multiple domains will find themselves involved in interacting and engaging with a widening network of professionals and paraprofessionals.

The inevitability of dis-integration
In our view, collaborative inter-agency working around individual cases is much harder to achieve than much of the extant literature implicitly tends to suggest. There is room for further analysis of the factors contributing to successful collaborative working between agencies around individual casework, or, more pertinently, the unintended barriers to such working. AMBIT aims to try to make sense of such difficulties in an explicit way and to develop purposeful and proactive strategies to address them.

Rather than accepting repeated reactions of surprise, disappointment, or irritation when evidence of dis-integration across a network reveals itself, AMBIT invites workers to anticipate these difficulties. For AMBIT, it is a fundamental assumption that dis-integration is the natural, expected state of affairs in any such network, and *not* a falling away from an idealized collaboration, however much this integrated working may be prescribed or expected. That is not to say we accept or minimize the harm of dis-integration in this work, just that an expectation that it would be any other way is an invitation to the kind of blame and recrimination that adds only heat, and little light, in the day-to-day work. This is not a new finding, and goes right back to early understandings of splitting in organizations (Main, 1957). The question that follows such an expectation is not, then, *why* dis-integration has erupted (and who is to blame), but *how* it is manifesting itself on this occasion, and what can be done to minimize its impact. It is not surprising that a network of workers with different trainings—framing their understandings of difficulties in different professional languages, and coming from different agencies with differing responsibilities toward a client—find it hard to develop shared understandings of the client's difficulties and shared approaches to what is likely to helpfully address them, let alone agreements about who is best placed or responsible for delivering those interventions. Let us consider another case example.

> A young person shows violent behavior at school. The social worker considers this behavior to be linked to undisclosed violence at home. The school feels that exclusion is necessary on the basis of maintaining a consistency of approach and setting boundaries in relation to aggressive and violent behavior ("Rules are rules, and we have a responsibility toward the other children in our care"). However, the social worker is more organized around ensuring that matters of risk and safety in this specific case are properly addressed. In the social worker's mind, it seems probable that exclusion from school will increase the risks of the young person either being exposed to more negative events at home or becoming more involved in delinquent or antisocial behavior in less controlled settings. For the social worker, the young person's continued attendance at school may be a key aspect of managing ongoing risks.

In this way, the positions of the two main workers involved in the case may be significantly different, and they may each feel that the other is behaving in ways that are unhelpful. This common scenario conveys what we call a dis-integrated network, in which well-intentioned and constructive workers end up in conflicted positions regarding the needs of a client.

There are other reasons for the persistence of dis-integration in even the best-organized and most well-intentioned networks. First, professional networks in any locality are often large, so it is generally impossible for personal relationships to develop across all the workers in all the agencies. Thus, a kind of shorthand develops by which agencies become "known" to one another. We have referred to this as a kind of "mythologizing" about agencies. An agency, and all the workers working for it, is often (quite naturally) characterized by a worker in another agency on the basis of their last memorable contact. We also tend to form more powerful impressions when things go wrong than when they go without a hitch. So, there is a tendency for biased negative feedback about this large system to be privileged over positive affirmations that things have gone, and can go, well. Agencies and individual workers are all vulnerable to these local mythologies that abbreviate and pigeonhole what is actually complex work that carries a range of successes and failures. A GP practice is described as "chaotic," a consultant (and, by extension, their whole service) is "really a golf player with a part-time clinic," a housing department "just likes to say 'No,'" etc. These characterizations may partly be a sort of "gallows humor" in a tough working environment, but they also evidence a seriously damaging lack of *respect for local practice and expertise* (another element of AMBIT's principled stance, described in Chapter 1). Explicitly or implicitly, such attitudes will be communicated to our clients, and in many ways serve to recreate what is often a familiar experience for them—a range of "responsible adults" around them who all seem to be at each other's throats. Even if parents do not conduct their arguments in plain sight of their children, one can be sure that the children know more about how the parents feel about each other than the parents like to think.

Second, it is easy to experience the very act of accepting a referral to one's agency as evidence of the earlier failures of another agency ("If the school had provided a bit of pastoral care early on, this family wouldn't be filling my clinic today"; "If the child mental health services had just treated this kid, his family wouldn't be needing all this extra social care input that we're being asked to provide").

Third, we often receive biased negative feedback about other workers or agencies directly from our clients. This is somewhat understandable, and may not simply mean that the other agency is no good ("That psychiatrist was awful. He never had any time for me—he just wanted to tick me off on his list and make another appointment"). It is not uncommon for a client to invite a new worker into a positive relationship by stressing the shortcomings of a previous relationship, even if in so doing they gloss over some of the very helpful things that the previous worker or agency achieved. The client in this situation may be more interested in trying to point out what they would like from a new relationship (someone who could spend some time with them) than in trying to give an accurate appraisal of the psychiatrist. In the client's mind, there may well be an assumption that the worker already knows that psychiatrist much better than they do. Another motivation for our clients to emphasize the least helpful elements of a previous worker's input may be to encourage the new worker into making greater efforts on their behalf. To hear another worker or agency criticized by a client is, if we are honest, sometimes a tempting invitation to show that we can do better than that—implicitly or explicitly, our clients may use this knowledge as another tool to try to get the very best out of a new worker. The result is another source for the drip-feed of biased negative feedback about the wider network.

Finally, as a worker it is an understandable temptation to call into question the judgment or behavior of another professional in front of a client. Consider a domestic building project: it is not uncommon for the bricklayer to suck his teeth and raise an eyebrow at the way the foundation trenches have been dug, or for the carpenter to point out the wasteful way in which the electrician has laid the cables. While there may be some truth in these criticisms, the actual function of that conversation may be much more about the worker's wish to be seen as the trustworthy chap who will "tell it as it is" and who is "on your side." We will cover more of this in the section about positioning theory later in this chapter.

So, in spite of well-intentioned workers and managers, there are many forces and factors at play that mean that the best multi-agency and multi-professional networks are constantly subject to dis-integration. How best to address this situation is one of the key themes of this chapter. Most current efforts toward integrated practice are completely consistent with the overall AMBIT approach, but, in our view, address only part of the story. Although increasing structural integration of services may contribute to improving network practice, we argue that differences in how frontline workers become positioned around a client will continue to present significant challenges to how effectively the networks that gather around specific individuals function. Dis-integration is inherent in these networks and not merely a symptom of structural/organizational failure (or, in the vast majority of cases, of individual malpractice). It is important to emphasize that AMBIT does not disagree with the need for change at an organizational level. Although supportive of the general direction of restructuring services to foster more integrated practice, the AMBIT approach avoids proposing a single concrete way for such restructuring to be carried out; this will inevitably be shaped by many local geographical, cultural, and political factors. In a complementary way, AMBIT aims to address the problems of how frontline workers with different intervention models, professional languages, and specific responsibilities toward the client can understand each other's dilemmas more accurately (through adopting a mentalizing stance to these dilemmas) and incorporate such beliefs into supporting effective collaborative practice.

Why do helping networks matter?

All clients have some sort of troubles in their journey from childhood to adulthood. Many of these may be common, such as being in love with someone who ignores you, or feeling that you are not clever enough (or not as clever as your sister), or feeling horribly unsettled by your family moving house, or disliking your parents for not understanding you better (or not giving you the money you need). Some clients must deal with less common problems, like having a mum with cancer or carrying the secret of their dad's violence to their mum, or being anxious about being pregnant. Despite the severity of some of these types of troubles, the majority of psychological help for people in these types of predicaments is probably provided informally—by the family and social network of which they are a part, with parents playing a greater or lesser role in orchestrating such help. For most young people, this is how they get through things.

For some clients, this "natural networked ecology of help" does not function very well, or perhaps not at all. Instead of a client experiencing their family, parents, or peers as being able to understand them (and love them) through their difficulties, they may experience others as critical, blaming, unsympathetic, or worse. In such circumstances, the attachment system may become overwhelmed by contradictory impulses—both proximity-seeking and avoidance—being triggered toward the same person. One of the aims of the AMBIT approach is to try to reactivate and remodel vestigial secure attachment processes, enabling the attachment system within a family (or more widely) to function more adaptively in response to a client's emotional turmoil and distress. In addition, and appropriate to the adolescent process of moving beyond the immediate family system, the aim might be to try to harness wider social networks to contribute to the process of recovery. In this way, for example, helping to reconnect a client to activities they had engaged with and gained from previously (such as re-joining a drama group) would also be part of trying to enable the network to function effectively.

In the AMBIT approach to networks, we are trying to do two things in parallel: we are trying to enable the client to rediscover the capacity to establish a degree of trust in some key people around them, and at the same time we are trying to reawaken the capacity of those around them to be responsive to opportunities that may occur only fleetingly in the dance of validation and invalidation, vulnerability and omnipotence, helplessness and hopefulness. After periods of unresponsiveness, it is very easy for those momentary efforts by clients to explore relaxing their vigilance to pass unrecognized by professionals who have been bruised in earlier battles with them. So, essentially, networks matter in AMBIT because they provide the context in which a client may be presented with the opportunity to rediscover epistemic trust (trust in communication from another person; see Chapter 2). Critically, we see the establishment of trust in the individual keyworking relationship as only the first step; what we seek is the next step, in which the client is enabled to become more outward-facing and to test this same attitude and approach in relation to well-chosen individuals in their wider social network.

We would not wish to equate professional networks around the client as having the same significance as family relationships. Professional networks matter because they may mimic the way that, in some families, extended family relationships can provide a degree of counterbalance to the vicissitudes of primary attachment relationships. In the same way that grandparents or aunts and uncles may be able to provide a trusting relationship that is less emotionally loaded (and so less challenging of mentalizing capacity in the here and now) than those with parents or siblings, so it may be possible for professional workers to develop and support a client's capacity to mentalize their situation in a calmer way than is possible with the parent(s) or primary carer. Close attachments (especially to family members) are the crucible in which mentalizing develops, but they are also the places where misunderstandings and misattributions most hurt, making mentalizing most fragile.

However, the challenge at present is that professional helping systems tend to prescribe who the client should speak to about a range of matters rather than responding to the client's preferences about who they feel able (or motivated) to speak to and share things with. In our experience there are often people in a client's life (a youth worker, a sports coach, or a college tutor) who, either currently or in the past, have had a useful and important relationship with the client, but who are discounted from the possibility of offering help in relation to more emotional or troubling issues. In AMBIT we invite curiosity about whether this always needs to be the case. Even if such relationships are only ever invoked in "as if" scenarios (a kind of "virtual systemic therapy"), this technique at the very least models a respect for the client's experience of past help ("So it seems your football coach, Mr Smith, often came up with good advice in the past—and he understood you pretty well. If you imagine he'd been here, just sitting and listening quietly to all you've been telling me, what do you think he'd be saying if we turned to him for help now?").

Creating mentalizing networks and organizations

The theory of mentalizing and epistemic trust has, as we have argued, rich implications for thinking about what encourages organizations, institutions, or, in fact, any social group to operate in more effective and humane ways—in other words (in our terms), in a way that supports balanced mentalizing and is able to resist slipping into non-mentalizing modes even when under high levels of pressure or in the face of conflict. We have, elsewhere, called this "mentalizing the system" (Bateman & Fonagy, 2016), and this more systemic application of mentalizing theory has some bearing on working with networks in the field of mental health work, and the demands on mentalizing that such networks can create. In this section we give a brief overview of how mentalizing theory can help us make sense of networks and organizations, and how we can create networks that are more mentalizing. We argue that mentalizing organizations are much better placed to support integrated networks.

All organizations are defined by their culture (their traditions and self-perceptions) and by the characteristics of their current leadership. Organizations can thrive as effective entities in an ongoing way only if they are able to "learn"—that is, if they are able to respond and adapt to circumstances (see Chapter 7 for more on this). This open approach to learning is possible only if the organization's culture and leadership permit and encourage it. The extent to which an organization can be defined as a "learning organization" depends on the extent to which its members maintain a position of epistemic trust toward the information they receive each from another—in other words, can they accept the general validity and applicability of the knowledge in each other's heads about how to do this work? In turn, the process by which epistemic trust is stimulated within a system is dependent on the capacity of the leadership and management of the organization to stimulate it.

As we discussed in Chapter 2, being mentalized—feeling understood because one is being treated as an agent with a mind of one's own—may be one of the fundamental and generic *ostensive cues* (a signaling system used by the person who wants to communicate something to another that acts as a "key" opening a communication channel between their mind and the other person's) for the creation of epistemic trust. An organization is a learning organization only to the extent that its members permit themselves to be influenced by those around them in this way. This may sound like a statement emanating from a 1970s West Coast encounter group, yet there is some wisdom in it. The speed of knowledge transfer is a key marker of an organization's success. If we have to explain something only once and it is immediately understood and acted on, independent of our supervision and oversight, then the system will function better than if we have to repeat our explanation because it was not truly believed and the substance of it was lost behind a curtain of deceptive superficial compliance. This is not to say that trust is invariably best and that vigilance has no role to play. There is such a thing as healthy skepticism, after all. But when we are not in a position to be able to judge the accuracy of a piece of information or knowledge, we have to make a judgment on the basis of our relationship with, and the cues emitted by, the person communicating that information.

This is perhaps most obvious in a hierarchical system where communication comes from a leader. Effective leadership demands effective communication. A leader is ultimately effective only if they are believed and treated as a reliable source of information by those they are attempting to lead (i.e. influence). Leaders need to be listened to as well as being simply heard. They can achieve this only if they model sufficient levels of mentalizing to generate an atmosphere of interpersonal respect and trust, and thus create a wider climate that supports mentalizing in members of that network. It is the understanding that members of a social system feel toward each other that fuels the capacity for them to learn from each other, which is the backbone of a learning organization. We suggest that an institution or agency that has relatively high levels of epistemic trust will have certain features that ensure the success of communication systems within that organization. These features, which may be thought of as *institutional ostensive cues*, and which need to be put in place and consistently modeled by the leadership, are probably highly varied, but they have *respect for agency* as the key common characteristic. This is written into the AMBIT stance as the principle of "Respect for local practice and expertise," which is always in some tension with its paired partner principle, "Respect for evidence," so there is an appropriate balance to be found; we explore this tension in more depth in Chapter 7.

The distinction we are describing here applies as much to peer-to-peer networks as to hierarchical ones. The relationship between appropriate attribution of agency (respect for local practice and expertise) and the capacity to influence applies equally whether the person in question is your manager or your colleague. However, the quality of communication within the organization may be a powerful influence that defines the efficiency of peer-to-peer knowledge transfer. There must be a broad awareness of the general intentions of the organization by all those within it, otherwise the motives of others can never be clear. The clarity of the mission will determine not just that individuals set their *personal* goals in a reasonably coherent manner, but that they are able to function together as a unit *because they understand what each other is trying to do*. Remember that without understanding the other person's actions in some kind of context that includes their understanding and motives, it will always be hard (perhaps impossible) to trust the information they provide, in which case we may need to test their communication by checking their figures, their sources, and their logic. If one is unable to do this, we must take the information "at face value," which means *just take it, but not take it in*.

So, how can we be sure we understand the intention behind the actions of a colleague? In general, unless we know him/her very well, much of what we have to go on is simply our understanding of the context—that is, the overarching aims of the institution within which he/she is operating. This is why institutional mission statements are of value. In order for my colleague's actions to make any sense, I must first be aware what organizational goals he/she is working toward, and when and how the organization would see these goals as having been successfully achieved. At a lower level of abstraction, we might consider (much more practical and concrete) tasks as opposed to goals. To understand the other person's task enough to provide meaningful feedback for them, I must not only understand the specifics of what they are trying to do in the here and now, but also their perception of whether this is, or is not, a challenging experience. Beyond this, any presumed understanding of my colleague's intentionality is likely to be helpful only insofar as I can also understand that my *own* behavior may well appear equally inexplicable to my colleague. All this interpersonal predictability and understanding is relevant, not for its own sake, but because understanding the actions of others and feeling that one's own actions are being accurately interpreted create a background of trust that accelerates the transmission of information across the network. Under those conditions, information is trusted, because there is epistemic trust.

What do we consider to be the hallmarks of a system where interpersonal understanding is sufficient to create a background of epistemic trust and the efficient transfer of relevant knowledge? Some features of a successfully mentalizing social system are obvious and follow from what has already been stated about individual mentalizing:

- The tone and culture of the institution are relaxed and flexible, not stuck in one particular point of view;
- There is an element of playfulness, with humor that engages rather than being hurtful or distancing;
- An element of problem-solving by "give and take" between perspectives pervades;
- Advocates should be able to describe their own experiences and inquire about others' experiences, rather than themselves defining other people's experiences or intentions;
- There is an atmosphere that conveys individual ownership of behavior rather than a sense that this is something that simply "happens" to them;
- There is curiosity about other people's perspectives, and an expectation that one's views will be extended by others.

In contrast, a non-mentalizing social system, by its very nature, disrespects or overrides individuals' subjectivity and sense of agency. This re-creates the evolutionary environment that encodes for (triggering, as it were) self-sufficiency, non-collaboration, and defensiveness. It is in such a climate that bullying behavior is far more likely to take place.

Non-mentalizing social systems tend to also generate fear and, as a consequence, an overwhelming desire for protection and security (proximity-seeking). If a sense of safety is not forthcoming, a consequent hyperactivation of workers' attachment systems ensues: the absence of safety generates further anxiety, which in turn intensifies the activation of the attachment system and the desire for even more proximity-seeking ... and so on. The increased level of arousal will undermine the capacity for balanced mentalizing and leave individuals within these systems interacting with predominantly non-mentalizing modes of social thinking. Such social systems, once established, can be self-reinforcing; therefore, despite the emotional instability they produce in individuals, as social systems they are highly stable. This is because non-mentalizing undermines the very social mechanism that could alter its character: human collaboration.

A vicious downward spiral of non-mentalizing takes place within such a disorganized social system, in which the frightening, undermining, frustrating, distressing, or coercive interactions on the part of one person elicit a powerful emotional response from another. This overwhelming emotional response in the second person reduces their capacity to mentalize: their poor mentalizing undermines their ability to understand or even pay attention to the feelings or perspectives of others. Other people appear incomprehensible and opaque; their intentions and feelings appear misaligned or in outright opposition to the individual's. The response on the part of that person is to try to control or change the behavior of others, or of themselves. This leads them to embark on frightening, undermining, frustrating, distressing, or coercive interactions. And so the cycle of powerful emotions, poor mentalizing, and so on, continues.

The non-mentalizing modes, discussed in Chapter 2, come into operation at a systemic level as well at the level of the individual. In a social system in which *psychic equivalence* dominates, ideas and thoughts are regarded as having the power of brute reality. In terms of institutional culture, this translates into a stance whereby the power of thoughts is regarded as so great as to require total control. Criticism—or even negative thought contents—cannot be sanctioned because the ideas become terrifying, real possibilities acquiring such power that they actually come to constitute a very real threat. The paranoid way in which totalitarian regimes tend to treat critical thinking is a good example. Often very particular and immovable solutions to understanding social reality are adopted, with no tolerance for alternative perspectives. Understandings of what might be going on in people's minds are simple, "black and white," and rigidly held.

In a social system in which the *pretend mode* of non-mentalizing predominates, ideas become decoupled from physical reality. It is a social world where ideas have no consequence: endless pseudo-communication and "busyness" result in no meaningful progress or outcomes. Because anything other than one's own thoughts and feelings seems unreal, selfishness and extreme egocentrism are permitted. Worse, because other people's minds are not, fundamentally, felt to exist, interpersonal aggression and even intentional harm are made possible. We tentatively offer as a systemic illustration certain religious communities where such pretend, superficially extremely caring and concerned, communities can engage in spiritual debate but at the same time show extreme cruelty to individual members of their group or people in their care.

In a social system in which the *teleological mode* of non-mentalizing predominates, other people's agency—their thoughts, beliefs, and behavior—is understood only in terms of observable action. Actions have a physical outcome and are regarded as true indicators of the intentions of the other. Similarly, changing the mental state of another—getting someone to change their perspective—is seen as being possible only as a consequence of physical acts. This legitimizes and gives a valid place to the use of physical aggression, the threat of harm, or, in less overtly dramatic ways, the overuse of formalized complaints processes. For people to reveal their intent in such a system, physically demonstrative acts are required, such as payment, acts of subservience, or retributive justice.

These accounts of the impact of non-mentalizing modes when they become generalized across a social system indicate the high significance of maintaining balanced mentalizing, both within a team and across a system. The creation of a mentalizing organization is dependent on activating secure attachments by creating and sustaining an attitude of compassion and concern. Excessive activation of attachment feelings, as can happen in traumatized social systems, risks hyperactivation of attachment and a reduction in balanced mentalizing. Furthermore, the creation of a mentalizing organization depends on enhancing the curiosity of members of the community in relation to each other's thoughts and feelings, and the ability to identify when mentalizing has turned into pseudo-mentalizing—that is, pretending to know. There needs to be a focus on the presence (and, to an extent, the inevitability) of occasional misunderstandings and respectful uncertainty about others' mental states, coupled with a curiosity about the minds of others.

Mentalizing and curiosity across networks

In trying to promote systemic mentalizing in the context of a network, in AMBIT we adopt and adapt a range of approaches and skills that we would also use in relation to working directly with our clients (see Chapter 4). So, we start by encouraging *curiosity*—an explicit interest in trying to understand the position and experience of other workers in the network, using the mentalizing stance. The AMBIT approach invites a worker to apply this curiosity to both the professional and non-professional networks around the client. The assumption is that knowledge of these two networks may provide rich information about the nature of the client's difficulties and, even more importantly, may help to identify who could play an important role in helping the client with their current difficulties. This may require persistence. Experience suggests that many of the clients being seen by AMBIT-trained teams tend to minimize, or even be quite dismissive about, the possible contributions of both their non-professional and professional networks. In response to questions about who might be helpful in dealing with their current difficulties, clients or family members often provide very thin descriptions of their network, so that potential helpers are implicitly discounted. Such a response is consistent with our formulation that many of our clients have a poor internal relationship to help; their expectation of the world is that real help is unlikely to be accessible to them, and still less "helpful." For this reason, we encourage AMBIT-trained workers to map professional and non-professional networks in explicit ways, either separately or together, in order to try to identify possible additional sources of help.

As previously described, many agencies will appropriately assume a role in trying to address the difficulties of highly excluded and hard-to-reach clients. As with the example of Jo at the start of this chapter, it is not uncommon for professional meetings to include a group of as many as 20 professionals from a wide range of agencies, with up to, say, five or six of these professionals being named as specific workers for the client in relation to particular aspects of the work. Many of these workers may have only quite occasional or superficial levels of face-to-face contact with the client (in network science (Scott, 2013) these would be described as "weak ties") but may be named as holding important professional responsibilities for some aspect of their current needs, such as, for example, school attendance or adherence to the terms of a Court Order. It is often unrealistic to expect a client whose capacity to make almost any positive help-seeking relationships may be minimal to engage with a group of this size. The AMBIT approach advocates that reducing the numbers or paying careful attention to sequencing the input of those who work directly with the client may add value, especially if doing so promotes higher-quality relationships with those workers who continue face-to-face contact. In network science these contacts would be called "strong ties" and, as indicated above, it is common that the number of strong ties within any individual network may be quite small, suggesting that this may be regulated by internal constraints rather than external opportunities. The work of Ungar and colleagues (2013), who looked at young people with complex needs engaged by multiple services, supports this. Their careful analysis suggested that in this population it is the quality of relationship and the perceived helpfulness of a service that promote resilience, not the number of different services involved. More, in this sense, is often less.

Systemic thinking and positioning theory

As acknowledged throughout this book, the AMBIT approach draws heavily on systemic thinking and practices. In this section, we discuss positioning theory as a valuable way of making sense of some aspects of the way networks function. Positioning theory (Harre et al., 2009) has been adopted by systemic practitioners as a way of making sense of people's behavior in complex systems, providing a theoretical understanding of how workers in different agencies become positioned with respect to each other—in the case of AMBIT, this is around the needs of their shared client. Positioning theory brings together systemic thinking and a number of other ways of making sense of human interactions. One of these ways is *role theory*, which considers how shared understandings about specific roles in a system develop and are themselves subject to change, and how those roles themselves influence and change the behavior of the people who find themselves "playing" them in a system. Another way of making sense of human interactions comprises the broad area of psychological research summarized as *intersubjectivity*, of which the theory of mentalizing might be seen as one of its finer fruits. Additionally, positioning theory tends to focus quite explicitly on the different kinds of language that tend to get used in (or are invited by) particular kinds of exchanges or discourses between specific positions. For instance, the kinds of language typically used between "helper" and "helped," between manager and employee, or between two experts from two different fields of work will be quite different, and will often serve to reinforce the positions that each of these players takes up or has imposed upon them.

Positioning theory starts from an assumption that all social systems operate in ways that construct sets of shared definitions and rules. Some of these are implicit and others explicit, but collectively they define the different roles and duties required to make that system function. In other words, there is no universal and objective understanding of what a "therapist," a "social worker," a "youth worker," or a "client" is, or what they do; there are only constructed versions that may be more or less local and more or less shared by the players in any specific network. This is what is meant by a "social constructivist" analysis.

People are positioned with respect to their rights and duties out of first-order self-constructions of identity/role (e.g. "I am a social worker") and second-order constructions (or narratives) of identity/role by others (e.g. "Social workers are mainly concerned with child protection"). The theory emphasizes that the interaction of these constructions is fluid and continuous, and is mediated predominantly through language—that is, by the ways people in networks talk about each other. The value for AMBIT lies in the idea that workers in a network reciprocally (and often implicitly, rather than explicitly) contribute to the narratives about each other, which "positions" individual workers. This impacts (helpfully or unhelpfully) on their capacity to fulfill their duties and make use of their rights and authority. Such positioning is also done by clients. The task for an AMBIT worker is to explore and perhaps challenge polarized constructions of workers and their positions within a network (e.g. "She's indispensable, but *he's* useless"), with a view to enabling workers within a network to adopt increasingly authentic positions with respect to their rights and duties.

Positioning theory starts from a social constructivist analysis of the social interactions that influence both implicit and explicit roles and duties. It aims to replace the more fixed construct of *roles* with a more dynamic changeable notion of *positions*. Positions arise out of interactions and implicit negotiations, so that a person becomes "positioned" both by their own role, their beliefs about this, and their own actions and values, but also by the beliefs, actions, and values of others. Much of this process is implicit, and the positions adopted are rarely named. For example, in a family an older sibling may adopt a position of responsibility for their younger sister who has a long-term condition, and this position is implicitly (and gratefully) endorsed by their single parent, which might confer some rights as well as responsibilities on the older sibling. However, the position may not be explicitly acknowledged, as in the naming of their role as a "young carer."

The value of positioning theory for AMBIT is that it provides a richer framework to make sense of the experience of professional networks around a client than is conveyed by the more static concept of the "professional role" with its attendant core competencies, responsibilities, and authority. Although it does not replace the first-order concept of role, it provides a second-order refinement that captures key elements of network functioning that are not otherwise satisfactorily addressed or acknowledged.

In professional networks around a young person, the roles and duties of individual workers may be very explicit and clearly named; for example, social workers have an explicit role with demarcated duties (e.g. child protection) prescribed for them. Similar levels of explicit prescriptions and demarcations would be true of, for example, nurses, psychologists, youth workers, psychiatrists, and teachers. The AMBIT approach does not aim to alter these fundamental roles, but uses positioning theory to explore the way people with specific and relatively fixed roles become variably positioned through interaction with others around a particular case. We have already referred to the fact that in AMBIT we refer to the position of the "keyworker," even though there may also be formal roles in the network with the same title; a professional network may either implicitly or explicitly agree to position one individual within the network to act as keyworker for the case. AMBIT argues that the experience of the client (how *they* act to position certain workers in this way) should be a very important consideration in such calculations, and that moving from implicit to explicit recognition of this position is important—not least for clarity of communication across such networks.

Balance and unbalance: Working across multiple domains versus taking responsibility for integration

The target group of clients for AMBIT-trained teams need help in a whole range of life problems, which usually include (but are rarely limited to) family relationships; housing or care needs; school/college/employment problems; peer-group relationships; negative patterns of behavior such as substance misuse, aggression, or social isolation; or other more specific mental health difficulties such as the effects of trauma. Inevitably, this requires different agencies to work together; at the same time, these same clients may find it hard to engage and work with staff from several different agencies simultaneously, and the agencies not uncommonly find themselves "treading on each other's toes." The dilemma broached in this section is how to reconcile covering all of your client's many needs by helping across many domains, with the need to avoid overwhelming the client with too many different workers and apparently contradictory interventions. For the AMBIT-trained worker, the aim is to achieve the best (or the least bad) balance. On the one hand, the worker must ensure that work is occurring across a sufficiently broad range of domains to cover all the client's needs and the factors that may perpetuate their problems, which inevitably involves what may be a wide network of helpers. On the other, they must take responsibility for using whatever ambit (sphere of influence) they have in helping to shape an approach that is integrated (or, simply, that "makes sense") from the client's perspective (see Figure 6.1).

As previously described, AMBIT proposes that smooth collaborative network functioning does not automatically happen, despite good intentions. Our assumption is that networks are often (perhaps always) implicitly conflicted (or "dis-integrated") in either minor or major ways, and that these conflicts tend to be more severe in outreach or particularly complex cases because they tend to be associated with larger networks and higher levels of risk, which have a higher negative impact on mainstream agencies. For instance, there is much more at stake in terms of service provision (starting with costs) if a young client is at risk of becoming looked after ("taken into care"), needing specialist educational provision, or needing to go to hospital. The paradox is that because the clients we target usually have problems that extend beyond the domains of any single agency, joint agency approaches are essential, but our clients also tend to be

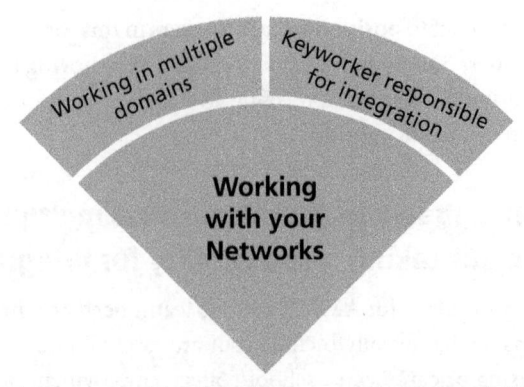

Figure 6.1 Working across multiple domains versus taking responsibility for integration.

highly resistant to the approach of an army of different workers; in addition, as those workers come from different service and professional cultures, they too are prone to fall out with each other.

Why should these clients require such complex service provision? This may be obvious, but is worth stating. Severe mental health problems in socially excluded clients are very rarely, if ever, disconnected from the broader context of these people's lives. Efforts to improve these clients' mental health problems must almost always be linked to improving their access to school/college/work, engaging them in positive, enjoyable activities, and supporting them to be part of constructive peer groups and functioning families, in having a place to live, and in negotiating their way through the pitfalls of the legal system. In this way AMBIT is very rarely just about individual therapy. As we have acknowledged, in seeking to address problems across the multiple domains in which those problems have co-evolved, the number of agencies, workers, models of working, and explanations for what is "wrong" inevitably multiply. An AMBIT-trained worker may discover considerable demand for efforts to engage and help to coordinate other agencies in providing the most appropriately attuned, contextually adapted, integrated, and timely help for their client. This can easily feel like an "extra" to the core task that their formal role describes.

Even the best-integrated and sequenced series of interventions may also require a high level of basic "shepherding" support to encourage and enable a client (perhaps with a troubled history of relating to adult help and authority) to try out new experiences that are offered by other services. The individuals in these (often quite large) professional or paraprofessional networks will all have their specific roles and areas of expertise, and are likely to have developed their own views (e.g. about the mental health needs a client may have) through lengthy professional training or years of work experience. Youth workers, teachers, social workers, housing officers, and all the rest may present to the client a bewildering array of serious-minded adults, all trying earnestly to engage the client in conversations about the difficulties in the client's life, following, as they must, their own obligations to make an appropriate assessment. This can be overwhelming.

Aside from the fact that they work in teams with specific remits to work in specific domains of a client's life, these different workers may also have spent many years training in quite specific models—not only for making sense of the various difficulties, but also for intervening helpfully. Each model or intervention carries its own theoretical framework for making sense of things, and often a whole "language," too (and AMBIT is no different in this regard). We have previously described this as contributing to a "Tower of Babel" experience for the client—a cacophony of earnest workers who may all seem to be enthusiastic and sincere, but who speak in different tongues, and occasionally (at least as it may appear) in direct opposition to one another. Whether or not this fits with the reality from the workers' perspectives, this is not uncommonly the impression that complex networks give to the clients they are organized around. In responding to this situation, the AMBIT worker may need to spend time with the client explaining how the various people approaching them hold different roles and responsibilities, and also how the shared intention is for all to work together to develop a shared approach to their difficulties, however shakily this may play out in reality.

One of the challenges for an individual network around a client is that, although there may be a lead professional with an explicit role to increase communication and liaison across agencies, more commonly there is no single person either formally accountable for how the whole network operates, or authorized to direct the operation of all the elements of such a network. The governance structures, funding streams, operating principles, and performance criteria for the separate elements in a multi-agency network are often very different. Consequently, regardless of operational guidance, the capacity of such networks to work together in coherent and effective ways is largely dependent on the individual motivations and goodwill of the workers themselves. Indeed, some organizational systems may unintentionally *discourage* attendance or engagement in the networking aspect of this work. For example, methods of measuring staff activity that focus only on registering direct face-to-face contacts with clients will inevitably (although, as we emphasize, unintentionally) devalue time spent on such "network-focused" activity. In general, liaising effectively across a network of agencies can be extremely time-consuming, and in tightly target-focused services the priority for this less easily measurable work may be subtly demoted, especially for workers with extensive caseloads.

Although AMBIT was initially designed primarily to address the mental health needs of clients, it recognizes that many areas of their lives contribute to resilience and more effective coping. Re-establishing a client's engagement with, for instance, a local football team may have as much impact on their emotional wellbeing as active engagement in individual therapy. One activity does not replace the other, but, in our view, mental health services may have the tendency to be rather "therapy-centric"—or at least to offer a rather "industrialized" approach to help in which identified needs are matched to one or other "deliverer" of more or less pre-ordained packages of intervention. The metaphor we use here is that of parenting. Effective parenting recognizes that a parent promotes a child's development by using a wide range of methods, both encouraging experimentation and also adapting to feedback as to what fits each child uniquely. Most importantly, it is a combination of both action and sensitivity (there are direct parallels here to the principles of Active Planning, described in Chapter 3).

For these reasons the AMBIT-trained worker is encouraged to consider all areas of a client's life and not just the situation that is causing current concern. The AIM assessment (see Chapter 3) highlights this, requiring as it does the worker's specific ratings for the client's functioning across all areas of relationships, development, learning, pleasure, and recreation, as well as their symptoms, and their response to help. This also has the potential to identify strengths that may be discounted if the intervention is entirely problem-focused. Below are two case examples that illustrate this aspect of the stance.

Karen

Karen was a 15 year old who had become severely depressed following the separation of her parents several months prior to her referral. She had subsequently stopped attending school and was engaged in daily acrimonious exchanges with her mother, who was caring for her. Her father saw her each week but was more concerned about retaining his relationship with her than trying to be effective in helping her with her difficulties. The roots of her depression preceded the parental separation, as Karen had been prone to low moods for several years and had a very negative sense of self, which impacted on her peer relationships. She had a 3-year-old niece of whom she was very fond, and she greatly enjoyed helping her aunt look after her. As she became more depressed, she stopped visiting her aunt, and her aunt "didn't want to trouble her" when she was feeling so low. The AMBIT worker encouraged the aunt to retain contact and to invite Karen over to encourage Karen to help her with childcare. This strengthened Karen's sense of value to others and became an area of her life where she felt good about herself, as well as recognizing that her niece was genuinely good company for her, too.

Matt

Matt was 16 and had hated school for as long as he could remember. He was constantly in trouble and was at times violent toward both adults and peers. He was involved in stealing motor scooters and really liked the excitement of being chased by police when this had happened. Apart from scooters, he had always had his own bicycle, and from an early age he had learned how to mend every aspect of them. The AMBIT worker also had a bicycle, and on a day when he was supposed to be meeting with Matt, he had had a puncture. He called Matt and explained he was going to be late. Matt offered to fix his puncture for him, which, after some discussion between his AMBIT worker and another colleague in the team, was accepted. Matt did fix the puncture, and this was a very important experience for him, because he was trusted with taking the bike away to his home and bringing it back. He referred to this occasion often in his future work with his worker, because the experience of being trusted was so rare for him. Later, his worker helped him find a place on a local motorcycle mechanics project, which built on his confidence; his mechanical prowess offered a way for him to gain respect.

Techniques and skills

We will now describe a set of specific techniques that can be used to try to improve the way a network functions around a particular case. These are part of the AMBIT toolkit to be used when things need fixing: they are not expected to be used if they are not needed. All the techniques described here are described in the AMBIT manual (https://manuals.annafreud.org/—follow the links to AMBIT), which also includes many video role-plays to illustrate techniques more fully. It is important to recognize that, in spite of what we have discussed above, there are plenty of examples of casework in which the network functions perfectly well, so that the techniques described here may be unnecessary. If this is the case, then the focus should be directed toward other areas of practice. As ever, AMBIT offers a range of mentalizing techniques that offer modest (yet, in our experience, potentially transformative) ways to help networks function more effectively around specific cases.

The "un-service-centric" stance

In many ways, this barely qualifies as a technique, and could equally be described as "the client-centric stance." It merely follows on from the earlier discussion in emphasizing that the AMBIT-trained worker is encouraged to be curious as to who the client finds helpful, how, and why. Of course, in answering these kinds of questions the client will be mentalizing both themselves and their workers— and this offers opportunities for the worker to note and reinforce (by positively connoting) any such reflectiveness. The assumption is that the capacity to be helpful is not confined to professionals and that there are likely to be others in the client's life who may at times in their life be, or have been, helpful to them. This is not just about feeling supported emotionally, but may include people who have helped in practical ways around things that mattered to the client (e.g. fixing their bike, lending them some money, sticking up for them in the face of criticism, recognizing their good points). These relationships may not be functioning so well during the troubled and stressful time at which professionals get involved, so it may be necessary to invite the client to reflect back to when they were younger to recall events and relationships that had felt supportive or safe. Sometimes this may involve, for example, memories of a now-absent parent, older siblings, grandparents, or primary school teachers. It may also include professionals such as classroom support workers, sports coaches, or youth club workers. Besides offering an opportunity for the client to reflect on (and teach the current keyworker) "what approaches work best for me," these conversations may also be very helpful in thinking forwards about who could be part of a group of people who might be enlisted to be helpful to the client in the future, perhaps as the current work approaches its conclusion.

Inquiries with the client around this should be informal and form part of initial conversations about getting to know each other.

> "I guess my job is about trying to find ways to be helpful to you. I wondered who you had found helpful about things in the past … What do you think it was that this person 'got' about how to be actually helpful for you?"
>
> "I have some idea that you really liked the dance group you were in a little while back. Who had encouraged you to get into that? Was that all from you?"
>
> "You mentioned a few times that you go round to see your nan sometimes. I wondered whether she was someone who you felt was supportive to you when you get a bit stressed … How do you think she manages to give you that confidence—that you can really rely on her?"

Sometimes these kind of inquiries reveal a great deal (particularly if a client cannot identify anyone at all); sometimes they evoke more conventional and defended responses. Often the client may have experienced the adult world as hostile, critical, and non-mentalizing of their situation, so it will not be unusual if they openly discount this approach, adopting a position that they "don't need help from anyone" and are quite capable of handling the situation they are in. This is particularly common in the adolescent years, in which a core developmental task is separation and the growth of independence, but a common detour is the denial of any needs or the denigration of healthy dependency.

Some clients may have experiences that suggest to them that help is more likely to be found in gang affiliations; these are unlikely to be profitably explored in the early stages of engagement and will likely be off-limits at first in conversations with professional workers, because of the likelihood of evoking strong loyalty binds, which could challenge the development of a new helping relationship. In these situations, some form of words that allows the worker to acknowledge the client's reality (that in their experience these relationships have been helpful) without getting drawn into collusion will be required. Rehearsing this with a colleague may be helpful, and this might in itself provide an opportunity for reaching out to another agency whose workers may have greater experience of negotiating such tricky territory.

AMBIT worker: "I want some way to acknowledge how important the gang is to Sara, but not for her to see me as supporting it or for her to see me as saying, 'It's either the gang or me!' because at this stage in my relationship with her I suspect she would choose the gang. How do you do that?"

Gangs worker: "I tend to be really upfront about who I am and what my job is, and use a bit of humor. I might say something like, 'Yeah, look Sara, I really get that those guys are your mates and they've stuck by you. I really mean that—I don't want to be disrespectful of that. But you know who I am and what I do, too, so you know I'm not going to say much else about that in case you think I'm telling you gangs are all great! I'm not in a gang, but I'm up for being helpful and straight with you.'"

Explaining networks to a client

Another approach—again, hardly a technique—is simply for the AMBIT-trained worker to offer to talk over with the client what the different workers and agencies do, and why they do what they do. The aim here is to try to move from implicit assumptions about why professional people do things, to having more explicit understandings about this. This is a form of mentalizing, in that it is exploring intentions behind people's behavior.

The starting point here is that the behavior of workers is often not as comprehensible to a client as those workers may assume. This is particularly the case for a client whose expectations from authorities or "helpers" in general may be colored by negative and/or non-attuned early experiences. For example, in exploring why a social worker was contacting their client quite frequently by phone, the client may reply that the social worker is "just doing her job" or that "she is just being annoying and doesn't trust me" or they may respond even more negatively: "She's deliberately hassling me, trying to wind me up." The purpose of these conversations is not simply to try to persuade the client that there may be other ways of understanding the motivations of the social worker. Nor is it to collude with the client's constructions, identify with them, and invite them to believe that you share such ideas about social workers in general. No, the task is to try to enable the client to begin to elaborate ideas about that *individual* social worker, to move from generalities (which are usually rather non-mentalizing) to more individual perceptions of people in their network.

Where it has been possible to move on from early, more defensive, conversations, it may be helpful to find opportunities to explore assumptions (or constructs) about such workers so that the client is better able to make sense of their actions. Facilitating conversations between the client and specific workers may be a further outcome of such work, which is about encouraging a proactive stance toward the identification, development, and (to quote one of the principles of the AMBIT stance; see Chapter 1) *scaffolding of existing key supportive relationships*.

David

David is 14 and has been using cannabis for three years. He has become increasingly involved in shoplifting and theft in order to support the cost of his substance use. He had engaged well with Sarah, his AMBIT worker, and there had been a recent positive change in his life in that his father, who had been violent at home and used cannabis himself, had recently left the family home. With reducing cannabis use, David was attending school more often and had engaged with a local canoe club, which he enjoyed. During this period, though, David was still prone to uncontrollable rages. Youth services, school, and social care services (who were working with his mother around the domestic violence) were all involved, and all had different approaches to responding to David's rages.

Having successfully engaged with the different agencies, Sarah found herself increasingly frustrated by the dis-integrated responses to David's anger. The school tended to be rather punitive in its response (emphasizing the need to "ground" David and respond with predictable consequences for his negative behavior), whereas Sarah had been trying to frame his anger more as a part of his withdrawal from high-level cannabis use. Although Sarah had some success in improving the degree to which approaches to David's rages were shared across his home and in other settings, there remained a wide diversity of responses. Rather than try to orchestrate the network further (over which she had no formal authority), Sarah recognized that she needed to help David make better sense of the wide variation of responses that he received in the different settings in which his angry outbursts occurred. Exploring specific incidents and the different ways other professionals had responded enabled David to make sense of others' behavior better, and helped him to anticipate slightly better the different staff behaviors in different settings. This provided a degree of containment that enabled the network to persist through a very difficult two-month period for David.

Mapping networks—the Pro-Gram

In AMBIT we have developed a very simple method of mapping out all the professional relationships in a client's life. We call this simple tool a Pro-Gram. Visually, the Pro-Gram is similar to a genogram but focuses on the professional network.

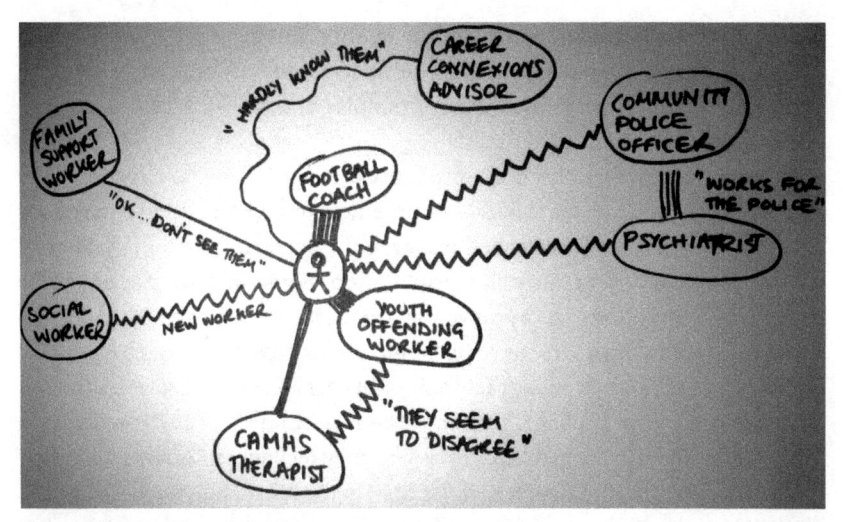

Figure 6.2 Pro-Gram example.

The basic idea is to make a drawing or map with the client placed at the center of the piece of paper, and then to position professionals in the network in relation to them (see Figure 6.2). This is the equivalent of a physical sculpting exercise (see below), but conducted on paper. Professionals positioned closer to the client on the Pro-Gram have a stronger relationship (one that the client identifies as being more helpful, or more understanding of their predicament) than those positioned further away. The aim is to be as inclusive as possible, to include teachers/tutors at school/college, and other workers who may appear at first sight to be rather peripheral.

In addition to mapping the relationships that these "nodes" in the network around the client have with the *client*, the Pro-Gram should also attempt to map how the client perceives these people relate to *each other*; where the different workers are laid out in relation to each other on the paper may also be very telling (*Client*: "My Youth Offending Team worker doesn't seem to agree at all with my therapist"; *Worker*: "Then they'd better be on opposite sides of the paper!").

The diagram can also be used in a developmental sense in that it may highlight previous relationships with professionals who are no longer active. For example, a relationship with a previous social worker that was felt to be helpful may be usefully included, to give a prompt on how current relationships might learn from this past success. A simple method for doing this is to discriminate between "live" and past relationships by using two different colors to mark these names on the diagram. The quality of relationships can be indicated—straight lines for positive relationships (thick for more significant ones) and zigzag lines for negative/conflicted relationships. The method can be adapted according to the AMBIT worker's own individual style; this is a tool for thinking rather than an attempt to quantify reality. Further examples of completed Pro-Grams can be found in the online AMBIT manual.

A common observation about this process is that both the client and the AMBIT worker learn new things about the network. Often, people may have become discounted, appearing at the edge of the paper, but revealing potential for development as a result of this exploration. Some may be placed on the periphery because they are perceived by the client to be unsympathetic (e.g. the school Head of Year: "He never liked me") or as powerless (e.g. the Housing Officer: "He just told my mum that we couldn't get a flat exchange even though he knows this place is dangerous for me to live in now"). The depiction of a fairly sparse and discounted helping system may feel uncomfortable and often unjustified in respect to people's efforts to help the client, but may indicate the bleakness of the client's *perceived* situation. This is social exclusion mapped as it is experienced. As our understanding of epistemic trust (see Chapter 2) suggests, the extent to which the client sees others as understanding their specific predicament will influence whether this trust is gained—with which comes curiosity and openness to learning from what others have to say next.

The intention is for this exercise to be a starting point for exploring the way the AMBIT worker may become positioned on the map. Who should the worker be close to? What sort of person should the worker be most like, or most unlike? Who would it be useful to speak to about what? For the network to work better to address all the client's needs, who in the network should be closer to who else? Once again, the client may be at a loss about many of these things. The point of this exercise is to make the implicit lack of knowledge and emerging understandings a bit more explicit, and in the process, hopefully, enhance understandings in small ways. The intention is not to overwhelm the client with too much information all at once, or to elaborate a complete rebuild of a network that neither the worker nor the client may have the authority to enforce, but instead to find small ways of improving how the network might function a little better.

Eli

Eli (age 17) had been excluded from college and was expected to attend a meeting there during the following week to plan his return. He said that he didn't know when the meeting was and what would happen at it. He was undecided whether he would go, but knew that he would be permanently excluded if he did not attend without a reason. His worker imagined that Eli felt anxious, angry, and perhaps worried that he would be shamed at the meeting.

In his Pro-Gram, Eli had placed his school Head of Year surprisingly close to the middle of the sheet, not as far away from him as several other teaching staff. When the worker inquired about what the Head of Year was like, Eli said that she was "strict but fair." This contrasted with a number of other school staff, who were more friendly but unpredictable from Eli's point of view. He was particularly friendly with the teacher who ran the special needs department, whom he liked because he "joked about" more than the others. The AMBIT worker suggested that she could phone the Head of Year now, during their meeting, and check out when the meeting at college was and what would happen at it. She could conduct this phone call in front of Eli, warning the Head of Year that she would be on speakerphone, so that Eli could ask things himself if he wanted to, or just listen. This call happened and a plan was agreed between all three people as to what Eli needed to do to prepare for the meeting at his college. The AMBIT worker agreed to support Eli in attending the meeting.

Sculpting a network

This technique is really just a three-dimensional version of the Pro-Gram, quite literally "positioning" characters in different roles within a specific network. It can be used by teams or groups of workers to try to make sense of a complex network around a client in a very concrete and direct way. The technique is used routinely in AMBIT training, and often elicits observations and reflections about the complexity and difficulty that many networks present both to the client and to the individual workers in the network. The technique is fully described in the online AMBIT manual and is summarized here. The aim is to visualize and to some extent "embody" the large and complex networks around clients, to take multiple perspectives from the positions of various protagonists, and to map out dis-integrations in physical space. Ultimately, it aims to identify perhaps a handful of small maneuvers or conversations that might reduce the negative impact of dis-integrations that have been identified. All that is needed to complete this exercise in a group of people is plenty of space to enable people to move around on their chairs. Begin by organizing the group to sit in a large circle.

The exercise involves inviting one person (or a small group) to describe a clinical scenario from their experience and to provide a brief history of the case. First, one of the team is asked to represent the client by sitting on a chair in the center of the group. The rest of the exercise involves positioning other figures in the client's network in ways that best reflect their relationship with the client and with each other. This follows common-sense ideas, so that close relationships are positioned close together, looking at each other, and distant relationships are placed further apart. Groups will develop their own creativity around this basic process and it is not necessary to be too prescriptive about the way it unfolds; nor does the process require high levels of creative expression (this has been described as "the lowest form of role-play"). For example, groups may want to consider whether they want people seated facing each other (an indication perhaps of support), next to each other (an indication of loyalty but difficulties), or turned away (an indication of conflict). It is helpful for the actual professional in a network that is being sculpted *not* to be sitting in "his/her" chair (i.e. representing their own position in the network), as this allows them to get a different perspective on their position.

The selection of who is included is often interesting and informative. The immediate family usually comes first, then extended family, peers, and friends, followed by significant others (pastor, imam, sports coach, etc.). The idea is to let professionals see themselves as "late visitors" to an existing network. How do they position themselves? Who are they close to and distant from? Having positioned themselves, participants in different positions are invited to reflect on what it is like to be in those positions and where they would like to be. Once the network is fully "sculpted," the facilitator may invite members of the group to walk around the sculpt, taking in the different perspectives, or to attempt to reorganize the network in physical space in ways that they think the client and family could start to experience as more accessible, helpful, and so on.

Our experience of this exercise is that it often evokes strong feelings—even heated discussion—between different "positions." People may become quite animated about trying to "solve" the network, and feelings of frustration or powerlessness can easily be experienced. The intention is to enable these observations to be reflected on and, if possible, to avoid becoming drawn into trying to solve very specific difficulties at this stage (it is useful to remind participants that this is not the real network, only their collective imagining of it!). What may be useful is to try to identify one or two key conversations that may enable the network to function better (see "Connecting conversations," below).

Another variation on the same theme, adopted by some AMBIT-influenced teams, has been to have a set of small cards made up, upon which are all the names of the "usual suspects" in an extended network, as well as some blanks. These are kept on the table around which the team meets to discuss cases; where appropriate, they can be used to map out a Pro-Gram of a client's network during a case discussion, which can then be moved around as more ideal configurations, and the strategies to achieve these, are considered.

The Dis-Integration Grid

The Dis-Integration Grid is another simple aid, designed to enable the AMBIT worker to work systematically to mentalize the behavior of individuals in the network around a client, and the relationships of these individuals with each other. The intention is that this exercise should lead to actions (based on a better mentalized understanding) that may ultimately, for example, reduce conflict in

Table 6.1 The Dis-Integration Grid

Levels of dis-integration	Young person	Parent/carer	Other person/ agency (name)	Other person/ agency (name)
Explanation "What's the problem?" (Why is it happening?)				
Intervention "What to do?" (… that might help …)				
Responsibility "Who does what?" (Who's responsible for doing this?)				

the network or strengthen a shared narrative so that workers in the network feel more validated and/or supported, and the client's experience is of more coherent and attuned collaboration to provide help.

The design of the grid (see Table 6.1) has been kept as simple as possible so that it can be used just by having a blank piece of paper and drawing out the grid by hand; alternatively, printed copies can be made from the template available in the online AMBIT manual.

There are three rows in the grid, linked to three key questions, namely:

- **What's the problem?** This probes the worker's best estimation of each member of the network's "Explanatory model" regarding the principal difficulty they see as needing help;
- **What to do?** This probes the worker's best estimation of each network member's "Intervention model" regarding what needs to happen to make a start in improving the problems they have highlighted;
- **Who does what?** This probes the worker's best estimation of each network member's "Responsibility model"—their understanding of who is responsible for whatever interventions they see as necessary in the system.

In the work of multi-agency and multi-professional networks, it is generally the case that the most common forms of misunderstanding (we might say "mis-mentalizing") or conflict occur at one or more of these levels, and these questions simply provide a systematic set of "mentalizing prompts" to explore these.

The columns in the grid (there can be as many as required) represent the key people in the client's network. The grid can include the client and their carers if this is useful, or it can just focus on a number of core professionals in the network. The selection of who should be included in the grid is left to the discretion of the AMBIT worker based on what, ideally, needs to be understood about the functioning of the network. The grid can be completed in different settings: either by oneself, in conversation with someone in the team—even during a multi-agency meeting (this often prompts collaborative work to complete it), or with the client/family themselves, as a means of explaining the network to them.

The AMBIT worker is invited to write down a small number of core statements in each box: bullet points about what they believe the particular person in the network understands the problem to be, what they believe should be done about it, and who they see is responsible for doing this. As much as possible, workers are advised to write short statements that, if the person in question were to read them, they might nod and say, "Not bad, that's pretty much how I see it." Of course, the AMBIT worker cannot possibly know as a fact what members of the network think and feel about these questions without going to the person to check. However, this is a *mentalizing* exercise, not a factual assessment. Where there are complete blanks (e.g. "I simply don't know what the psychiatrist would say is the problem!"), this might be a useful prompt to communication and exploration with that professional. The intention is to enable the worker/team to create an overview of their best estimation of the states of mind of the chosen people in the network. Later in this section, we provide a worked example that shows some of the types of issues that may emerge through doing this exercise.

The questions for each row are deliberately designed to avoid jargon and to invite speculation about the "bottom line" beliefs that a worker may hold. For example, a school Head of Year for a young person might believe that the main problem is the inability of the parents to provide adequate care, that the appropriate intervention is for the young person to be taken into care, and that social services are responsible for doing this. The social worker (who knows that, whatever concerns there may be about parenting, this family does not pass thresholds for the forced removal of the child) may believe that the problem is primarily due to cannabis use, that the young person needs treatment for their drug use, and that the health care system should be providing this. The point

TECHNIQUES AND SKILLS | 245

of this technique is to encourage purposeful and systematic mentalizing of the behavior of colleagues in the network.

While this can also be done with a client as a way of helping them make sense of a large and complicated network, this tool was developed primarily to enable the AMBIT worker to consider the states of mind and intentional stance of different workers in the network. Using this systematic approach to mentalize the network has two main intended outcomes. First, it shifts workers away from non-mentalized ways of explaining the behavior of colleagues, which, as we suggested near the start of this chapter, may fall back on default themes of individual lack of competence or motivation, or even malice, as explanations for other agency workers' behavior. Likewise, it addresses the risk of workers being influenced by negative professional and agency narratives about the work of other agencies, which easily crystallize into unhelpful stereotypes or mythologies.

Second, this approach is designed not just to help identify the most destructive or risky dis-integrations in a client's professional network, but to develop an understanding of them that is contextualized and sensitive to the different perspectives rather than essentially blaming. This means that, within the limited time available to work on strengthening a client's network, a worker is more likely to invest their time in brokering the most important "connecting conversations" (see below), with a view to repairing the most critical weaknesses in the fabric of a network that is endlessly fragile and perhaps inevitably somewhat threadbare.

Case example

Michael (age 14) lived with his maternal grandmother. Both his parents had severe substance misuse problems and Michael had been cared for by his grandmother since he was 4 years of age. He had attended primary school regularly, but his attendance at secondary school had always been problematic. He disliked school because he found reading difficult and easily felt humiliated by this in class. He had started smoking cannabis when he was 12, which was provided to him by his uncle, and his use was now increasing. He had started to become linked to a local gang of mainly older boys who were involved in dealing drugs, who used him as a "runner" to deliver drugs to their customers. His grandmother was rightfully worried that he was becoming involved in petty crime to fund, among other things, his cannabis use. The key people in his professional network were a youth worker who he respected, the school SENCO, his Head of Year, and a social worker from a recently formed Family Support Team, where he had just been referred.

The youth worker in the local young people's substance use service had recently received training in AMBIT with their team, and used the Dis-Integration Grid to map out the beliefs of the network and to mentalize how the different people in the network were feeling about Michael and their work with him (see Table 6.2). From this, it was clear that there was a substantial conflict between education workers and social services

Table 6.2 Michael's completed Dis-Integration Grid

Levels of Dis-Integration	Grandmother	Youth Worker	School SENCO	Young Person	Social Worker
Explanation "What's the problem?"	Peer group relationships and links to gangs	Use of drugs	Family lack authority to support school attendance	No money	Lack of parental monitoring (but not at threshold for removal) Peer group influences
Intervention "What to do?"	Send him to boarding school	Engage with drugs team Alternative friendship group	Remove from family into foster care	Get money to stop offending	Youth work Drugs work Parenting work with grandmother
Responsibility "Who does what?"	Education authority	Drugs and alcohol team Youth club football team	Social care	My dad	Youth Services drug service Social worker

workers about the most appropriate interventions, which appeared to be paralyzing support for any other options apart from Michael's removal from his grandmother's care (even though such a dramatic intervention was not seen as appropriate—or even possible—by the agency that would have to enact it).

On Michael's part, as a result of this network paralysis and his sense that no-one else seemed to know or agree what to do, he could see little relevance in many parts of the network. His disengagement was amplified particularly because his own belief was that his main problem was his lack of money; this was fuelled (the youth worker tentatively surmised) by his sense of fury at his father's betrayal and abandonment of him to start a new life elsewhere.

The grid highlighted the likelihood that, although there was collaboration between the agencies, there was a lack of a shared understanding of why Michael had such difficulties, and also a lack of an authentically shared plan. This reflective process helped to galvanize the AMBIT-trained youth worker into trying to broker and facilitate two "connecting conversations" (the process involved is described in more detail later in this chapter). The first conversation was between Michael and his grandmother, to talk about money and the sad and unfair reality that his father (despite Michael's sense that it was his duty) was not likely to contribute to Michael's upkeep. The second was between the social worker and the SENCO at the school, and was more delicate; as a youth worker in a separate team, the AMBIT-trained worker had no mandate or authority over either of these agencies. However, in response to the youth worker reflecting a reasonably accurately mentalized understanding of these other workers' dilemmas, they both became curious about this new perspective on the functioning of the network as a whole, and a conversation did take place. This allowed the social worker to explain to the SENCO the frustrating reality of legal thresholds for the possibility of removal of a child (which Michael's predicament did not meet) and the value that the school could bring through supporting the community-based plan that was being shaped. The point of mapping disintegration in the network—however this is achieved—is to try to support the network so that it becomes more effective in its work with the client.

When completing a Dis-Integration Grid, it is not uncommon for significant differences in key beliefs and intentions to be highlighted between professionals linked to different agencies. These differences are sometimes so stark that it seems quite evident that the network is unlikely to function effectively so long as they persist. It is hard to convey how powerful a 15-minute exercise can be in indicating how the network is (or is not) actually functioning. Apart from clarifying what is happening, it is important to highlight that the grid should always prompt workers to consider how they can take responsibility for trying to improve this, bearing in mind the fact that their ambit (sphere of influence) may be limited.

Focusing on trust as well as expertise: Positioning theory

In AMBIT, a great deal of significance is given to the recognition (and, to use our language, the *marking*) of actual existing relationships that the client already has with family members, peers, and professionals. In particular, AMBIT strives to promote the importance of the position of a worker who has the most trusting relationship with the client (the person who, at least in the client's mind, is "key" to their seeking and receiving help). This person may not have the highest status in the network, or the specific specialist skills most relevant to the client's immediate problems, but their relationship may represent an opportunity for the client to experience some sense of trust in another person and gain a "window" into the world of being helped. Put starkly, the dilemma may be between offering help from someone with the right skills (e.g. a nurse with experience in working with self-harm) but with whom the young person has no relationship of help, versus help being offered by someone who is already trusted by the client (e.g. a classroom support worker who does not have the skills around the specific problem and is worried by it). For AMBIT, the task of the network as a whole is to find a way of working together to bring these two elements together through collaborative practice.

The worker who has some level of trust with a client is holding a position. Such a position is not fixed and may change (other workers may join them there as time passes), but it cannot be simply assigned to someone else as part of a job description.

For individual cases, a joint agency plan can be formulated, according to which the worker who has the position of "knowing the client best" may, for example, be asked to communicate with the client about the network in general, or to act in a kind of chaperone role, introducing another worker whose specialist skills are required. This would be adopting a position that may appear quite similar to the more formal meaning of the "keyworker" role. However, in networks, there is often no-one with explicit authority across the network for assigning these roles, and positions, in contrast, are not appointed so much as they emerge. In contrast to formal roles, positions adopted by individuals in a network, once recognized, may be negotiated between colleagues (is this helpful position to be recognized and strengthened, or is that unhelpful one to be diluted and shifted?). This may be done either implicitly or explicitly, but will always occur within the context of hierarchical organizations that are themselves bound by local protocols, commissioned targets, and professional codes. A worker's authority and capacity to adopt and use (or attempt to shed) particular positions with respect to the professional network is partly determined by the constraints and opportunities given them by their host agency. In a multi-agency network, the potential for this kind of adaptive positioning (in which different workers might, for instance, adopt more or less central positions at different times with respect to the core challenges for the client) is likely to be determined largely by the quality of the interpersonal and inter-agency relationships that exist across it. Increasingly mentalized understandings of each other's formal roles and dilemmas make such flexibility more possible. Such a cultural shift inevitably takes time, and is likely to proceed as a series of small incremental advances, rather than being something that can be managed into existence through a single large-scale reorganization alone. Nonetheless, it will be apparent that strong support from senior managers is an essential component in the process.

Common positions in a network

The AMBIT worker is invited to make sense of the network around a client in terms of not just formal roles, but also the positions adopted by (or, to some extent, assigned to) individual workers. A number of common positions that result from, or contribute to, dis-integration may be helpful to recognize within a network. Here, we describe a few examples; it is likely that specific local networks, laboring under their own local constraints and challenges, will be able to identify examples of these or others that are particularly pertinent for them.

For example, one worker in the network may feel that their agency is the lead agency for the case. A social worker with a client on a child protection plan may feel that safety issues should be the overarching consideration for everyone in the network, and that collaboration is fine as long as it is organized around this key issue. The social worker is positioned by their own agency and the context as a lead professional in the network, even though this may not necessarily be how other parts of the network perceive this (at worst, in their eyes, the social worker may find themself positioned as a self-appointed controller). In parallel, a Youth Offending Officer may simultaneously consider that the requirements of a Court Order in relation to the client/family are non-negotiable with respect to the rest of the network. In this way a network may become increasingly organized around dilemmas as to whose case this is. This is difficult to resolve when several agencies simultaneously feel that they are holding non-negotiable responsibilities that cannot be compromised by other agencies, and require leadership positions in the network. Such difficulties around the position of "leadership" may lead to clients having a series of appointments with different professionals that are at least in part determined more by the requirement for each agency to discharge its formal responsibilities (or, worse, to assert dominance) than the need for a shared intervention plan.

Theories about personal responsibility may also influence how different workers become positioned. For instance, there may be significant differences in their answers to the question of how much the client has created or contributed to their current difficulties. Some workers may feel that the client needs to recognize the consequences of their negative behavior and that avoiding issues of personal responsibility is unhelpful, whereas others may highlight disadvantage and negative events as ways of explaining current difficulties. Sometimes, for example, a school may feel that exclusion is important in order to communicate boundaries about what is acceptable, and that the client must take responsibility for their behavior. However, this may create anxiety for the social worker, who may be concerned about the risk of increasing negative behavior when the client is not in school. In this way, it may be helpful to consider who in the network is taking the position (or being positioned) as the one trying to establish a boundary for the client.

Moreover, workers may become positioned around the question of "Who knows the client and the family best?" This may be linked to the question of "Who is most likely to be experienced by the client as being helpful to them?" or "Who is most liked by them?" For example, a worker may become quite identified with the client, and in consequence might distance themself from the rest of the network—supported by a belief that most of the main agencies don't really understand the client at all. Alternatively, staff in a school may feel that they have a greater understanding of the client than other agencies because they "have the young person all day." Other workers' knowledge about the client may be discounted as "not knowing what they are really like." In this way, workers may become positioned around the quality of their expertise about, or relationship with, the client, as a way of ensuring that their view about the client should prevail in decision-making around case management.

Case example

A teaching assistant at a secondary school has developed a strong relationship with a young person who has very poor attendance at school. The Education Welfare Officer (EWO) has been referred to the young person because of the severity of their absence from school. A meeting of professionals is called by the social worker involved in the case because of increasing concern that the family is unable to cope with the young person when they are out of school, and all the other risks that this entails. At this meeting, the education system is represented by the EWO; the teaching assistant is not invited. This process "positions" the relationship of the teaching assistant with the young person as not being of value in trying to address the young person's increasingly severe problems. The teaching assistant feels that he understands the young person better than everyone else, and that the higher-status professionals do not really understand the young person. This position is unintentionally communicated to the young person by the teaching assistant in his ongoing contact with the young person. This unhelpful positioning is challenged by the AMBIT worker by asking the teaching assistant to help with making sense of the young person's problems and by inviting the teaching assistant to meet with him and the young person together.

In trying to address aspects of how professionals and non-professionals become positioned in a network around a client, the AMBIT worker is rarely able to orchestrate explicit changes to such positions. The skills and techniques described here are captured by usual methods of collaborative practice, but with an effort to develop an enriched understanding of the way that networks are not simply made up of formal roles and responsibilities—and that the helping process also involves attention to the subtle but crucial positioning of helpers, both by each other and by the client. The sort of conversations that may be helpful between people in the network in resolving such positioning dilemmas are covered in the next section.

Connecting conversations

Connecting conversations may arise either out of issues identified from the Dis-Integration Grid or from observations based on positioning theory. Connecting conversations are perhaps the main method of intervening in the professional network around the client. On one level, these simply involve conversations by the AMBIT worker with others, with the explicit intention of helping to rebalance network relationships or facilitating more effective network relationships (we could describe this as a state in which there is more accurate mentalizing on each side). Often, the AMBIT worker may be trying to facilitate conversations between others in the network, something that depends as much on diplomatic skills as anything specific to AMBIT.

The purpose of connecting conversations

The key idea about connecting conversations is that they are not just about liaising across a network with a view to improving information sharing, or general communication, or being supportive, etc. These functions are undoubtedly helpful, and AMBIT would not wish to discourage such a core activity. The idea of connecting conversations is about more than just information-sharing; these conversations have the explicit intention of trying to improve understanding across a network—that is, for professionals within a network to develop a more mentalized understanding of each other's experience and work. Put another way, a connecting conversation often involves paying more attention to the functioning of the network (or the quality of the relationships) than to the content of the material being shared (or not) between workers. This has some parallels with parenting: one of the key issues may be less about the particular style of parenting that one parent adopts but more about the degree to which it is shared with the other parent, or the degree to which differences may trigger conflict between them. A shared approach, or one in which differences between parenting styles are handled explicitly and respectfully, may be more significant than the precise contents of such an approach.

Connecting conversations arise out of reflections about how the network is currently functioning—accurate mentalizing of the different "players" in the network, as it were—either through discussion of a completed Dis-Integration Grid for a particular case, or from observations about how workers are positioning themselves, or becoming positioned, in the network.

In the example of Michael, discussed earlier, the AMBIT worker may aim to facilitate a few key conversations in the network that address some of the issues highlighted by the Dis-Integration Grid. In Michael's case, the AMBIT worker acted to facilitate a conversation between the SENCO and the social worker about how to develop a shared formulation and plan regarding how to support Michael. The intention was to find ways in which both agencies could support the grandmother's authority more effectively. Next, a conversation between Michael and his grandmother about money was also highlighted—how much money Michael would have each week, how this could be arranged in ways that were consistent and open, and how Michael could understand the severe constraints on his father in respect of Michael's wish that his father would supply extra cash.

Pragmatic aspects of connecting conversations

Connecting conversations also take into account the fact that working in a network can involve a large amount of time. Professionals' meetings, child protection planning meetings, liaison arrangements with agencies such as schools, and other network processes are all highly labor-intensive, especially if the hours required to find a suitable time for the various participants are factored in. If connecting conversations are to be useful, they will have to be woven into such existing arrangements rather than being additional processes and burdens to staff. As much as possible, the intention is to try to use existing protocols and processes (e.g. meetings that are already part of the program) as opportunities for this kind of enabling work directed at whole-network functioning. In terms of how a team takes this on, it is important that this work is regarded as a mainstream component of working practices rather than allowing it to be side-lined as a sort of luxury add-on, or a special example of "going the extra mile."

So, if they are to become a part of ordinary practice, connecting conversations must often be brief. The AMBIT approach encourages their design to be realistic about, and sensitive to, the pressures and demands of many frontline workers. For example, in any particular case, the AMBIT worker may be invited to consider how best to use 30 minutes in any week to spend specifically on trying to enable that particular network to function better. The aim is to reduce the burden of network processes rather than increase them. In our view, idealized descriptions of networks operating through regular well-attended network meetings are often highly unrealistic (even if desirable) when applied to the experience of very busy and often stressed frontline workers in different agencies. Full network meetings can rarely be convened quickly, often requiring at least a two- or three-week delay in order for diaries to be coordinated. This kind of delay may be out of step with the situation the network needs to address.

A second pragmatic aspect of influencing a network is for the worker to consider the question of what their sphere of influence (ambit) is for a particular case. This is not a technique, but an effort to encourage reflection on what is the appropriate level of influence that a worker can expect to have within a network. This will be different not only for each worker, but for each of a given worker's cases. One of the characteristics of a network compared with a managed system is that members of a network do not necessarily have any formal authority over the actions of others in that network. As we described earlier in this chapter, coordinated and shared approaches to the care of clients can be achieved only through negotiation and creating a climate in which staff from different agencies listen to and respect each other's practice and expertise. It is common for psychologists to have a view about whether a young person should be looked after by the local authority, and for social workers to have beliefs about which young people should be admitted to hospital. Such beliefs may be sincerely held, but acting upon them may be neither the responsibility nor within the authority of the roles that the different agencies hold. In this way, effective networks need to respect local practice and expertise and accept the judgments of others, even if such judgments are different from their own. Creating a culture of cross-agency respect is one of the core aims of the AMBIT approach.

As always, the final point is that (rarely, but certainly occasionally) it is appropriate, and still need not be disrespectful, to challenge the decisions or attitudes of workers in other agencies. Sometimes it is hard for an AMBIT-trained (or, indeed, any) worker to avoid the conclusion that it is necessary to try to persuade others to act differently, or even to protest about the actions of other agencies. Clearly there are times when this will be necessary and appropriate to the needs of the client and their family, or to longer-term working in the network. To elicit such a connecting conversation in the most productive way, we would recommend that it should always be preceded by a process of "Thinking Together" with a team colleague (see Chapter 5) in order to mentalize and reflect on the issues and the likely states of mind involved as carefully as possible. The section on graded assertiveness in Chapter 5 may also be relevant in such circumstances. It is quite understandable that feelings of anger and frustration with the perceived actions of other agencies sometimes come to dominate judgments as to what is the appropriate position for an AMBIT-trained team to adopt around a particular case. The important thing here is to enable action to take place, sometimes assertive action, in the context of recognized states of mind, rather than just issuing reactions to specific events and/or unquestioned beliefs about the work of another service.

Techniques in connecting conversations

There is, then, the potential for positions adopted by different individuals and agencies in the network to become polarized, fixed, and oppositional. Under such conditions, the task of accurately mentalizing the different people in the network becomes much harder. The job for the AMBIT worker is to try to identify such polarizations and to see what adjustments could be offered to address them. Just as in face-to-face work with a client, the more that the worker can accurately mentalize their professional colleagues, the more likely it is that professional trust (trust based on acceptance of professional qualifications and roles) can become *epistemic* in nature—allowing new insights to be heard, taken in, and generalized to the work and to future interactions.

In general, positions are likely to become more fixed if they are perceived as being attacked, criticized, or invalidated by others. Connecting conversations that start from the position of trying to persuade others about the correctness of one's own position are unlikely to result in increased fluidity of positions within the network. So, the purpose of connecting conversations is to create dialogues that move in a different direction. It is not necessarily as helpful to become concerned about proper technique around this as it is to have a sense of one's intentions—what one is trying to facilitate—namely, an opening up of dialogue from closed to more open perspectives. Everyone will have their own approach to this, but some preparatory advice and two techniques will be mentioned here, both of which involve the use of the self as a way of facilitating change.

Preparation

In preparing for a connecting conversation, it is critical that the worker ensures that their own intentions are clear—that they have mentalized themself as well as the other "players." Thinking Together with a colleague or supervisor is advisable before engaging in the exercise. Two helpful questions that a worker might ask themself are:

> "What *don't* I know about this situation that is leading me to think about it differently from her/him?"
> "What information do I have *that I may not have communicated clearly enough* in order to make better sense to people holding these different points of view?"

Technique: joining

For example, in the example mentioned earlier, where the school took a position of "setting a boundary" for the young person in relation to their behavior, the AMBIT worker may see this as the dominant narrative that the school is representing and so would seek ways to amplify some of the more marginal narratives of other agencies, and the ways they, too, might share this concern. The AMBIT worker seeks opportunities by which the school can recognize that other agencies share the sense of the importance of boundary-setting for this young person, rather than leaving the school staff to feel that they alone are standing up for the importance of this. For example, there may be opportunities for the school's representative (e.g. a senior teacher) to experience the social worker as someone who is equally concerned about negative behavior, and to hear more about how this becomes enacted in the social worker's sessions with the young person. The teacher will need to experience any professional talking to him/her about this issue as genuinely recognizing their own very real dilemma, not merely categorizing them as harsh and punitive.

The AMBIT worker may try a number of methods to increase the fluidity of positions within the network, rather than allowing them to become increasingly polarized. The example we give above is an example of a "joining technique," where the aim is to join temporarily with the position of the other. Explicitly supporting the other's initial position can help to create a richer description of what it represents, and to invite curiosity about other positions. If, as in this example, the teacher believes that excluding the client from school would be helpful, then the aim in joining in this way would be to "really work this through," developing a narrative about how this might work out in the longer term, so that it is then possible to start to construct a more detailed plan about how to contribute to this approach. What could be done to try to make this work better? What help could you offer to the school in relation to this? What ideas does the teacher have about how the young person's learning could be supported out of school? Do they have ideas about how the positive relationships that the young person has with other pupils could be supported, and the negative ones discouraged?

Technique: "use of self," or help-seeking
The second technique is to offer to shift one's own position or, to put this more simply, to ask for help. This may arise when the worker feels that the outcome for the client is not improving, and although having a view about this situation, recognizes either a lack of understanding of the client's predicament or a sense of helplessness around such circumstances. The task here is more to use one's own self to model a capacity for uncertainty and openness in order to enable more fluid dialogue. For example, a conversation might begin with the AMBIT worker saying, "I wondered if I could ask for your help with Sam. I have been working with him for several weeks but I don't feel that I am getting anywhere.

I'm aware that you have known him for much longer than me and imagine that you know him much better. Could I ask for your thoughts about why he gets so stressed about things some days?"

System transformation: Increasing mentalized understandings across the network

Techniques that involve shifting positions within a network clearly overlap with techniques supporting a mentalized understanding between colleagues. The potential pitfalls remain similar. It is pointless to set out to try to *make* others in the network "mentalize more," whether about themselves, the client, or others in the network. The primary task is to focus on *one's own* effort to understand things as well as possible, because it is accurate mentalizing that brings about more accurate mentalizing, not simply telling someone to do it! For example, it may be helpful to recognize that one's own behavior may not make as much sense to others as we may expect. One feature of active mentalizing is the capacity to imagine how one may appear from the outside. To make oneself more predictable and understandable, it is generally useful to broadcast one's intentions about the purpose of the conversation ("I really want to make sure that I am not unintentionally undermining your work with Kelly, as I know you are really trying to get her to talk more with her mum, and I'm aware my meetings with her might not be necessarily seen as helping this") and, if possible, to "mark the task" ("Can we brainstorm a bit for the next few minutes to get some ideas about how I can best frame my work in the light of this?") so that others can start to see how you see things. This may also include respectful aspects of self-disclosure, such as, for example, acknowledging "feeling a bit clumsy in my work with this client." The importance of sharing individualized aspects of one's own experience in this way is that it can help facilitate a more mentalized dialogue about the client's needs with colleagues, by reducing professional defensiveness.

Another technique to promote mentalizing can be to join the other worker in imagining what the client might make of the conversation that is taking place while the current predicament is worried about and worked through. "If X was able to listen to us talking about this, I wonder what they would make of it? What do you think about this? I find it hard to know." The aim here is try to enable workers to look at their own state of mind from the outside by imagining it being viewed by the client.

Perhaps, more broadly, connecting conversations may provide an opportunity to voice just how difficult the task is that all workers are grappling with, and especially perhaps in relation to our own experience. The important thing is to recognize this difficulty, but to do so in the authentic context of our joint and individual efforts to help the client. Of course, facilitating a conversation that acknowledges a sense of professional helplessness without offering any paths forward is unlikely to be helpful. A mentalizing stance is supported by connecting this "noticing and naming" of a dilemma with the underlying intentions of workers—to be helpful to their clients, and to provide a well-run service. Of course, there are all sorts of other motivations that may be present and may be much less easy to acknowledge, such as a wish to place the problem with others and/or to reduce one's own workload. We realize that in relation to such issues, the initial stance of acknowledging our own vulnerability or limitations could potentially be described as naive. Despite this, we hold to our view: if we are to facilitate trust across a network, we may need to start with the courage to demonstrate a trusting stance, until shown that this is not appropriate to a particular case.

Explicitly acknowledging integrated working

Some AMBIT-influenced teams have adopted a practice of intentionally looking out for, and providing, written acknowledgement of instances of positive integrated work from colleagues in other teams. A simple letter or e-mail is sent to a worker in another agency (preferably copied to their manager) to acknowledge how helpful their contribution was and very briefly describing what it was that was experienced as being so helpful. Such letters are best kept short and to the point, and a set pro forma is best avoided, as this undermines the fact that something quite specific and individual is being acknowledged.

> Dear Anne, Just a quick e-mail to thank you for all the work you did with Azeem and me. It was great to work so closely with you on this, and I'm particularly grateful for the way you helped encourage Azeem to start seeing me—he didn't much want to at first. You always seemed to speak with Azeem about all the different workers in his (complicated!) case with such care and respect, and I'm sure that helped him make sense of us all, as he clearly trusted you, and for us to work with him. Looking forward to an opportunity to work together again! Best wishes.

This is not just one of the most basic forms of behavioral intervention—positive reinforcement of a desired behavior—it is also a purposeful attempt to put into practice the AMBIT stance principles of showing respect for local practice and expertise, and taking responsibility for integration. In a sense, it is a small but purposeful attempt to counter the drip-feed of biased negative feedback about networks and their functioning that we described at the beginning of this chapter.

Limitations and challenges

Privileging client contact

The AMBIT approach aims to be as network-focused as it is client-focused (and team-focused, and learning-focused!), and the encouragement of communication and collaboration between different agencies is a core part of this work, not a "luxury extra." This may appear to have intrinsic common-sense value in improving the quality of practice. However, for some services this type of work is not seen as being quite as crucial or valuable as the direct work with a client. More problematic is that some services are paid only for the direct (face-to-face) work they do with a client. Although in the UK some commissioners of services have started to recognize the value of joint network approaches, the more dominant approach is for commissioners to try to ensure value for money by monitoring (and paying for) only direct contact with the client. This narrow definition of value can produce major constraints on joint working and can lead to all agencies becoming narrowly focused on achieving as many appointments with clients as possible. In such contexts, work directed at network functioning may be seen as mere "icing on the cake," to be squeezed into time between appointments, and in such cases is likely to be inadequate to the task. It is important for workers trained in AMBIT to be clear about the degree to which managers and commissioners genuinely support the high importance of networking tasks that the AMBIT approach asserts. For example, if a client is referred to an AMBIT-trained team and the team feels that help would be much better offered through supporting an existing relationship that the client has with, say, a probation officer, this indirect work through the probation officer needs to happen in such a way that it does not disadvantage the service in terms of the income it may receive in relation to its casework. In one AMBIT team, achieving this required renegotiation with commissioners and the definition of a specific new intervention modality, which they called "Structured Consultation."

Confidentiality

Good-quality networks need to share information. Except in the rare instances where safeguarding concerns preclude it, information-sharing needs to take place transparently with the client and carers. In general, our experience is that families prefer networks that communicate well, as this improves their experience of care. However, for some clients and families this raises very major anxieties about stigma and the threat of loss of privacy, or other negative consequences. For some families or individuals whose motivations are more perverse (where hidden abuse is still ongoing, for instance), a well-functioning network that shares information is the last thing they want.

It is not uncommon for the process of beginning to engage with help to raise anxiety about the inevitability of repetitions of previous betrayals, disappointments, or humiliations in relation to caregivers or authorities. A common way for clients to try to address such anxieties may be to invite the worker to feel that they alone have some capacity to be trustworthy—that all the others in the network are not trustworthy, or have already proven themselves inadequate, so the AMBIT worker should not share information with them. This is a form of positioning by the client—inviting the worker into the elevated position of "super-helper" by denigrating the other members of the network—and should be resisted. It easily becomes a negative collusion about how useless the adult world is in general, or this professional network is in particular. This adds to the biased negative feedback about local agencies that is often a subtle but pernicious factor in maintaining dis-integration.

For the AMBIT worker, as we discussed in Chapter 5, the aim is to model a sense of helpful connection with their core team by emphasizing how much they rely on the support of their colleagues in order to be able to think effectively about their clients' problems. This explicit referencing of professional relationships as being helpful to the worker is intended to demonstrate to the client that having helping relationships is healthy and commonplace, and *not* cause for shame or humiliation. Hopefully this serves two purposes: first, as a starting point for developing ways of sharing information with the wider network that the client can accept as being part of their being helped, and second, as a modeling of help-seeking (by the worker in their relationships to other parts of the network) that the client might later try to emulate. Clearly, any issues of safeguarding always override such considerations; the AMBIT approach is always to respect local protocols of information-sharing (albeit that an AMBIT team may also play an active part in influencing positive improvements to such protocols) and to recognize that it is not possible to devise a system that will work the same way for every family.

Pragmatic constraints on network practice: time

There is no doubt that attending to the way in which a professional network functions has the potential to take up a great deal of time. There are some obvious examples of this with respect to professionals' meetings, safeguarding meetings, and so on. Not only are the meetings themselves time-consuming, but arranging them can be extremely hard work, as professional diaries are often congested and inflexible. We recognize that it is far from helpful to burden professionals with additional demands on their time, particularly if such work is not given the same importance as face-to-face work. The intention around connecting conversations is that they are light-footed and, where possible, brief and pragmatic. Our experience is that these conversations usually take place in the form of phone calls or e-mails to colleagues, often with the aim of reducing unnecessary work and communication.

The AMBIT approach is not about increasing the number of professional meetings, but more about trying to ensure that where such meetings take place the AMBIT worker attends to the process of the network itself, and not just the information about the client. Our hypothesis is that if the network works better, this will reduce anxiety in the network and reduce the demand for professional meetings prompted by such anxieties. Finally, connecting conversations are best seen as an ongoing process, not as major "once-only" events that are expected to solve things. A wise colleague refers to "laundry basket" conversations in relation to the same phenomenon in families (referring to the need for parents to accept the necessity of giving apparently endless reminders, sometimes for years, in relation to an adolescent whose dirty socks need to be picked up from the floor and placed in the basket as they cannot apparently remember to do this of their own accord). We suspect that adolescents, unlike complex networks, have a stronger track record of getting the message in the fullness of time.

AMBIT and a keyworker system

AMBIT is an approach to working with hard-to-reach clients that encourages effective joint agency working. It is not a pro forma for restructuring inter-agency processes. Whatever the nature of local cross-agency protocols and practices, workers will need to make sense of each other's behavior, trust each other's judgment, and be attentive to how they are being positioned in the professional network. The degree to which local agencies would wish to formally adopt a keyworker system in the AMBIT sense, dependent upon a "team around the worker" and recognizing and supporting a "key" worker who has been positioned as such by the client (as opposed to being appointed to a formalized role), is outside the authority and remit of AMBIT. To attempt to do so without intimate knowledge of a specific service ecology would risk presenting a service with a set of blunt (and ultimately teleological) demands for explicit roles and responsibilities that carry the risk of as many unintended harms as there are intended benefits.

We recognize that this would be a particularly major undertaking if the service included statutory responsibilities around, for example, safeguarding, school attendance, and offending, where designated services (and individual workers) hold formal responsibilities for community outcomes around such needs. Our experience in training communities of teams in a local area is that it is important to be clear that AMBIT is not a management system for introducing structural change. Its primary focus is on improving the experience and practices of workers and clients around processes of help, and, while it adopts a multi-agency stance about this, it does not advocate specific new and concrete cross-agency practices. The AMBIT position is to respect local practice and expertise, and if cross-agency changes arise in the fullness of time—influenced by a number of local teams adopting an AMBIT approach—then this would be a fine outcome, so long as outcome evaluations show corresponding improvements in the capacity of the professional networks to function well. We are aware that there have been many policy initiatives aimed at increasing integration between agencies, and although we are clearly in sympathy with such developments, we recognize that this is a huge structural undertaking that is beyond the scope of AMBIT alone.

Conclusions

Addressing the inevitable dis-integrations in multi-professional and cross-agency working is a core aspect of the AMBIT approach, as it is part of the AMBIT stance to consider the full range of different domains of a client's life that need attention and help. But cross-agency working is often hard to make sense of (i.e. to mentalize) and is not always characterized by reciprocal and trusting professional relationships. The AMBIT approach makes use of both systemic thinking and mentalizing in developing knowledge, techniques, and practice for this important area of work in order to enable professional networks to function more effectively together. As well as sharing plans and liaising with each other, AMBIT workers are also invited to ask, "What is it like to be … the social worker, the psychiatrist, the teacher in this particular case with this individual client?" "Is it dispiriting or enjoyable, satisfying or undermining, for this worker to try to help this client?" These questions seem to us to be as important as simply sharing demographic or narrative information about the case. Similarly, recognizing how a worker becomes subtly positioned by the client ("You are the only one who understands me") or by other agencies ("This is really your agency's responsibility, not ours") as part of a collaborative approach to help is often crucial as a way of understanding tensions and difficulties that are common (indeed, we would argue that they are inevitable) between agencies working in this field. If such difficult work is to be successful, then the aim of these practices is to generate renewed understandings, to make better sense of the complex behaviors enacted by other workers and ourselves, to make sense of how difficult this sense-making (mentalizing) is in such fraught contexts, and to attend to the need to maximize trust between workers.

References

Bateman, A. W., & Fonagy, P. (2016). *Mentalization-Based Treatment for Personality Disorders: A practical guide* (Oxford, UK: Oxford University Press).

Children's Workforce Development Council. (2009). *The Team Around The Child (TAC) and the Lead Professional* (Leeds, UK: Children's Workforce Development Council), http://webarchive.nationalarchives.gov.uk/20130401151715/http://www.education.gov.uk/publications/eOrderingDownload/LeadPro_Managers-Guide.pdf, accessed 24 Jan. 2017.

Department for Children, Schools and Families. (2008). Children's Trusts: Statutory guidance on inter-agency cooperation to improve well-being of children, young people and their families (London, UK: Department for Children, Schools and Families), https://www.education.gov.uk/consultations/downloadableDocs/Childrens%20 Trust%20Statutory%20Guidance.pdf, accessed 24 Jan. 2017.

Department of Health, & NHS England. (2015). *Future in Mind: Promoting, protecting and improving our children and young people's mental health and wellbeing* (London, UK: Department of Health, & NHS England), https://www.gov.uk/government/uploads/system/uploads/attachment_data/file/414024/Childrens_Mental_Health.pdf, accessed 24 Jan. 2017.

Harre, R., Moghaddam, F. M., Cairnie, T. P., Rothbart, D., & Sabat, S. R. (2009). Recent advances in positioning theory. *Theory & Psychology* 19: 5–31. doi: 10.1177/0959354308101417

HM Government. (2003). *Every Child Matters* (London, UK: The Stationery Office), https://www.gov.uk/government/uploads/system/uploads/attachment_data/file/272064/5860.pdf, accessed 24 Jan. 2017.

HM Government. (2013). *Working Together to Safeguard Children: A guide to inter-agency working to safeguard and promote the welfare of children* (London, UK: HM Government), http://media.education.gov.uk/assets/files/pdf/w/working%20together.pdf, accessed 24 Jan. 2017.

Holme, P., & Saramäki, J. (eds.). (2013). *Temporal Networks* (Heidelberg, Germany: Springer).

Lewis, T. G. (2009). *Network Science: Theory and applications* (Hoboken, NJ: Wiley).

Lord Laming. (2009). *The Protection of Children in England: A progress report* (London, UK: The Stationery Office), http://dera.ioe.ac.uk/8646/1/12_03_09_children.pdf, accessed 24 Jan. 2017.

Main, T. (1957). The ailment. *British Journal of Medical Psychology* 30: 129–45.

Munro, E. (2011). *The Munro Review of Child Protection: Final Report. A child-centred system* (London, UK: The Stationery Office), https://www.gov.uk/government/uploads/system/uploads/attachment_data/file/175391/Munro-Review.pdf, accessed 24 Jan. 2017.

Royal College of Psychiatrists, National Institute for Mental Health in England, & Changing Workforce Programme. (2005). *New Ways of Working for Psychiatrists: Enhancing effective, person-centred services through new ways of working in multidisciplinary and multi-agency contexts* (London, UK: Department of Health), http://eprints.nottingham.ac.uk/788/1/NWW_Psychs.pdf, accessed 24 Jan. 2107.

Scott, J. (2013). *Social Network Analysis* (3rd edn, London: Sage).

Sloper, P. (2004). Facilitators and barriers for co-ordinated multi-agency services. *Child: Care, Health and Development* 30: 571–80. doi: 10.1111/j.1365-2214.2004.00468.x

Turnell, A., & Edwards, S. (1997). Aspiring to partnership. The Signs of Safety approach to child protection. *Child Abuse Review* 6: 179–90.

Ungar, M., Liebenberg, L., Dudding, P., Armstrong, M., & van de Vijver, F. J. R. (2013). Patterns of service use, individual and contextual risk factors, and resilience among adolescents using multiple psychosocial services. *Child Abuse and Neglect* 37: 150–9. doi: 10.1016/j.chiabu.2012.05.007

Wasserman, S., & Faust, K. (1994). Social network analysis in the social and behavioral sciences. In: *Social Network Analysis: Methods and applications*, pp. 3–27. Cambridge, UK: Cambridge University Press.

Chapter 7

Learning at work: Toward a learning stance in teams

Introduction: Learning invites participation

Making team learning a central part of the AMBIT approach—one of the four core quadrants of the AMBIT wheel—has surprised some people. In this chapter we aim to explain some of the rationale for this, but also to convey the potentially exciting aspects of this feature of the approach. Rather than AMBIT being a model that is "done to you" as practitioners, the aim is to enlist everyone's much-needed expertise in the process of delivering successful help to our clients. Just as our clients don't much like—or benefit from—being passive recipients of someone else's ideas, however good they may be, we believe that the AMBIT approach truly comes alive only when teams collaborate (internally and, ideally, externally too) in the process of gaining and sharing knowledge, skills, and experience. An important part of what our clients achieve when an effective helping relationship is established is the move from passivity, hopelessness, and despair toward a stance in which they have a sense of agency around at least some aspects of their life. We aim to mirror this process in the way AMBIT is experienced by teams who adopt this approach; it is intended to be an active collaboration that makes as much use of everyone's knowledge and skills as possible. In truth, this work is so tricky that we probably cannot afford to do anything else. We would like you to feel that this chapter is an invitation to join AMBIT, to join in by finding ways to contribute the things you know or discover that work, and to bring your creativity and enthusiasm to the party.

In Chapter 1, we briefly described how the AMBIT model closely aligns with the overall framework of a learning organization, and described some of the reasons why we feel this approach is helpful for working with young people with mental health difficulties and other comorbid problems. This chapter continues this theme, looking at the fourth quadrant of the AMBIT model, "Learning at Work," and applying a mentalizing framework to explain how teams learn together.

AMBIT emphasizes learning for a number of reasons.

1. Contrary to the belief of many practitioners, implementation science (e.g. Meyers et al., 2012) suggests that health and welfare teams do not readily take

up new ideas or new methods of intervention, particularly if they already have well-established methods of practice. Although many teams engage in ongoing processes of team and case discussion, our observation is that this may not lead to much team learning. It is not unusual for teams to have somewhat repetitive discussions about similar dilemmas and issues that do not lead to any systematic progression in shared responses by team members. This may occur for many reasons, such as general stress, conflict within the team, the absence of a shared intervention model, or the lack of a structured approach to supporting "team memory," meaning that insights into improved practice may be acclaimed but are quickly forgotten.

2. Formal research evidence about what is effective for the clients of AMBIT-trained teams is either very limited or non-existent. Given the present state of knowledge, we do not know as much as we need to about providing effective help. This suggests that alongside our reading of research (*evidence-based practice*), we also need to learn from our experience as much as we can, and to try to capture effective ways of working so that others in the team—and workers in other teams—can gain from this. This is commonly called *practice-based evidence*.

3. In a recent meta-analysis, Weisz et al. (2013) noted that in the (disappointingly rare) instances where comparisons have been made between manualized evidence-based treatments and "treatment as usual" (TAU; sometimes referred to as "Usual Care"), evidence-based practice showed only relatively modest advantages over TAU. This finding led the authors to conclude that "the EBPs [evidence-based practices] have room for improvement in the magnitude and range of their benefit relative to usual clinical care." Nonetheless, most trials suggest that, on average and with local exceptions, interventions in manualized formats are somewhat more effective than benignly intentioned eclecticism. Among other things, Weisz et al. (2013) suggest that more focus should be placed on identifying the effective components of TAU, which can do surprisingly well. Our approach is completely in tune with this, and aims to engage teams in identifying the effective aspects of their practice in more systematic ways.

4. AMBIT is a team approach (see Chapter 5) in that the whole team is encouraged to share responsibility for the work of any individual case worker and to provide help to each other as required. This requires that team members develop a shared approach to common challenges in the work. However, this does not develop automatically just by workers working alongside each other. As we discussed in Chapter 6, workers may have very different ideas about what represents an appropriate response to a complex situation. Our

experience and reading of the literature suggest that "Learning at Work" must encompass a range of quite specific ideas and techniques, all aimed at helping to develop a core of shared practice, based as much on the team's different experiences of working on other cases as on the current state of the scientific literature. Without developing such processes, team members may continue to respond to common situations in very diverse and even divergent ways, and in doing so struggle to offer the support that the "Team around the Worker" (see Chapters 1, 4, and 5) suggests.

5. Explicit learning requires both individual courage and a contained and safe team environment in which team members can share their uncertainties, mistakes, and worries about lack of progress with some clients. These rather "negative" experiences are the preconditions for learning, and a climate that disallows acknowledging or thinking about them will hamper team learning. However, such a climate can be hard to establish in a context where the consequences of making mistakes (e.g. in child protection cases) or fear of professional shame about perceived lack of competence can make such dialogue extremely anxiety-provoking.

The AMBIT approach proposes that learning as a team needs to be given an explicit place in the routine work of *every* team. It requires a move from implicit processes ("just getting on with it") to explicit processes ("sharing how we do it, and why"), and from implicit learning to explicit learning. This is what the effective delivery of the AMBIT approach rests on, so it cannot be allowed to be seen as just peripheral or aspirational. In the AMBIT wheel this is represented in symbolic terms, placed as it is in the bottom quadrant, where the wheel makes contact with the ground and achieves traction. In our view, learning will not happen unless the processes that support it are transparent, effective, agreed upon, and constantly worked on by the team. This chapter describes the knowledge, skills, and practices that support learning within AMBIT-trained teams.

We will briefly describe the ideas underpinning "learning organizations," particularly the work of Peter Senge. We will explain how these ideas relate to mentalizing, to required AMBIT competencies, and to outcomes, and how the process of *manualization* may provide a vehicle to support a team's learning capacity. We will then describe a series of techniques and ideas about team learning, and will consider in detail the obstacles that can arise in establishing a learning culture in a team, as well as ways of creating such a culture.

We have come to realize that, perhaps even more than for the other aspects of AMBIT practice, this element of the AMBIT approach requires effective leadership—not just within the team, but supported at senior management levels. This in turn demands confidence among senior staff. We hope that, if not already, then at least by the end of this chapter it will be clear that the confidence in leadership that we refer to here is not of the blind or self-congratulatory variety, but one much closer to what has been described earlier in relation to the features of good mentalizing. This includes the capacity to tolerate not-knowing in one's own mind, all the while making the effort to remain mindful of, and curious about, the other minds in the team or wider system. Beyond that, the effective leader will use this capacity to create meaningful and coherent narratives, to develop explicitly intentional plans to address these, and to explain these in terms that make sense to those whom they intend to influence. This is no small feat, and most effective leaders will acknowledge that the team members they lead are critical ingredients in helping them toward such ideals. Leadership requires effective (and, we would argue, mentalizing) followership for it to be effective.

Knowledge and theory

Learning teams and learning organizations

In his book *The Fifth Discipline*, Peter Senge (2006) describes ideas about the "learning organization," its value, barriers that inhibit it, and ways to support its development. His work was in relation to business and management theory, but the language and ideas about the learning organization have propagated well beyond this field, and we were pleased to find a very close fit between his ideas and those that we had been developing in relation to AMBIT. Two aspects of his thinking seemed to us to be particularly pertinent to AMBIT—namely, his ideas about the importance of sharing each other's "mental models," and the role of team learning. We shall briefly review both of these.

For Senge, one of the major tasks for an organization is to enable staff to explore and make explicit basic assumptions about what may underpin problems and decisions in their work; for those with a more psychological orientation, these might be described as *constructs*. This work of clarification is supported by developing reflective practice within the organization: exploring differences between espoused theory and what is done in practice, through the process of balancing *inquiry* and *advocacy*. Senge proposes that the exploration of mental models is an active process between colleagues that entails a balance between exploring the ideas held by a colleague (inquiry) and also being able to be transparent about one's own ideas (advocacy). Too much inquiry without advocacy does not promote collaborative learning, and vice versa. Senge's "exploration of mental models" is consistent with a mentalized approach to team practice. It is easy to see the links between this balancing act and the tension between *sensitive attunement* (or the inquisitive mentalizing stance) and *broadcasting one's intentions* that we explored in Chapter 3 in the discussion of Active Planning. In describing the balance required in Active Planning, we created a third position, which is *planning*—in other words, the current best approximation or "map" of our shared understandings and intentions. The process of manualizing that we promote (described below) offers an explicit, and additional, method for teams to explore espoused theory measured against their actual practice.

In considering the process of team learning, Senge emphasizes the difference between *discussion* and *dialogue*. Discussion is characterized as being a process of passing things back and forth between people in order to see which idea will prevail—or "win." Dialogue is different and, as Senge puts it, refers to the "free flow of meaning between people." In dialogue, people are no longer primarily in opposition but are participating in developing common meaning. One feature of dialogue is that "people become observers of their own thinking"—in our language, they mentalize. This needs three conditions: all participants must suspend their assumptions (again, translating this into mentalizing language, this means avoiding the pitfall of psychic equivalence); all participants must view each other as "colleagues"; and there must be a facilitator who "holds the context" of dialogue (in AMBIT teams, this would be the overarching intention to provide more effective help).

In contrast, non-learning teams tend to be characterized as either "conflict free" (on the surface) or "highly polarized." Defensive processes that block dialogue are common and pervasive, often involving aspects of either hierarchy and power (e.g., "I don't want to show my boss that I don't feel confident about what to do") or an over-identification with one's role or position that ignores the purpose of the wider system (e.g. "I am a social worker; it is not my role to address X or Y"). Learning teams are certainly not free of defensive processes, but they aim to expect and actively look for them, and, on recognizing them, to address them by adapting—including efforts to learn from the experience and minimize the likelihood of similar barriers causing harm in the future. So, for AMBIT teams, staff are encouraged to find ways to share mental models and increase dialogue together. Later in this chapter we will describe methods and techniques to achieve this.

Team learning and quality improvement

Within mental health services, evidence of the effort made to create learning within services is not confined to the literature on learning organizations. There is a growing literature that describes the fact that organizational factors, in addition to evidence-based practice (e.g. Glisson et al., 2010), contribute to improved service effectiveness. The impressive work of Glisson and colleagues (Williams & Glisson, 2014; Glisson & Hemmelgarn, 1998) in developing the

Availability, Responsiveness, and Continuity (ARC) model has shown that addressing both organizational culture and climate can exert significant positive impacts on outcomes—to a similar degree as introducing evidence-based practice. The features of a service with a positive culture and climate (see also Chapter 5) have much in common with what the literature on learning organizations promotes: values, outcomes, and processes that are open to ongoing scrutiny, reflective practice, and adaptation.

Alongside this, quality improvement, defined as "better patient experience and outcomes achieved through changing provider behaviour through using a systematic change method and strategies" (Øvretveit, 2009, p.8), also has the potential to contribute to team learning. In general, however, many quality improvement methods often rely heavily on data systems that may be experienced by frontline teams as being motivated by organizational priorities for change (e.g. resource efficiencies) rather than having application to client care. The focus for AMBIT is less on these more structural processes of change and more on the relational components of teams that support mentalized practice. It is clear that the literature on organizational learning referred to above indicates how difficult this task is; there is no simple or mechanistic formula for how to promote team learning. The challenge, then, is to find ways of converting a general set of ideas and principles into clearly recognized practices that can help to shape the culture of a team and the way it actually works. We, too, do not believe that there is a single set of arrangements that would universally suit all teams that have been trained in AMBIT, so from the outset we have tried to develop a set of techniques to support learning that can and should be adapted to specific service contexts. Most prominent of these is the development of the "wiki" AMBIT manual (a wiki is a website that can easily be edited by its users; see later for more explanation of how wikis work). Local versions of the manual can be individually tailored, through small iterative additions and improvements that a local team makes, in order to fit local contexts—building on the core content of the approach, which itself inches forwards, curated by the AMBIT project and shared as a (we hope and intend) robust foundation to build upon. This commitment to supporting the capacity of teams to adapt general ideas to local circumstances is central to the AMBIT approach.

Team learning and client outcomes

One of the biggest drivers in supporting team learning is the capacity of a team to review and understand the outcomes of its work (Bearman & Weisz, 2015; Wolpert et al., 2012). The active inquiry as to whether the intervention being offered is actually being experienced as helpful to the client is important for several reasons. First, because the process of helping others is a human process rather than a technology (Munro, 2011), requiring feedback and sensitivity in order to avoid the possibility that workers fall into psychic equivalence, convinced that they are being helpful when this is not actually the case (Whipple et al., 2003). Also, evidence-based practice has demonstrated that, even with the most effective interventions in mental health work (e.g. cognitive-behavioral therapy (CBT) for anxiety; Reynolds et al., 2012), a significant proportion of young people do not improve despite being offered these "gold standard" treatments (Weisz et al., 2013). It is easy to see that there is a need to have active methods for identifying at an early stage those clients who are likely to improve on the basis of what we are doing, and those who may not. This information may lead to teams identifying interventions for clients who are less likely to benefit from the standard help offered by the team at an earlier stage, and modifying care provision appropriately. However, the implementation of an outcome-led approach is not easy; often, systems impose a high administrative burden on staff, and work on outcomes may subsequently become more focused on data entry (data traveling upwards to some distant and managerial observer) rather than data outputs or feedback (data feeding the downwards flow of information—about where we are and where we are heading—to the worker and client) (Wolpert et al., 2012).

Systematically evaluating the outcomes of the work of a team may have a range of important functions, including being able to justify further funding of the service. But, in our view, it also offers the possibility for a team to learn about the factors that lead to better outcomes (Jacob et al., 2017). In AMBIT, we do not propose a uniform approach to outcome evaluation, but we do insist that outcome evaluation of some form must be an integral part of a team's work. The online AMBIT manual (available via https://manuals.annafreud.org) provides a range of outcome measures, including the AMBIT AIM (discussed in Chapter 3), which, if used in its interactive online format, can support decision-making about possible interventions by tallying scores against simple algorithms that highlight rational intervention priorities. In line with the deployment-focused approach to model development (Weisz & Gray, 2008), many AMBIT-trained teams have carried out local evaluations about specific aspects of their work. These are often compiled as reports to support local decision-making about the value of different services being offered, and a number of these reports have been published (Fuggle et al., 2016, 2015; Griffiths et al., 2016). Some of these evaluations are more fully described in Chapter 9. These provide explicit examples of a further way in which teams can learn about their practice, so that the process of learning is not only about their experience as practitioners but also occurs through more systematic evaluation of the impact of the service on their target population. The intention, which is hardly original but is worth stating explicitly, is that such learning should contribute to ongoing service improvement and adaptation (recorded and broadcast through local team manualizing, which we cover below) so that evaluation work is never reduced to a process of feeding back to service stakeholders, but also stimulates ongoing learning for the team itself.

Team learning and AMBIT competencies

Competency frameworks have been recognized as a key component of creating clear ideas about the learning and training needs of different staff teams (Roth et al., 2010; Roth & Pilling, 2008). For mental health practice in the UK, competency frameworks have been developed for both adult and child mental health practitioners by the Centre for Outcomes Research and Effectiveness (CORE) at University College London. These competency frameworks have provided essential guidance about the skills and knowledge therapists need to deliver specific evidence-based interventions.

Following this line, AMBIT has developed two competency frameworks: one for individuals, and one for teams. These are fully described in the AMBIT online manual. For individual team members, AMBIT has 20 core competencies, grouped into three categories, which are listed in Table 7.1.

For AMBIT, the greater challenge is the degree to which these individual competencies develop into a team approach that is able to deliver on the team competencies listed in Box 7.1. In this respect, we see the team as a whole being fundamentally greater than the sum of its parts. An AMBIT team could be identified as having four core competencies mirroring the AMBIT wheel, with the addition of the need to evaluate client outcomes.

Each of these competencies has been further elaborated in the web-based manual[1]. There, for each of the five competencies, we have included a list of possible alternative ways in which this aspect of team practice might be demonstrated. Teams can make their own judgments as to what parts of the model to use, but we suggest that it is vastly preferable that this is marked as something explicitly chosen rather than something that happens by default. In keeping with much of the thrust of our argument, we are hesitant about appearing to reduce a competency to a single practice. This would be unhelpfully teleological, but at the same time, if there is no explicit way by which a competency could be observed to be taking place, there is a possibility that the competency itself

---

[1] https://manuals.annafreud.org/ambit/#%5B%5BAMBIT%20Team%20Competencies%5D%5D

Table 7.1 Individual practitioner competencies

	Part A: Knowledge for AMBIT
1	Knowledge of the theory of mentalizing
2	Knowledge of the AMBIT approach
	Part B: AMBIT Practice
3	Ability to use mentalizing in their work with clients and their families/carers
4	Ability to apply mentalizing to work with colleagues
5	Ability to apply mentalizing to work across agencies and see problems from multiple institutional standpoints
6	Ability to intervene in multiple domains
7	Ability to scaffold existing relationships to provide help
8	Ability to Think Together with colleagues
9	Ability to assess network functioning using a Dis-Integration Grid
10	Ability to manualize specific local practice
	Part C: Advanced Competencies
11	Knowledge of the common difficulties of "hard-to-reach" clients and their families/carers across multiple domains
12	Knowledge of attachment theory and help-seeking as a way of making sense of "hard-to-reach" clients
13	Knowledge of systemic principles that inform the AMBIT approach
14	Ability to engage with clients and their social context
15	Ability to complete an AIM assessment
16	Ability to develop a mentalized formulation of the client's difficulties
17	Ability to develop a shared care plan with the client
18	Ability to support the measurement of individual and team clinical outcomes
19	Ability to identify with, and access support from, the wider AMBIT community of practice
20	Ability to reflect on one's own and the team's fidelity to AMBIT

may be marginal to mainstream teamwork. As ever, the AMBIT approach is to try to balance top-down definitions with appropriate local adaptations.

Team learning and manualizing

In AMBIT, manualizing has a key place in the overall approach. We emphasize that manualizing, like mentalizing, is a verb; it is an ongoing activity that is a

> **Box 7.1 AMBIT team competencies**
>
> 1. Mentalize the Client
> 2. Mentalize the Team
> 3. Mentalize the Network
> 4. Learn as a Team
> 5. Evaluate Client Outcomes

key part of the life of an AMBIT-trained team. What is the difference between the manual (a noun; a thing) and manualizing (an activity)? The core content of the AMBIT manual (the basic wiki that all teams start with) supports learning by providing information and training materials online with open access to anyone who wishes to view them. The manual also contains all the teaching materials used in the basic four-day AMBIT training, including videos of the teaching sessions. Teams trained in the method are given a brief training on how to navigate and use the manual, bearing in mind the large amount of material that it contains. But this is just the starting point. In addition, each AMBIT-trained team is provided with its own version of the manual, which it can amend and update according to its own local circumstances and needs, without changing the core content that is shared with all AMBIT-trained teams. This will be described more fully in the section on web-based manuals later in this chapter. For now, the key principle is that this function supports workers and teams to move from implicit to explicit practice, reflecting on their work, and recording and broadcasting the conclusions of their dialogue in a publicly accessible web-based format. This provides a method for teams to consolidate and clarify their shared experience and update their knowledge and practice. Of course, this could be done using a folder kept in the office, but folders get lost and lack the capacity for energetic engagement that comes when a team knows that the fruits of its shared thinking will be available for all to see.

So, what does manualizing look like? Manualizing takes place in a team meeting and is a shared effort by the team to become explicit about its practice by writing clear descriptions of how it does common tasks, and why it does them in *this* way, rather than *that* way. These can range from complex issues—for example, how we work with clients at risk of sexual exploitation—to specific recent new information about a new substance being used by young people in the local area. Key "good practice" points from the reflective dialogue in the meeting are generated, written down, agreed, and then uploaded to the local AMBIT manual for future reference by the team.

Manuals and intervention fidelity

Intervention manuals have a range of functions, of which conventionally the most prominent may be that they provide the means for improving and assessing the degree to which an intervention is delivered properly against explicitly agreed standards of care. Because of its importance, this aspect of manuals is considered here in some detail, even though this function is not afforded quite as much prominence in AMBIT as it is in some other intervention manuals.

One of the things that most evidence-based approaches have in common is some form of intervention manual. Manuals, at their most basic level, exist to record key practical steps and techniques in order to promote reliable repetition of effective practice. It is against such *manualized* practice that some measure of adherence or fidelity to the method can be measured, and verdicts about the effectiveness (or not) of such worker behaviors can be arrived at. Valid evidence for the effectiveness of an intervention can be gathered only if:

1. The full range of therapeutic practices that make up the intervention is adequately manualized, so as to capture the range of appropriate responses and protocols (ones that many experienced workers in the field will tend to follow implicitly rather than with explicit reference to a manual);
2. There is evidence that the practice of workers in the field has been faithful to the practices recorded in the manual. Without this, outcome measures may simply be measures of non-specific effects (e.g. a worker's personal charisma and ability to connect with clients), and there is no means of teasing out and then disseminating the effective components of such practice through training.

It is not hard to see that a difference exists between how a manual may be used in a highly specific and focused "unimodal" intervention (e.g. CBT for a specific phobia) and the kinds of wide-ranging "multimodal" interventions across multiple domains (of which AMBIT is an example). This is not to say that examples of the latter interventions have not employed and benefited from manuals, however. There are some useful learning points from an earlier approach to multimodal intervention that has been influential in the development of AMBIT.

As an important example of the use of a conventional (paper-based) treatment manual, one of the most advanced versions of robustly manualized practice, which affords powerful and impressive levels of attention to enhancing worker fidelity to the model of practice, is multisystemic therapy (MST; Henggeler et al., 1996). MST has subsequently been adapted in numerous ways, extending its application beyond its original constituency, which was conduct-disordered young people. One of these adaptations (Henggeler et al., 2002) was a version designed for young people with substance use disorder (SUD)—an excellent diagnostic category for capturing a population of complex, comorbidly affected, and hard-to-reach clients. When the four-year follow-up of the original study of MST for adolescents with SUD showed somewhat disappointing results, learning took place. A cognitive-behavioral ("contingency management") module drawn from another evidence-based approach (the Adolescent Community Reinforcement Approach; Godley et al., 2002) was subsequently grafted on to the MST manual, and this further adaptation showed greater success in one US study (Henggeler et al., 2006). The MST model's SUD interventions are primarily behavioral with some cognitive components, in an ecosystemic (Bronfenbrenner, 1986) framework, and are strictly abstinence-based (it must be noted that this excludes a significant proportion of young people at the more severe end of the spectrum, or those with more chaotic lives, who would not voluntarily sign up to the program). Some forms of this approach have been tested in mandated settings in concert with "Drug Courts," and in others it has been acknowledged that there has been a relatively high degree of "informal mandation."

It is of interest that research on MST has placed a great deal of emphasis on the need for workers to maintain fidelity to the manualized models of practice. There is some evidence that it is through increased fidelity to the MST program that associated improvements in outcomes for young people are achieved (Schoenwald, 2008). This certainly supports the general finding that manualized interventions achieve better outcomes than "eclectic" approaches, although, as we will explain below, this is by no means an emphatic advantage. Moreover, without much more detailed process research it still remains rather unclear whether these objective clinical improvements resulted because the specific details of protocols and sequencing set out in the MST manual were carried out faithfully, or whether they could have been attributed to other factors. For instance, it is possible to hypothesize that improvements in outcomes might also be an unintended benign effect resulting from the positive feedback that is given to the worker about their "fidelity score," which is an intrinsic part of the MST Intensive Quality Assurance (IQA) program and involves detailed semi-independent observation of workers' practice. For instance, a worker who is adhering closely to the MST manual will receive regular positive feedback in supervision about his/her high Therapist Adherence Measure (TAM) scores; this may in turn be expected to have a confidence-building and energizing effect on their performance with their clients. Conversely, a worker whose creative attempts to respond adaptively to their perception of the client's immediate needs (veering away, if only temporarily, from the strict manualized content) may result in poor TAM scores, and subsequent negative feedback that might be demoralizing and demotivating.

The application of the MST IQA methods (which include regular independent phone contact with the young person and their family to ask about the content and style of sessions, measured against the manualized intervention, with fidelity scores fed back to therapists in their supervision) was formally assessed by Henggeler et al. (2008). A group of 30 practitioners were taught how to deliver a manualized contingency management intervention for adolescents with cannabis abuse problems. These practitioners were assigned either to the IQA process, or to a single "workshop-only" training. The IQA intervention showed mixed results; there was an increase in the application of manualized cognitive-behavioral techniques by practitioners in the IQA group over practitioners in the workshop-only group, but not in the application of contingency management monitoring techniques (which are the harder aspects of contingency management for workers to achieve, requiring workers to request from their clients regular urine samples for analysis, etc.). The authors of that study suggest this may indicate a "ceiling effect," above which even these intensive fidelity-monitoring structures and techniques cannot push workers. So, even with highly intensive and expensive quality monitoring and feedback systems, shifting practitioners' behavior toward fidelity to what is written in a manual is still very challenging.

Can intervention manuals be co-produced?

As mentioned above, John Weisz and colleagues (Weisz et al., 2013; Weisz & Gray, 2008) have remarked upon the successes of TAU/"Usual Care" that is often used as the control condition in randomized controlled trials (RCTs). While often less effective than the robustly manualized intervention models that are under investigation in such RCTs, TAU also quite often performs surprisingly well. To this end, Weisz and colleagues have referred to the need to "study Usual Care with care," and they develop this theme in what they refer to as the "deployment-focused" approach to the development of innovative interventions. In contrast to the more standard approach of first developing a (manualized) intervention and then setting up an RCT to test it, in a deployment-focused approach, multiple iterations of a draft method of working are tested in real settings, with feedback from each iteration leading to subsequent adaptations of the draft, aiming to advance practice incrementally. This approach has been highly influential in the development of AMBIT, and to our focus on learning at work as a critical component of good practice.

An important attempt to avoid the unintended consequence of manuals leading to poor attunement with the experience of clients ("following the manual, not the client") is represented in a recent body of work that contrasts the kind of all-inclusive packages of evidence-based practice (that tend to insist on an all-or-nothing approach to the implementation of their model, manuals, and supervisory systems) with what have instead been termed "evidence-based components of practice" or "empirically supported principles of change" (Chorpita et al., 2005; Rosen & Davison, 2003). Work in this field attempts to break down large "unitary" treatment models (which are actually composites, composed of multiple smaller elements of practice that may or may not be coherently linked in a single theoretical framework) into their constituent parts. Explicit in this field of research, too, is a challenge to increasingly large and powerful organizations that may assertively "brand" or market their "packages," claiming and marketing intellectual property even though the work builds on many theories and practices that have evolved from preceding work.

We do not want to undervalue the genuinely valiant efforts that have been made to develop real evidence about what interventions are most effective for the kinds of complex clients that AMBIT wishes to help. However, insisting that only the wholesale implementation of these packages is truly evidence-based, and that a judicious and purposeful adoption of components of their practice is not, is actually in itself relatively thinly evidenced. There is a risk that such an all-or-nothing "brand lock-in" approach to the dissemination of best practice might paradoxically act as a barrier to dissemination, especially in an economic context that places at severe risk investment in services for young people with complicated problems. Moreover, if ongoing adaptation and modification of current best practice are not allowed (or encouraged, even) and accepted as necessary by the funders/commissioners of services (on the basis that they can invest only in evidence-based intervention packages, which could be defined as those able to raise the enormous cost and effort of running RCTs), there is a risk that manuals and evidence-based practice could actually work to prevent innovation and further improvement.

The activity of manualizing treatments is clearly, and rightly, here to stay. However, AMBIT's manual is designed somewhat differently from traditional manuals, in that it aims to engage workers in local teams in the co-production of these documents, blending centrally sourced material based on evidence-based practice with their own locally generated practice-based evidence. It is an as yet formally untested hypothesis that workers, or teams, that write (or at least co-author) their own manual are more likely to adhere to it—although there is some evidence to suggest that where practitioners are encouraged to use manuals in a more flexible way, greater adherence to manuals is observed (Wilson, 2007).

This is the approach that has been adopted by AMBIT, in an attempt to balance the benefits of well-evaluated interventions with the need for local attunement. This approach has been implemented using web-based technology in the form of wikis, and is described in detail in the section on techniques and skills later in this chapter. The key idea is that each AMBIT-trained team has a version of the core manual but can adapt this to their own client group and local context. In doing so, the core manual is retained, so that there is no risk of altering the fundamental tenets of the approach. It is adaptation around a core set of knowledge and practice.

Balance and unbalance: Evidence-based practice versus practice-based evidence

There are many comprehensive discussions about the benefits and limitations of evidence-based practice (e.g. Fonagy et al., 2015) and we will not aim to repeat all of these here. For AMBIT, the aim is to hold a balance between what is known to be effective from research (the AMBIT stance of "Respect for evidence") and what is known to be helpful from the experience of frontline workers (the AMBIT stance of "Respect for local practice and expertise") (see Figure 7.1).

The challenge is to create a culture of curiosity as to what works so that both evidence-based practice and local practice-based evidence are open for scrutiny and discussion in their application to a particular case. In this way, the discussion is not so much about whether, for instance, CBT for social anxiety is a good approach to working with a client who cannot travel to college, but whether this is the best approach in this particular case. If we then choose to take a different approach, can we do this in such a way that we learn whether it

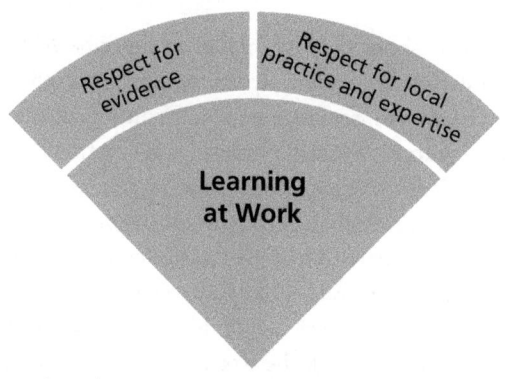

Figure 7.1 Evidence-based practice versus practice-based evidence.

turned out to be any better? This is what we aim to achieve by some of the methods outlined later in this chapter, including the process of manualizing itself.

Intervention manuals are a key part of evidence-based practice. The evidence points clearly to an advantage (even if not an overwhelming one) for outcomes associated with their use, as opposed to working by instinct or intuition. Despite this, it is not uncommon for practitioners to experience a tension between prescribed practice from a manual and their own beliefs about what would be useful in an individual case. Although many therapists are positive about treatment manuals in general (Langer et al., 2011; Najavits et al., 2000), this is not always the case (Borntrager et al., 2009; Addis et al., 1999; Parloff, 1998), and even the "manual enthusiasts" note the need for improvements to make them more accessible and useful for the practitioners who are the primary intended audience for these documents (Wilson, 2007), and also to allow flexibility in the ways in which their content is implemented (Borntrager et al., 2009; Kendall et al., 2008).

Among the reasons cited for the lack of enthusiasm for manualized treatments, one of the most common is the concern that adherence to procedures manualized by a remote "expert" may result in the loss of fluidly responsive, intuitive, and creatively adaptive ways of approaching work. Workers' own experience (and research, as documented by Orlinksy et al., 2004) suggests that this adaptability is necessary to retain therapeutic engagement, without which there is unlikely to be much effective therapy. The concern is that slavish adherence to a manual may generate a rather mechanistic (teleological) response to a situation, with too much focus being placed upon the worker's ability (in measurable ways) to work according to the instructions in the manual, rather than offering more attuned, reciprocally enlightening interactions that offer the hope of stimulating epistemic trust and therapeutic learning on the part of the client. If manuals are still better than no manuals, the question must be how to reduce this risk.

Let us first be clear about the risk, and then describe AMBIT's attempt at a solution. A blunt-edged, poorly adapted therapeutic approach may well be perceived by the client as insensitive and non-contingent (i.e. lacking any fit to their immediate perceived social, physical, and emotional needs). This is an example of the kind of aversive experience that Gergely and Watson (1996) have shown to be in direct contrast to the kinds of contingent responses in caregiving relationships that are understood to drive the earliest development of mentalizing. The problem arises when, rather than clarifying and addressing the psychic reality of their client's lived experience of need ("I need you to give me some space because I don't trust you"), the worker works according to preconceptions about what is good for their client. These preconceptions may be defined by the worker's reading of the treatment model (or manual) they are trying to follow. This may be done in a distinctly teleological (or, one could say, "mechanical") fashion, or at worst the model may be taken as an absolute truth (adopting a psychic equivalence mode of thinking) against which the failure of a case to progress is blamed on the worker, or worse, the client. Dozier et al. (2008) have shown that clients' experience of non-contingent responses by well-intentioned therapists attempting to follow manualized instructions may trigger disruptive memories of neglect and abandonment, and other studies replicate such findings in terms of clinical outcomes if adherence to the manual is adopted in what we have termed a teleological fashion (Castonguay et al., 1996). Comas-Díaz (2006) has highlighted the risk that manualized evidence-based practices may represent an implicit imposition of the therapist's own cultural assumptions upon the client.

As already described, there is a constant challenge in blending evidence from research with local expertise—those lessons drawn from workers' lived experiences with their clients, in the streets, youth clubs, family homes, offices, or clinics where "real life" face-to-face therapeutic work is done. In AMBIT we believe that both forms of expertise are valid, and the major challenge is for teams to develop a culture in which both have a legitimate place in case discussion and intervention planning. How does this work in practice? Let us take a specific example.

> A client has started to work with an AMBIT worker and has begun to talk about wanting to find out whether she could attend college again. The focus of the discussion about this goal has been about what sort of course she would like to do, and how she felt about her previous experience of college. However, little action has taken place, despite the worker and client making plans for her to contact the college, and so on. Gradually, the worker begins to feel that something is being avoided, and it emerges that the client is extremely anxious about traveling on public transport, which would be necessary if college were to be a realistic option. The client wants to see if she could cycle there, but the worker believes that the distance is too far and that cycling will not be sustainable. An evidence-based approach would be to try to address the client's social anxiety using methods of graded exposure as part of a CBT approach, although this is a technique that the AMBIT worker does not feel confident in using. The AMBIT manual provides information about the CBT approach to anxiety, and the worker receives some help from one of the other members of the team who is more familiar with this approach. The focus of the worker's sessions with the client increasingly moves from meeting in cafés to combining these meetings with supported travel on buses until the client begins to feel more able to travel alone.

This relatively simple example illustrates the way an AMBIT worker is encouraged to move away from their usual practice by considering what is known to be more effective in dealing with a particular problem. However, there may be times when local expertise may not be consistent with what is recommended in general from the evidence. For example, for young people out of school, the evidence would suggest that the longer a young person is out of school, the more difficult it is to support their return. This has led to an approach that encourages a rapid return to school. Once a young person has been out of school for several months, they may well have developed a new routine of life, so that school routines may seem a distant memory. However, let us imagine that the school that a particular client is enrolled with has a local reputation for prioritizing academic achievement over aspects of pastoral care. Pupils returning to school have often been poorly supported, and in their experience, not welcomed back. Efforts by the AMBIT worker to engage school staff in developing a support plan for return are not reciprocated. The parent of the client has a very negative experience of the school and does not authentically support return to that school, and instead looks to find a place for their child in a different school. Again, the general evidence would suggest that changing school as a solution to school difficulties often makes things worse (Hattie, 2008), so that this solution is also not ideal. In this case, the AMBIT worker is faced with balancing the wishes of the client, the views of the family, the local service ecology, and what is generally known from research to be most likely to be effective. In our view there is no absolute formula for how these considerations should be reconciled, but we suggest that, as much as possible, these dilemmas should be shared with the client in developing a collaborative approach to the predicament. Resolving such dilemmas relies upon effective team working in which the open discussion of dilemmas is welcomed. If concluded successfully, there may be scope for the team to reflect and record what they saw as the key learning points, ready for when a similar conundrum arises again, as it most likely will. In this way, learning as a team cannot be separated from how the team functions more generally (see Chapter 5), and this team learning is what we will focus on next.

Techniques and skills

Working things out together as a team

There are two key components to this process. The first is for teams to develop a culture of open, supported conversations, meetings, and discussions about key issues that arise in enabling clients to achieve positive outcomes—that is, to create a culture of learning as a central part of team functioning. The second is to develop a method by which the richness of such discussions is systematically recorded so that teams explicitly develop shared expertise around their work. This is the function of manualizing; the specific nature of AMBIT manuals will be described in the next section. Here we want to focus on the culture and practices of shared learning that are essential to the manualizing process.

For an AMBIT team, learning arises out of consideration of live issues. The process is not about spending time writing out procedures describing what people should do in response to standard situations. That form of manualizing, often exemplified by team policies around health and safety (and obviously not unimportant in itself), can often be experienced by frontline staff as defensive, bureaucratic, and remote. The purpose here is to engage in issues that are truly relevant to the direct working experience of the team. Here are some examples of the sorts of issues that teams consider together:

- How do we make sense of a client's aggression toward his/her parent, and how much do we need to do in order to protect the parent?
- How much should we focus on a client's shoplifting when there seem to be much bigger problems in their life?
- How should we "do" text messages with clients? Do we reply at weekends?
- Is it OK to meet a client with other members of their gang?
- What should we do if we are aware that a client may be carrying an offensive weapon?
- We are trying to re-engage a parent with their 15-year-old daughter. There is a high level of distrust in the relationship. What is the balance between the needs of the client and those of the parent?

These types of dilemmas often arise in live case discussions and the solutions are usually far from clear-cut; this is what makes them so difficult. The purpose of the team discussion is to generate some specific ideas in relation to the individual case, and then to extract some shared ideas about good practice in this sort of situation for the future. The underlying intentions are twofold: first, to build shared ideas about good practice so that clients generally experience the team as having a coherent, although not uniform, approach to their predicament, and second, so that the explicit culture and clear practice principles that the team develops in this way equip team members to support one another better as a "team around the worker."

To achieve this, teams are encouraged to manualize their practice together regularly, as part of the ordinary cycle of team meetings—identifying areas where clarification or improved techniques will be likely to help, or marking existing individual strengths that could be shared more widely across the team. Here are a few examples: one or two cases may come up that highlight the need for more attention to documenting how the team manages transitional arrangements with other local services; the successful involvement of another client in a local voluntary project may prompt work first on brainstorming and then on creating a simple database (or even just a list) of other local projects that clients may benefit from, along with principles and tips on how signposting clients to these can be most successfully conducted; some teams report that "strengths-based" sessions, in which workers name and describe techniques that other particular team members have demonstrated particular skill at, are a good place to start for a team new to manualizing—particularly if those team members agree to the uploading of short video clips of them role-playing these techniques.

> "Last week I was with Sarah and she has the best way of introducing the tricky subject of safe sex to vulnerable clients I've ever seen! Just the right balance between humor, naming the awkwardness, and getting the message across. Sarah, could you role-play that conversation, with me as the client? We could video it on my phone and upload it to our manual. If you're shy about doing it to camera, you could direct me to play the part of you."

This process requires careful choreographing to ensure that what is manualized can be as representative of the whole team's views as possible, and to avoid manualizing becoming the province of a select group of enthusiasts within the team. We have been encouraged by early experiences, reported by AMBIT-trained teams, of manualizing as a means of supporting the team to develop its own sense of identity and shared mission, as well as stimulating interest and engagement in (and fidelity to) manualized content. The intention is that, incrementally, a team's local version of its manual comes to represent the collective thinking of the team, and to serve as a powerful tool for inducting new staff and retaining the contributions of those who have moved on.

The team process in developing shared ideas

Several elements of this practice have been designed to help encourage this process, which is undoubtedly an alien activity for most teams. First, we use an analogy between this tentative offering of "where we have got to as a team so far" and the mentalizing stance of a therapist (described in Chapter 4). It is the sharing of mental models, as suggested by Senge (2006), supported by a process of dialogue, in which our own thinking becomes the matter of inquiry—as "This is how I see it" rather than "This is how it is." We propose that the team that is *manualizing* its practice is also in the business of *mentalizing* its practice. Just as the mentalizing therapist attempts to share the extent (and limits) of their understanding of a client as explicitly as possible, presenting their thoughts as "works in progress" that are intended and expected to be improved upon as understanding grows (rather than as statements of fact, which, given that they relate to another person's subjective experience, would be an example of psychic equivalence), so the team broadcasts its best collective understanding of the issues to date.

Our experience of team manualizing is that it may evoke strong beliefs and feelings in team members. In our view, this indicates that the team members are addressing live issues rather than abstract policy, but also that a bit of structure for this process is necessary and helpful. For manualizing in team meetings, we suggest that it may be useful to assign certain roles to enable the process to function well. The three core roles in a team learning meeting are a *chair* (whose role is to enable all voices in the team to be expressed, and hold the context, which is to help the team serve its clients' needs more effectively), a *scribe* (who writes down key points on flip chart paper, or types notes with the text projected on to a screen, allowing the whole team to observe and comment on what is written), and a *manualizer* (who works directly with the team's local version of the online manual—a role that is sometimes also adopted by the scribe). Experienced teams will often edit their online manual "live" during these meetings (see below), which adds a certain amount of energy to the dialogue by marking very explicitly the fact that what the team comes up with is part of the "flag under which they sail." Such manualizing activity does not need to be a long process; it can take 10 minutes if that is all the time available or needed, although many teams find that setting aside an hour every few weeks as part of the normal round of team meetings is a more effective strategy.

In practice, the effort to achieve team consensus about good practice around particular aspects of practice is often challenging. The discussion may result in the scribe having noted a range of somewhat disparate observations and ideas from different team members. Differences of views may emerge between staff within a team for a wide range of reasons, including coming from different professional backgrounds or differing levels of seniority, or other reasons. The process of writing down these differences on a flip chart or translating them directly into the manual enables the team to see ideas and the degree to which these are shared. There is a deliberate process of making things explicit. This is like offering the team a mirror so that they can see their ideas in combined form—either complementary, or dis-integrated. In many ways this is the most important aspect of the process and may result in the team beginning to mentalize themselves and each other better, to recognize individual viewpoints, and to find compromise and respect about these ("So in this kind of situation, Tom would generally do X, but Ali would do Y. OK, these are different approaches; are there circumstances in which they might see the alternative as a useful option?"). In some discussions a consensus of good practice may be easily achieved. In others, the recognition of diverse viewpoints may be what becomes "manualized"—with the risks and benefits of a range of options listed out.

One common criticism of this process is that teams do not have the time for this sort of activity—that it is a luxury too far, and unsuited to a world of austerity and lean working. However, we have come to see that something akin to manualizing takes place in all teams anyway—at least in terms of team discussion about how to do something better; this is what happens in many (most?) team discussions. Often, however, the ideas generated from such discussions may not be brought to a shared conclusion, and general learning points are not recorded in an easily accessible place. So, for example, a team may have a discussion about the eligibility criteria for access to their service in relation to a particular referral. In some cases, the points raised from such a discussion may be used to amend or supplement the referrals policy, which may then be filed away where it is not always easy to find, or not thought about much. In contrast, in an AMBIT team, the outcomes of such discussions are consistently entered into their own local version of the AMBIT manual. In this way it is not so much that the AMBIT team is doing something that other teams do not do; it is that what is done is being explicitly valued and there is a deliberate effort to draw discussions together to shape a broadly shared and coherent approach. The team's local online manual becomes a record of their thinking and development as a team; for example, pages written last year may be revisited in the light of experience, and corrected or added to.

The AMBIT approach to web-based treatment manuals

AMBIT uses what is known as "wiki" technology for treatment manualization. This section will describe the structure and function of the AMBIT wiki manual, as well as the ways in which this technology is used in an effort to connect practitioners in geographically disparate teams via a community of practice (Lave & Wenger, 1991). It is recognized that some of this material may seem alien to some workers, and distant from the exigencies of working in the field, but it is hoped that readers will persevere at this point to grasp the essentially practical aspects of this evolving method of developing and sharing best practice and evidence as they emerge.

The AMBIT manual is not a paper-based document, but exists on the internet as an expanding set of interlinked websites, accessible via smartphones, tablets, laptops, or desktop PCs. Technically, these are a particular type of wiki known as "TiddlyManuals" (so named because of the "TiddlyWiki" software that powers them). The word *wiki* (derived from the Hawaiian word for "quick") simply refers to a set of interlinked web pages covering a specific area of knowledge, which are *editable by the users* (rather than being an entirely "top-down" dissemination of expertise). While some wikis (the most well-known of which is Wikipedia) are radically open and can be edited by anyone at all, TiddlyManuals are closed documents that can only be edited by members, as befits documents relating efforts to deliver evidence-based practice. Further, using ground-breaking new technology developed by an open-source (see below for a definition of this term) community of computer programmers, the wikis that AMBIT uses have a number of additional and unique functions.

In particular, these wikis are able to incorporate the public content from one wiki into the content of another, so that the manual (website) seen by a user who opens it in their browser is in fact built from content provided from multiple layers, each layer having explicitly demarcated ownership. At the very bottom "layer" is very boring content (unless, of course, you are a technophile) that is merely computer code laying out the basic architecture and functions of the wiki; this is unseen by the visitor. Above that are the many pages of foundational or "core" content that are edited and curated by the AMBIT project's central authorial team, attempting to integrate a range of evidence-based components of practice. This core content is "projected upwards" into the top layer, which comprises the multiple individual *local* TiddlyManuals (a new one of which is opened for, and subsequently owned by, each new AMBIT team that is trained), where the local manualizing that we have been describing is saved.

This structure is represented diagrammatically in Figure 7.2.

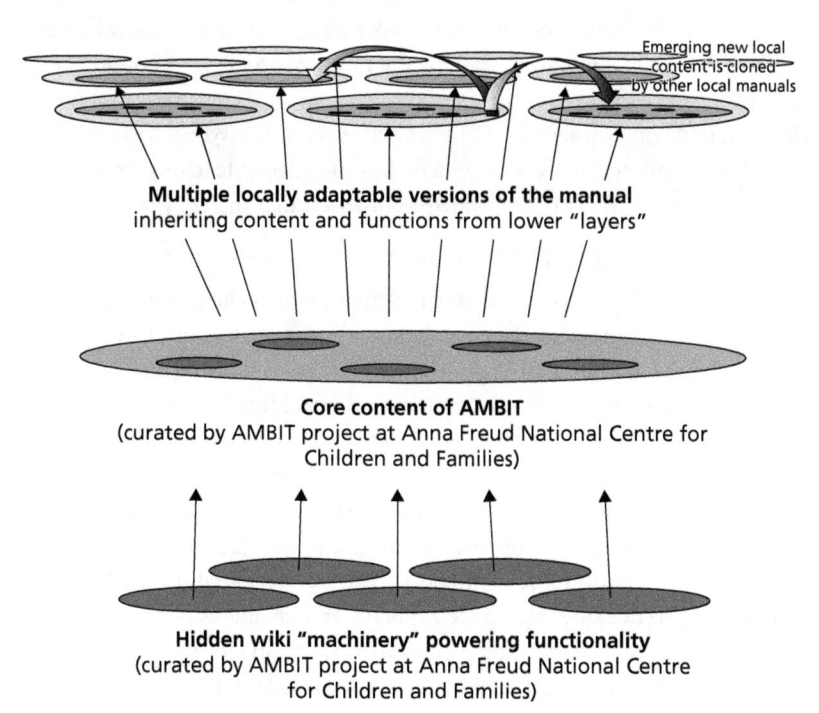

Figure 7.2 Structure of the AMBIT online manual.

New elements of practice that one team documents about its own practice and learning in this way can easily be "cloned" by another team and then, if necessary, further customized, leaving acknowledgments on the new page and the originator's page that this has been done. If new local material arises that has evidence of effectiveness and utility (for instance, if a local page is widely cloned by multiple other teams—suggesting that its contents are indeed useful), then the AMBIT project at the Anna Freud National Centre for Children and Families can choose to clone it into the core content—at which point it will automatically be included in *all* local versions. In this way the AMBIT manual functions as a large knowledge management system that is adapted as knowledge advances.

Local AMBIT TiddlyManuals can be found at the signposting site https://manuals.annafreud.org by following the links to AMBIT.

As with any website, an AMBIT manual can be viewed by the user reading from page to page as in a conventional book, or they can follow a non-linear path via *hyperlinks* that highlight specific words or phrases throughout the text; clicking a link opens a new page that offers greater depth of discussion about the topic that was highlighted by the link. In addition, there is a search bar that can be used to look up specific words or phrases. Broader topics are grouped under "tags" (these are what a conventional book might refer to as chapter headings, although in a wiki—unconstrained by the physical ordering of bound paper—the same page can belong to numerous "chapters"). Pages may contain text, pictures, embedded webpages (from other parts of the World Wide Web), or embedded windows that stream video clips of didactic teaching, role-plays of techniques, etc. This is rich multimedia content rather than dry text.

Creating localized content above the core AMBIT content

The core AMBIT content is the starting point, which each team can (and we think should) customize in their local manual. This can be done by either overwriting particular inherited pages that do not quite work in their own local context, or improving upon existing material, or adding brand new pages integrated and interlinked alongside the existing content. Local manuals are thus co-constructions that draw together centrally curated evidence-based practice and locally generated practice-based evidence. When a local team overwrites local content in their local manual, the original pages (curated by the AMBIT project team) remain untouched and so can be compared against new local versions (differences are thus made explicit). Wiki manuals publicly broadcast each team's current understanding of itself, its work, and its onward learning, as they incrementally blend local expertise and knowledge with externally derived evidence-based content. In keeping with this fluid learning structure (rather than being based on fixed assumptions about knowledge), AMBIT has been referred to as an *evidence-oriented* approach.

At the time of writing there are nearly 200 local versions of the AMBIT manual in existence—from both statutory and voluntary sector teams across the UK and abroad. Following a brief AMBIT training, team members should understand how to access and browse the core AMBIT manual. This provides detailed material on the core AMBIT approach, extensive information and teaching on mentalizing, and comprehensive information on the four quadrants of the AMBIT wheel. The manual also includes basic evidence-based information and guidance on methods relevant to the client group, such as systemic practice, CBT, and motivational interviewing. This core manual comprises over 1,000 pages of material developed over more than a decade of the AMBIT project's life; of course, these are linked and tagged to avoid the reader being overwhelmed with detail that they do not need!

Using the manual to guide decisions about the best forms of help

Given a large book of "how to do this work," most practitioners would struggle to know where to start in relation to a specific question about practice, and in one sense the AMBIT manual is no different. Time spent reading or browsing the AMBIT manual, so as to familiarize oneself with the content and layout, is a good investment. We are reasonably confident that with its multimedia content, and its deliberate use of a somewhat informal style, it is not unmitigatedly dry. Navigating the manual is in many ways like navigating any other website, but in some ways it is different—there is video guidance on how to find your way around. There is a contents bar and a search facility, as with most other websites. The pages in the manual are all deeply interlinked with each other, so that it can feel as though, rather than just reading text in a linear way, the reader explores in three different dimensions: not just from the top of a page to the bottom, but "sideways"—scanning other pages that fall under the same broad chapter headings (tags, in the language of wikis) as the current page, and "depthwise"— exploring content in more depth that is accessed via a specific hyperlink in the text of the current page.

Once a worker has basic proficiency in finding their way around, the manual may provide a useful planning aid before a session. In keeping with the emphasis on evidence-oriented approaches to working, the AMBIT manual also has a wide range of outcome measures built in, and these—particularly the AMBIT AIM—can also offer a way into the content that is most pertinent for a worker. The AIM assessment is described in some depth in Chapter 3, and we refer readers back to this discussion for more detail. While the AIM can be completed as a paper-based measure, it is designed to be interactive when it is used in the online manual, and offers an additional pathway into the content of the manual. Entering scores for any or all of the 40 items in the AIM allows the user to generate lists of suggested interventions based on those scores. These lists (which can be sorted and ranked in different ways) offer direct links to relevant content within the manual, so, by identifying (and rating) one or more issues highlighted by the AIM, a worker can directly generate a list of possible interventions that are worth considering for use with their client.

Reducing training costs

A major driver in the development of AMBIT has been the effort to reduce training costs in order to bring trainings within the financial reach of teams whose budgets are severely constrained. Because the entire didactic content of the training is provided as freely accessible videos embedded within the manual, along with many detailed training exercises (tested in multiple trainings, and described in sufficient detail to steer AMBIT trainers, to avoid pitfalls), local teams can easily use these resources themselves in locally run "top-up" sessions. The intention in creating this resource has been to enhance local capacity and "agency," and the number of days of face-to-face training required has been very significantly reduced from the earliest efforts (see Chapter 11 for more details on training).

The manual is designed increasingly to act as a resource for ongoing locally organized training events. As the manual is freely available online, it is theoretically possible for a team to substantially self-train, and work is currently underway to look at ways to further develop this approach by training local trainers via reciprocal "buddying" arrangements with other local trainers from neighboring teams. These workers attend training sessions at intervals over a number of months, between which they support each other to train their own teams locally, supported by the rich content of the online manual and web-based supervision. The intention is to embed greater local expertise in teams, reducing reliance on (often prohibitively expensive) external expertise.

Reflective tools to support learning

So, in keeping with Senge's (2006) encouragement of the learning organization (discussed at the beginning of this chapter), rather than seeking to establish itself as a rigid "one-size-fits-all" method of working, AMBIT promotes a constrained autonomy of learning and development by local teams that, having received initial training, iteratively and incrementally build their local expertise and cultural attunement upon a core of more or less evidence-based material (which itself ratchets forwards with the incremental gains of knowledge from scientific research). What follows are some other ways in which this incremental and iterative approach to team learning is supported.

Using scales to reflect on individual and team strengths and uncertainties

Team manualizing can also be supported by more explicit processes of inquiry about the way the team is working. Here, we describe a series of scales that can be seen as prompts for systematic mentalizing of a team's practices. Vulnerabilities or gaps that are identified might trigger a local training "top-up" session and some manualizing to address them.

The tools described below are freely available to access and download from the web-based AMBIT manual.

The AMBIT Practice Questionnaire (APQ)

This is a newly developed set of 15 questions that probe an individual's current experience of working in their team. The APQ broadly explores the core elements of the AMBIT wheel and is written without jargon so that it can be applied to teams before any training and then repeated after training to look for evidence of change. By collating a whole team's answers, areas of shared strength and of vulnerability can be identified.

The AMBIT Competency Scale

This allows team members to rate themselves in terms of how confident they feel about each of the AMBIT competencies listed earlier in this chapter, in the section entitled "Team Learning and AMBIT Competencies" (scoring: 0 = *Not confident*; 1 = *Becoming confident*; 2 = *Confident*). We prefer to start with explorations about confidence, as in our experience it is rare for the competencies to be completely outside a worker's skills, but the issue is more about whether the worker has the confidence to use these skills in practice. For example, developing competency in explicit mentalizing is not so much a case of learning a new skill as of learning how to identify times when it may be useful, and then having the confidence to use the techniques involved. Starting with an exploration of workers' confidence is a way of engaging a team in thinking about their own strengths and allowing them to describe and reflect upon any anxieties.

AMBIT team competencies

Similarly, we have developed a set of five *AMBIT team competencies* (described earlier in this chapter) that look more at the function of the whole team, to supplement the reports of individual practitioners. These competencies again essentially reflect the four quadrants of the AMBIT wheel, along with the need to evaluate client outcomes. The purpose, again, is less about adopting a position of expertise and more as a way of stimulating reflection for the team as a whole. For AMBIT, the task is always to move beyond reflection to a process of team learning by aiming to capture reflective processes in a systematic way, combining reflection with manualization. Starting with a process of looking at existing competencies may then enable a team to identify areas in which they would like to strengthen as a team, as well as recognizing what they feel confident about in their work.

The AMBIT Practice Audit Tool (APrAT)

The APrAT is a similar tool—another short questionnaire—that enables team members to review *specific cases* that they have been (or are still) working on. It probes the degree to which actual work done has involved all four quadrants of the AMBIT approach. Our experience is that it is not uncommon for one part of the AMBIT approach to become somewhat lost as a result of preoccupations about some specific issue. Collating a number of APrAT results across a team provides an opportunity to look at that team's practice and identify any common themes indicating a loss of balance at the level of the system. This should lead on to considering ways in which local practice could be developed to reduce any such unbalance in the work. Again, this is likely to provide an opportunity to manualize local practice.

A community of practice

As well as promoting local manualization, we emphasize the fact that teams that take up this aspect of AMBIT practice become active participants in a growing "community of practice" (Wenger, 1998; Lave & Wenger, 1991)—this has become an increasingly key concept in AMBIT. Lave and Wenger (1991) described communities of practice following an anthropological study of apprenticeship. They found that as much (or rather more) learning of a specialist craft was transmitted *between* apprentices (especially from apprentices who were a year or two ahead to ones newer to the trade) as was "handed down" from acknowledged experts. In mentalizing terms, we can assume that one apprentice is more likely to experience the sense that another apprentice has "understood my dilemma here," and will be better able to imagine and engage with the difficulties encountered, than a lofty expert (who may be perceived as more distant from the anxiety and uncertainty of the street-level worker); as we have seen, these are the conditions in which epistemic trust may be triggered whereby learning is facilitated.

Communities of practice are not new; they stem from medieval trade guilds, or earlier still. In such "professional" communities, groups of practitioners collaborate formally or informally to compare and share ways of working, so as to grow and sustain a quite particular knowledge base about "what works, in which situations" (situated learning). Anyone who has worked in health or social care will recognize the tendency for colleagues to enjoy "talking shop," even when supposedly off-duty, and in a sense this is exactly what sustains communities of practice. It is a pleasure to share your own "workarounds" and, magpie-like, to steal those of one's colleagues.

With the advent of the web, the opportunities for supporting this form of learning have multiplied. We argue that the very novel format of the AMBIT manual is a particularly powerful tool in this respect. The local online versions of the manual include multiple "windows" on to the recent manualizing activities of *other* teams, so that practice developments authored elsewhere can be compared, shared, and even cloned and customized between teams. As mentioned above, locally evolved practice developments that have positive clinical outcomes or other indications of value (for instance, widespread adoption by other teams) may be moved into the "core content" curated by the AMBIT authorial team. Once a page is added there, it is automatically included in all local versions, and in this way emerging best practice can be shared widely and rapidly. The opening page of the AMBIT manual includes a link to a list of up to 20 page titles that have most recently been edited by local teams; bringing recent activity to the surface in this way is designed to act as a stimulus to teams that were previously less engaged with this aspect of practice.

An open-source approach

The AMBIT approach to creating open access to information has been strongly influenced by the "open-source" method of software development. Open-source projects take an alternative approach to the methods traditionally pursued by large commercial software developers, and have in many cases (e.g. the freely available Firefox browser, or the many variants of the Linux operating system) provided remarkably effective products distinguished by their fast, highly adaptable nature—responding to changing threats and demands—and by their inventiveness. Instead of concealing the source code (the "inner workings" of a piece of software) with encryption and then selling occasional upgrades to license holders, open-source projects take completely the opposite line, publishing all of the source code openly on the web at the earliest opportunity and inviting collaboration from a wide community of mostly voluntary contributors, whose collective efforts can often outstrip the more product-focused efforts of commercial development teams. Open-source projects harness the common human enthusiasm for sharing expertise and contributing to making things work better. Such enthusiasm is a quality shared, the AMBIT project believes, by many of the individuals who choose to work with multiply vulnerable young people.

Thus, AMBIT positions itself as a collaborative, open-source approach to the development of innovative therapeutic practice, rejecting a silo mentality toward the holding or commodification of expertise. Instead, it actively promotes the sharing of knowledge in ways that allow low-cost dissemination. It promotes local innovation and adaptation of its own evolving materials, alongside robust testing. It enthusiastically invites opportunities to operate as the TAU/"Usual Care" or control arm in RCTs, on the basis that any learning from such trials can be incorporated into AMBIT's own subsequent iterations and shared among the community of workers.

Limitations and challenges: Staff experience of learning and manualizing

As Senge (2006) has emphasized, the creation of learning cultures within organizations presents greater challenges than might be expected. We have learned through working with many teams that the creation of an explicit culture of learning rarely happens quickly, and that for many teams the process of manualizing may, at least at first, appear to be more of a burden than a benefit. In seeking feedback from teams about what they have most valued about the AMBIT approach, the capacity to support learning through manualizing is often the least valued. The reasons for this are not entirely clear, as training in new methods of working may be quite highly valued by the same staff teams. We have come to see that it is crucial to focus more on learning as a culture than on learning as a product. As a product, it is likely it will be experienced by staff as either burdensome ("I suppose we need to manualize this discussion"), time-consuming ("We can't afford to use team meetings for this"), or exposing ("I'm not sure that I want our commissioners to be able to read about some of our challenges in our work"). However, despite this initial tentativeness, engagement with the online manual and the amount of work being shared across the community both continue to grow steadily. In 2015, the core AMBIT content on the web received over 40,000 page views by nearly 3,500 users, across nearly 6,000 sessions with an average duration of over five minutes—and this figure does not count any views of local versions of the manual. Compared with sites such as Amazon or Wikipedia, this is clearly a tiny "footfall," but in relation to time that might be spent on a traditional treatment manual, we are encouraged. Nearly every week there are up to ten new local adaptations or additions, shared from teams across the world, and covering a wide range of topics. Our impression is that once a team has established online manualizing as part of its work, it tends to stick. So, what do we consider to be the barriers to establishing a learning culture in newly trained AMBIT teams?

AMBIT-trained teams often include staff who have had very advanced training and possess high levels of expertise. This expertise is of value to the team, to the clients and their families, and to other agencies. In effect, it is what people are paying for. So, to acknowledge uncertainty in an expert system is a complex process; being able to find a balance between certainty and uncertainty, and between decisiveness and caution, depends on there being a degree of confidence within the team. In our experience, how the leaders of the team operate around this issue is often crucial. If those with more influence and power have the confidence to model a position of not-knowing (at least temporarily), then it is more possible for others in the team to behave in the same way. It seems to us that there is a need for *confident not-knowing* (what the systemic therapist Barry Mason (1993) has described as "safe uncertainty"). This is the learning position, conveying an optimism that "we may not understand this yet, but we will be enriched in thinking about it, and may come to understand it better." This is in contrast to a *defeated* sense of not-knowing, which can be associated with feelings of hopelessness and incompetence, and is not conducive to learning.

A second barrier to learning is the anxiety evoked by the lives of the clients we are aiming to help. People who are suicidal or who are self-harming and doing dangerous things both make us anxious and (particularly if they are young) evoke strong feelings of responsibility in adults positioned as helpers or responsible authorities. Such feelings of anxiety and responsibility can strongly challenge the capacity of teams to hold a mentalizing stance and the capacity to recognize a degree of not-knowing and uncertainty about a case. For isolated practitioners, these mentalizing challenges are likely to be overwhelming. What is needed are team relationships in which trust and non-blame are strongly established. Although the AMBIT training may present our aspirations about how teams can learn together, in practice the authentic development of team trust in relation to learning together takes time to establish. It is probable that overemphasizing the role of the physical act of manualizing too early may compromise efforts to create a more learning culture. With hindsight, we think it is possible that our early efforts to promote online manualizing may have made it harder for some teams to establish a learning culture because the imperative to manualize may be experienced as anxiety-provoking rather than reassuring. Experience shows that in teams there will usually be one member who is the least "technophobic," and that identifying this person and supporting them to take a lead in uploading material, and sharing their expertise, is helpful—in fact, once people have done it a few times, the process is very simple (indeed, one of the authors of this book is not known for prowess in this field, but copes with ease!).

At present, the process of manualizing in AMBIT aims, over time, to produce an explicit and rich description of detailed aspects of frontline practice within a team. It emphasizes the need to move from implicit practice ("This is just how I always do it") to explicit consideration of both principles and techniques with respect to specific cases. This, in our view, is really only the first stage. Over time, we would want to develop ways in which additions to the manual can result in predictions, which can then be evaluated. This is essential in addressing the challenge that, while practice-based expertise may appear convincing, it still might not actually work. So, for example, if a team comes up with a new way of supporting a client to get to college, can this suggestion be linked with robust observations about when this has worked (or not)? At present this is still a little way off, but without this next stage the current manualizing approach is vulnerable to the criticism that the suggested "good practice" has not been meaningfully evaluated.

Conclusions

The AMBIT approach argues that the creation of a culture of team learning is an essential component in improving outcomes. With a generous open-source community of programming collaborators, we have been part of the development of a highly adaptable and innovative technology that supports this process, using TiddlyWiki software. In the resulting wiki, and over the past decade, we have written the AMBIT manual and built a rich training resource to support team development. We now recognize that the deep structure of interlinking that characterizes the format of the AMBIT wiki manual has almost certainly influenced the integrative nature of AMBIT—as content has emerged, been recorded, and been subject to incremental revisions over the years.

However, AMBIT is not simply a "tech project," and equal focus needs to be given to establishing a culture of learning that enables "balanced uncertainty" to have a voice in the work of the team. We believe that this supports the process of mentalizing and models the need to avoid forms of non-mentalizing that may be unintentionally supported by usual team processes, professional isolation, and the nature of the work. It seems to us that teams are easily prone to forms of non-mentalizing such as psychic equivalence (e.g. a concrete and inflexible approach to diagnosis), teleological thinking (e.g. insistence on having a safety plan in the notes over having a safety plan that might work), or pretend mode (e.g. losing focus on an immediate risk through musing on how the predicament relates to what happened when the client was younger). As we have described earlier, non-mentalizing states are not necessarily unhelpful, but if left unchecked they can lead to patterns of team interaction that restrict reflective exchange and reduce effective communication. In this sense, the purpose of team learning is the same as that for families: to enable people to reflect on their lived experience in such a way that new solutions can be allowed to emerge. In the wider AMBIT "family" of teams, it is also the intention that those emerging solutions that are transferable beyond the specific location in which they arise should also be easily, effectively, and freely shared.

References

Addis, M. E., Wade, W. A., & Hatgis, C. (1999). Barriers to dissemination of evidence-based practices: Addressing practitioners' concerns about manual-based psychotherapies. *Clinical Psychology: Science and Practice* 6: 430–41. doi: 10.1093/clipsy/6.4.430

Bearman, S. K., & Weisz, J. R. (2015). Review: Comprehensive treatments for youth comorbidity—evidence-guided approaches to a complicated problem. *Child and Adolescent Mental Health* 20: 131–41. doi: 10.1111/camh.12092

Borntrager, C. F., Chorpita, B. F., Higa-McMillan, C., & Weisz, J. R. (2009). Provider attitudes toward evidence-based practices: Are the concerns with the evidence or with the manuals? *Psychiatric Services* 60: 677–81. doi: 10.1176/appi.ps.60.5.677

Bronfenbrenner, U. (1986). Ecology of the family as a context for human development: Research perspectives. *Developmental Psychology* 22: 723–42. doi: 10.1037//0012-1649.22.6.723

Castonguay, L. G., Goldfried, M. R., Wiser, S., Raue, P. J., & Hayes, A. M. (1996). Predicting the effect of cognitive therapy for depression: A study of unique and common factors. *Journal of Consulting and Clinical Psychology* 64: 497–504.

Chorpita, B. F., Daleiden, E. L., & Weisz, J. R. (2005). Identifying and selecting the common elements of evidence based interventions: A distillation and matching model. *Mental Health Services Research* 7: 5–20. doi: 10.1007/s11020-005-1962-6

Comas-Díaz, L. (2006). Cultural variation in the therapeutic relationship. In: C. D. Goodheart, A. E. Kazdin, & R. J. Sternberg (eds.), *Psychotherapy: Where Practice and Research Meet*, pp. 81–105. Washington, DC: American Psychological Association.

Dozier, M., Stovall-McClough, K. C., & Albus, K. E. (2008). Attachment and psychopathology in adulthood. In: J. Cassidy, & P. R. Shaver (eds.), *Handbook of attachment: Theory, research and clinical applications,* 2nd edn, pp. 718–44. New York, NY: Guilford Press.

Fonagy, P., Cottrell, D., Phillips, J., Bevington, D., Glaser, D., & Allison, E. (2015). *What Works for Whom? A Critical Review of Treatments for Children and Adolescents* (2nd edn, New York, NY: Guilford Press).

Fuggle, P., Bevington, D., Cracknell, L., Hanley, J., Hare, S., Lincoln, J., … Zlotowitz, S. (2015). The Adolescent Mentalization-based Integrative Treatment (AMBIT) approach to outcome evaluation and manualization: Adopting a learning organization approach. *Clinical Child Psychology and Psychiatry* 20: 419–35. doi: 10.1177/1359104514521640

Fuggle, P., Bevington, D., Duffy, F., & Cracknell, L. (2016). The AMBIT approach: Working with hard to reach youth. *Mental Health Review Journal* 21: 61–72. doi: 10.1108/mhrj-04-2015-0012

Gergely, G., & Watson, J. S. (1996). The social biofeedback theory of parental affect-mirroring: The development of emotional self-awareness and self-control in infancy. *International Journal of Psychoanalysis* 77: 1181–212.

Glisson, C., & Hemmelgarn, A. (1998). The effects of organizational climate and interorganizational coordination on the quality and outcomes of children's service systems. *Child Abuse and Neglect* 22: 401–21.

Glisson, C., Schoenwald, S. K., Hemmelgarn, A., Green, P., Dukes, D., Armstrong, K. S., & Chapman, J. E. (2010). Randomized trial of MST and ARC in a two-level evidence-based treatment implementation strategy. *Journal of Consulting and Clinical Psychology* 78: 537–50. doi: 10.1037/a0019160

Godley, M. D., Godley, S. H., Dennis, M. L., Funk, R., & Passetti, L. L. (2002). Preliminary outcomes from the assertive continuing care experiment for adolescents discharged from residential treatment. *Journal of Substance Abuse Treatment* 23: 21–32.

Griffiths, H., Noble, A., Duffy, F., & Schwannauer, M. (2016). Innovations in Practice: Evaluating clinical outcome and service utilization in an AMBIT-trained Tier 4 child and adolescent mental health service. *Child and Adolescent Mental Health* doi: 10.1111/camh.12181 [epub ahead of print]

Hattie, J. (2008). *Visible Learning: A Synthesis of Over 800 Meta-Analyses Relating to Achievement* (Oxford, UK: Routledge).

Henggeler, S. W., Clingempeel, W. G., Brondino, M. J., & Pickrel, S. G. (2002). Four-year follow-up of multisystemic therapy with substance-abusing and substance-dependent juvenile offenders. *Journal of the American Academy of Child and Adolescent Psychiatry* 41: 868–74. doi: 10.1097/00004583-200207000-00021

Henggeler, S. W., Cunningham, P. B., Pickrel, S. G., Schoenwald, S. K., & Brondino, M. J. (1996). Multisystemic therapy: An effective violence prevention approach for serious juvenile offenders. *Journal of Adolescence* 19: 47–61.

Henggeler, S. W., Halliday-Boykins, C. A., Cunningham, P. B., Randall, J., Shapiro, S. B., & Chapman, J. E. (2006). Juvenile drug court: Enhancing outcomes by integrating evidence-based treatments. *Journal of Consulting and Clinical Psychology* 74: 42–54. doi: 10.1037/0022-006X.74.1.42

Henggeler, S. W., Sheidow, A. J., Cunningham, P. B., Donohue, B. C., & Ford, J. D. (2008). Promoting the implementation of an evidence-based intervention for adolescent marijuana abuse in community settings: Testing the use of intensive quality assurance. *Journal of Clinical Child and Adolescent Psychology* 37: 682–9. doi: 10.1080/15374410802148087

Jacob, J., Edbrooke-Childs, J., Law, D., & Wolpert, M. (2017). Measuring what matters to patients: Using goal content to inform measure choice and development. *Clinical Child Psychology and Psychiatry* 22: 170–86. doi: 10.1177/1359104515615642

Kendall, P. C., Gosch, E., Furr, J. M., & Sood, E. (2008). Flexibility within fidelity. *Journal of the American Academy of Child and Adolescent Psychiatry* 47: 987–93. doi: 10.1097/CHI.0b013e31817eed2f

Langer, D. A., McLeod, B. D., & Weisz, J. R. (2011). Do treatment manuals undermine youth-therapist alliance in community clinical practice? *Journal of Consulting and Clinical Psychology* 79: 427–32. doi: 10.1037/a0023821

Lave, J., & Wenger, E. (1991). *Situated Learning: Legitimate Peripheral Participation* (Cambridge, UK: Cambridge University Press).

Mason, B. (1993). Towards positions of safe uncertainty. *Human Systems* 4: 189–200.

Meyers, D. C., Durlak, J. A., & Wandersman, A. (2012). The quality implementation framework: A synthesis of critical steps in the implementation process. *American Journal of Community Psychology* 50: 462–80. doi: 10.1007/s10464-012-9522-x

Munro, E. (2011). *The Munro Review of Child Protection: Final Report. A child-centred system* (London, UK: The Stationery Office), https://www.gov.uk/government/uploads/system/uploads/attachment_data/file/175391/Munro-Review.pdf, accessed 24 Jan. 2017.

Najavits, L. M., Weiss, R. D., Shaw, S. R., & Dierberger, A. E. (2000). Psychotherapists' views of treatment manuals. *Professional Psychology: Research and Practice* 31: 404–8. doi: 10.1037/0735-7028.31.4.404

Orlinksy, D. E., Ronnestad, M. H., & Willutski, U. (2004). Fifty years of psychotherapy process-outcome research: Continuity and change. In: M. Lambert (ed.), *Bergin and Garfield's Handbook of Psychotherapy and Behavior Change*, pp. 307–90. New York: Wiley.

Øvretveit, J. (2009). Does Improving Quality Save Money? A review of evidence of which improvements to quality reduce costs to health service providers (London, UK: The Health Foundation), http://www.health.org.uk/sites/health/files/DoesImprovingQualitySaveMoney_Evidence.pdf, accessed 24 Jan, 2017.

Parloff, M. B. (1998). Is psychotherapy more than manual labor? *Clinical Psychology: Science and Practice* 5: 376–81. doi: 10.1111/j.1468-2850.1998.tb00157.x

Reynolds, S., Wilson, C., Austin, J., & Hooper, L. (2012). Effects of psychotherapy for anxiety in children and adolescents: A meta-analytic review. *Clinical Psychology Review* 32: 251–62. doi: 10.1016/j.cpr.2012.01.005

Rosen, G. M., & Davison, G. C. (2003). Psychology should list empirically supported principles of change (ESPs) and not credential trademarked therapies or other treatment packages. *Behavior Modification* 27: 300–312.

Roth, A. D., & Pilling, S. (2008). Using an evidence-based methodology to identify the competences required to deliver effective cognitive and behavioural therapy for depression and anxiety disorders. *Behavioural and Cognitive Psychotherapy* 36: 129–47. doi: 10.1017/S1352465808004141

Roth, A. D., Pilling, S., & Turner, J. (2010). Therapist training and supervision in clinical trials: Implications for clinical practice. *Behavioural and Cognitive Psychotherapy* 38: 291–302. doi: 10.1017/S1352465810000068

Schoenwald, S. K. (2008). Toward evidence-based transport of evidence-based treatments: MST as an example. *Journal of Child & Adolescent Substance Abuse* 17: 69–91. doi: 10.1080/15470650802071671

Senge, P. (2006). *The Fifth Discipline: The Art and Practice of the Learning Organization* (rev. edn, New York, NY: Doubleday).

Weisz, J. R., & Gray, J. S. (2008). Evidence-based psychotherapy for children and adolescents: Data from the present and a model for the future. *Child and Adolescent Mental Health* 13: 54–65. doi: 10.1111/j.1475-3588.2007.00475.x

Weisz, J. R., Kuppens, S., Eckshtain, D., Ugueto, A. M., Hawley, K. M., & Jensen-Doss, A. (2013). Performance of evidence-based youth psychotherapies compared with usual clinical care: A multilevel meta-analysis. *JAMA Psychiatry* 70: 750–61. doi: 10.1001/jamapsychiatry.2013.1176

Wenger, E. (1998). *Communities of Practice: Learning, Meaning, and Identity* (Cambridge, UK: Cambridge University Press).

Whipple, J. L., Lambert, M. J., Vermeersch, D. A., Smart, D. W., Nielsen, S. L., & Hawkins, E. J. (2003). Improving the effects of psychotherapy: The use of early identification of treatment failure and problem-solving strategies in routine practice. *Journal of Counseling Psychology* **50**: 59–68. doi: 10.1037/0022-0167.50.1.59

Williams, N. J., & Glisson, C. (2014). Testing a theory of organizational culture, climate and youth outcomes in child welfare systems: A United States national study. *Child Abuse and Neglect* **38**: 757–67. doi: 10.1016/j.chiabu.2013.09.003

Wilson, G. T. (2007). Manual-based treatment: Evolution and evaluation. In: T. A. Treat, R. R. Bootzin, & T. Baker (eds.), *Psychological Clinical Science: Papers in honor of Richard M. McFall*, pp. 105–32. New York, NY: Psychology Press.

Wolpert, M., Ford, T., Trustam, E., Law, D., Deighton, J., Flannery, H., & Fugard, R. (2012). Patient-reported outcomes in child and adolescent mental health services (CAMHS): Use of idiographic and standardized measures. *Journal of Mental Health* **21**: 165–73. doi: 10.3109/09638237.2012.664304

Chapter 8

"It was somebody I could trust": A descriptive case study of one young man's experience with an AMBIT-influenced team

Introduction: Experience and expertise

This chapter presents an account of a conversation with a young person with past experience of being cared for by a team strongly influenced by AMBIT. The team is a young people's substance use service (referred to here as the "YPSUS"). As a descriptive case study, this chapter is less an evaluation of the effectiveness of AMBIT or this service, and more an exploration of one young man's experiences. We privilege his own words to begin with, and then in the latter parts of the chapter we frame these with commentary, linking the experience of Thomas and his keyworker to AMBIT-influenced theory and practices. The intention was to glean insights into what difference, if any, AMBIT principles and practice might have made to Thomas's experience of care, perhaps providing pointers for future study.

Ethical considerations

The subject of the case study, Thomas (a pseudonym to protect his confidentiality), has capacity and gave informed consent to participate in this exercise, and we are hugely grateful to him for his generosity in doing this. Thomas is no longer in treatment with the substance use team (he was four months post-discharge at the time of writing) and has had editorial control over what has been included.

Method

A loose semi-structured interview was used to ensure that key topics of interest to readers (namely those relating to the core stance and practices of AMBIT) were explored, while giving Thomas the opportunity to tell his own story.

The reasons for selecting Thomas to take part in this case study were twofold. First, while the specifics of his individual and systemic circumstances are of course highly unique to Thomas, his case was in some key ways typical of the sort that AMBIT was developed to help (see Chapter 1). He had a poor history of forming effective helping relationships and he had multiple synergistic difficulties, and these resulted in the involvement of multiple workers, creating a complex professional network at risk of dis-integration. Second, and perhaps less typically, Thomas is an extraordinarily coherent narrator, and generous. He was keen to contribute to this book. He felt confident that he was sufficiently recovered from his difficulties to engage in an interview without the process upsetting his wellbeing.

Thomas's verbatim account is offered in its entirety to start with, in order to give voice to his experience and to enable the reader to come to their own conclusions about what might be learned from it. This is followed by the worker's commentary and reflections, quoting from the source material.

Interview (verbatim account)

Worker: Can you start by telling me what was going on when we first met?

Thomas: I was smoking a lot of cannabis. I was doing speed, cocaine, all sorts of other drugs. Never nothing hard like heroin, it was just stupid party drugs. Just going out and getting drunk all the time. Having house parties at my house. My house used to get trashed. And I didn't care because I was always off my face. My life was miserable. Depressing. I didn't have any money, didn't have any nice stuff. I was always sort of just being given stuff, as a hand-me-down. It made me feel like a bit of a tramp really, and I didn't like that.

W: Who were you seeing back then?

T: I was seeing [the housing support worker], [the adult drug service], [the youth worker], [the information advisor], and my GP. I was on the waiting list for adult mental health services.

W: What was it like seeing [YPSUS]?

T: At first, seeing you [YPSUS] was nerve-wracking because I didn't know you and I get really wary around other people. As time went on I got to know you, and become quite good sort of friends, as such. And all in all you kind of really did help me quite a bit.

W: Was there anything different about [YPSUS] compared to other services?

T: Definitely. I think with sort of [the local adult drug service] and stuff like that, there's a lot of people to handle. Whereas [YPSUS] sort of go one on one and they do help you. They muddle through your problems and help you out with other stuff as well. So it's not just drugs and alcohol, it's other stuff as well.

W: What sort of stuff?

T: Well, at the time I had house robberies. I've had people walk in my house with samurai swords and stuff like that. And you helped me out with that, because that was sort of like the PTSD.

Depression, that was another thing. And I think, at the time I was seeing you, my brother was trying to commit suicide and I had that all on my shoulders as well. I think the case of looking after my brother from the age of 16 didn't really help. Once my brother got his new girlfriend I kind of went out and just got absolutely shit-faced because I knew that I could leave him in safe hands. So I just kind of let off a lot of steam, because at the age of 16 normal sort of 16-year-olds are going out and getting shit-faced and using drugs. And when I was 16 I was looking after my brother, so by the age of 19 I was sort of thinking I was 16 because I didn't get to have that whole "kid getting drunk and having drugs and stuff." And actually—not doing what I wanted to do—but experimenting with drugs and alcohol, and I think it just went wildly out of control. Really quickly.

W: Was there anything else different about [YPSUS] or me?

T: It was somebody I could trust. With somebody that's had a lot of trust issues—it's a case of people screwing him over and nicking stuff of his and it's—it's definitely an element of trust issues. And as you came in I didn't trust you but then as time grew on I come to trust you and sort of—you looked out for me, sort of thing.

W: How did you start to think you might be able to trust me?

T: Just the way I could tell you stuff and just get it all off my chest and you wouldn't—unless it was that I was going to harm somebody, and then you'd have to tell somebody because there's certain protocols in place—but other than that it was confidentiality and I think that did help a lot.

W: Was there anything else?

T: The food and that. The munch. Taking me to KFC [chicken shop] and that. That was awesome. It was a case of—even when I had no food, it was like, "Come on then, let's go and get some coffee" or "Let's go out," just get me out of the house, 'cos being in the house too long can sort of mess with your head a little bit, so that kind of helped in another way. You wanted to get me out of the house.

W: What did the getting you food or coffee do? Why was that important?

T: Because throughout my life I've not had a lot of people who care about me, and that showed that you cared, which I don't think a lot of drugs and alcohol nurses would do. So ... [sighs].

W: So it showed that I cared, and that helped you to trust me?

T: Yeah, definitely.

W: How else did you know that I cared?

T: Um ... it was a case of when I was getting in relationships and stuff, you were sort of warning me "Be careful" because if not they're going to hurt you and you're going to be back the way you was, and sort of stuff like that. Just small stuff—it makes a difference.

W: Was our relationship the same as other relationships you've had with workers before?

T: I think I've had this sort of relationship before but it was kind of "Get me to a certain point then drop me from a height." So a lot of people sort of ... they'd get me over what needed to be done, and then that was it. But [my YPSUS worker] kind of did what needed to be done and sort of ... slowly fizzled it out, not just dropped me as and when I'd finished doing what I needed to do. So that kind of helped a lot.

W: You said about your relationships with other people. Was there anything in the work we did that helped, or made a difference to, other relationships?

T: In the end it's all down to what *I* do, but having somebody there to influence you does help a lot. Sort of—don't get me wrong—I've been in and out of relationships with girls and it sort of ... it always ends horribly wrong. But ... I kind of accepted that, but you did help me when I was going through a messy patch with one of my ex-girlfriends. And I think that helped because it did fix it for a little while and then, sort of, there was no love there. It was just sort of, "Ah, you do my head in, piss off" sort of thing.

W: How did I help?

T: It was a case of just warning me to be careful and take it slow. But I kind of ... me being me with my ADHD, sort of ... I jump into things, and I don't think about it. So I think that kind of helped.

W: Do you think you got better at ... were you able to slow things down before "jumping into" things? Has that changed?

T: The impulsivity of ADHD—it's kind of "Ah fuck it. Jump into it and think of it later," and it's always going to be like that, but—I know this is sort of wrong, because this is a sort of drug and alcohol thing—but the cannabis kind of calms me down.

I have calmed down since you've known me. When you first met me I couldn't sit still. It was probably me growing up as adult … but I do find that cannabis helps me calm down and get perspective on life.

W: What about your relationships with your family?

T: My family relationships have always been up-down, up and down. Either we love them or we hate them, but family's always going to be family. You're always going to love them.

W: Are there any conversations we had that were helpful with your relationships with your family?

T: Yes and no. I'm a very hot-headed person so I kind of walk into a room and if someone's got a problem, something to say, I'm like: "What's your problem then?" So that's kind of what sparks it off usually, with mum and dad, and my brother and sister. But I think a lot of the time, you kind of advised me and there was me being me—just blatantly ignored it. Being a hot-headed douche.

W: You say that, but actually when I first met you, you basically weren't talking to your parents at all, and now you've got to a point where …

T: It's like you love them or you hate them, it's like Marmite. I think as I've grown older, as well, getting mature as well, I think I've realized that life's too short. I've seen a couple of my family members pass away, sort of thing, and I think that just seeing, and being there, when that happened and stuff, I think I kind of realized that you've only got one set of parents and you've got to sort of take it by the horns and grab hold of it while you've got it.

W: Has that realization changed how you are with them?

T: I'm still always hot-headed, but when it's a serious situation—like recently my dad's been in hospital, sort of thing—he had a kidney infection—I think I walked into the hospital and the first thing I done was I give my dad a cuddle—and it's a weird thing because my dad and I never got on. We've always had our problems, but just in a serious sort of context like that, it's sort of, it's called for. And I know it's weird because man being man—it's sort of pride and … but I don't care about that. I just care about my family. I love my mum and my dad and my brother and sister. Don't get me wrong—they're all douchebags at some points in their life but I still love them and I just want them all to get on.

W: I guess one of the things I wanted to be able to do was help your relationship with them so that …

T: I think you have repaired the relationships a little bit, because me and my mum and my dad are actually talking now, whereas before we wasn't. And

I think also they respected the fact that I got help for what I had—taking drugs and stuff. I think it's because I got help with it, that they started talking to me. Because, with drugs, there is an element of trust with family members. They don't trust you because you're gonna rob from them for your habit. Don't get me wrong. I've never ever in my life ever robbed from my family for my habit. I always supplied it myself. My friends and I buy it so you can get shit-faced. I've never robbed from my family. I wouldn't do it, I don't think it's right. I've been brought up, if you've got morals, you've got somewhere to go in life.

W: You were saying [YPSUS] has been helpful—what has been helpful?

T: Well I've seen you and ... Helen [another worker in YPSUS, covering during a period of leave] ... I think when I saw Helen and you ... you were both on the same lines, exactly, which is kind of weird because you normally have two people who are two completely different people. But you was both on the same kind of lines. You were both caring, you both sort of wanted to help. And there's not a lot of people in life who want to do that. There's a lot of people who are sort of "Get on with your life, deal with it, you've made your bed—lie in it."

W: You've met a few of us ... So what was it like, even though you mostly saw me, knowing that I had a whole team of people who kind of helped me, and helped me to think about you? That they were there?

T: I was quite surprised that a team like yourselves ... your team ... they're caring, they want to see the best in the person, they want to make that person a better person than when they first walked through the door ... First impressions count. What were your first impressions of me?

W: I was impressed by how much you knew about your situation. I know that sounds kind of silly, but you know how we were saying you sometimes can't see the wood for the trees ... but actually you told me: "You know, my glasses are broken, my teeth are sore ... I've got ADHD. I want to go to college, but my ADHD isn't treated." You had this awareness ... you had a lot going on ...

T: I think a lot of that was my fault. Pure and simple. Fact is ... when you first met me my house was a fricking dump because I used to have house parties and get shit-faced and trash things. But I think now I've learned self-respect. Sort of ... my house at the moment—I've got a TV, I've got stuff that is ... not essential ... but kind of essential because I spend a lot of time in my house and you get bored if you spend a lot of time in your house.

W: Yeah, you definitely look after this place now. It looks homely.

T: ... ish.

W: No, it does.

T: ... ish!

W: My overall impression of you, and I think the whole team would say this as well, is that you are a really impressive guy. You've been through a lot, you've had a lot of challenges that aren't your fault ... you've had some traumatic stuff happen to you ... but you put this smile on and you battle on through it. And you're kind and friendly, and have great social skills. Maybe that's something that's changed actually ... When we first met, you'd be swearing out on the street, even if there were kids and an old lady nearby, but now you're super good at ..."

T: Keeping a lid on it?

W: Yeah, but also being "Hi! Thank you! ... please." You make people smile.

T: There's two people I can thank for that. Yourself and my best friend. 'Cos he's 27 and he went to school with my cousins and he's sort of been a role model and he taught me stuff. When I scratched his car, he had a go at me and went "I don't care, just pay the money." We're fine again now. He's a role model, as such. Don't get me wrong, I have got some douchebag mates. They do some stupid stuff when they're drunk. They shaved a mate's eyebrows. When he was asleep.

W: You said your friend had mainly been a role model. How did I help you with that social skills stuff?

T: I think it was a case of—not a case of you having a go at me, but a case of "Oh that wasn't called for was it" or "Well that wasn't needed" and just it helped me sort of kick myself up the bum and say "What are you doing? Sort your life out!" So, thank you.

W: Thank *you*—you've taught me a lot. We were talking about the team and you said it was a surprise that they all cared about you as well and saw the best in you. What about the way you saw doctors in our team? Was that different to how you've seen doctors before?

T: Well it's not like a GP who you sort of go to. You knew they were there if you needed them, the other end of a phone call. With doctors, my doctors especially, you ring up and not that I've ever done it ... you're bleeding from your arms and it takes four hours to get through to them. Whereas if I left you a message, the next day you'd get back. It was quick. If I needed to talk about something it was "OK then, we'll sort it out" right there, as and when you knew what was happening. And the doctors on the other hand, when I had blackouts and I couldn't remember anything, you got on the phone to [the team doctor]. Next two to three days, there was a prescription waiting.

"There you go, sort yourself out mate." It was a kind and friendly service sort of thing. Always polite, always nice. Don't get me wrong, you can get some snotty doctors out there, do you know what I mean?

W: Did you like that they came here?

T: Yeah, because then if something was up I could have a chat with them or that sort of thing.

W: Thinking back to all the people you had in the beginning … what was that like having all those people involved?

T: It was alright but they kind of … I think a lot of them were sort of … they were trying to get me into a job … more than trying to sort my personal health out. So I think [my housing support worker] was trying to get me into another house or at least get me ready for moving on to the next house. [The information advisor] was trying to get me into a job. [The youth worker] was trying to … to be honest I don't know what the frigging hell [the youth worker] was there for. [The youth worker] didn't do anything to be honest. Me and [the information advisor] go back a long way … I knew her when I was at school so me and her have got that kind of close friendship like we can always chat, and if I went in there today she'd be "Ooh 'ello! 'Ow you doin?'" sort of thing. But they're all trying to focus on all different aspects of my life, whereas you were trying to sort out my drugs and alcohol, [the information advisor] was trying to do one thing, [the housing support worker] was trying to do another, and everyone was trying to do something else and no-one was caring about how I felt inside and how I was reacting with stuff. Whereas your team, they kind of cared about what was going on in my life and how things were going and *where* things were going as such.

W: So different people were trying to do different bits …

T: Whereas the main important thing nobody really cared about, apart from your team.

W: How did you feel about how I spoke to [the housing support worker], your GP, and [the youth workers]?

T: You did a brilliant job 'cos like I'd go into my doctor's—if I had to sort out my PIP [Personal Independence Payment] claim, say—you'd write a letter. We had your support—the whole team's support—and I think that kind of influenced a lot of people into helping me, which kind of helped a lot.

W: Did you feel like … it sounds like in the beginning …

T: … It was all quite muddly.

W: Did you feel like it got a bit clearer? Do you remember we all met?

T: Yeah, that was with you, [the housing support worker], [the youth worker], [the information advisor], mum, dad, [the housing manager].

W: Did that help the muddle?

T: To be honest, at that point I was either tired, stoned, or drunk. I don't know, but either way I don't think I paid attention to that meeting. I think I was like "Ah, piss off, dickhead" and all the rest of it. I don't think I paid much attention to that meeting. If we had that meeting now, I think it would be a very, very, very different occasion.

W: Do you think the process of getting everyone together was helpful?

T: It was helpful, but it was a pain in the ass, getting everyone in the same room on the same day.

W: Did any of the work that we did, or conversations we had, change the way you think, change the way you think about these things?

T: In which aspect?

W: In any aspect.

T: It did. I think it taught me to self-evaluate my life. So, I think we've already spoke about this earlier, but … when I was going through a hard time you sort of helped me, sort of "Right, just step back, evaluate your life and see what's going on" and I think at that point I did actually do it and it kind of "Wow, not everything is what it seemed."

W: So almost like a stepping outside and looking at yourself from the outside?

T: Yeah, and that was without drugs!

W: Did it change the way you think about or look at other people?

T: What do you mean by that?

W: Well you said you started to look at yourself from the outside, did you start to think more carefully about people?

T: No—to be quite honest. I think a lot of it was that I needed to sort myself out before I could help other people.

W: Yeah. Did anything we talked about help you to understand other people and what they do?

T: No, I never understand people in general! People in general are weirdos.

W: Did you know what I was thinking?

T: Pretty much. I think your aspect of it was "Sort your life out! Seriously," you're a good person, you're a nice person.

W: How did you *know* what I thought?

T: I think a lot of the time it was sort of—not aggressive—but sort of you just wanted me to succeed. I think a lot of people don't show that, like, they don't show that "I want you to succeed." I mean a lot of my friends are like "Why don't you get a fucking job, you lazy bastard?" and it's like … ahh … I'm trying to sort myself and I don't want to hear it, I don't really care for "You're a lazy bastard." But I think the way that they put it, and the way that you put it, it's not the same. But I think you've both got the same intentions. Of trying to help me out, trying to sort me out, try to get a job, try to get a life. And yeah I think they cared as much as you cared but they say it differently.

W: Oh that's interesting, so you do think about their intentions?

T: Yeah I do think about their intentions. I question it.

W: So how did you know what my intentions were?

T: I didn't. But over the last three or four months, since we've not spoken, I've thought a lot about it. And I think, look! I think I thought about the way you kind of tried to help me sort my life out, have a better life in general.

W: You said you knew my intention was to help you. Does that have to do with how you knew you could trust me?

T: Yeah. I don't know what it is and it's weird, but as a person normally you can tell . . . from people's body language. And I think your body language was sort of "I want you to succeed, I want you to have everything that you want. But I can't make those decisions for you … you've got to make those decisions on what you do and how you play your life out."

W: I wonder what my body language was?

T: Ah, that would be telling!

W: I'm really interested in this … do you think you would be able to tell a worker who was just like …

T: If someone walked in now you could tell from their body language whether they were angry, sad, happy. Do you know what I mean? It's the way that they walk, their posture, their presence. You feel a vibe off them, and the vibe I got off of you was "I want to help you. I want you to sort your life out and have a good life."

W: Do you know what the body language was?

T: It's hard to explain. It was a mixture of … how do I put it … "I want you to succeed. I want you to enjoy life." It's just weird, I can tell but I can't explain it. I think it's your self-confidence, the way you were happy all the time, that helped me out a lot. You're a happy person.

W: Do you remember that time when you'd had a bad night the night before and you'd been hitting the wall with the bar from your weights ... and I came round and you started to tell me, and you picked up the metal bar thing ...

T: Yeah and you started to get nervous.

W: Yeah, and I said let's go out for a walk. Do you remember that day?

T: Yeah. I do. Shit. I remember that day quite well. And I think after that day I kinda stopped drinking as much, because I think I was quite heavily intoxicated from the day before and going for that walk I think that calmed me down a bit and stopped the whole anger and the "grrrrr" in me and I think 'cos—to be quite honest—I've not had a proper beat-the-crap-out-of-someone fight in years, I've had fights ...

W: Do you remember what I said?

T: I can't remember. We walked down the side of the river bank.

W: You remember that I told you it made me a bit ...

T: I know it made you nervous, not nervous, more ... I don't know, scared? Is that the word?

W: Yeah, a little bit. What impact did that conversation have?

T: There's one thing that you need to know, right, I would never ever hit a woman. I don't agree with it. I think that any man that lays his hands on a woman is a fucking coward. But I think that day someone had riled me up and I was proper on one and I think I've not been like that for a little while because I've calmed myself down. I smoke weed, but I don't drink as much. The impact had a chain reaction, as such. Sort of, that day that I noticed that I scared you, it kind of hit home that "You don't go getting violent in front of a woman. It's not right and you shouldn't do it." I think that's what stopped me from smacking [X's mum] in the face later, 'cos I think I had a flashback of that day with you, and I did think ... I was gonna, I was *SO* gonna. I never had a woman square up to me like that ... but even though she starts tearing my hair out I just pulled away and said "Get lost, just go away. I don't fancy punching you."

W: You had a flashback to our conversation and that stopped you?

T: Yeah. I was like "Woah!"... This might sound sexist ... women aren't as physically strong as men, they have their own strengths ... but a lot of women are more vulnerable than men.

W: So although you said you're as impulsive as ever, you did think before acting then?

T: Yeah, there's a first time for everything. If I'd have hit her, I wouldn't be here today. I don't know if he would, I don't know if he wouldn't, but her sister's husband is a massive-time traveler, and his sons would set fire to you ... He's lumped me one, because he's her sister's husband.

W: On that day, for you to be able to stop and think ... that really made a difference.

T: Yeah. Part of it was as I was getting tensed up I was like ... just breeeathe. And calm down a little bit. And she was getting in my face and I was like ... arghhh ... my hands were tensing and [X] and [Y] saw it ... The thing is [my brother] was on her side ... I had a go at him about that the other day ... "What sort of family are you—not to back your own up, but you'll back her up instead? I've been there through everything with you and you've just gone 'fuck off' pretty much. That's the way it felt." And he said: "That's not what it meant" and I said "That's what it felt like."

W: It's good you were able to tell him how it *felt*.

T: Yeah, if you don't tell him, how's he supposed to know? It's the same with everyone. No-one's a mind reader. If you've got a problem with someone, bring it up. Talk about it.

W: So in that moment were you able to do that—"look at it from the outside" thing?

T: No. If I'd have done that I'd have walked away a long time before in that argument!

W: Yeah, it's hard. Is there anything else you want to say?

T: Thank you?

W: Ah, you don't have to say that.

T: No I do, because you've made a massive impact on my life. It helped me a lot and do you know, honestly to god I wouldn't be here today if it wasn't for [the YPSUS team]. Suicide. There was a few times I thought about my ex-girlfriend and all the rest of it and I'd try and slit my wrists and ... bad times ... But now everything's good.

W: Are there any other particular conversations or sessions we had that stand out?

T: Ooh. There's been millions of conversations. The one when I was in KFC. We sat in the car at KFC. We had a massive conversation about my mum and dad and the way that ... sort of ... the drugs doesn't help and stuff. That helped.

W: Do you remember what it was about?

T: I think a lot of it was about how … not you saying this, but me … I was sort of saying "I only get one set of parents" and you said "Well that is very true" sort of thing, and you were very supportive when I was going through a bad time and I think that helped quite a bit.

W: OK, and that stands out?

T: It stands out because there's not many out there who are willing to help someone like myself and other people who are in my predicament.

It's your presence. Just you being there. When you've got someone like yourself who is willing to take your time up to sort of sit in a car, buy me some food, have a chat … it's brilliant. It's absolutely brilliant. I could go from being depressed, hate myself, being miserable and then I'll talk to you and that will give me a buzz for a few days like "la la la" and then something will happen again and then I'll see you and it'll be like "la la la la la" again and that's how it would go. I like talking to people—my own company scared me. If I sit here, I'll think. And if I sit here and think, shit just comes back and it just hits me like a ton of bricks and I'll be like miserable for days. Until somebody talks to me and then I'll be like "ho ho hum" … sort of doodling along as I go through life.

W: Was there anything I did … and it's OK to say this … that made you cross? Or didn't feel helpful?

T: No.

W: What about like …

T: No no no, with me I've always been brought up … be upfront about it … if you don't like something, tell people how you feel. Don't hold it back.

There was one day … I don't think that it was the case that you were angry … there was a day I told you I'd used cocaine and it was anger, it was disappointment. Always disappointment with you. It was a case of "Oh really? You didn't really need to do it" … It's not your fault … it was a case of you're disappointed because you want to see me succeed.

W: How did you know it was that?

T: Body language. You were sort of "Ah really …?"

W: It sounds like you're getting better at working out what's going on for people?

T: Yeah.

W: I'm interested in this. How you *know* my intentions were good? Do you think you've got better at that?

T: Reading people? Definitely.

W: Do you do that more with your parents now?

T: No. With my family it's like bleeehhghh!

W: What about your friends?

T: Yeah … and I'm better at knowing what I do that annoys people … I'm better at reading people and it means I'm better at not annoying people … but also if I really want to piss people off, I'm better at that too!

W: So, understanding what you do that pisses people off helps you to not do it …

T: And it also means I can do it really well! [laughs]

W: Thank you for talking about all this.

T: No, thank you.

W: Is there anything else that stood out about [YPSUS]?

T: No … I think we've talked about everything to be honest.

Commentary by worker

The situation

Thomas referred himself to the substance use team having met one of the team's support workers at an outreach event. At the time he was 18 years old and under the care of an adult substance use service, but wasn't turning up to his appointments there. The age criteria for the local adult service and the young people's substance use team are deliberately designed to overlap, with both services accepting 18- to 21-year-olds. Services were commissioned in this way with the intention of enabling vulnerable young people to access care from the service most appropriate for their individual needs, in recognition of the difficulties many young people experience in accessing services primarily designed for older adults. After a period of discussion and liaison, it was agreed that Thomas's needs were not being best met in the adult service, and his care was transferred to the young person's substance use service (here referred to as YPSUS). At that time, Thomas was using multiple substances:

> "I was smoking a lot of cannabis. I was doing speed, cocaine, all sorts of other drugs. Never nothing hard like heroin, it was just stupid party drugs. Just going out and getting drunk all the time. Having house parties at my house. My house used to get trashed and I didn't care because I was always off my face. My life was miserable, depressing."

In addition to the substance use, Thomas had numerous difficulties across multiple domains of his life: he was living independently after his relationship with his parents had broken down, and was struggling with independent living skills; he was a carer to his older brother; he had mental health problems (post-traumatic symptoms, anxiety, and depression); and he was seen by professionals as vulnerable to exploitation. The parties at Thomas's house became a problem. His house became a place for local youths to drink and use drugs, and police were called out on several occasions to respond to the antisocial behaviour of his peers. Consequently, he was at risk of eviction. His house got "trashed," as he describes above, and—worse—his acquaintances stole from him:

> "I had house robberies. I've had people walk in my house with samurai swords and stuff like that . . . that was the PTSD."

Thomas's post-traumatic stress disorder related to events in his earlier childhood. He had also been low in mood for several years, and had been diagnosed with ADHD at a young age. He had been treated with pharmacological and psychosocial interventions by Child and Adolescent Mental Health Services (CAMHS) but was lost to follow-up after turning 17 years of age. In Thomas's case the most significant gap in services resulted from the lack of any local service for adults with ADHD to be transitioned to from CAMHS. Thomas transitioned instead on to a general adult mental health service waiting list, but moved address—becoming unreachable—before reaching the top of the list. He had fallen out of the education system too. He had had a chequered academic career, having been excluded from multiple educational placements, and at the time of referral he was "NEET" (not in education, employment, or training).

Thomas now—demonstrating his capacity to mentalize—has some ideas about how and why things might have become particularly difficult toward the end of his adolescence. He describes caring for his older brother, who was permanently disabled by an accident:

> "My brother was trying to commit suicide and I had that all on my shoulders as well. I think the case of looking after my brother from the age of 16 didn't really help. Once my brother got his new girlfriend I kind of went out and just got absolutely shit-faced because I knew that I could leave him in safe hands. So I just kind of let off a lot of steam, because at the age of 16 . . . normal sort of 16-year-olds are going out and getting shit-faced and using drugs. And when I was 16 I was looking after my brother, so by the age of 19 I was sort of thinking I was 16 because I didn't get to have that whole 'kid getting drunk and having drugs and stuff'. And . . . experimenting with drugs and alcohol, and I think it just went wildly out of control. Really quickly."

Working with your client

Building a relationship

Thomas describes his trepidation about meeting a new professional after his self-referral to the substance use team:

> "At first seeing [the team] was nerve-wracking because I didn't know the person and I get really wary around other people."

It is not a surprise that Thomas felt this way. To minimize this anxiety associated with building new relationships, and based on the AMBIT principle of the primacy of the keyworker relationship, the YPSUS developed a policy that wherever possible the same worker offering the initial assessment goes on to become the allocated keyworker within the service. The establishment of this relationship is an essential task in the initial phase of AMBIT work (see Chapter 3). Previously, there had been more separation between the processes of assessment and treatment, and these were often carried out by different people. This is just a small example of the kind of "local adaptations" that AMBIT encourages teams to make, incrementally trying to improve their offer of help through a judicious balancing of evidence-based practice (where it exists) with respect for local practice and expertise (or practice-based evidence.) This policy seeks to minimize the risk of frustration or being overwhelmed by requirements to relate to multiple new professionals—not least the risk that in the moment of crisis when assessment often occurs, a young person begins to build a degree of (epistemic) trust with the assessing worker, only to have to start from scratch with another worker if accepted into treatment. Importantly, the intention behind this policy is communicated to young people from the outset. This approach is certainly not unique, but is in contrast to some other service models, which prioritize flow and effectiveness by ensuring timely assessment by one worker, followed by allocation to another worker for intervention. Of course, there are benefits to the latter model, but we suggest that these are mainly for young people who are able to tolerate multiple workers.

Thomas noticed the difference in service design between the substance use service and other services in terms of the immediate allocation of a single worker:

> "I think with [other services] and stuff like that, there's a lot of people to handle. Whereas [the substance use team] sort of go one on one and they do help you."

Trust

Thomas talks about the relationship with his keyworker developing over time, despite his initial fears:

> "As time went on I got to know you and become quite good sort of friends, as such. And all in all you kind of really did help me quite a bit."

Asked what had made it possible for this to happen, and what was different between this relationship and other relationships he had had with professionals, Thomas referred to the development of trust in the relationship:

> "It was somebody I could trust. With somebody that's had a lot of trust issues—it's a case of people screwing him over and nicking stuff of his and it's—it's definitely an element of trust

issues. And as [my keyworker] came in I didn't trust [her] but then as time grew on I come to trust [her] and sort of—[she] looked out for me, sort of thing."

He has some ideas about what made it possible for him to trust his keyworker over time:

"I could tell [her] stuff and just get it all off my chest and [she] wouldn't—unless it was I was going to harm somebody, and then [she'd] have to tell somebody because there's certain protocols in place—but other than that it was confidentiality and I think that did help a lot."

Also:

"The food and that. The munch. Taking me to KFC and that. That was awesome. It was a case of—even when I had no food it was like 'Come on then, let's go and get some coffee' or 'Let's go out,' just get me out of the house, 'cos being in the house too long can sort of mess with your head a little bit, so that kind of helped in another way. [She] wanted to get me out of the house."

Here, Thomas describes his own perspective on what, in the keyworker's mind, was an explicit effort to offer contingent care based on *sensitive attunement* to his current perception of his needs and his mental state. The worker's efforts to achieve and sustain this attunement were directed by the goal of generating the experience for Thomas that his worker was someone offering help with a good "fit" with his perception of reality (see Chapter 4). This in turn supports the development of epistemic trust—trust in communication from another—which we understand as the cornerstone of helping relationships (see Chapter 2). Of course, there is potentially a circularity here: do we become helpful (i.e. effect meaningful change) when our clients have learned to trust us, or do our clients begin to trust people who have first been helpful to them (i.e. those who have actually effected meaningful change)? There is evidence suggesting that this relationship between alliance and outcomes works in both directions, but here we are stressing the former, as we see this as the *first* barrier to effective work. In support of this, Falkenstrom et al. (2013) found that positive measures of therapeutic alliance in one session predicted positive clinical outcomes in the next session.

In the scenarios described by Thomas, the keyworker was operating on a pre-existing plan for the sessions—perhaps trauma-focused work, or psychoeducation around substances—but, upon finding that Thomas had not eaten properly for several days, or was agitated after being alone in the house, needed to adjust these plans. Balancing adherence to pre-existing plans for care (interventions designed to tackle "upstream" difficulties nearer the "source") with sensitive attunement to issues in the here and now may have multiple benefits (this is described in Chapter 3—"Active Planning").

In the example of the keyworker taking Thomas to get some food when he had not eaten, there are long-term benefits from offering the experience of sensitive attunement and so supporting the development of epistemic trust. For Thomas, this attention to his needs was important, and facilitated the development of trust because:

> "throughout my life I've not had a lot of people who care about me and that showed that [she] cared, which I don't think a lot of [workers] would do."

Asked if that helped him to trust his keyworker, Thomas replied:

> "Yeah, definitely."

In addition, however, and in the more immediate term, getting some food for Thomas may have supported the effectiveness of the pre-existing intervention plan. Still hungry, Thomas's capacity to mentalize and to engage helpfully in the planned intervention would most likely be very low. Once fed, however, he and his keyworker were more able to return to the planned interventions. Creating a small budget to facilitate such flexibility is another example of adaptation, and was justified to commissioners on the grounds that this is a very small investment compared with the cost of a wasted session.

Being available

In addition to (or perhaps supportive of) being able to trust his keyworker, other aspects of the relationship with his keyworker and the wider team were important to Thomas:

> "It's [the keyworker's] presence, just [them] being there. When you've got someone like that who is willing to take [their] time up to sort of sit in a car, buy me some food, have a chat … it's brilliant. It's absolutely brilliant."

He spoke particularly of the importance of being able to get hold of someone when he needed to:

> "It's not like a GP who you sort of go to. You knew [YPSUS] were there if you needed them, the other end of a phone call. With doctors, my doctors especially, you ring up and not that I've ever done it … you're bleeding from your arms and it takes four hours to get through to them. Whereas if I left [my keyworker] a message, the next day [she'd] get back. It was quick. If I needed to talk about something it was "OK then, we'll sort it out" right there, as and when [the keyworker] knew what was happening. And the doctors on the other hand, when I had blackouts and I couldn't remember anything, [my keyworker] got on the phone to [the YPSUS doctor]. Next two to three days, there was a prescription waiting. "There you go, sort yourself out mate." It was a kind and friendly service sort of thing. Always polite, always nice. Don't get me wrong, you can get some snotty doctors out there, do you know what I mean?"

Promoting mentalizing

Thomas talks about how the work he did with his keyworker resulted in some changes in the way he thinks:

> *"I think it taught me to self-evaluate my life ... When I was going through a hard time [my keyworker] sort of helped me, sort of 'Right, just step back, evaluate your life and see what's going on' and I think at that point I did actually do it and it kind of 'Wow, not everything is what it seemed.'"*

This encouragement to "step back" and "self-evaluate" is Thomas's account of his keyworker's efforts to promote mentalizing. Thomas also refers to improvements in his ability to try to make sense of others. Talking about the intentions of different people who have tried to help him, he demonstrates his capacity to think about the intentions that underlie the behaviours of others:

> *"I think a lot of the time it was sort of—not aggressive—but sort of [my keyworker] just wanted me to succeed. I think a lot of people don't show that, like, they don't show that 'I want you to succeed'. I mean a lot of my friends are like 'Why don't you get a fucking job, you lazy bastard?' and it's like ... ahh ... I'm trying to sort myself and I don't want to hear it, I don't really care for 'You're a lazy bastard.' But I think the way that they put it, and the way that [my keyworker] put it, it's not the same.* **But I think [they've] both got the same intentions**. *Of trying to help me out, trying to sort me out, try to get a job, try to get a life. And yeah I think they cared as much as [my keyworker] cared, but they say it differently ... Yeah I do think about their intentions. I question it."*

Thomas talked about how one does this:

> *"If someone walked in now you could tell from their body language whether they were angry, sad, happy. Do you know what I mean? It's the way that they walk, their posture, their presence. You feel a vibe off them. It's hard to explain."*

Thomas recognizes that making sense of others is more difficult in some situations:

> *"With my family it's like bleeehhghh!"*

However, he talks about his efforts to help his brother to mentalize him following an argument in which Thomas felt his brother was on the other party's side:

> *"I had a go at him about that the other day ... 'What sort of family are you—not to back your own up, but you'll back her up? I've been there through everything with you and you've just gone "fuck off" pretty much. That's the way it felt'. And he said 'That's not what it meant' and I said 'That's what it felt like'... If you don't tell him, how's he supposed to know? It's the same with everyone. No-one's a mind reader. If you've got a problem with someone, bring it up. Talk about it."*

Interestingly, Thomas recognizes that the ability to mentalize people more accurately can be used toward both good and bad ends:

> *"I'm better at knowing what I do that annoys people ... I'm better at reading people and it means I'm better at not annoying people ... but also if I really want to piss people off, I'm better at that too! [Understanding what pisses people off] also means I can do it really well!"*

Broadcasting intentions

Thomas recalls a particular session in which his keyworker shared her thinking and feelings out loud (see "Broadcasting Intentions" in Chapters 3 and 4). His keyworker had arrived at Thomas's house for a scheduled session that day to find holes all over one of the walls of his sitting room. Thomas explained that he had become very upset the night before and had picked up a metal pole and repeatedly hit the wall, creating large holes in the plaster. As he recounted his distress from the night before and the incident that had caused it, he became increasingly agitated and he demonstrated his story by picking up the pole and swinging it around in front of the keyworker. Wishing to ensure her own safety, and to punctuate Thomas's non-mentalizing state of mind, she suggested that she and Thomas go for a walk, having observed in the past that this was an effective way for Thomas to reduce his emotional arousal and restore his mentalizing. According to Thomas:

> "We walked down the side of the river bank ... Going for that walk I think that calmed me down a bit and stopped the whole anger and the 'grrrrr' in me."

Once Thomas was calmer, his keyworker asked Thomas to mentalize her by asking how he thought she might have felt when he was shouting and swinging the metal bar around in front of her. He wondered whether it had scared her, and she shared with him that it had, a little:

> "I know it made [her] nervous, not nervous, more ... I don't know, scared? Is that the word?"

Thomas talks about the impact of that realization:

> "I remember that day quite well. And I think after that day I kinda stopped drinking as much, because I think I was quite heavily intoxicated from the day before ... I think that day someone had riled me up and I was proper on one and I think I've not been like that for a little while now because I've calmed myself down ... The impact had a chain reaction, as such. Sort of, that day that I noticed that I scared [my keyworker], it kind of hit home that 'You don't go getting violent in front of a woman. It's not right and you shouldn't do it.'"

Most interestingly, Thomas talks about generalizing this learning, from a session with his keyworker over a year ago, to a recent incident in which he was in a confrontational interaction with another older woman:

> "I think that's what stopped me from smacking [her] in the face, 'cos I think I had a flashback of that day with [my keyworker] and I did think ... I was gonna, I was SO gonna. I never had a woman square up to me like that ... but even though she starts tearing my hair out I just ... 'Get lost, just go away. I don't fancy punching you'... I was like 'Woah!'... This might sound sexist ... women aren't as physically strong as men, they have their own strengths ... but a lot of women are more vulnerable than men."

Thomas reflects on how the situation impacted upon his own mental state, and how he noticed this and recognized the need to manage it before being able to think in a different way:

> "Part of it was as I was getting tensed up. I was like … just breaaathe. And calm down a little bit. She was getting in my face and I was like … 'arghhh'… my hands were tensing."

We do not think we are reading too much into what Thomas describes here to say that this describes the beginnings of a change now generalizing beyond the specific relationship with his keyworker where this new understanding was first articulated. Thomas describes the signs of an emerging capacity for conscious inhibition of violent impulses, and this seems to have been mediated by the earlier experience of explicitly mentalizing fear in another (trusted) person, his keyworker, which was neither repudiated by her nor resulted in reciprocal threats or recriminations. Perhaps, during that "mentalizing walk," Thomas also recognized that his keyworker had, on her part, also been able to mentalize his own distress at having caused her fear (unintentionally, it would seem), and she had been able to use this understanding in a way that he experienced as benign, contingent, and understanding. It is this recognition of self, as it is represented accurately in the mind of the other, that is the key to epistemic trust.

Repairing relationships

A key task for an AMBIT-influenced team, which supports the Ending Phase (see Chapter 3), is the practice of scaffolding existing relationships. As described in Chapter 4, this element of the principled AMBIT stance describes explicit efforts by the keyworker to help strengthen or build around the client a reasonably reliable and sustainable network of relationships that is able to provide ongoing support and help. For Thomas, this work commenced quite early in the intervention journey, through family work, with the aim of bolstering Thomas's resources and resilience, and reducing the likelihood that family conflict would destabilize things. The aim was to create the capacity for him to maintain improvements in his wellbeing beyond the ending of his relationship with his keyworker.

Of his relationships with his family members, Thomas says:

> "I think [my keyworker has] repaired the relationships a little bit, because me and my mum and my dad are actually talking now, whereas before we wasn't. And I think also [mum and dad] respected the fact that I got help for what I had—taking drugs and stuff. I think it's because I got help with it, that they started talking to me. Because, with drugs, there is an element of trust with family members.
>
> Recently my dad's been in hospital, sort of thing—he had a kidney infection—I think I walked into the hospital and the first thing I done was I give my dad a cuddle—and it's a weird thing because my dad and I never got on. We've always had our problems, but just

in a serious sort of context like that, it's sort of, it's called for. And I know it's weird because man being man—it's sort of pride, and ... but I don't care about that. I just care about my family. I love my mum and my dad and my brother and sister. Don't get me wrong, they're all douchebags at some points in their life but I still love them and I just want them all to get on."

"Slowly fizzling out"

Reflecting on what was different about his engagement with his YPSUS keyworker compared with other relationships with professionals in the past, Thomas referred to differences in the amount of time dedicated to the Ending Phase of the relationship:

> "I think I've had this sort of relationship before but it was kind of 'get me to a certain point then drop me from a height'. So a lot of people sort of ... they'd get me over what needed to be done, and then that was it. But [my YPSUS keyworker] kind of did what needed to be done and sort of ... slowly fizzled it out, not just dropped me as and when I'd finished doing what I needed to do. So that kind of helped a lot."

Chapter 3 details the critical importance of the Ending Phase of AMBIT work, and how preparation for that ending starts at the beginning of the relationship. Thomas refers to previous helping relationships that he thinks ended rather too suddenly, dropping him "from a height" upon completion of care plan goals. Mentalizing Thomas for a moment, we wonder whether such an experience of ending being perceived as too sudden may have been particularly bruising for him after the painful breakdown in his relationship with his parents, resulting in him being asked to leave home. Thomas refers to having "this sort" of relationship with other workers prior to his contact with the YPSUS keyworker, so we can suppose that significant attachments were formed in those relationships. If that is so, then it is not surprising that he experienced the abrupt end of those relationships as having been "dropped."

Thomas's perception that his work with his keyworker "slowly fizzled out" may have a basis in two intentional practices undertaken by the keyworker. First, the prospect of the inevitable ending of the work was discussed explicitly from very early on in the relationship, making it clear that a good attachment was desirable, but in pursuit of particular goals for Thomas, and thus timelimited. Second, the intensity of intervention was tapered off slowly toward the end of Thomas's engagement with the service. Once care plan goals were more or less achieved, the focus of the work shifted toward maintenance, and weekly appointments became fortnightly, then three-weekly, and so on, over a period of several months.

Working with your team

Much of Thomas's testimony about his experience of the AMBIT-influenced substance use team revolves around his relationship with his keyworker, rather than his experience of specific interventions or of the functioning of the team as a whole. Given AMBIT's emphasis on the centrality of a secure relationship with a keyworker, this is perhaps unsurprising, or at least reassuring.

However, as we have learned in Chapter 5, successfully establishing a powerful keyworking relationship is not without risk. Describing his relationship with his keyworker, Thomas said that, after initial distrust on his part, they became "*sort of friends*," indicating perhaps a degree of rapport that was different from, but reminded him of, friendship. We hypothesize that this was a key ingredient in Thomas's progress, for the reasons outlined above. However, this degree of "closeness" to Thomas's own difficulties and distress also impacted upon his keyworker's own state of mind, putting at risk her capacity to mentalize both herself and Thomas, and thus, ultimately, her capacity to be as helpful as possible to Thomas. AMBIT stresses the importance of the keyworker being "well connected to the team" to counter such risks. This phrase describes not just a culture of "team support" but of quite explicit efforts by team members to support one another's mentalizing capacity in this anxiety-provoking work. Home visits, conversations in cars and in fast-food establishments, and walks by the river characterize the kind of outreach work Thomas's keyworker engaged in with him. This may have been key in supporting and maintaining his engagement in treatment, but also required the keyworker to work autonomously, often quite isolated from her team.

The YPSUS team uses a number of the team-based techniques outlined in Chapter 5. Team members encourage a strong culture of explicit help-seeking between colleagues. The Thinking Together process is used both informally and more formally in weekly group supervision. Much of this work goes on "behind the scenes" from the client's perspective, but YPSUS also makes efforts to share something of its team approach quite explicitly with clients.

Thinking Together between the worker and another team member is sometimes conducted in front of the client in the same room (not dissimilar to systemic therapists' use of a "reflecting team"). Alternatively, it may take place via a mobile phone switched to loudspeaker mode, so that the client can listen in and contribute as they see fit. In such circumstances, the keyworker does make it clear to the client that this is a conversation primarily designed around themself as a worker getting help (ensuring a plan is sound, developing new ideas, balancing risk with care, etc.); the invitation to listen is so that the client has access to this thinking in a transparent way, and, although they are welcome to join the conversation, they should not feel obliged to contribute. Thoughts or "take-home messages" from team conversations about a client's predicament are shared with the client by the keyworker, mentioning team members who have helped move thinking forward by name, where possible. This models a positive relationship to help—that workers, like anyone, can be helped to better understand things or to gain fresh perspectives by thinking things through with trusted others. It also marks the keyworker–client relationship as a helping relationship, and not an "exclusive" friendship or any other category of relationship.

Asked about his experience of knowing that his keyworker had access to a team of people who helped her to help him, Thomas explained that:

> "I was quite surprised that a team like [YPSUS]—they're caring; they want to see the best in the person, they want to make that person a better person than when they first walked through the door."

It is interesting to note that here Thomas describes, and *attributes shared intentions to*, a team of people he either has not met, or has met on only a handful of occasions. Separately, Thomas referred to his experience of meeting another member of the team who was observing the practice of his keyworker (for training purposes):

> "I think when I saw [the other team member and the keyworker they] were both on the same lines, exactly, which is kind of weird because you normally have two people who are two completely different people. But you was both on the same kind of lines. You were both caring, you both sort of wanted to help."

In this brief anecdote Thomas finds these two workers to be "on the same lines," and the hope is that his observations and description reflect the effect of a team with a developed culture around shared understandings of mentalizing, and explicit efforts in practice to adopt a mentalizing stance.

Working with your networks

"Not just drugs and alcohol"

When Thomas referred himself to the substance use team he had problems in multiple domains of his functioning: he was using drugs and alcohol in risky ways; was getting into fights and had close calls with the police; was struggling to live independently after being thrown out of home; was being exploited by others who used his flat as a place to use drugs; had a difficult relationship with his parents, with infrequent contact characterized by conflict; was low in mood; had untreated ADHD; was not in employment, education, or training (NEET); was caring for his brother; and had unmet physical health needs (his eczema was flaring up, he needed new glasses, and he experienced significant dental pain). It would have been hard to claim that any single difficulty was the "primary problem." Rather, these difficulties were interacting synergistically. For example, Thomas managed his distress arising from relationship difficulties and caring responsibilities by using drugs and alcohol—and his drug and alcohol use led to further conflict with his parents. Impulsivity resulting from

ADHD made it harder for Thomas to manage his money, and he was often without food and in debt to his landlord. This in turn became a further stressor, maintaining his low mood and substance use, and so on. When Thomas first referred himself to the substance use team it felt, he said, like he had a "mountain" to climb to get back on track.

He appreciated that the substance use team were interested in the whole picture, despite their relatively narrow "formal" area of speciality and responsibility:

> "[YPSUS] muddle through your problems and help you out with other stuff as well. So it's not just drugs and alcohol, it's other stuff as well."

The muddle

As is commonly the case for young people who have multiple difficulties, Thomas had multiple named workers, across multiple agencies:

> "I was seeing [the housing support worker], [the adult drug service], [the youth worker], [the information advisor], and my GP. I was on the waiting list for adult mental health services."

Navigating this network of support was not plain sailing:

> "It was alright but they kind of ... I think a lot of them were sort of ... they were trying to get me into a job ... more than trying to sort my personal health out. So I think [my housing support worker] was trying to get me into another house or at least get me ready for moving on to the next house. [The information advisor] was trying to get me into a job. [The youth worker] was trying to ... to be honest I don't know what the frigging hell [the youth worker] was there for. [The youth worker] didn't do anything to be honest ... But they're all trying to focus on all different aspects of my life, whereas you were trying to sort out my drugs and alcohol, [the information advisor] was trying to do one thing, [the housing support worker] was trying to do another and everyone was trying to do something else and no-one was caring about how I felt inside and how I was reacting with stuff."

AMBIT holds as a core assumption that, when young people have multiple problems and thus multiple workers are involved, the kind of dis-integration described by Thomas above is the norm. Thomas describes a number of workers, each—we can assume—with good intentions but with different priorities, although it appears that Thomas was not clear on what exactly the priority was for the youth worker. Again, we suggest that it is not unusual for a client and/or their family to be unclear about the priorities or the role of one or more workers in a crowded network. As Thomas says:

> "It was all quite muddly."

Addressing dis-integration

Thomas had clear substance use needs, and it would have been reasonable to agree a transfer of responsibility for Thomas's substance use care from the adult substance use service (with whom he was struggling to engage) and for YPSUS to offer straightforward substance use interventions in its place. However, it was not obvious that adding an additional worker, or new interventions, to the muddle was going to be helpful to Thomas's overall wellbeing where other well-intentioned and very capable workers were struggling to be effective.

It appeared that workers were each pulling in different directions—directions that were all ostensibly reasonable and helpful when considered individually, but in combination were ill-sequenced and even contradictory. This was not due to lack of communication between the parties. On the contrary, the network was reasonably well functioning in that, on the whole, workers were aware of one another's involvement, roles, and planned interventions. There was plenty of communication in terms of keeping one another up to date about their involvement and Thomas's progress. What was lacking, from an AMBIT viewpoint, was explicit sharing by workers with one another of (a) how they understood the nature of Thomas's difficulties, and (b) how they thought their combined interventions would fit together or be experienced by Thomas.

So, rather than adding to the dis-integration by immediately offering another worker and further interventions, risking at best not being very helpful, or at worst, causing damage to the existing network and Thomas's wellbeing, Thomas's keyworker decided first to intervene (with Thomas's permission) at the wider network level. This work started with mapping out a Dis-Integration Grid (see Chapter 6) with Thomas, then writing a letter to all involved parties to share Thomas's and the keyworker's understanding of the current situation and suggesting that it might be helpful for a new meeting to be arranged by the lead professional for all to share ideas about how best to deliver and sequence interventions. This was offered as a view from "the edge of the pond," with great care taken to maintain the stance of "Respect for local practice and expertise." The underlying assumption in this communication was that Thomas, his family, and existing professionals in the network were best placed to make such decisions, rather than the "Johnny-come-lately" substance use team keyworker.

This meeting took place and the professionals involved agreed that it would be helpful to sequence interventions intelligently, based on priority (e.g. first addressing problems that were a risk to Thomas's immediate safety) and a shared understanding of the primary direction of influence between Thomas's different problems (e.g. helping Thomas to manage his agitation and ADHD better *before* offering him a further educational placement might help to avoid setting him up for yet another failure). For some workers in the network, this meant offering less help, not more, initially. At this meeting it was also decided that Thomas's substance use needs would be better met by YPSUS than the existing adult team, as the young person's team had the expertise and (perhaps at least as important) the capacity to offer the outreach approach that Thomas was likely to benefit from. A transfer of care was therefore agreed.

Thomas does not recall getting much from this meeting himself:

> "To be honest, at that point I was either tired, stoned, or drunk. I don't know, but either way I don't think I paid attention to that meeting. I think I was like 'Ah, piss off, dickhead' and all the rest of it. I don't think I paid much attention to that meeting. If we had that meeting now I think it would be a very very very different occasion … It was helpful, but it was a pain in the ass, getting everyone in the same room on the same day."

However, he did appreciate the different approach taken by YPSUS:

> "... the main important thing nobody really cared about, apart from [YPSUS]."
> "[YPSUS], they kind of cared about what was going on in my life and how things were going and where things were going as such."

Learning at work

During the course of working with Thomas, one old and two new issues arose that stimulated discussion and reflection in the wider team in team manualization sessions (see Chapter 7). These areas of interest were by no means unique to Thomas's case, but brought into sharper focus areas of practice that, although they may lack a powerful evidence base in literature, nonetheless shape local practice in important ways.

First, existing practice around how the YPSUS team used its small budget to provide coffee/sandwiches or other food for its clients was raised in a team meeting. Specifically, there were questions about the extent to which a worker could claim expenses for such an outlay, and how the team was justifying this outlay to its commissioners. Discussion in a team manualizing session took place, and notes on "Staff Expenses" were updated in the YPSUS team's online manual, which included clarification about what a staff member can and cannot claim for from petty cash, and the principles behind this approach. The team clarified its understanding that the offer of food or drinks to a client is not simply a routine offer, nor even a standard "carrot" to help engagement, but instead should be specifically indicated on the grounds of (a) basic physical needs, which, if not met, would hinder mentalizing in the session (see Maslow's hierarchy of needs; Maslow, 1943), or (b) that doing so allows the worker to demonstrate sensitive attunement specific to the situation and in keeping with the process of Active Planning (see Chapter 3).

Second, the use of text messaging between the worker and Thomas contributed to a wider discussion in the team about this, which ended with the drafting of learning points in the local online manual about how to ensure that text messages are properly documented, and how to clarify to clients that this is not an appropriate channel for emergencies, as they are not accessed out of hours.

Finally, this case contributed to team discussion and manualization about how a worker might judiciously share their emotions with a client in certain circumstances, and more generally describing the team's approach to therapeutic relationships so that Thomas could describe his worker as being "like a friend," but nonetheless remain within a firmly boundaried relationship. As a result of these discussions, a new page on "How do you answer questions inviting personal disclosure?" was created in the team's online manual, documenting the team's most up-to-date collective thinking about this.

Summary

Besides the general limitations of the single-case study methodology used, we must note some more specific limitations and potential for bias in this exploration of Thomas's case. Thomas could be described now as a "happy customer" of the AMBIT-influenced team in question and, as such, although it meant that he was willing to agree to help us in writing this chapter, it also meant that he was unlikely to make negative comments about his experience (when asked by the interviewer, he said he "would not change anything" about his experience). Moreover, the interviewer was his old keyworker, and this would have made critical comments about the service he received even harder for him to offer.

We hope that, notwithstanding these limitations, something of the quality of the relationship was communicated. Of course, no case is being made for any direct causal link between Thomas's positive outcomes and the influence of AMBIT on the team he worked with. Rather, we hope that this case study illustrates some of the principles and practices promoted by AMBIT, and explores one young man's experience of these.

We are very grateful to Thomas for his time and generosity in helping us to write this chapter.

References

Falkenstrom, F., Granstrom, F., & Holmqvist, R. (2013). Therapeutic alliance predicts symptomatic improvement session by session. *Journal of Counseling Psychology* **60**: 317–28. doi: 10.1037/a0032258

Maslow, A. H. (1943). A theory of human motivation. *Psychological Review* **50**: 370–96.

Chapter 9

There is no such thing as a standard AMBIT team

Introduction: An operating system for multiple programs

The purpose of this chapter is to provide the reader with a range of examples of how the practice of AMBIT has been developed by different teams. As we have described in previous chapters, AMBIT emphasizes the importance of adaptation to the local service context and the local needs of the target population of a service. The intention is that AMBIT provides an overall framework to support a multidimensional process of help. It is a bit like a computer operating system such as Windows (although the open-source Linux system would be a truer comparison), which supports a huge range of different software programs, enabling the individual user to use it in many different ways. AMBIT provides a platform by which more specific forms of help (e.g. evidence-based methods of addressing mental health needs) are delivered in ways that are more accessible to clients who have very little confidence that the "standard software" will work for them.

What sorts of teams have been trained in AMBIT?

AMBIT has provided training for approaching 200 teams working with hard-to-reach clients; mostly these teams work with young people with severe and complex needs, but some work with adults. Although AMBIT was initially developed as an approach for adolescents, and remains developmentally attuned, there is nothing in the core features of the approach that limits its applicability to a specific age group. Most of the teams we have trained to date have been based in the UK, but the approach has also been adopted by a range of teams in the USA, Australia, and across Europe. Some of these are mental health outreach teams containing a range of health care professionals, including nurses, psychologists, psychiatrists, family therapists, and social workers. Other teams are more linked to social care systems and focus on young people at risk of entering the care system, at risk of exploitation, or at risk of offending.

In the UK there is also a range of services provided by charities and voluntary sector organizations that target highly disadvantaged young people—for example, those who are homeless, those with substance use disorders, and those at risk of sexual exploitation. Many workers in these teams may not be formally qualified health or social care professionals, although they may be highly experienced with the particular client group that is the focus of their team. To add to this diversity, not all of the teams that we have trained use an outreach approach, although most do—that is, they establish contact with clients in community settings rather than relying entirely on clients coming to them. Some teams with which the AMBIT project has worked operate with a not dissimilar population, but in inpatient, residential, day-hospital, or prison settings.

In general, the teams we have trained comprise between 6 and 15 staff, and usually include a team manager. Some teams will have a clinical supervisor who provides supervision for all of the team, while other teams may have a range of supervisors related to different professional groups. The teams we encounter often have a relatively flat hierarchy, with strong values of shared decision-making and transparency. Many of the teams include service users as part of a steering group.

The teams we train tend to have a number of shared values and contexts. First, they have a commitment to working with disadvantaged clients and their families. Second, they tend to have strong beliefs about the value of real-life experience in conducting this work with clients; this underpins a belief in the value of workers having an implicit "feel for the work," which is very different from what can be gained from more formal types of training. Third, they are often functioning in unstable service settings, whether in the public or charitable sector, in which ongoing funding uncertainties and sector reorganizations create a stressful backdrop to their work. Additionally, many teams have relatively limited resources for training and supervision. Fourth, they place a high value on engagement with clients—that is, to demonstrate a capacity to relate to the lives of their clients that is believable and authentic. Following engagement with the client, there is often rather less clarity about their intervention model, and the "model" followed may vary quite significantly between team members, often according to their previous training, experience, and expertise.

Our experience is that different teams have different requirements in the task of making the "operating system" that we referred to above work better. For some teams, the main focus may be on developing mentalizing skills for their work with clients. Other teams may focus more on improving the function of broader locality-wide networks of help.

The aim of this chapter is to illustrate how different teams have taken different aspects of the AMBIT model to improve their existing practice. In our view, all four quadrants of the AMBIT model deserve attention, but some teams may already be quite highly developed in relation to one or more of these quadrants.

For example, some teams may already have very well-developed methods for supporting each other's work ("Working with your Team"); AMBIT training may lead to relatively little change in this area, while other areas of work might be more powerfully influenced. In these circumstances, what may be valued by the team is what AMBIT can add through defining and enriching existing team competencies.

The teams describing their work in the following sections of this chapter represent a range of different ways of offering help to highly troubled young people. They comprise a mainstream NHS mental health adolescent outreach team; an inpatient adolescent unit; a community youth project involving young people as workers; a highly specialist residential care and treatment service; an intensive outreach treatment service; an integrated social care and health team; and a substance misuse service. This diversity of teams represents the variety of services relevant to the multiple needs of the clients for whom AMBIT has been designed. However, these teams are by no means equivalent in terms of the level of prior training their staff will have had. Youth service-led projects may be staffed by youth workers who are highly experienced, but who have had relatively little professional training compared with psychiatric nursing and medical staff. Psychologists (clinical and educational) and social workers will also bring an extensive range of prior training, and this will influence the degree to which aspects of the AMBIT model are experienced as new or are seen as variations on familiar ideas and practices. In our experience, these workforce differences also influence the way in which teams experience the AMBIT approach. For example, for some staff trained in youth work, the concept of mentalizing may be very helpful, but the technical "psychology language" may be significantly off-putting. In response to this variability, AMBIT sets out to create some shared language across these professional boundaries. We recognize that the degree to which this is achieved will often depend on the existing skill mix within the team.

We invited a series of teams that had received the AMBIT training to describe what they had found valuable about the AMBIT approach, and what parts of the model they have adopted as part of their practice. The following sections describe their perspectives and highlight the diverse range of contexts in which these teams work.

The influence of AMBIT on seven teams and services

AMBIT in a CAMHS adolescent outreach team: The Bexley experience—*an account by Sarah Harmon and Peter Slater*

Prior to the existence of the Bexley CAMHS (Child and Adolescent Mental Health Services) Adolescent Team, increasing numbers of adolescents with mental health problems from Bexley in south-east London were being admitted to psychiatric inpatient units, where they were staying for increasing periods of time. The local CAMHS and commissioners recognized that lengthy inpatient stays have a number of disadvantages: they can be traumatic; young people become dislocated from their families, social networks, and support structures; and their education is disrupted. The evidence suggests that inpatient care is neither always necessary nor always the most effective way to help young people with significant mental health needs (National Institute for Health Research, 2008). Finally, young people and families prefer to be treated within their communities (Children's Commissioner for England, 2007).

Consequently, a multidisciplinary adolescent mental health team was created with the purpose of providing community alternatives to inpatient treatment. This new team consisted of nurses, psychiatrists, psychologists, a psychotherapist, a family therapist, an occupational therapist, and an outreach support worker. The young people we supported in the community presented with problems such as depression (76%), suicidal ideation (57%), suicide attempts (20%), self-harm (57%), and psychosis (13%). Many young people were struggling with more than one of these problems simultaneously.

When we were working with adolescents who posed such a high level of risk to themselves, anxiety levels within the team could understandably be very high. From our AMBIT training we learned to accept that this anxiety was to be expected and to recognize the impact it was having on our ability to mentalize our clients, ourselves, and each other. We recognized a tendency within the team to operate in a teleological mode in relation to the young people (i.e. to do something for the sake of doing something) when anxiety was high, and in psychic equivalence mode (i.e. how we see it is how it is) in relation to each other, leading to strained relationships within the team.

The AMBIT approach gave us a language that clinicians from varied trainings and orientations could identify with and use to communicate with each other, as well as allowing us to voice the continual balance that we needed to strike between thinking and action. Particular emphasis was placed upon incorporating components of stance and practice such as the "well-connected team" and "scaffolding existing relationships." Through the adaptation of "supervisory structures," a culture of mentalizing was integrated not only into our work as individual clinicians, but also within the day-to-day life of a team working in close proximity with each other, as well as within the network of other agencies supporting our client group.

When working with such adolescents and their families, who often present with disparate and fragmented external and internal states, the need for a well-connected team was paramount. Sustaining frequent and close communication between team members and a capacity and willingness to mentalize each other's experience, along with "Thinking Together" exercises when anxiety levels were high, was invaluable in keeping thinking and reflection alive in the face of high levels of affect. Such confusing and unpredictable presentations often led to fragmentation occurring in the support services around a young person. We found that by adopting the AMBIT stance and practice of "scaffolding existing relationships," there was less opportunity for dis-integration in the network of support around the young person. It also increased the capacity for identifying existing levels of resilience within the young person and their family.

One way in which we adapted the "supervisory structures" already in existence, in order to support mentalizing in the team, was in the changes we made to our team meetings. We moved from having one long team meeting per week—at which an attempt was made to discuss many cases, but which tended to be dominated by those who provoked the most anxiety in team members—to holding three different types of meeting, each with its own purpose. A brief meeting at nine o'clock every morning was used to discuss those young people presenting with the highest risk and to agree action plans for managing the risk that day. A one-hour formulation meeting once a week was used to discuss a complex case involving several team members and agree our formulation and, based on this, the care plan, all in language that can be shared with the young person and their family. Another hour-long meeting, held weekly, was a team supervision group with the purpose of helping restore mentalizing in any team member/s who felt "stuck" or in conflict in an ongoing case. None of these meetings is unique in mental health services and all have been borrowed from other teams we have visited or worked in. What is more specific to the Bexley CAMHS Adolescent Team is that all meetings use the structure of Thinking Together for their case discussions, with the chairperson having the task of keeping the speaker focused on "Stating the Case" and the team having the task of mentalizing their colleagues and the young person and family.

Case example

K was a 16-year-old female referred by the emergency department of a local hospital having taken a substantial overdose (not her first). She was serially self-harming her upper body, and spoke of pseudo-hallucinations, a recent expulsion from school, and ongoing experimentation with drugs. There had earlier been an acrimonious parental separation, and she had previously made and then withdrawn an allegation of sexual abuse against her mother's partner. K initially refused to have any parental involvement in her care. K and her mother both blamed each other for the other's deep unhappiness and distress.

K was discussed in team supervision following a difficult meeting with K and her mother, resulting in K threatening a further suicide attempt. Her mother stated that she would hold the clinicians involved responsible should K kill herself, because they had not admitted her to an inpatient psychiatric unit. During supervision, the purpose of bringing K's case to the meeting was initially defined (*Marking the Task*): the clinicians involved felt stuck. This was followed by a brief summary of the case for those team members who were not familiar with it (*Stating the Case*) and then a description of the recent difficult session, including the clinicians' own thoughts and feelings at the time. The team then supported the clinicians in mentalizing first themselves, and then K and her mother (*Mentalizing the Moment*). The clinicians involved were feeling resentment about who was to take the lead, and some blame around why the case had become so stuck. They found it very useful to think about how their own difficulties appeared similar to the fragmentary quality of K's own internal and external states and the persecutory nature of K's relationship with her mother. This process helped the clinicians to have a better understanding of K and her mother's experience, which in turn led to some ideas about the way forward (*Return to Purpose*). For example, there was a need for one clinician to be the keyworker working with K and coordinating her care, as well as a role for another clinician to work with her mother and the family. This was felt to be of particular importance given the level of hostility between K and her family at that point in time, but with a view to bringing K and her mother to work together at a later stage. Other supportive networks were identified and integrated into the plan (*Scaffolding existing relationships*), in this case a healthy network of friends and a supportive form teacher who recognized K's potential and who was keen to support K's reintegration into school.

As in many instances, we made use of the AMBIT approach to provide and protect a structured reflective space for joined-up thinking and collaborative working, which are invaluable in our work. By helping to contain anxiety within the team we were then better able to apply thinking states to managing the risk levels of the often highly dysregulated young people under our care. The team was better able not only to think about and adapt how we structured contact with our patients and their families in order to better engage with them, but also to recognize the importance of improving communication between team members and with the services we work alongside.

AMBIT in an inpatient setting: The experience of the Darwin Unit—*an account by James Fairbairn*

The Darwin Centre is an adolescent inpatient unit. We have 14 beds and admit young people aged 12–17 years experiencing complex and severe mental health difficulties. Young people are usually admitted with suicidal and self-harming behavior, and most arrive in a position of "high risk." Many of the young people have complex trauma histories, and most struggle greatly to manage emotions, often feeling overwhelmed and frightened, and without a coherent sense of self. Finding words to express or make sense of feelings and experiences can be a huge challenge for the young people we see. In this environment there are multiple factors that impact on our capacity as workers to mentalize. High emotion and distress are easily amplified and transferred around staff and patients on the unit.

How have we applied AMBIT? It has given us permission to stop, notice, and think about our feelings. The power of unconscious processes within inpatient units, and the potential for harm when unhelpful dynamics are acted out, is well documented (Menzies, 1960). We have used AMBIT as a framework for noticing our (the team's) feelings and responses to the work and patients. We have explained and reminded ourselves in mentalizing terms why it is crucial to make sense of our own feelings and responses to the work. We have defined our weekly staff process group as a forum for mentalizing ourselves and the young people, and we have become explicit about our rationale for this: that in order to reduce the chances of difficult feelings or reactions being acted out with the young people, we need to understand our own feelings and responses.

We have always held a weekly team case formulation meeting. We have come to see that this is implicitly about mentalizing; if we can develop a more shared, complex, and psychological understanding of a young person, we are less likely to resort to prementalizing explanations for their behavior, such as, "It's not mental health, it's just behavioral." Such descriptions stop us from thinking creatively and finding new opportunities to intervene. They can also lead to more punitive and less therapeutic responses. Under the influence of AMBIT, we have come to use this time explicitly to protect and support mentalizing, asking each person to say how they have been feeling in relation to the young person. We then consider what this might tell us about the young person and we work to identify the potential traps or patterns that we might get stuck in with them. We have used AMBIT to notice and normalize the impact of distress and emotion on all of us, and to create a shared language for this. It is very validating to know that we *all* lose the capacity to mentalize and that we *all* have a responsibility to help each other regain it.

We practice Thinking Together as part of our AMBIT induction for all new staff. Our experience is that this approach has not become embedded across the whole team. Nurses and health care assistants say that it can be difficult to use Thinking Together around crisis points, particularly at nights or weekends when there are fewer staff able to take a position at the "edge of the pond" (see Chapter 5). At these times, finding a physical and mental space to "think together" means two staff leaving the main ward area. This is a challenge when a number of young people may need immediate support, which must be shared across a few staff.

In our ward induction we now present the barriers to Thinking Together on the ward in these kinds of situations, and then we brainstorm how we might still manage to regain our capacity to mentalize in this context. Ideas that are regularly used on the ward include noticing each other's level of emotion and asking, "Do you want to take five minutes off the ward?", phoning the on-call nurse to think things through, and going individually off the ward for a short break. We use AMBIT to emphasize the importance of finding space to think when emotion rises. It gives us a clear rationale for why this is essential in managing high-stress situations.

AMBIT has also shaped the way we think about relationships between staff and young people on the unit. The strongest and most influential connections usually develop with the staff who have most contact with the young people. This is often our nurses or health care assistants. Rather than using a single "keyworker" model, young people are allocated a care team consisting of one nurse and two health care assistants on admission. There is an emphasis on the care team taking a lead in getting to know a young person and being in charge of administrative tasks such as updating and communicating care plans. However, we now pay close attention to *all* the relationships that develop naturally between staff and young people. These relationships are often with a member of the care team, but this is certainly not always the case, and there are not uncommonly one or two other staff members with whom the young person may also find their own "good fit." It is in these "patient-selected" relationships that we often see the most trust develop. Before AMBIT, the capacity for therapeutic change through such relationships was not fully recognized, and they would have been side-lined. We now notice and highlight the importance of these relationships, and where possible these workers are supported in taking a more central role in a young person's care and treatment. In some cases we reallocate members of the original care team, although often this is not necessary as we can be flexible across allocated team structures.

Some of the important work that happens through these relationships includes: having therapeutic and personal conversations that might not be possible with any other team member; supporting young people to manage their therapy by joining family or individual sessions; coming to ward rounds or care planning meetings to help other staff explore the young person's perspective; taking on an outreach role through supporting young people at home both pre- and post-discharge; facilitating and joining community appointments or other meetings with a range of professionals involved; and being the named person on shift that the young person will call to think things through. The shift work of the nurses and health care assistants means they often spend long periods, including weekends, evenings, and nights, on the ward. This presents opportunities for infinite different conversations and interactions with the young people. Within the "key relationships" described here there is then a valuable opportunity for the young person to have an overall experience of a relationship that feels safe and in which they feel understood. It is this that we see as leading to therapeutic change.

Applying this model on the ward has many complexities and is not without problems. Having a close and trusting relationship with a distressed young person is certainly demanding. There have been times when team members have felt overwhelmed or overburdened by the intensity of these relationships, particularly when they might be the only person on the unit whom a young person really feels they can trust. These situations can throw up complex boundary issues, and sometimes splits in the team form around these difficulties. Finding a balance between making best use of these relationships and the wider team feeling able and empowered to carry out their own work with the young person can be tricky. There are times when a number of young people orientate toward one or two workers, and this is a challenge that needs to be thought about in the team. These issues underline the importance of those workers with the key relationships being held in well-connected ways to the team, through supervision, the forums described above, and additional informal support. An important part of the psychologist's and systemic psychotherapist's roles on the ward is to provide support and thinking space for those workers when they find themselves in "the middle of the chaos." Above all, we have strengthened our recognition of the need to be open about issues when they arise and think them through together as a "well-connected" team.

AMBIT in a community youth-led service: The example of MAC-UK—an account by Olive Moloney and Sally Zlotowitz

MAC-UK is a charity founded in 2008 to radically transform mental health and wellbeing services for the UK's most excluded young people. MAC-UK has developed an innovative, evidence-based model, "Integrate," which grew from the ground up, working alongside those it sought to help. It is owned and customized at a local level to wrap mental health and wellbeing support around youth-led activities. The approach draws heavily on psychologically informed thinking, integrates health and social care, harnesses experts by experience (young adults who have experienced similar problems to the client group), and intervenes and creates change at multiple levels, from the individual and peer group through to the community (Zlotowitz et al., 2016). In partnership with multiple agencies, including the NHS and other statutory services, four projects implementing the Integrate model have been piloted across London, specifically focusing on young people who are affected by "street gangs."

AMBIT has been incorporated into the Integrate project's practice, with the staff teams being some of the first teams in the UK trained in AMBIT. All aspects of AMBIT are embedded; however, there have been several components that have helped the projects to fly. One specific example is how mentalization-based thinking has informed communication between the young people and young adult (expert by experience) employees and the mental health-trained employees. Differences in ideas and perspectives that relate to a whole range of practice have arisen from having people with lived experience as part of the team. We have found that by using explicit mentalizing techniques, both the mental health-trained staff and the experts by experience have been helped to understand and appreciate each other's different perspectives; this can then be built upon within practice. They have learned from each other.

For instance, experts by experience have often told mental health practitioners that they "ask way too many questions"—that young people can feel "psychologized" and consequently "back off." So they have helped psychologists to learn to balance their curiosity, ensuring it is mixed up with humor and flexibility. Experts by experience have helped mental health workers to mentalize the concept of "respect" and how this can play out in the projects. Explicit broadcasting of intentions and regular manualizing of team practice have been used to support Integrate practitioners in managing personal and professional boundaries and ensuring shared understandings around these issues. In street- and community-based work this has been important, and even more so for the experts by experience, who already know the young people from their community with whom they are working. Furthermore, the team has worked at becoming well connected through daily morning handover meetings, team formulation meetings, and regular clinical supervision. This ensures not only a constant feeding back of the perspective of the experts by experience, but also that they experience themselves as being well supported. The emphasis has been on quick and accessible peer supervision using an AMBIT framework, so that those with different background experiences can "think together" and this can enrich the solving of a dilemma.

MAC-UK has found that AMBIT provides a flexible and instructive framework for supporting Integrate teams in implementing the Integrate model. Young people involved in the projects have provided overwhelming feedback that they feel they can trust Integrate practitioners. They have fed back that Integrate practitioners have taken them and their life circumstances seriously and don't dismiss their concerns, and the evidence is that this has been linked to the privileging of "mentalized" relationship-building in the team's practice. Such feedback is, in our view, at the heart of what drives the Integrate practitioners to keep going in what can be complex and challenging work.

AMBIT in a specialist residential care and treatment service—an account by Stephen R. Mandler

Yellowstone Boys and Girls Ranch (YBGR) is a non-profit, multi-service organization providing mental health treatment and support to children, young people, and their families based in Billings, Montana, USA, and the surrounding rural regions. We serve children and their families in the community, in schools, and in homes, as well as at our longer-term residential treatment program, which accepts children with serious psychiatric disturbance from across the USA.

The YBGR Child and Adolescent Residential Treatment Program accepts young people with very severe problems. At any time, there are about 70 young people, who stay in care from three months to a year or more if required. They range in age between 9 and 18 years and comprise both sexes, from all states of the USA. Most of these young people have had many previous emergency psychiatric hospital placements, other residential treatment attempts, intensive outpatient efforts, and involvement with the criminal justice system for violent behaviors. We serve young people who are in foster care after being removed from their homes by the state government owing to serious sexual or physical abuse and neglect. Many of the young people began using hard drugs as early as 7 years of age or even younger; sometimes the drugs were provided by their biological parents. Additionally, we treat serious self-harmers who try to cut or burn themselves to the point of being severely scarred. We have young people who are intent on suicide and very seriously depressed.

In July 2012, the YBGR executive team made a decision to pursue an organization-wide approach to care based on the relationship between attachment processes and the development of the capacity to envision mental states in self and others (Fonagy & Target, 1997), and also inspired by the idea of "Mentalizing Communities" (Twemlow et al., 2005). At YBGR we hoped to create a culture that viewed the behaviors of both young people and their families in treatment, and the adults who care for them (e.g. therapists, mental health workers, nurses, dining hall staff, gardeners), as having a basis in early life experiences. Our stance was that, for workers and clients alike, the nature of their own attachment in formative years would affect how they received and delivered care.

Prior to the implementation of the mentalization-based approach, we observed that well-intended, college-educated adults charged with the day-to-day care of young people were often brought to extremes of emotions and sometimes non-therapeutic actions in the presence of "acting out" by the young people. In these environments, non-mentalizing could become contagious, and thus an environment intended to be therapeutic would cease to be so. Communication between workers often broke down or became inefficient. To address this problem, we rolled out three areas of staff training—mentalization-based treatment (MBT), implementation of the Reflective Care Program, and AMBIT team training, as described below.

1. **Mentalization-based treatment** for children and families is an approach to treatment for families with children aged 6–18 years. First, a cohort of

ten leading and supervising YBGR clinicians traveled to the Menninger Clinic in Houston and underwent intensive didactic training followed by an in-vivo training composed of intense role-playing. Later, a group of clinicians from the Menninger Clinic traveled to our campus and trained all of our licensed therapists in MBT; this training included a strong role-play component.

2. YBGR developed, in collaboration with the Center for Reflective Communities in Los Angeles, the **Reflective Care Program**. Reflective care focuses on developing and enhancing our staff members' capacity for reflective thinking. It is an approach to training non-therapists in the concepts of mentalizing and allows for a form of group supervision that encourages workers to discuss the powerful thoughts and feelings elicited by working with children with severe attachment disorders. Through this protected and limited self-disclosure, staff members have found that they are less prone to enter non-mentalizing states while at work.

3. **AMBIT team training** from the Anna Freud National Centre for Children and Families was offered to a large proportion of our staff. We have subsequently completed an ongoing year-long supervision of the implementation effort. In the time since the original AMBIT training, we have completed two locally run organization-wide trainings modeled on the original AMBIT training. AMBIT has brought together mentalizing, its application to the very severely and comorbidly affected young people and their families that we serve, and an organizational style of communication that has facilitated efficient teamwork within our organization and with multiple partnering agencies (our wider "network").

Preliminary results suggest that therapists and direct care staff at YGBR find great value in a mentalization-focused treatment model for the young people and especially great value in AMBIT. Feedback was provided by a number of workers in the service. Some of the benefits identified were increasing communication among team members and the value of each young person having one central person (akin to a "keyworker") to speak/work with, which facilitates better relationship-building. One staff member commented:

> "One of the pieces of AMBIT that I especially value is the focus on the strong therapeutic attachment with the client. The focus is not on roles, degrees, or experience of individual working with the child, but on the person who has the strongest relationship and connection with the client."
>
> "I find it extremely useful and necessary to have an AMBIT facilitator at our own team meetings. It is a valuable tool to keep the meeting on track and talk about cases/issues in a way that gets to the point and makes sure the person seeking feedback gets what they need."

Another member of the team described the value of the AMBIT approach as follows:

> "Utilizing AMBIT has been essential to my role as a school-based therapist, because it has helped keep sessions focused and on task. I have found it also incredibly useful in staff meetings to be sure the task at hand is identified in a clear, understandable manner; this keeps the time from 'getting away' by keeping participants focused and on track rather than chasing rabbit holes. Using AMBIT in therapy has been beneficial to assisting youth in staying on track and in the moment and really processing their thoughts/feelings without allowing them to 'avoid.' I find the concept brings out thought-provoking insight and interactions and sometimes it even 'buys time' to assist me in thinking about what I want to say or where I want to go next with a youth by putting the focus back on them and helping the youth verbalize what they need rather than allowing them to look to me to provide an answer or 'give advice.'"
>
> "Most importantly, AMBIT gave a 'name' to something I was already doing and it helped me feel validated that my work was meaningful and helpful."

A number of important challenges were also highlighted by members of the team, reflecting a range of organizational obstacles commonly experienced by many teams. When working in community teams through community-based services, not all members of that team have been open to utilizing the AMBIT approach. It has also been difficult to sustain the approach, as not all members of our team here have been trained in AMBIT. The current system (bigger than YBGR itself) is not set up to embrace this model, as all team members need to have specific requirements to be met for state rules. The prior qualifications of staff in the services have varied, making it difficult for different people to take on the keyworker role. The notion of a keyworker is also extremely difficult to implement, as there are many different pieces at play. Expectations of specific role positions, billable time, clinical responsibility, and guardianship make it more difficult for us to put AMBIT's version of the keyworker model into practice. Lastly, as one team member poignantly commented, "*I feel that AMBIT is a workable program, but changing one's personal habits to institute the AMBIT program, thus facilitating the 'AMBIT way,' is a very human challenge.*"

An important aspect of the work of the service is that we have seen a marked reduction in incidences of physical restraint, seclusions, and emergency intramuscular injections for agitation. The service approach is that we never want to lay hands on a child or young person to restrain them; however, because they frequently engage in potential self-harm and harm to others, we must step in to protect them. We are highly trained and use de-escalation approaches that are certified as approved approaches. We call these special procedures seclusions, restraints (non-mechanical), and relocations (technically a restraint, but involves moving a child into a safer area to assist in de-escalation). We aim for no special procedures to be used, and for many young people they are never required. We have had a substantial decrease in all types of special procedures since the implementation of mentalization-based approaches (of which AMBIT is one). It is our hypothesis that this new approach to care is largely responsible for those changes. We believe that we will also show a decrease in the use of chemical restraint (an intramuscular injection into the gluteus of a combative and restrained child or young person), which would make the findings, if true, even more powerful.

Despite accepting children and young people with very severe behavioral and emotional problems throughout this time, and with the approximate number of clients served remaining the same, we have evidence of a very significant drop in the number of special procedures after adopting the new approach to care. Over a four-year period there has been a reduction in the average number of all forms of restraint from 148 separate incidents a month to 39 incidents a month, a reduction of approximately 70%. The majority of this decline actually occurred before the AMBIT training took place, but the team's belief is that the consolidation of mentalizing processes advocated by AMBIT has continued to strengthen this process of reducing instances of special procedures. Table 9.1 summarizes the data so far. There are more data to be collected, but we think this accurately depicts the improvements in clinical culture and quality of care over the past two-and-a-half years. We believe that if we can gather information on staff injuries, and intramuscular injections given to young people, it is likely that a similar decline will also be shown.

Table 9.1 Average number of special procedures per month at YBGR

Year	Average seclusions per month	Average restraints per month	Average relocations per month	Average total per month	Comments
2011	52.17	97.17	9.75	149.33	Before implementation of mentalization-based approaches (numbers from years prior to 2011 are similarly high)
2012	51.25	50.00	32.58	101.25	Marked decline in the number of procedures following the introduction of mentalization-based approaches toward the second half of 2012
2013	29.42	44.00	28.50	73.42	Continued decline
2014	13.70	21.80	12.50	38.00	Continued decline

AMBIT in an intensive treatment service: The experience of Lothian CAMHS—*an account by Fiona Duffy*

The Lothian CAMHS Intensive Treatment Service (ITS) is a multidisciplinary NHS service designed to meet the needs of young people with severe mental health difficulties through intensive community treatment. The ITS is not a crisis service (this remains the remit of on-call psychiatry) but instead offers responsive planned care. It is designed to prevent hospital admissions where possible by offering community-based care packages, but also facilitates appropriate admissions to a 12-bed generic NHS adolescent inpatient unit (IPU) serving the south-east of Scotland. The ITS covers a mainly urban area where, as of 2011, 160,379 residents were aged under 18 years. It is designed to supplement existing services, rather than hold independent caseloads, producing fewer transitions for young people, as they maintain contact with outpatient CAMHS workers and community resources throughout ITS intervention. Young people meet criteria for the service if, as a result of severe mental health difficulties, the assessment or management of their risk or functioning requires appointments in excess of what mainstream CAMHS is able to provide. Interventions are multidisciplinary and eclectic, and include risk assessment; monitoring of physical and mental health; evidence-based individual, family, and group therapies; medication; case management; and support in accessing external community agencies and education. Flexible packages of care aim to reflect ongoing need, and interventions take place within the young person's home or community. Development of the CAMHS ITS and associated service redesign has been shown to significantly reduce median length of IPU stay, and to reduce admissions of young people to adult psychiatric wards by 65% (Duffy & Skeldon, 2013), and has produced significant improvements in associated clinical outcomes (Duffy & Skeldon, 2014).

Lothian CAMHS Tier 4 services (over-12s day services, an early psychosis service, and the ITS) were trained in AMBIT between 2011 and 2012. Our more intensive community services were initially targeted, but the combined training of multiple teams within the service at once was agreed in order to encourage the development of a common language and a shared philosophy across services. However, it quickly became apparent that not providing similar training to some of our colleagues, for example to those working in mainstream CAMHS and our inpatient unit, could create potential for "system dis-integration." This led us to provide an additional introductory AMBIT training for our colleagues in associated teams.

Post AMBIT training, the element that has continued to be used most frequently within the ITS is the concept of the "Team around the Worker," and specifically the use of Thinking Together consultations, or—as we came to know them—"AMBIT moments." Working with young people and their families when in crisis, in an outreach capacity, is inherently anxiety-provoking and potentially isolating for clinicians owing to the community outreach component of the work. Working with families in highly stressful circumstances creates the potential for a temporary loss of mentalizing in workers, which may in turn lead to crisis-based decision-making, which is often of little long-term benefit to the young person and their family. Indeed, the proposition within AMBIT training—that such a temporary loss of mentalizing is inevitable in the work we do—was experienced as reassuring and reinforced the perspective that seeking support from colleagues within the team was not a weakness, but an essential component of our job. This philosophy was supported by our CAMHS management, who recognized the need for a high level of connectedness between team members and supplied them with Blackberries (smartphones) to support contact between members of the team via phone, text, e-mail, and sharing of clinical diaries, enabling a reflective forum to gather at short notice via electronic media.

Within a busy service, the process of negotiating Thinking Together (see Chapter 5), being explicit about why this is requested, and creating shared understandings of the boundaries of these discussions, reduced frustration and misunderstandings and supported transparency in the team's thinking, while also modeling appropriate help-seeking for our service users. This has allowed team members to temporarily take time out of highly emotive situations when they recognize the potential for a loss of mentalizing, and to maintain a sense of connectedness with a "safe base" while working in an outreach capacity.

As a team we continue to struggle to incorporate the AMBIT manualization of our practice. While there is a clear understanding of the importance and value of manualization, as an NHS service we initially struggled with the technology required to sustain this practice within team meetings (e.g. wireless connections, compatible browsers), and as a result of not immediately incorporating this practice post-training, the act of regular team manualization was lost. The importance of running regular top-up AMBIT continuous professional development slots also became apparent when, as the time post-training extended, we noticed we had begun to "lose" some elements of the AMBIT wheel, and the underpinning rationale of some of the practice. Finally, there is a recognition that changes in staffing are to be expected, so the development of an ongoing internal training program was essential to support new clinicians joining our AMBIT-informed teams, ensuring the long-term sustainability of the model.

AMBIT in a multi-agency team: The experience of the Adolescent Multi-Agency Specialist Service—*an account by Laura Talbot*

The Adolescent Multi-Agency Specialist Service (AMASS) is a multi-agency team based within Islington Children's Services in North London, made up of specialist staff from social care, health, employment, and education services. The team works jointly with existing case-holding and fostering social workers to improve outcomes for young people aged 10–16 who are on the edge of care or at risk of placement breakdown and are exhibiting challenging behaviors. The team offers an intensive community outreach intervention to families for up to a year, in order to increase the stability of the young person's home or foster placement. The AMASS intervention is goal-based and is informed by behavioural and systemic approaches.

The team holds a caseload of up to 12 families in the intensive phase at any one time. AMASS senior social workers join with the case-holding social worker to meet twice weekly with the parent/carers. The young person is allocated a keyworker—the assistant psychologist, outreach worker, or education coordinator (a teacher)—who takes an active role in building a relationship with the young person, often on an assertive outreach basis. Having separate workers for the parent(s)/carer(s) and the young person enables relationships to be built with different parts of the family system in a way that keeps different people's needs in mind. The aim across the intervention is that the parent/carer and young person might be supported, via their respective relationships with workers, to engage in joint sessions with a shared focus.

The AMBIT framework influences the practice of the AMASS team in multiple ways, which have developed and continue to evolve over time. Some of the key AMBIT ideas and practices by which the team have been influenced are outlined below, with reference to the area of the AMBIT wheel to which they most closely relate.

Working with your Client: Improving the relationship to help

Workers make no assumptions about a young person or family viewing themselves as in need or want of help; indeed, many of the clients are explicitly non-help-seeking. The team's initial stance is therefore to be explicit in stating an intention to help, and being curious about the family's previous experiences of "helpful" and "unhelpful" help. Over the course of the intervention, the team aims to increase a family's capacity to seek and use help effectively. Keyworkers aim to create opportunities for young people to try out help-seeking in a graded and gradual way (e.g. by starting with practical rather than emotional needs, which may feel like a safer place to start).

There is an explicit focus on aiming to build epistemic trust. Workers recognize the importance for both parents and young people of having an experience of workers who try to understand what it is like to be them. Workers make explicit efforts to share their best guesses about this with family members, in order to build relationships where exploration of, and learning about, different ways of doing and being feels safe.

Collaborative approaches to goal-setting are underpinned by workers' active avoidance of making assumptions about a young person seeking help; instead, they try to exhibit curiosity about what, if anything, young people would like to be different in their life. To hold a balance between supporting young people's self-efficacy and upholding safeguarding responsibilities, workers are also encouraged to make explicit to young people the worries/hopes that they might have for them in order to ensure that risk issues are included as part of the focus of the work. Using Active Planning, workers aim to bring an explicit plan and purpose to each session. Young people's workers use written tools to support their session planning, to ensure that thinking and planning are not lost if a session does not take place in the planned way. Explicit agreement is sought from young people about the session agenda, whether informally in conversation or by bringing a written agenda. Workers balance following an agenda with the need to be flexible in adapting the focus according to young people's changing needs.

Scaffolding existing relationships is also a key part of the work of the team. Workers are interested in who is important to the young person and how they can be involved in supporting the young person to reach their goals. This might mean including members of the young person's family, peer group, or professional network directly in sessions, or introducing these people in "virtual" form—thinking with the young person about ways in which they might be able to help them toward their goals (e.g. a friend texting the young person in the morning to help them wake up for school).

Working with your Team: Group supervision

Group supervision takes place each week, and includes all team members and also the case-holding social workers for each case; the social workers are expected to attend for a specific time slot in this meeting (and prior negotiation means that their management facilitates this). Supervision is a space to reflect, review progress, and set goals. There is a focus on purposeful case discussion (e.g. using the Thinking Together framework to explore dilemmas). The team have written a wiki entry on "black holes" that the team can fall into during supervision, and how to avoid these (e.g. "storytelling"—a version of the pretend mode, for which the team culture gives explicit permission to interrupt/be interrupted).

Within a multi-agency team that shares a caseload, it is important that the roles and responsibilities of each team member are explicit, so that they can be easily understood by both clients and the network. Having recognized the gap between the job description and what the role looks like in practice, the team have manualized the key practices/functions that are most valued and effective in each role, in order to promote effective practice and to ensure continuity in the event of staff changes. Team members have recorded videos of themselves talking about their role, and these are included in the wiki.

Working with your Networks: Addressing network dis-integration

Key members of the professional network are invited to group supervision in order to promote network integration. The team aims to give other professionals an experience of being mentalized by the team, in order to nurture the network's capacity to sustain a mentalizing stance in relation to their clients and other colleagues. The team aspires to support networks to configure around families in the way that makes most sense to the families, by reducing the number of professionals where there is overlap, and supporting families to understand the roles/intentions of everyone in their professional network. The team will join with professionals who have strong relationships with young people—where these already exist—to support their work indirectly if this is felt to be helpful, rather than seeking to replace them.

Learning at Work: Openness to team learning

The AMASS team has historically placed a high value on learning and improvement. Being open and willing to learn together has been an explicit part of the team culture, which the team seeks to preserve across (or in spite of) a changing team membership. This has been achieved by Thinking Together as a team about what enables the team to maintain this stance and the conditions that promote team learning and improvement. This is revisited whenever there are staff changes, with thought given to how new team members can both be acculturated into the existing team culture and feel empowered to make new contributions. The team has weekly manualization sessions in which one team member takes on the role of "wiki champion" in order to keep alive in the team's mind the endeavor to record local practice. The team meets together for 30 minutes per week to create a wiki entry together. The "wiki champion" keeps a running list of topics that the team could manualize as they arise; they might include capturing *things that worked well* (e.g. "top tips" for getting a parent and school working effectively together) or brainstorming *solutions to a particular kind of dilemma* (e.g. how to respond to personal questions from young people). The team aims to ensure that the wiki process captures how this thinking will be translated into practice, so that the balance between reflection and action is maintained. As part of the team learning, the team managers construct a service improvement plan using the AMBIT framework. The plan consists of goals that the team will work toward, covering each of the areas of the AMBIT wheel. These goals are worked upon collaboratively with the team, using time in fortnightly team meetings as well as in smaller working groups outside this space.

AMBIT in the Cambridgeshire Child and Adolescent Substance Use Service—*an account by Verity Beehan*

The Cambridgeshire Child and Adolescent Substance Use Service (CASUS) is a community-based outreach treatment service for young people up to the age of 18 and is part of the local NHS Mental Health Trust. We also have a commission to work with a small selection of 18- to 21-year-olds whose needs would not be well met by the adult substance use service. We are a multidisciplinary team who primarily offer treatment for substance use disorder. However, the young people we work with could often be deemed to be "hard to reach," with multiple complexities and vulnerabilities; therefore, not uncommonly, we offer dual-diagnosis work for young people where their substance use and mental health are linked, and where they would find it difficult to attend clinic-based settings (i.e. mainstream CAMHS). Since we cover a large geographical area, the appointments are offered to young people in whatever place feels right for them—at home, at school, at the GP surgery, or in the worker's car, traveling to get a McDonald's.

CASUS has been using the AMBIT model since the service was commissioned in 2010. There are many aspects of the model that are hugely helpful to our work with service users and within the team. I feel the main aspect of the AMBIT model that has been—and continues to be—hugely successful for us is the principle of the "Keyworker well connected to the team" and our use of Thinking Together within this. It would be fair to say that it has taken us time to get used to this approach in the discussions we have with each other. Thinking Together refers to the specific conversations we have with one another about clinical issues; it is an approach whereby we use a set format to enable us to make the best use of our conversations with colleagues. This may occur in the office or when we are out in the community; the conversation may be between just two members of staff, or it may be in front of the young person, with a member of the team talking things through over a phone switched to loudspeaker.

Following a clear structure, Thinking Together conversations involve:

1. Marking the Task ("What do I want out of this conversation?")
2. Stating the Case (giving the bare bones, trying to avoid storytelling)

3. Mentalizing the Moment (where a colleague helps to mentalize the worker/young person/network)
4. Returning to Task ("Have I got what I needed from this conversation?").

We have also adopted a very similar format within our weekly clinical meeting. I feel that as a team we initially struggled somewhat to follow this format, as we had a tendency to go off into storytelling while worrying about a case. It could also be disconcerting, especially at the beginning, to call a colleague for help and then to be stopped and asked to mark the task before going into any detail—more so when we were feeling unsure about what we wanted from the discussion. Now, having experience of this aspect of AMBIT, I feel it would be alien *not* to use this structure in our conversations, as a large part of their effectiveness comes from the worker first having to consider what they actually want from the conversation. Cutting out storytelling seems to help reduce the collusion that used to happen when we would go into storytelling, and it makes the discussion much more objective.

If appropriate, these Thinking Together conversations can also occur in front of service users: this enables us to display our own help-seeking behavior to them, reinforcing our messages about mentalizing going "off track" in times of stress and worry. More recently, we have implemented a duty worker system that involves all clinical staff. The duty worker is assigned for the day and is available to the rest of the team to facilitate Thinking Together conversations. Therefore, despite our autonomous (and often quite physically isolated) ways of working, as a worker you never feel alone; there is always someone available. As a team, we are encouraged to talk about our anxiety in the work we do with our clients. This is another hugely important aspect of the model, in that, by being encouraged to talk about our worries surrounding service users, we do so without fear of being criticized. As a result, we are not holding risk in isolation, but sharing risk management as part of a multidisciplinary team.

> **Case example**
>
> Recently, I went to visit one of my service users, "Jodie" (name and details anonymized), who had given birth one week earlier. On my arrival, Jodie's mother said she was worried that Jodie appeared very low in mood and was withdrawing from the baby. I went to speak to Jodie in her room; both subjectively and objectively she appeared low in mood, and she disclosed she was experiencing intrusive thoughts of harming the baby and this was making her feel suicidal. Having worked with Jodie for a long period of time, and feeling exceedingly worried, I shared my concerns with Jodie and we went downstairs to speak with her mother.
>
> Explaining that I was feeling very worried and wanted to ensure that we got Jodie the right help, I said I was going to call my colleague to consider the best way forward. During my call I explained that I needed to think together with them, and marked my

task and stated the case. The first thing my colleague did was to mentalize *me*; this greatly helped me to externalize (and validate) my worry. Exploring the options open to us, we decided an on-call mental health assessment was urgent; however, we were aware that it was late afternoon and services would soon be closed for the day. We divided up tasks and agreed to speak again shortly. I supported Jodie and her family while also calling the local crisis team, and an on-call assessment was arranged. Debriefing with my colleague afterwards enabled me to let go of the situation, as opposed to going home and worrying more about it. I felt reassured through this conversation that we had done everything we could.

When visiting Jodie some weeks later, during a discussion about mentalizing she reflected that it was helpful for her to see my mentalizing go off track, as it showed her that we are all human and that the important thing was to use someone close to help us get our thinking back on track.

Conclusions and reflections

Approaching 200 teams have now been trained in the AMBIT approach. From the sample of teams described above, it is clear that it has been adopted by a very wide range of teams and services working with targeted client groups for whom the priority need and the key outcome may be very different. We suggest, however, that although the teams vary greatly in terms of structure, skill mix, workforce backgrounds, and the types of intervention they use, it is probable that the clients vary somewhat less. Our conjecture is that the scenario is rather like the well-known story of a group of blindfolded individuals examining, by touch, an elephant. The people who can feel its legs may believe that they are in front of a very different beast from the one being held by those who have grabbed its tail or its ears. But, of course, while the legs, ears, and tail are extremely different, they are all "elephant." The AMBIT approach asserts that similar broad structures and techniques can be applied to working with this group of clients, no matter what the immediate orientation of the particular team is. Furthermore, we suggest that it would probably be valuable to help the various teams to work together with the understanding that they are all connected to a single difficulty—namely, a client with multiple and severe needs.

In this chapter we have illustrated that different teams will be tasked to deal with different aspects of this problem, and that subsequently it is not surprising that they emphasize different aspects of the AMBIT approach. For some teams, the focus has been on addressing staff isolation, high anxiety, and reactive decision-making by introducing Thinking Together as a core aspect of good practice. For others, the emphasis has been more on consolidating mentalizing as part of effective work with young people. And for others, the value of ongoing model development through manualizing has been highlighted.

For all teams, it can be difficult to sustain AMBIT practice owing to inevitable changes in staffing over time. However, we are aware that for one team (AMASS) there has been a complete turnover of the original staff team and a change of all the supervising managers over the eight-year period in which the service had existed at the time of writing. Despite this, the team has retained a very strong AMBIT approach through having a weekly group supervision combined with a clear commitment to ongoing manualizing (often done in the same meeting). As a concrete example of how manualizing has helped AMASS with this common problem, an assistant psychologist was attached to the team for a year, during which time she developed the use of AIM cards (see Chapter 3) as an assessment and engagement technique. In the course of this project, she created some video of her role-playing the use of this tool, which was uploaded to, and remains on, the team's local online manual—her lasting legacy to the team. For AMASS, as well as many other (but by no means all) teams, manualizing has been shown to make a valuable contribution to the induction of new staff into the team's culture and practice. It has been a surprise to us that the ongoing process of trying to make explicit what a team does has had a significant impact in sustaining the AMBIT approach, alongside its original intention of encouraging local adaptation to specific service ecologies and populations of young people served.

References

Children's Commissioner for England. (2007). *Pushed into the shadows: Young people's experience of adult mental health facilities* (London, UK: Office of the Children's Commissioner), http://dera.ioe.ac.uk/18763/1/Pushed_into_the_shadows.pdf, accessed 26 Jan. 2017.

Duffy, F., & Skeldon, J. (2013). Innovations in Practice: The impact of the development of a CAMH Intensive Treatment Service and service redesign on psychiatric admissions. *Child and Adolescent Mental Health* **18**: 120–3. doi: 10.1111/j.1475-3588.2012.00659.x

Duffy, F., & Skeldon, J. (2014). A CAMHS Intensive Treatment Service: Clinical outcomes in the first year. *Clinical Child Psychology and Psychiatry* **19**: 90–9. doi: 10.1177/1359104512468287

Fonagy, P., & Target, M. (1997). Attachment and reflective function: Their role in self-organization. *Development and Psychopathology* **9**: 679–700.

Menzies, I. E. P. (1960). A case-study in the functioning of social systems as a defence against anxiety: A report on a study of the nursing service of a general hospital. *Human Relations* **13**: 95–121. doi: 10.1177/001872676001300201

National Institute for Health Research. (2008). *Alternatives to Inpatient Care for Children and Adolescents with Complex Mental Health Needs* (London, UK: National Institute for Health Research), http://www.nets.nihr.ac.uk/__data/assets/pdf_file/0009/81468/RS-08-1604-141.pdf, accessed 26 Jan. 2017.

Twemlow, S. W., Fonagy, P., & Sacco, F. C. (2005). A developmental approach to mentalizing communities: I. A model for social change. *Bulletin of the Menninger Clinic* **69**: 265–81. doi: 10.1521/bumc.2005.69.4.265

Zlotowitz, S., Barker, C., Moloney, O., & Howard, C. (2016). Service users as the key to service change? The development of an innovative intervention for excluded young people. *Child and Adolescent Mental Health* **21**: 102–8. doi: 10.1111/camh.12137

Chapter 10

Adopting the AMBIT approach to changing wider systems of help

Introduction: Extending the ambit of AMBIT

In the previous two chapters we described the impact of AMBIT: first, on the life of a young person (see Chapter 8) and then on the work of a number of teams trained in the AMBIT approach (see Chapter 9). We now turn to considering the potential impact of AMBIT on helping systems as a whole. Here, we are setting out our larger ambitions about improving ways of helping children, young people, and their families. Although AMBIT was originally specifically designed for young people who are not seeking help, we believe the approach has potential value in considering how services for children and families in general may be delivered.

We do not underestimate the scale of the task in seeking to improve services, and recognize that there are many aspects to improving outcomes for children and young people. We will start with a somewhat bleak (but not unique) review of the current provision of child and adolescent mental health services (CAMHS). In our view, the difficulties for such services cannot be solely attributed to a lack of adequate resources, although this clearly and significantly exacerbates existing problems. Our proposal is that service difficulties are also amplified by an unbalanced emphasis on, first, the structural aspects of helping systems, and second, fragmented ways of defining need. Put more concretely, we will argue that the division of helping systems into health, social care, and specialist educational provision poorly serves the needs of children, as does the definition of needs in terms of those agencies. Our belief is that effective helping systems need to prioritize three key principles that are at the center of the AMBIT approach, namely that:

- Help is a relational human process, involving trust
- Effective help is nearly always the result of collaboration between a number of people

- Effective collaboration is underpinned by a mentalized understanding of both our clients and the other helpers.

These are our starting points in looking more widely at helping systems for distressed children and their families. We will then describe a new approach to service design known as the "THRIVE" framework and explain how AMBIT is particularly pertinent to one specific part of this model. Finally, we will briefly describe some preliminary examples of how AMBIT may be used as a method for whole-system change.

Current problems of service provision for young people with mental health and other needs

The description of mental health service provision for young people that follows is primarily based on developments in, and the experience of services in, the UK. We hope that the general themes from this discussion will be applicable to international contexts, but acknowledge that the details will vary considerably between countries. Certainly, our experience of training teams from the USA, Australia, Spain, the Netherlands, Switzerland, and elsewhere suggests that the same basic dilemmas tend to occur. Services for clients with severe and multiple needs—especially, but not exclusively, if they are young—are provided by a wide range of agencies, organized loosely into services provided by educational, social care, health, justice, and voluntary sector organizations. It is in the nature of mental health needs that they impact on areas of functioning covered by all these different services, and so help-seeking and help-giving for mental health needs (in more or less formally organized ways) actually take place across all of these services. In other words, help for mental health needs is—quite appropriately—not confined to mental health services per se. From the perspective of the client, their mental health needs are intertwined with their (frequently multiple and severe) other needs, and so cannot be addressed by an isolated mental health agency; they get anxious about meeting their social worker, they feel overwhelmed by helplessness and hopelessness while considering options with their college tutor, and their paranoia interferes with their ability to comply with a Court Order. Unfortunately, this simple observation is not mirrored by the way services are designed for such young people. The challenge is how to create helping systems (i.e. systems that really help) in such circumstances.

The need for a cross-agency approach

As we have outlined, the majority of clients seen by AMBIT-trained teams are unlikely to have a mental health difficulty that is not linked to difficulties in other areas of life, such as education/employment, the home environment, parents/carers, and often conflict with the police and justice system. Considering mental health problems, in young people especially, in strict separation from their family, social, and educational context is not consistent with what we know from developmental and social science, which shows clear and significant associations between contextual factors and mental difficulties.

As a more concrete example, a 14-year-old with depression who has significant literacy problems may be helped to cope better with her depressive feelings by evidence-based therapy for depression, but her mood may also benefit from adaptive help for her literacy problems, either through the provision of additional educational support or by adjusting her school timetable to reduce the demand for high-level literacy skills, or by being supported to attend vocational projects such as a motorbike maintenance or hairdressing apprenticeship. Both individual therapy and "environmental" changes are likely to improve the young person's mood, even if only one of these interventions is explicitly addressing mental health. This multifaceted approach is exactly the kind of "bundling" of knowledge and practice from different areas of experience that most parents are familiar with in helping their own children—that is, combining emotional and practical help. When problems are more complex and severe, it means that an effective response to mental health problems will inevitably require help from a combination of agencies and individual workers. However, it is in trying to coordinate such care across largely separate service systems that frontline practitioners are presented with some of their most considerable challenges.

The recognition of this problem is far from new; we do not claim any originality in stating these issues. Over the past two decades, a range of solutions has been proposed in the UK to address this issue, perhaps starting with the highly influential NHS Health Advisory Service Thematic Review entitled *Together We Stand* (NHS Health Advisory Service, 1995). The review advocated a four-tier model of service provision and delivery, and provided a framework for the expansion of the function of CAMHS from a clinic-based specialist service for severe and complex mental health needs to providing a more broad-based set of services and interventions across four tiers of service. Tier 1 interventions were to be carried out by non-specialist practitioners in community settings (general practitioners (GPs), school nurses, etc.), often with formal access to consultation from specialist practitioners. In Tier 2, single mental health practitioners based in community settings (schools, local GP surgeries, etc.) would provide early interventions and preventive work. Specialist multidisciplinary teams provided more specialist Tier 3 work, predominantly based in outpatient clinics (although, more recently, many teams have developed outreach services that are sometimes referred to as "Tier 3-and-a-half"). Tier 4 referred to highly specialist inpatient settings.

Although not explicitly intended by the review, there were two important consequences of the developments it advocated. First, it broadened the function and responsibilities of CAMHS so that CAMHS increasingly came to be seen as the agency responsible for the emotional wellbeing of children and their families. An example of this would be the psychological wellbeing of children in care, or children with disabilities. For what was still a relatively small service, this expanded scope and range of responsibilities was far beyond what CAMHS was actually capable of delivering. It could be argued that an unintended effect of this change, made out of the best of intentions, was that the wide range of other professionals involved with caring for and educating children became somewhat deskilled in relation to addressing the mental health needs of the children with whom they worked. This was no longer "in their remit," but, at a more subtle level, because of the new emphasis on specialism in CAMHS, many of these other workers perhaps began to perceive themselves as lacking the necessary skills and qualifications to venture into this territory.

Second, the tiered system became a criteria-driven delivery model, in which young people and families were passed between services if their needs did not fit the criteria of a particular tier. Services were designed on the basis of identifying specific needs and then matching these needs to appropriate resources. So, for example, a young person with depression would be seen either at Tier 2 for moderate depression, or at Tier 3 if their depression was more severe. The problem was that very often the level of severity of mental health problems fluctuated, resulting in young people being moved from one part of the service (and one worker) to another. Equally damaging was that families were positioned as passive recipients of services rather than active agents in a process of help and recovery.

The gap between demand and resources in CAMHS

By 2014, specialist provision for children and young people's mental health in the UK was causing increasing concern in relation to its ability (or otherwise) to meet the range of young people's mental health needs. These concerns gave rise to the creation of a Government Task Force in Children and Young People's Mental Health, which, in 2015, produced the report *Future in Mind* (Department of Health, & NHS England, 2015). Evidence presented to this group has suggested that current public sector provision faces a range of severe difficulties in meeting the population's needs. At present there is a lack of adequate service and treatment data in relation to what is currently being provided and how beneficial such treatments are proving to be. Despite such limitations, it is widely recognized that a major gap exists between need and provision. For example, the last UK epidemiological study (Green et al., 2005) suggested that, at that time, less than 25–35% of those with a diagnosable mental health condition accessed support. For young males, only 13% with depression received any form of professional help. These figures would clearly be considered scandalous if applied to any significant physical health need for young people that had the potential to have a lifelong impact—just as depression in adolescence may do.

These difficulties have been exacerbated by an increasing incidence of certain types of mental health problems in young people, particularly self-injurious behavior (Madge et al., 2008). This potential increase in demand on services has coincided with significant disinvestment in public sector provision for mental health services, including CAMHS (YoungMinds, 2015). Significant reductions in staffing and range of provision, due to reductions in public sector commissioning budgets, have been reported in many services. Some services have reported staff reductions as large as 50%. This suggests that the minority of young people who manage to access services at present is likely to become even smaller over the next few years.

In addition to increasing demand and reduction in available services, there is also concern about whether the current design of services is fit for purpose in relation to the needs such services are intended to address. Some of these design problems have been recognized over a long period of time—notably the division of specialist services between education, social care, and health referred to earlier. As suggested throughout this book, this fragmentation of service provision fundamentally impacts on all aspects of specialist interventions, leading to organizational complexity and poor knowledge about the options for broader cross-agency intervention on the part of both frontline workers and families. Regular major reorganizations of health, education, and social care services have added to this difficulty. Proposals to achieve greater integration of services for children and young people have been made repeatedly over the past 15 years, including initiatives such as Children's Trusts (Department for Children, Schools and Families, 2008) and a major UK program called "Every Child Matters" (HM Government, 2003). Despite central government policy support, real integration of local authority provision and NHS services never really took place. This service fragmentation has been sustained by a commissioning system that is divided between education, social care, and health, with yearly commissioning cycles and funding often guaranteed for only 12-month cycles.

Service reorganizations have not been effective in addressing these problems

Although we share many of the opinions put forward in these reports about the problematic current state of service provision and the model that underpins it, we perhaps differ in that we see the problems as more severe than even this disappointing picture presents. We are hugely concerned that this context results in a repetitive cycle of structural reorganizations (a teleological response at the level of the system, as it were) and ongoing criticism of frontline practitioners working in CAMHS and other agencies (the kind of attributional error that is commonly associated with psychic equivalence). For instance, in addition to the lack of integration and short-term commissioning cycles described above, there has been ongoing criticism of CAMHS for offering a poor delivery model that makes treatment relatively inaccessible, particularly to those families who need it most. Traditional clinics and appointment-based systems have been shown to create barriers for families with the most severe needs; these families are likely to need services provided in ways that are more community-focused and integrated with existing resources in their children's lives, such as in schools and nurseries. However, the resources and systemic, organizational, or political levers to facilitate changes on this scale have simply not been present. As well as poor access, CAMHS has also been criticized for not having explicit systems by which parents and young people can make informed choices about options for help (Harper et al., 2014; Robotham & James, 2009) and for having long waiting times. In conclusion, the current position of CAMHS seems to be unsustainable. There is clearly a need for a radical overhaul of the design of CAMHS that goes far beyond just adequately resourcing an outdated model of service delivery.

Important challenges need to be faced with respect to the demand for interventions that follow evidence-based practice. Although evidence-based interventions may be the most effective form of help currently known, it is also known that a significant proportion of young people receiving well-conducted evidence-based interventions show relatively little, if any, improvement (Weisz et al., 2013). Societal and commissioning expectations about the appropriate service response to the lack of improvement in a problem remain unresolved. If a young person receives treatment for depression and shows no improvement in their mood on completion of the treatment, what is the appropriate response to the young person? Should we continue a treatment that has not been shown to be effective for this client? As one commissioner said to one of the authors, "You can't just abandon them." This powerful sense of responsibility around the needs of children and young people is not easily resolved, set as it is against the simultaneous demands to reduce waiting lists and improve access. At present, in the face of poor outcomes, families may be offered longer or repetitive treatment cycles, which are often no more effective in terms of outcomes than the first treatment (Weisz et al., 2013).

The AMBIT approach to service improvement

So, how does the AMBIT approach relate to these wider challenges? First, aside from our strong emphasis on the notion of the team as the fundamental unit of local learning and staff support, AMBIT does not propose a specific structural redesign of services as a method of creating more effective helping systems for young people and their families. We recognize that some structural arrangements are more facilitative of cross-agency working than others, but we believe that cross-agency working, and the inevitability of "dis-integration" in these contexts, will remain a feature of the offers of help that many families receive—whatever the future design of services turns out to be.

The emphasis in AMBIT is to assume that there will always be differences of views and perspectives between practitioners involved in helping young people with severe and multiple needs; this principle of dis-integration has been described in detail in Chapter 6. AMBIT proposes a radical realignment of expectations so that dis-integration is seen as the natural resting state of all multi-professional or multi-agency networks—something that is to be expected and addressed rather than triggering (non-mentalizing) reactions of blame and shame. We do not believe that this dis-integration can be eradicated through structural change—that is, by creating a unitary managed system (perhaps the health and social care equivalent of totalitarianism!). To advance another analogy, even in the most effective parenting, disagreements, misunderstandings, and misalignments in respect of parenting "methods" are common between the parents. Translating this concept to the arena of health and welfare provision, what is crucial for effective care may be somewhat less about agreement and perfect alignment (helpful though that would be) and more about the ability to recognize different points of view and to collaborate and arrive at a shared approach in practice. In our view, this provides a crucial template for what is needed in cross-agency working—namely, the capacity to expect and recognize misunderstandings and to develop a shared approach that is *organized around a mentalized understanding of the needs and wishes of the client* rather than the requirements of the specific agency in which a worker is employed. As we have described throughout this book, AMBIT uses a mentalizing approach to address these inevitable challenges. This approach is partly based on common observations of the degree to which negative emotions and beliefs influence relationships between agencies, often acting to obscure their shared intention, which is to help the same young person. This mimics the way that persistent negative emotion between parents is known to have a negative impact on the development and wellbeing of many children.

Faced with such a range of difficulties, what can be done? In our view, there are many key components to improving the effectiveness of services for children and young people with mental health needs. For example, we need to stop seeing service restructuring as a solution to the goal of service integration, as each restructure destroys years of relationship-building within helping systems. We agree that a new approach is needed, and we will now set out some starting points, from an AMBIT perspective, as to what this approach should look like.

AMBIT's starting points for whole-service design

First, AMBIT proposes that services should be designed in ways that are consistent with what is known about processes of help-seeking and help-giving. Second, it supports a widespread commitment to increasing shared understanding and practice between services and agencies—operating on the belief that truly effective help is always fundamentally a collaboration between helpers, as well as between helper and client.

The need for professional systems of help to be modeled on helping processes

The design of services needs to be built upon an understanding of the complex process of help-seeking and help-receiving. This is not a mechanical or industrial process concerned with addressing the delivery of a package of "needs" defined by a professional and medical system. Instead, it is a highly individualized and dynamic process, involving key themes of trust, personal agency, choice, cultural beliefs, and life expectations. Processes of help need to be placed at the center of the whole system. This stance has a number of immediate consequences. First, it highlights the fact that *the vast majority of psychological help for children and young people is provided by families or carers*—albeit supported by agencies such as schools, nurseries, youth clubs, and sports clubs. The majority of psychological help for children takes place in the context of those carers who are most present. Moreover, processes of help during periods of psychological distress for a child (e.g. the death of a grandparent) or life changes (e.g. moving school) or negative circumstances (e.g. a parent losing their job) are intrinsic to the very process of childhood itself. Perhaps the most elaborated area of research where this has been demonstrated is in attachment theory. Attachment is a help-seeking and help-delivery/receipt system, which is highly biologically determined, and which involves crucial reciprocal functions on the part of caregivers to reduce threat and provide safety in response to the child's fears, apprehensions, and distress. If the system "works," the child develops the ability to tolerate distress, to explore the physical and psychological world, and to learn. In a community, these processes underpin a vast swathe of "psychological" care, which quite obviously dwarfs the work of a small professional system of help. What is critical is that professional systems of help, such as CAMHS, social care, youth offending services, or education, do not undermine the capacity of these intrinsic systems of help-seeking and receiving, unintentionally leading them to function less confidently and effectively.

Starting with a focus on "helping systems" repositions the function and purpose of professional systems as to how they facilitate and strengthen this wider function. Another aspect of this starting point is perhaps equally important. Psychological problems of childhood may perhaps be conceptualized as a combination of some form of distress (e.g. a specific trauma, a peer-group rejection, a form of maltreatment) and the inability of the intrinsic helping ecology around the child to respond effectively to the distress. For example, a young person experiencing depression may be having to cope with unanticipated, confusing, and hard-to-name feelings and states of mind, but also with parents who may misinterpret these difficulties as being "part of adolescence," "bad behavior," or some other characterological flaw. In this circumstance, the young person may experience the parents as adopting a critical stance toward them (e.g. in response to their not getting out of bed until the afternoon). So, instead of experiencing the relationship with their parents—the attachment system—as providing help, the young person discovers that their place of safety has become a place of threat and criticism. We propose that, for a significant proportion of mental health needs, the difficulty is often a combination of the primary distress with the failure of existing helping systems to respond effectively. It is, in more ordinary language, a "double whammy." We are suggesting that this "double whammy," although not a feature of all cases referred to CAMHS, is an important component of many mental health presentations; as we have described earlier, it is almost universally the case that clients who are the target group for teams working to the AMBIT model have experienced such a combination of factors.

This focus on the helping process provides two starting points for how services may be more effectively designed. First, it emphasizes the importance of helping families to be positioned in ways that nurture and support their own capacity to provide psychological help for their children (rather than "exporting" these responsibilities). Second, it suggests that services may need to be designed as much around enabling a family to engage in processes of help as in treating the problem itself. Many families who are referred to CAMHS have histories of very poor experiences of help-seeking, both within their own families and with professional helping systems. An obvious and concrete example would be a parent who themself was in care as a child, and who had very negative experiences in care (and prior to care), and who may be extremely reluctant to engage with helping agencies based on this previous experience. Again, we make no claims that this is an original or new observation.

The conclusion from this is that mental health services for children, young people, and their families need to be designed to support and harness the ways in which families already help each other, and to use this as a starting point for many forms of help. This approach of considering "How can a service help a family to manage a problem?" is consistent with models of self-management in physical health care, although these need to be adapted to include consideration of how families can be strengthened to discover their own capacity to be helpful to each other. (In AMBIT, this is directly addressed by the principle of "scaffolding existing relationships.") In many mental health presentations, it can be striking how the nature of the problem tends to invalidate the usual helping systems. Parents will often say that they don't know what to do, that they feel useless and demoralized, and that the type of problem that is affecting their child never happened to them when they themselves were young. This "shock of the new" means they do not have a learned model of response, which often leads to anxiety, anger, frustration, a sense of helplessness, and other indications of the collapse of the helping system within the family. This can occur in areas of life other than just mental health—for example, with a teenage pregnancy or very "successful" adolescent online gambling. The aim for services in this context may—if they are to be most effective—be less about becoming involved in the specific problem and more about enabling the usual systems of care, negotiation, and help to become reactivated.

This means that we need services that are designed to work with clients and their families/carers who may have a very poor relationship to help, who may not be actively help-seeking, and who may have no trust that others are likely to be able to help them. Such services will need to provide more personalized care and be co-designed by clients and their families/carers, and may well need to focus (perhaps initially, at least) much more on establishing processes of trust-building than on directly addressing a problem as it is perceived by other agencies. In practice, such services are likely to be less clinic-based and appointment-focused, and will need to develop a form of expertise that is consistent with such objectives. In our view, AMBIT has begun to map out some of the features of such a service, but we see this as only a starting point from which much more will need to be done.

Using mentalizing to increase collaboration between agencies

A second foundation of the AMBIT approach to whole-service development is the need to increase effective collaborative practice between the different agencies that work with children/young people and families (or carers). As we have described earlier, we do not believe that structural integration of specialist services for children and families across education, social care, and health is currently possible, nor do we believe that it would be sufficient. We are only too aware of the complexities in the implicit demands upon services. We would generally aim to work within the constraints of the existing flawed structures, on the assumption that whatever structures are in place are likely to be flawed, albeit in different sorts of ways.

There are two main reasons why we see this as necessary. First, as stated previously, it makes no sense to disconnect the mental health problems of a client (especially a child or young person) from the context of their life. The impact of parenting, marital and family relationships, quality of schooling, and economic disadvantage (to name just a few factors) on a child's emotional and psychological wellbeing is not in question. Successful interventions to address a child's mental health needs cannot be teased out from such "environmental" factors—and this is already widely recognized. There is little point in, for example, treating a client's depression if they are still exposed to ongoing domestic violence at home underpinned by parental alcohol abuse. Or rather, the treatment must include the context.

Second, families and parents report frustration at the fragmentation of services (Department of Health, & NHS England, 2015). This frustration is often reported in relation to the need for them to repeat information about their lives and problems to different people in different settings, but more generally the system often just appears extremely complicated even to those who work within it; it is often difficult to know which service or worker does what. Certainly, from the point of view of many young clients, these professionals are all just adults giving advice or telling them what to do; the different training backgrounds, managerial systems, and commissioned priorities that support each one may be much less apparent to the client than they are to the professionals who do this work. As professionals in the system, our understanding of different agency tasks and boundaries is often at odds with a client's assumption that we all work for different departments of the same "State" (just as the geography teacher, the school nurse, and the groundsman all work for their school and therefore share a degree of authority over the young person). In this sense, these clients offer us an important and often overlooked reminder: diverse professionals do indeed share an *intentional* state (to help), notwithstanding the labyrinthine organizational structures that have developed to support this function. We are at risk of repeating ourselves when we say that these themes have been extensively documented and our observations are not new. The legal infrastructure of the statutory responsibilities held by various different agencies makes sharing information and the tasks linked to these responsibilities a continual challenge. For example, social care has overall responsibility for child safety. Other agencies clearly share responsibility for child safety, but the final responsibility for ensuring the investigation of maltreatment and the implementation of a child protection plan remains unambiguously with social care.

These two AMBIT starting points—of focusing on helping processes and the need for integration across agencies—are consistent with a new approach to conceptualizing children's and young people's mental health services that is known as THRIVE. We will now provide a brief summary of THRIVE, as we believe that it provides a useful framework for the type of service problems AMBIT is trying to address.

The THRIVE framework for child mental health services

The THRIVE framework has been developed out of a collaboration between clinicians and mental health specialists from the Anna Freud National Centre for Children and Families and the Tavistock and Portman NHS Foundation Trust in London, led by Professor Miranda Wolpert (Wolpert et al., 2015). The model is intended less as a fixed "engineering plan" for organizational rearrangement, and more as a set of principles and processes that can be adapted to local commissioning demands.

The THRIVE framework conceptualizes mental health services for children and young people and their families as needing to deliver four overlapping functions. These are not tiers and do not necessarily translate into the work of specific teams. The model anticipates that teams are likely to have the capacity to deliver more than one function in order to sustain continuity of care where this is possible. The four functions are summarized in Figure 10.1.

The four types of activity in THRIVE

The first function (upper left quadrant in the diagram) has been called "Getting Advice." This function involves helping families and young people to get advice on working out how best they can address their difficulties themselves, without relying on significant involvement with professional services. This may involve a range of different forms of help, including:

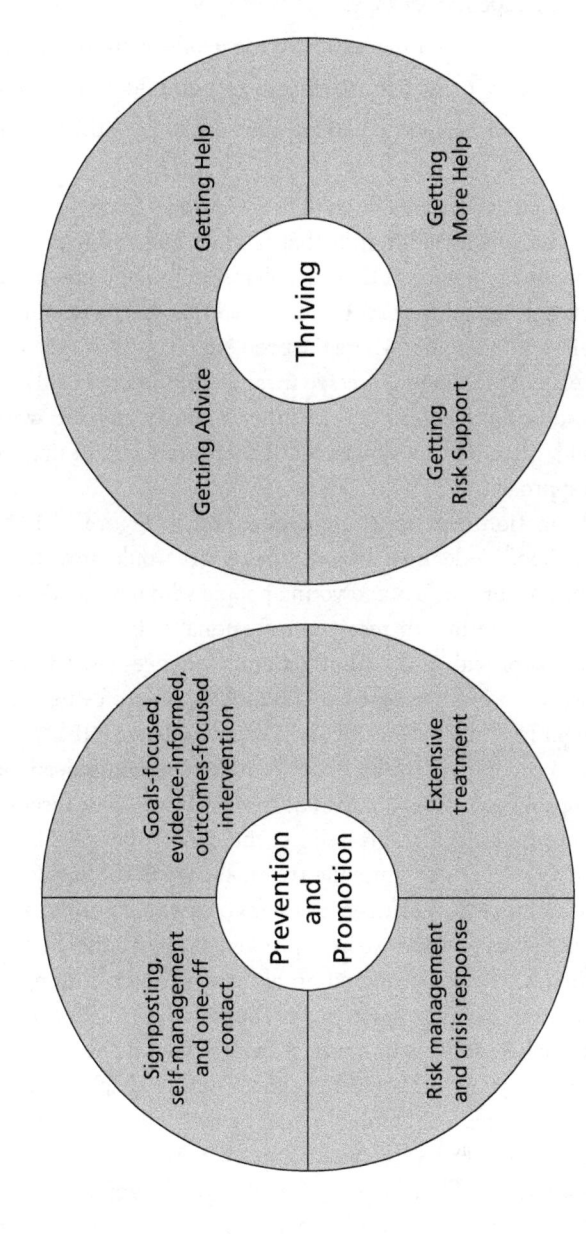

Figure 10.1 The THRIVE framework.

- Learning about the nature of the problem (psychoeducation)
- Receiving telephone advice and support
- Using online therapeutic packages
- Joining a support group for parents or young people with similar problems
- Being offered access to positive activities, e.g. sports clubs or youth groups
- Advice about services, particularly those available within schools and nurseries, etc.

The predominant language and culture of the "Getting Advice" function would be educational, and the assumption is that families and young people will be able to learn about the nature of their problems and then come to their own ways of addressing such difficulties. It is expected that this form of help will be particularly relevant to families where the problem is relatively recent in onset. It is not assumed that problems addressed through this function will necessarily be less severe; some families with severe difficulties may prefer to work in this way. This would, of course, be challenged if there were child safety concerns related to this approach.

The second function (the upper right quadrant in Figure 10.1) has been called "Getting Help." Under this function, the service would provide evidence-based interventions for families and young people who have made an explicit choice that they would like to receive professional help for their difficulty. The service would provide a time-limited and evidence-based intervention; where possible, this would be based on national-level professional guidance (e.g. the National Institute for Health and Care Excellence (NICE) guidelines in the UK). The outcomes of the approach would be monitored, so that progress (or lack of progress) against *individualized* goals would be discussed with the family as the treatment progressed. At the end of the specified number of appointments or length of time, the treatment would be reviewed. Those young people/families who had achieved their goals would be discharged from the service; those who continued to have problems would either be discharged (if that was their wish) or be offered an alternative intervention, involving either "Getting More Help" or "Getting Risk Support" (see below) or "Getting Advice" (as described above). In contrast to the "Getting Advice" function, the predominant language and culture of the "Getting Help" function would be around health, so that the families would be aware that they were coming to the service for a specific treatment for a specific problem. "Getting Help" is not a function associated with the provision of ongoing support; as mentioned above, the interventions offered under this function are limited by time or by a number of appointments.

"Getting More Help" is the third function of the model (the lower right quadrant in Figure 10.1). In line with the evidence, a significant proportion of young people and families (depending on the type of problems) can be expected to continue to have problems at the end of an evidence-based treatment. These families would be offered a choice as to whether they would like to receive additional help. This help would not involve extending the previous intervention in response to poor outcomes. A different, perhaps higher-intensity, time-specified intervention would be offered if further help were to be given. This function is likely to be focused on young people with more severe needs, including, for example, young people who need to attend inpatient care because of the severity of their self-harm or suicidality, or those who have emerging chronic and serious difficulties such as psychosis or behavioral patterns suggestive of personality disorder. As with "Getting Help," the predominant language and culture of "Getting More Help" would be health-related, so that families would be aware that they are coming for a specific treatment for a specific problem. Again, this function does not offer ongoing support.

The fourth function for a CAMHS service operating within the THRIVE framework (the lower left quadrant in Figure 10.1) is called "Getting Risk Support." This function is focused on families with significant mental health needs who have not benefited from evidence-based treatments or who do not wish to make use of such help. In general, the families involved at this level may not be actively help-seeking, although they may make use of services on a crisis basis, such as attending hospital emergency departments, or through having to attend court as a consequence of offending behavior. These families are likely to have major difficulties in helping relationships, both within the family and also in their interactions with helping agencies. The aim of this helping function would be to avoid the risk of more aversive outcomes (e.g. offending, self-harm, early pregnancy, sexual exploitation, gang membership) and to offer long-term joint agency support work with the aim of establishing a degree of trust so that the family may begin to access other forms of help over time. Compared with the other functions provided within the THRIVE framework, this function would not be time-limited, but would invest in establishing relationships over time so that aspects of trust in the helping process may develop. The language used within this function would be that of social care, and the working model would be a joint agency support plan. In our view, the group of families and young people who are most likely to be helped by this function are those for whom the AMBIT approach has been specifically designed.

The THRIVE framework fully supports the need to integrate services for families where possible. This may take place in a number of ways—from more structural developments, such as joint agency local budgets, to more process-oriented developments, such as collaborative protocols between agencies regarding referral pathways between partner agencies. Projecting forwards, such efforts to integrate could, for instance, include joint intake systems, so that the allocation of cases to the social care or mental health systems could be accomplished jointly with the agreement of the client and family/carers. Such developments are not new, and have been implemented in different ways in many services through the initiative of local partnerships to improve systems. However, they remain partial, and are vulnerable to being disbanded during periods of reduced public sector investment.

For some time, some services in the UK have been structurally designed to include staff from different agencies. The Youth Offending Service is such an example, in that, within it, education, health, mental health, social care, and youth justice staff work together under a single management structure. Similarly, some disability teams have been constituted as joint agency teams that aim to address children's needs in a more holistic way. We recognize that joint agency integrative models of service delivery are not unique to the THRIVE framework, and that most thinking about the future design of services is broadly sympathetic with such developments. The challenge is to translate such aspirations into systems that operate effectively in practice. It is this challenge that we will now try to address.

AMBIT and THRIVE

The earlier chapters of this book outlined an approach to working with "hard-to-reach" young people in families who may not be help-seeking, and who may be antagonistic to mental health services. We believe that this approach fits well with the function of "Getting Risk Support" in the THRIVE framework. Furthermore, we tentatively suggest that AMBIT has developed a degree of face validity in its value in working with this group of families and young people. In Chapter 9, we showed how the AMBIT approach has been adopted by a range of teams—from social care, youth offending, the voluntary sector, health services, and more. AMBIT has been specifically designed to be accessible to teams that have a wide range of skills among their staff, from the very highly trained to those who have had relatively little formal training but who may have a wealth of local knowledge and life experience to offer. All these teams share a focus on families and young people with severe and long-standing life difficulties, who have often had very troubled relationships with helping agencies. Our feedback from the vast majority of teams that have completed AMBIT training is that they experienced AMBIT as recognizing and validating the nature of their work and the challenges it throws up, and that it has provided them with ways of changing their approach to very difficult cases in a positive and constructive way.

At the time of writing, the THRIVE framework is being explored in 11 "demonstrator" sites across England. The aim is to test out the core principles of practice in these settings in order to support implementation at local level. Intrinsic to this approach is that much of the work around the details of delivery will be determined by the local context and the existing local relationships among key services. As with families, the investment in THRIVE is in relationships as much as in structures. Structural arrangements are important, but the degree to which services experience each other as trustworthy may be equally crucial in developing effective helping systems for families and young people.

AMBIT and whole-system change

Overall, the AMBIT approach represents a major shift in the conceptualization of helping systems within CAMHS. It profoundly challenges the linearity of the traditional (we have described it as "industrial") referral system in which, first, a service receives a referral from an agency for help with a specific problem, and then—following assessment, and assuming appropriate thresholds are met—the referred-to service "accepts" that referral and begins work with the client. In contrast, under the AMBIT model, a worker is not expected to start a process of help; they are expected to *join an existing helping system*. Obviously, however, for many clients arriving at an AMBIT-influenced team (and, indeed, for their AMBIT keyworkers) it may be very hard to see that any such system already exists, or that any help is taking place at all.

We have come to see this apparent absence of a pre-existing helping network as a systematic effect of the process of seeking help from agencies in a multi-agency network. The process often evoked is one in which other help that clients are receiving (either from other professionals, or from their wider informal network of family, friends, peers, neighbors, or colleagues) is not revealed. The reasons for this tendency for clients and helpers to "miss out" reports of existing helping systems are varied. First, it may be due to an implicit understanding of service thresholds ("If I already have access to existing help, I may not be deemed deserving of your help"). Second, it may be because of implicit assumptions about how help-seeking happens ("I must show my needs to the helper, not my resiliencies. It is for the helper to find out resiliencies, and not for me to reveal them—or, even worse, to boast about them"). Third, and perhaps most dramatically, based on very negative expectations about the harm that so-called "helping" authorities might actually do, there may be such a complete denial of any need at all on the part of the client and/or family that to couple this with reports of any other help-receiving from elsewhere in the wider network would challenge their image of invulnerability, and the client and/or family thus self-censor ("I am fine. There is no problem. Why would I need help from anyone?"). Finally, there may be a systematic drive to minimize the significance of other helping relationships *on the part of the helper*, especially if they are alert to, or anxious about, the fact that the very best help they can offer may still be of limited value ("What if I am no good at helping people like this?"). In such cases, the worker may be influenced by "face-saving" motivations; it is tempting to overlook pre-existing sources of help that (especially if they are actually helpful) might implicitly add a further challenge to the worker's own tenuous sense of how helpful they really are. These and other complications in what we refer to as the "relationship to help" will, by now, be familiar themes to readers of this book.

Some examples of AMBIT whole-system projects

The AMBIT project began by trying to articulate an approach to working with clients (at the time, focusing on young people) who were not seeking help from professional agencies. This remains the core focus of the project, and the main focus of this book. However, the project has also become involved in a series of projects that have entailed changing wider systems, rather than working with individual teams. We will now briefly describe a number of these initiatives.

The AMBIT project has been commissioned to train groups of teams within the local area in three different London boroughs. In each borough, this work has involved training over 100 staff, drawn from a range of service teams that were identified as working with broadly similar client groups, with the explicit aim of increasing understanding between these different teams and of creating a shared language between them.

Under these large training programs, staff from specialist educational services, social care teams, youth workers, youth offending services, and mental health teams have jointly received training in AMBIT. The focus has been on helping teams to articulate and sustain shared ideas around engagement, communication, and processes of help (mentalizing), case discussion ("Thinking Together"), network working (the concept of "dis-integration," and the use of Dis-Integration Grids), and the development of local protocols (manualizing).

Local evaluations of these projects have reported qualitative changes in practice ("Could we discuss this in a more 'AMBIT' way?") and improved relationships between teams. One area that engaged AMBIT in multiple team trainings reported a reduction in referrals between the different services involved, which was attributed to the way staff had made more use of other teams or services to help them with their own clients, rather than reflexively referring the clients to a new service. In one borough, a structural change was implemented in which a "Transformation Team" was created with seconded staff from a wide range of different teams. This team was explicitly targeted to work with families with multiple and long-term problems that had made extensive use of multiple services over several years, but without much evidence of substantive positive change. The team explicitly adopted the AMBIT approach and particularly focused on *reducing* the number of agencies involved with each family at any one time.

Additionally, AMBIT has become involved in a number of forensic settings (e.g. adult prisons and secure units for young people) in which network issues arise in very powerful, but very different ways, compared with community settings. These interventions are in the very early stages and have been initiated by staff in forensic settings approaching the AMBIT project as they could see the potential value of the approach to their own setting. As we described in Chapter 9, a number of residential services (inpatient units and care settings) have found the AMBIT approach more applicable to an institutional setting than we had originally anticipated.

In our view, these projects suggest that AMBIT may have value in supporting substantial changes in the way local systems work in relation to families with multiple needs. Although some of these changes may be captured by quantitative changes in patterns of service use, such as referral patterns, we are more interested in how we can change the quality of relationships between services and teams so that a helping culture is amplified, with a positive acknowledgment of the value of the work of other teams with respect to our clients. For example, in our experience, frontline workers from one team rarely explicitly compliment the work of another team in front of their clients. Our conjecture is that helping systems around families would be more effective if teams explicitly communicated their positive evaluations of each other's work with their clients, and took a more explicit learning stance toward other agencies or workers that the client reports as being helpful to them. This would mirror the patterns known to be associated with effective parenting.

Another progression of the AMBIT approach to whole systems has been our increasing interest in exploring clients' experiences of help in a more systematic way. Increasingly, as AMBIT workers, we have become as interested in the histories of help-seeking and help-receiving that are reported by our clients as we have conventionally been in the histories of their problems. We are currently developing methods of enabling young people and their parents/carers to share their "helping histories" in a way that is not a lengthy interview of a linear progression of different interventions, but more a way that mutually explores their history of the helping process, in order to improve their experience of help in the future.

Despite the fact that we originally began developing AMBIT as an approach for "hard-to-reach" people, we are increasingly keen for services to move away from labels such as this. Such labels may easily be taken as pejorative and blaming of the client (they are "hard to reach" rather than "under-served"), but they also do nothing to make sense of (mentalize) our clients' behavior in relation to histories of help and experiences that have undermined their fundamental capacity to develop trust toward new agencies or workers. In line with some of this thinking, we have been pleased to discover that some teams use the Dis-Integration Grid (see Chapter 6) at the point of receiving a referral, as a way of making sense of the new request for help. Similarly, some teams have used the Pro-Gram (see Chapter 6) as a starting process with clients, as much as focusing on the referred "problem" itself. These whole-system applications of the AMBIT model remain a tentative development, but we are encouraged that they may represent important cultural changes in how teams conceptualize their work within wider helping systems.

Conclusions and reflections on AMBIT and whole-system change

The AMBIT approach to whole-system change has important similarities to the asset-based approach to community resilience specifically applied to the "community" of service providers working within children's helping systems. In *Building Communities from the Inside Out*, Kretzmann and McKnight (1993) present a powerful analysis of a pattern of potentially negative effects of using the traditional needs-based approach for communities requiring support. There are quite obvious parallel processes between this community- or system-wide analysis and our analysis of some of the common processes involved in help-seeking and help-receiving by clients or families that we offered earlier in this chapter (see "AMBIT and whole-system change").

Kretzmann and McKnight (1993) suggest that community leaders may find that the best (or perhaps only) way to attract additional institutional resources is to play up the severity of their current problems and minimize the strength of their local collaborations. Their success (as leaders) may be judged on how many resources are won for the community, not on how self-reliant the community has become. This parallels the "missing" existing networks of help that families and workers often fail to describe during the process of assessment. Such a narrative may lead communities (or families) to see themselves as deficient and incapable of taking charge of their lives and/or of their community.

Community members may begin to act like "clients" or "consumers" of services, with reduced incentives to be active agents in addressing their own needs. Local groups may begin to deal more with external institutions than with groups in their own community. This reinforces the notion that "only outside experts can provide real help" and further weakens neighbor-to-neighbor links.

"Help," in this stark description of the current system, is made available on the basis of categories of needs, rather than emerging through more integrated approaches based on the community's own problem-solving capacities. If all the problems we face are categorized as needs requiring specialist interventions, we see little hope of ever summoning sufficient external resources to solve them. An alternative approach is one that recognizes that it is the capacities of local people, and their associations, that result in the building of powerful communities. In *Building Communities from the Inside Out*, the thrust is toward communities being helped to build an inventory of their assets and encouraged to see value in resources that would otherwise have been ignored, unrealized, or dismissed. The parallel process between this notion of helping at a community level and that which AMBIT-influenced workers might be seeking at the level of the client or family/carer is, we think, striking and valuable.

Although, to date, the AMBIT approach has not indicated direct work with whole communities, it is already actively focused on developing resilience among the "community of helping agencies" (which we have referred to as a "community of practice"), and the themes raised by Kretzmann and McKnight (1993) have a familiar resonance to the way AMBIT aims to influence such systems. Rather than focusing on structure and resources, the AMBIT approach to whole-system change is to place emphasis on relationships and levels of understanding between individuals, teams, and agencies. The integration of services is not just a structural problem—that is, a problem of how resources are effectively managed—it is also a process of developing effective helping relationships within these systems; relationships that enable individual workers to develop and share their understandings with each other and their clients; relationships that open with the question of how collaborative help is taking place here and now, in each particular case.

Far from being a recipe for idiosyncratic and disorganized care, we believe that a mentalized helping system is likely to be both safer and more effective. It is through the gaps left by dis-integration—where failures of mentalizing across a system nurture untested assumptions, hot-headed impulsivity, or an absence of appropriate worry—that risk creeps into the system. A mentalized helping system is one in which different workers have explicitly shared intentions (remaining mindful of the client's mind and markers of successful help from the client's perspective) and can show respectful understanding of each other's minds. Regarding the beneficial impact on safety that a mentalized helping system might offer, repeated inquiries into child abuse suggest this is the case—that we should focus not just on effective liaison with each other ("who is doing what, when") but on genuine inquiry as to how each worker sees the client's situation, and why that might be so (Munro, 2011). With this approach, the effort to change whole systems is less about finding a formula for integration or the preferred structure, and more about investing in the age-old human challenge of enabling and supporting those involved in helping systems to see the world from each other's point of view. Although this aim may be criticized as being somewhat vague and elusive, it is no more than what is required between parents/carers so that they can carry out the day-to-day tasks of helping those in their care.

References

Department for Children, Schools and Families. (2008). *Children's Trusts: Statutory guidance on inter-agency cooperation to improve well-being of children, young people and their families* (London, UK: Department for Children, Schools and Families), https://www.education.gov.uk/consultations/downloadableDocs/Childrens%20Trust%20Statutory%20Guidance.pdf, accessed 27 Jan. 2017.

Department of Health, & NHS England. (2015). *Future in Mind: Promoting, protecting and improving our children and young people's mental health and wellbeing* (London, UK: NHS England), https://www.gov.uk/government/uploads/system/uploads/attachment_data/file/414024/Childrens_Mental_Health.pdf, accessed 27 Jan. 2017.

Green, H., McGinnity, A., Meltzer, H., Ford, T., & Goodman, R. (2005). Mental Health of Children and Young People in Great Britain, 2004. A survey carried out by the Office for National Statistics on behalf of the Department of Health and the Scottish Executive (Basingstoke, UK: Palgrave Macmillan), http://www.esds.ac.uk/doc/5269/mrdoc/pdf/5269technicalreport.pdf, accessed 27 Jan. 2017.

Harper, B., Dickson, J. M., & Bramwell, R. (2014). Experiences of young people in a 16–18 mental health service. *Child and Adolescent Mental Health* 19: 90–6. doi: 10.1111/camh.12024

HM Government. (2003). *Every Child Matters* (London, UK: The Stationery Office), https://www.gov.uk/government/uploads/system/uploads/attachment_data/file/272064/5860.pdf, accessed 27 Jan. 2017.

Kretzmann, J. P., & McKnight, J. L. (1993). *Building Communities from the Inside Out: A path toward finding and mobilizing a community's assets* (Evanston, IL: Institute for Policy Research, Northwestern University).

Madge, N., Hewitt, A., Hawton, K., de Wilde, E. J., Corcoran, P., Fekete, S., ... Ystgaard, M. (2008). Deliberate self-harm within an international community sample of young people: Comparative findings from the Child & Adolescent Self-harm in Europe (CASE) Study. *Journal of Child Psychology and Psychiatry* 49: 667–77. doi: 10.1111/j.1469-7610.2008.01879.x

Munro, E. (2011). *The Munro Review of Child Protection: Final Report. A child-centred system* (London, UK: The Stationery Office), https://www.gov.uk/government/uploads/system/uploads/attachment_data/file/175391/Munro-Review.pdf, accessed 27 Jan. 2017.

NHS Health Advisory Service. (1995). *Together We Stand: Commissioning, role and management of child and adolescent mental health services (NHS Health Advisory Service Thematic Reviews)* (London, UK: HMSO).

Robotham, D., & James, K. (2009). *Evaluation of the Choice and Partnership Approach (CAPA) in Child and Adolescent Mental Health Services in England* (London, UK: Mental Health Foundation), https://www.mentalhealth.org.uk/sites/default/files/CAPA_PDF.pdf, accessed 13 Feb. 2017

Weisz, J. R., Kuppens, S., Eckshtain, D., Ugueto, A. M., Hawley, K. M., & Jensen-Doss, A. (2013). Performance of evidence-based youth psychotherapies compared with usual clinical care: A multilevel meta-analysis. *JAMA Psychiatry* 70: 750–61. doi: 10.1001/jamapsychiatry.2013.1176

Wolpert, M., Harris, R., Hodges, S., Fuggle, P., James, R., Wiener, A., ... Fonagy, P. (2015). *THRIVE Elaborated* (No. ISBN 978-0-9931555-8-1) (London, UK: CAMHS Press), https://www.ucl.ac.uk/ebpu/docs/publication_files/thrive_elaborated, accessed 13 Feb. 2017

YoungMinds. (2015). *Millions of pounds in CAMHS cuts last year—infographic*, http://www.youngminds.org.uk/news/blog/2943_millions_of_pounds_in_camhs_cuts_last_year_-_infographic, accessed 27 Jan. 2017.

Chapter 11

Future ambitions for the AMBIT project

Introduction: Evidence and dissemination

AMBIT is ambitious. Over the past decade, the energy with which many teams have engaged with the basic ideas presented in the preceding chapters, using elements of the AMBIT approach to support significant and innovative efforts in their own work to help extremely excluded and disadvantaged young people and families, has been inspiring. This final chapter plots out some of the future directions and challenges for the AMBIT project at the Anna Freud National Centre for Children and Families, with the community of practice that has begun to develop around this approach.

First, we address the evidence: what there is so far in relation to AMBIT, what we lack, and how we might address these fundamental challenges in the years ahead.

We then turn to dissemination. Here, we really just follow our own advice, described in the section on Active Planning in Chapter 3; as much as we are keen to remain *sensitively attuned to an external reality* (in this case, by following and chasing down evidence about whether AMBIT actually helps, whether it is acceptable to clients and workers, etc.), we are also constantly interested in *broadcasting our intentions* (here, this means finding more efficient and effective ways of disseminating learning, and sharing what we currently believe to be the safest and most helpful ways of working). This balance between attunement and broadcasting is held in tension with the third position or element—our frequently adapted but broadly consistent *plan*—which is to broaden training opportunities and grow the AMBIT community of practice, thereby benefiting the project by accumulating learning from the many new iterations of natural field trials that are created in this way.

Related to dissemination, we briefly discuss future plans for the online AMBIT manual. We hope this resource will continue to improve—as a reference, a training aid, and a recording tool to support teams in clarifying their own identity, role, and approach, and also as a forum for interaction across the expanding AMBIT community of practice. For readers of a more technical inclination, the manual is a great example of how open-source technologies can seed and incubate innovation; the manual was developed to its current position on a shoestring budget, encouraging and facilitating the best of amateur enthusiasm and altruism. In 2017, a major new technical drive is underway to dramatically improve the user interface and add important social networking functions to the innovative web-based manuals. We see these changes as a major part of our mission of freely disseminating and sharing the best learning. If the web-based resources that we have developed ultimately come to allow teams to embark completely independently on these developments in practice, and at no cost, we would see this (our redundancy) as a particular triumph. We think this is rather unlikely, however, and so we also acknowledge and describe the benefits of involving external trainers, and briefly describe the development of training capacity and the expanding range of different training models that the AMBIT project has developed at the Anna Freud National Centre for Children and Families.

What is the evidence base for the AMBIT approach?

In earlier chapters of this book, we have described AMBIT as a set of organizing principles and practices based on well-established developmental (e.g. mentalizing) and systemic (including positioning theory) processes. AMBIT is also an approach that is seriously committed to the need for ongoing scrutiny through evaluation and evidence-gathering. We are only too aware of initiatives with good face validity, taken forward by well-intentioned clinicians, whose objective value to the group of clients they serve ultimately proves to be unfounded. We take the possibility of this risk for AMBIT very seriously.

The challenges of effective evaluation

Despite a growing range of early descriptive studies and local outcome evaluations, and evidence of enthusiastic uptake by the vast majority of teams that have received AMBIT training, we are well aware that, as yet, hard evidence about AMBIT is thin and needs to be thickened before robust statements can be made about its value. Amid these aspirations, the AMBIT approach presents a number of important challenges as to how such evidence might be gathered.

To start with, AMBIT is not a focused mentalization-based intervention, specifically defined in a "traditional" (i.e. fixed) treatment manual, so that face-to-face interventions can easily be evaluated alongside conventional treatment fidelity measures (does doing "purer" AMBIT equate with achieving better outcomes?). In addition to the very broad (and purposefully adaptive) range of face-to-face operations that an AMBIT-influenced worker may carry out in work with their clients, there is also a wide variety of team- and network-based practices that may also be deployed flexibly but are no less intrinsic to the AMBIT model than the worker's actions during the direct face-to-face client contact. However, this makes evaluations of AMBIT practice somewhat trickier. What, then, is being evaluated? We are committed to devising an open and integrative system, which must be explicitly adapted to local settings through local learning—hence our mantra that "there is no such thing as an AMBIT team" (see Chapter 9). We do not support the idea of developing another rigid system of helping, which may then be experienced as an imposition on local services in a way that undermines local expertise and experience (analogous to the one-size-fits-all and "service-centric" offers of intervention for families and young people that the THRIVE model, described in Chapter 10, challenges).

In addition to the breadth and fluidity of what an AMBIT-influenced approach might actually entail, another tricky challenge for evaluators is the way that our development model for teams shares much with our advice about the approach to clients. We start from positions of respect for how things are now. We explicitly invite teams to identify the aspects of their ways of working that are already successful (aspects that AMBIT should avoid harming) and the parts of the AMBIT approach that seem to them to add value to their current ways of working; we invite them to explicitly adapt the AMBIT model to their needs. This approach is radically different from the idea of developing a uniform model applicable to any locality or service structure. It is significantly different from, for example, mentalization-based treatment for adolescents (MBT-A), even though the MBT-A approach has been profoundly influential on the development of AMBIT. MBT-A is in many ways a more traditional treatment: it has a manual to ensure treatment fidelity so that it can be replicated accurately by appropriately trained teams in different settings; it is directed at a group of young people whose problems and needs are predefined and can be clearly identified; and the approach is now known to be helpful for this group, thanks to a well-conducted randomized controlled trial (RCT) (Rossouw & Fonagy, 2012). Thinking back to the THRIVE model of system change that we described in Chapter 10, MBT-A would fit more closely with the offers of help in the "Getting Help" or "Getting More Help" sections, rather than the "Getting Risk Support" section, where AMBIT is more focused. One can see the "Getting Risk Support" section of the THRIVE model as being suited to those clients or families who have exhausted the potential of existing evidence-based packages of treatment.

The AMBIT approach to model development

AMBIT's model development approach has been strongly influenced by three strands of thinking.

First, we have been influenced by the way in which innovations take place through start-up social enterprises and the impact of the internet on such developments. The process of *learning by doing, and improving in subsequent iterations,* characterizes much IT development, especially in the "open-source" model of development, in which software is continually upgraded in response to feedback from real-world applications; occasionally there are punctuated phases in which whole new versions are made available to clients, but mainly there is a constant "drip-feed" of minor improvements. This seems to us to have considerable salience in developing effective models of interventions for complex systems.

Second, as described in Chapter 7, we have been strongly influenced by the idea of *learning organizations,* so that teams are encouraged to become interested in developing ways of systematically improving the work that they do. This is a key part of the AMBIT model that is closely aligned with the emphasis on outcome measurement that, in the UK, the Children and Young People's Improving Access to Psychological Therapies (CYP IAPT) program has promoted. For AMBIT, the effort toward systematic improvement goes well beyond the routine measurement of clinical outcomes, their review, and subsequent adaptations to the offer of help in the light of these findings (although achieving this much alone would be a significant advance on a lot of common practice); it extends to a much wider range of team and worker behaviors, whose development is marked, tracked, and remembered by the team through the process of local manualization. In practice (probably particularly because of the very heterogeneous presentations of clients working with the wide array of AMBIT-influenced teams), we note the difficulty in finding and implementing common or universal routine clinical outcome measures for this work, and this is another important challenge. The AMBIT AIM measure, described in Chapter 3, may offer one blueprint for this, but other measures, such as The Current View (Jones et al., 2013), also offer promise. Expecting a universal measure that will be universally applied is almost certainly to wait for a dawn that will not arrive. Key to the success of any measure will be the extent to which workers see it as *measuring what matters*—both to their clients, and to them as practitioners in the field. The difficulty in moving workers toward the use of routine measures may also reflect the degree of "cultural shift" that such a development represents for some of the teams we have trained, which may previously have had little experience of using outcome measures.

Third, we have been influenced by service *quality improvement models* that aim to position individual workers as having agency and the capacity to make individual contributions toward improving the effectiveness of the team. This idea has been supported by the work of Glisson and colleagues around the impact of organizational culture and climate on clinical outcomes (Williams & Glisson, 2014; see also Chapter 5).

Fourth, we believe that AMBIT is a platform via which clients who are currently unable to use or access (or be "reached" by) evidence-based practice may come to benefit from such interventions. In other words, AMBIT may perform a "shepherding" function—bringing the client to the intervention, or the intervention to the client. The former would involve connecting the client to a service or worker who is able to deliver an evidence-based intervention, in a state of mind that is more ready to engage and open to trust. The latter might involve versions of evidence-based interventions that have been specifically adapted to be delivered in the field, perhaps by a less than fully trained practitioner, but thereby addressing barriers that have previously been identified as insurmountable. In this way, we would emphasize that AMBIT embraces evidence-based interventions within its overall framework.

Overall, these strands of thinking have led to an approach that is consistent with Weisz and Gray's (2008) idea of "deployment-focused model development," relying heavily on feedback by current users in the field to guide iterative refinement and elaboration of the initial ideas so that they incrementally become better adapted to real work contexts. However, we recognize that the risk with this approach is that it makes rigorous evaluation and testing of hypothesized mechanisms and techniques difficult, as the model is (at least in this active development phase), by definition, in a continual state of change.

Given these features, we think that the conceptual and developmental framework of AMBIT presents significant challenges in relation to the requirements for an RCT. However, while comparing AMBIT with another form of help by randomizing matched individual clients or families to different treatments may be difficult, it remains a high priority to find ways to achieve this. If, for example, AMBIT were being rolled out sequentially across an area where multiple teams serve neighboring localities, there would be scope for a form of randomization at a team level, with multiple-methods evaluation deployed to compare differences in outcomes. This is a study waiting to be conducted. We would prefer this to be done by assessors not connected to the program developers, as this is an obvious potential source of bias.

An evidence-informed approach

Our current approach to evidence with respect to the AMBIT model is to address the lack of formal RCT evidence in a number of different ways, described below.

1. **Developmental science.** We require that basic mechanisms supported by the AMBIT approach, such as mentalizing, are supported by developmental science. Mentalizing has a substantial theoretical and empirical base, with extensive studies of the association of mentalizing to attachment theory and to parent–child interaction studies (Fonagy et al., 2002). This may seem unremarkable, but it is not always the case that key therapeutic concepts related to work with children and young people are grounded in developmental science. For example, the idea of a "core belief" in cognitive-behavioral therapy (CBT) arises from adult theory of CBT, in which the developmental basis of such types of cognition remains unknown.

2. **Supporting existing evidence-based practice.** AMBIT functions as a platform within which existing evidence-based practice can be supported. We require that the interventions that we promote (e.g. CBT, motivational interviewing, family therapy) can be reasonably extrapolated to suggest the likelihood of effectiveness for the non-standard client groups or settings where help is offered. For example, we judge that mentalization-based interventions can be appropriately applied to work with "hard-to-reach" adolescents on the basis of two important areas of study. First, an RCT of mentalization-based treatment for self-harming adolescents (MBT-A) showed that this approach was more effective than treatment as usual, and was one of the first studies to show reductions in self-harm as a primary outcome in this population of young people (Rossouw & Fonagy, 2012). Second, mentalization-based interventions have an extensive evidence base for effectiveness with adults with borderline personality disorder (BPD). There are similarities between the types of presenting problems (impulsivity, self-harm, poor affect regulation) of adults with BPD and the younger people seen by teams using the AMBIT approach. The same principles apply in our support for evidence-based interventions, such as the use of motivational interviewing in working with clients with substance misuse problems (Jensen et al., 2011) or CBT to address problems of social anxiety (Spence et al., 2000), to give just two examples.

3. **Organizational research.** The basic processes of how AMBIT teams work together, and how they work with other agencies, are supported by research on organizational factors associated with effective health interventions, which suggests that team functioning may play a significant part in effective practice (West, 2012). Many of the principles of good practice

advocated by AMBIT are shared with other models. For example, the need to have clear treatment objectives, well-measured outcomes, and a shared, joined-up approach with other agencies is not controversial. In some senses AMBIT could be seen as having quite modest aims—to act as a systematic approach to documenting best practice as it is conducted in fieldwork with this client group.

4. **Local service evaluations.** Directly in parallel with its emphasis on local adaptations to the model, AMBIT strongly supports the need for local service evaluations. We have already described AMBIT as an example of a deployment-focused treatment development (Weisz & Gray, 2008). In many ways, AMBIT is still in the developmental phase of setting up multiple field trials and gathering feedback from them in order to refine the model, but there is certainly evidence that the core features of AMBIT have "settled down" considerably over the past three years, after a period of more dramatic development and change. There is also now evidence from a growing number of local service evaluations that supports the effectiveness and acceptability of AMBIT (see Chapter 9). For instance, the introduction of AMBIT appears to have reduced the length and frequency of hospital admissions in services in both Bexley (south-east London) and Edinburgh. There is evidence, too, that AMBIT-trained teams were effective in meeting commissioning targets. A number of local evaluations have taken place in recently established teams that were set up with clearly specified outcome targets set by commissioners. Perhaps the first of these was the Adolescent Multi-Agency Specialist Service (AMASS) team in Islington (north London), which was set up to work with adolescents in birth families at risk of family breakdown. The explicit objective of setting up this service was to reduce the number of adolescents coming into the care system. Ongoing evaluation indicated that 85% of referred adolescents remained with the birth family after the AMASS intervention (Fuggle et al., 2015). A local evaluation by the Cambridgeshire Adolescent Substance Use Service indicated positive results with respect to reductions in substance misuse, as well as positive client feedback on the acceptability of the approach, and subjective and objective impressions of impact on wellbeing (Fuggle et al., 2015). Measures of local improvements against predetermined training objectives, not unlike "goal-based outcomes" in clinical work (Law, 2013), are valuable. Qualitative studies of service users' experience of care, and of teams using AMBIT to influence their practices, while not so powerful in the hierarchy of empirical evidence, have much to offer, and are beginning to appear in the published literature (e.g. Griffiths et al., 2016).

5. **Local reports of practice changes.** Connecting AMBIT training to improved outcomes is supported by evidence from team self-reports that training in AMBIT results in changes in the team's practice. Without yet being able to define exact proportions, we know that a substantial and encouraging number of teams trained in AMBIT clearly adopt a number of the key components of the model in their work as a team following training. This is demonstrated by their ongoing feedback to the AMBIT project; examples illustrating this are presented in Chapter 9. However, it is clear that the degree of adoption, and the specific elements of the approach adopted, varies between teams. In our view, this is congruent with the need for local adaptation of the model to local client groups and service ecologies, but also with our knowledge that different teams embark on AMBIT training in different states of preparedness and from within often very different contexts. Learning more about what facilitates adoption, and the most common barriers to change, is an ongoing task.

So, our view is that overall, and to date, AMBIT provides a promising approach as a platform for working with clients who may present significant concerns for services, but who are not actively engaged in therapy or more formal methods of help. There is no question that more systematic research is needed to clarify the mechanisms and processes that AMBIT promotes. Such ongoing evaluation fits with AMBIT's values as a learning system. At its heart, AMBIT is an open system, and here is the real challenge (or invitation): its dissemination and development will be determined by the degree to which AMBIT-trained teams become increasingly engaged in the process of model development itself.

Our challenge is to find ways to help teams move away from a position of "passive receptivity" in relation to an externally devised therapeutic model, toward one in which the workers and their clients consider themselves as stakeholders and co-producers in the process of working out what intervention(s) works best for which client(s). To achieve this would be to mirror the form of dissemination that has been achieved in some open-source communities in the field of software development; it is a goal to which the AMBIT project continues to aspire.

AMBIT as a learning system

AMBIT is defined by both the needs of its client group and the values of its proponents. In this book, we have (we hope tenaciously) tried to hold on to and promote our aspiration to see the AMBIT project embody the features of a learning organization (as discussed in Chapter 7). The reality is that this is very hard to achieve, and even harder to sustain. There is little doubt that, in part, the stress we place on learning reflects the fact that AMBIT's development has so far been such a powerful learning experience for us.

We remain committed to the original values of developing an open helping system: one that supports each team's capacity for improving and developing their own work as they co-produce it. We also want to provide highly accessible training materials to support such developments in teams whose training budgets may be severely restricted. In the treatment development world, as we seek out increasingly effective practice programs (especially when these are directed at some of the most vulnerable clients, and build on the work of multiple previous generations of researchers and practitioners), we do not think it is unreasonable to articulate a battle cry along the lines of "intellectual property is theft."

Web-based developments in learning and evidence-gathering

From the core values outlined above we seek to take the AMBIT project forward by strengthening the community of practice, linked through an increasingly interactive web-based resource. Besides ambitions to significantly improve the online manual's navigability and technical performance, the 2017 development plan will boost its social interactive elements to support our aspirations for a learning community of practice. For instance, we will introduce practitioner discussion threads linked to specific pages, so that specific topic areas might gather small groups of interested workers discussing evidence and improvements; there will be more explicit marking and facilitation of the existing "comparing and sharing" functions in the manual, so that it is much easier for teams to browse and benefit from each other's local contributions and developments—cloning and customizing those that have value, allowing local "outbreaks" of improved practice to propagate to settings well beyond their origins; there will be much more active provision of feedback in response to contributions by local workers; and so on.

In addition to these developments to the web-based manual, there is also an intention to support the AMBIT community of practice in beginning to collectively share and pool data on client outcomes. This will be achieved using another innovative online service—a web-based shared database that has been co-developed by the Anna Freud National Centre for Children and Families and University College London, known as POD (http://www.annafreud.org/services-schools/services-for-professionals/pod/). Our intention is to integrate the existing online AMBIT manual with the POD system, which is already being used for a number of mentalization-based treatment studies and allows anonymized outcome data (relating to a wide and adaptable range of measures) to be entered very simply, by clients and workers in the field, via any web-enabled device (laptop, tablet, smartphone, etc.). As part of developing a more coherent process of evaluation and scrutiny of the AMBIT approach, we are working toward creating a community of multiple teams, in diverse settings, whose own local learning can be supported by using POD, while incorporating this work into a much broader collective study through the pooling of anonymized data. If teams found this data-collecting system useful for collecting information about their own local outcomes, client feedback, etc., then the pooling of anonymized data for broader analyses would be relatively simple to achieve. The challenge is to ensure that this kind of development does not take place in a top-down way, but that it represents an authentic co-construction of a process of learning between the communities of teams interested in this approach. In addition, we need to include our clients in a more direct way so that the process of learning is something in which they also become active partners. Some teams already invite clients to help co-produce pages in their local manual, for instance documenting what they taught their worker about "how to help somebody like me." We hope that readers from AMBIT-influenced teams will hear this as a rousing call to join us.

Broadcasting our intentions: Disseminating the model

We introduced this chapter by saying that in some ways our planning for the future development of AMBIT simply follows our own advice in relation to Active Planning, described in Chapter 3. A plan that is disconnected from effective ways to broadcast it (so that collaborators can opt in) or from sensitive attunement to the predicaments of those it seeks to address (so that there is an authentic relationship to help) is unlikely to go far. In the section above, on seeking evidence for AMBIT, we could argue that we have been trying to ensure there is an attunement to reality—does AMBIT actually help in the ways it says it is trying to help? We now move on to discussing our ideas for the dissemination of the model. This closely maps on to the notion of AMBIT broadcasting its intentions; the question then is whether others might want to travel with us.

The most common method of disseminating ways of working is the process of training. This is traditionally done by teams or individuals who attend training events in order to develop knowledge and skills linked to competencies (the AMBIT competencies have been described in Chapter 7). Training is all very well, but if it is the only way to bring about change in our wider world, then it is a bottleneck that will deprive the majority of clients of new ways of working, unless more creative ways of dissemination are developed.

For AMBIT, we have developed a basic four-day team training, which is delivered in blocks: an initial two-day introduction to AMBIT, a one-day training for "AMBIT leads," and a further one day for the whole team. The AMBIT lead is the person (or preferably two or three people) in the team who has been given responsibility for supporting and fostering the AMBIT model in the team. AMBIT leads are usually reasonably senior (or influential) members of a team, and hopefully enthusiasts for the approach, but, most importantly, they are workers who can command "clinical" respect from their colleagues. The AMBIT lead is given additional training, particularly in the use of the web-based manual in order to be able to make the material there more accessible to the team as a whole, as well as in using the many training exercises documented in the manual—these can be adapted to support brief local "top-up" training sessions.

At the time of writing, nearly 200 teams have received this basic training; sometimes this is delivered to one team on its own, but more frequently we have delivered training to several teams together. This multi-team approach has facilitated contact between teams and has generally been perceived as enriching the training experience by increasing the diversity of the group. The training events are generally rated very highly by the participants as being valid, relevant, and useful. However, the real challenge is not how much the participants appreciate the training, but the degree to which this training generalizes to their real work context. Whole-day training events are expensive for teams—and for training organizations. The basic training plan has been significantly influenced by the budgetary constraints of teams, particularly in the voluntary sector, for whom longer trainings would not be affordable. The four-day training for a team (three days for most team members, other than AMBIT leads) covers the basic competencies, but is a very brief period to cover the whole model. It is not surprising that the impact of four days of training on some teams is quite modest, although other teams have made quite profound and enduring changes based on this training alone.

To enhance the impact of the basic training, all the training materials are included in the web-based manual, which is freely available to anyone with internet access. The materials include video versions of all the key talks given as part of the training, and of group exercises where the participants have agreed to allow this video to be shared. The manual also contains extensive documentation of training exercises that have been found to be effective in training situations, which teams can practice in their own setting without the input (or expense) of external trainers. The intention is that this considerable training resource should greatly strengthen the capacity of teams, encouraging above all the generalization of experiences from the training event into real work settings by allowing local rehearsal and exploration.

More recently, we have further expanded our dissemination model by developing a training package for local trainers. This "Train the Trainer" approach requires two people from a team to attend a five-day training program to learn the AMBIT approach, and in addition, to learn how to train the rest of their team. Local training events are then facilitated by these new local trainers, preferably supported by other local trainers from nearby teams, as well as by telephone supervision from the AMBIT project base. This approach is still being piloted, but we are encouraged that it appears to provide opportunities to further increase access to the approach—for instance, to services where the whole team is unable to attend the standard four-day training (this is particularly the case for services providing residential or crisis care, whose teams cannot all be away simultaneously). We also like the idea that by training local trainers, we are disseminating expertise and emphasizing local capacities rather than encouraging dependency on an external agency.

We have come to see dissemination as multi-faceted; training on its own is rather unlikely to produce changes in staff practice that are sustainable over time. Implementation science (Fixsen et al., 2005) and the literature of organizational change (Miller et al., 2015; Grol & Grimshaw, 2003) have become increasingly crucial to us for understanding the mechanisms by which teams achieve sustainable change. This has led to an increasing focus on AMBIT as a project to support the production of effective and sustainable change in team practices, rather than "just" providing a training in a particular type of therapy. We have been increasingly impressed by the value we have discovered in stressing parallel processes between the ways of supporting and implementing positive change with our clients and their families, and the ways of achieving the same aims with teams and organizations.

Using this perspective, we have introduced an additional day of "pre-training," called a Preparation, Reflection, Evaluation and Planning (PREP) day. The purpose of this day is to provide a space for teams and services to think in a structured way about *why* they need training, and if they do, *what* they want and require from the training. The intention is to develop clear local service objectives that any subsequent training would need to aim to support (training "outcome measures," as it were). In terms that will be familiar if you have read Chapter 5, the PREP day is thus a focused attempt to help a team or service to "mark the task" for any future training. We are increasingly less focused on teams being trained in AMBIT as a starting point, and more interested in teams articulating what they would like to improve about their work, and then planning a training program using AMBIT materials that might support these objectives. For example, in a recent training project, we agreed with the service managers that one of the key outcomes of the training was to reduce the number of agencies offering direct help to individual young clients where such help was proving ineffective—that is, where more workers are brought in as a reflex response to poor outcomes or increasing risk.

Increasingly, we have been asked to support trainings that involve multiple teams, sometimes from across multiple systems in a locality, rather than single teams. On the basis of a series of broadly very positive early experiences of these locality-based multi-team trainings, we see this type of training as a possible pointer toward the future.

What are *your* intentions? Attuning trainings to trainees' intentions

Reading this book is not the same as taking part in training! However, we are aware that some readers who have got this far through the book may be considering whether AMBIT could be helpful for them in their work setting. This section invites you (and, ideally, your team) to reflect on whether this is likely to be the case. The online AMBIT manual includes two questionnaires: the AMBIT Service Evaluation Questionnaire (ASEQ) and the AMBIT Practice Audit Tool (APrAT). These tools have been developed to help teams and individual workers to probe some important areas: first, the extent to which their work is already congruent with an AMBIT influence, and second, to reflect upon any significant discrepancies in their existing practice from AMBIT theories that might prompt thoughts of doing things differently.

As mentioned above, the single stand-alone team consultation day (the PREP day) is designed to help teams "think together" about their own training needs. During this day we use a variety of group exercises to probe several key questions. We list these questions here, as they may be of value to teams considering training options for the future:

- **"What are this team's existing strengths, which any training should be building upon and be wary of undermining?"** Here we emphasize our respect for local practice and existing expertise, and the importance of avoiding "iatrogenic" harms from team training that paradoxically undermine the existing strengths in a team or system.

- **"Why would this team (which we assume contains a wealth of experience already) want or need any training at all?"** Here we are interested in a team's commitment to, and readiness for, change. Teams that have high levels of confidence that what they are already doing is the best that can be done are more likely to receive any group training as something imposed and unwelcome. Can the team can find a position that acknowledges its existing strengths and retains confidence that these are not under threat, and yet remains open and curious about opportunities for improvement in other areas of practice?

- **"What are the specific challenges in the work of this team that whole-team training might reasonably address?"** Here we are interested in being sure that the challenges that a team finds most salient are ones that AMBIT might have something to offer in order to help. A lack of skills in a specific evidence-based intervention such as trauma-focused CBT, for instance, would not best be addressed by AMBIT training. We are interested in probing how a team can reflect on the difficulties of its work, and whether it is able to extend its reflections (or finds it meaningful to do so) across the four main quadrants of AMBIT practice (working with clients, working with the team, working with networks, and learning at work).

- **"What outcomes would indicate the success of a team training?"** Here we look to develop SMART (specific, measurable, attainable, relevant, and time-limited) goal-based outcome measures with the team in relation to any proposed training.

- **"What are the most likely barriers to achieving these goals, and what might help to find ways through or around these barriers?"** Here we seek to establish realistic expectations of training, and collaborative solutions to likely problems in the implementation of any changes, particularly with a view to longer-term sustainability after any investment in training has been made.

This process enables us to tailor training to the specific needs and intentions of individual teams. For example, some teams have particularly wanted to focus on working more effectively with other teams in their local networks, and this has been given greater prominence in their training than other areas that they felt more confident about. This is what we mean when we say that there is no standard AMBIT training. The parallels between this flexibility and the therapeutic work that teams do with clients are obvious.

Dilemma: Adaptive training versus core curriculum

In relation to our wish to be adaptive in our training offers, we have also had to use the balancing influence of AMBIT—managing the risk that, under such conditions, teams may conceivably choose to work only on those quadrants with which they already have the easiest relationships, while ignoring those that are more challenging but perhaps more important. We are very interested in the areas on which teams appear to be less focused. Again, this parallels what might occupy a worker in considering what existing relationships and issues their client brings for them to work on. We have considered (and are still considering) offering a more modular type of training, offering discrete days that focus on separate quadrants of the AMBIT wheel. What causes us to be reticent in this is the concern that, given our hypothesis—that the balanced application of attention across *all four* quadrants is critical for safe, effective, and sustainable working—we might be doing a team no favors if it is "let off the hook" by not having to consider all four quadrants!

Dilemma: Affordable trainings versus available trainings

Another dilemma for us concerns the inevitable cost of trainings. Despite our ambition that the AMBIT online manual may at some point facilitate active relationships between reciprocating teams who might co-train each other using our materials, but without incurring any expert trainer or material costs, we are not yet there. Maybe a time will come when the funding available for training in this field is commensurate with the perceived need, and is justified by validated evidence, but we are far from that point. Until then, trying to develop ways of sharing learning that are affordable, accessible, and equitable remains a necessary challenge for us. As developers and trainers we would like to be redundant, but the demand for training remains stubbornly high. In the same way that, paradoxically, the "professionalizing" of mental health care for children may have contributed to a loss of capacity or sense of agency in wider systems, including schools and the family itself (see Chapter 10), we perceive significant risks attached to centralizing expertise in relation to improvement and learning.

Meanwhile, however, feedback tells us something contradictory. The many teams that have been through AMBIT trainings have mostly described in very positive terms their experience of working with other minds (the trainers) who are external to their own systems and are thus perhaps freed from some of the constraints within which each particular system has developed. In particular, there seems to be an implicit assumption that there is value in working with external minds that take a particular interest (and, rightly or wrongly, claim some expertise) in creating contexts where exploration and learning can take place. That is a long-winded way of saying that AMBIT trainees consider the *experiential* component of a team-based training as the most important. This makes sense to us: theories and facts can be gathered more efficiently elsewhere; what is critical is that a team can collectively mark a shared experience, so that later they can refer back to the shared meanings that this has generated. If culture is a system of shared meanings carried through time, then AMBIT training is largely about the purposeful development of a team culture. However, what this does not solve, but in fact exacerbates, is the problem of creating more training opportunities that are affordable for more teams. Much as we prize and value the skills, experience, and charisma of our growing team of AMBIT trainers, who are drawn from teams practicing AMBIT-influenced work, the solution is unlikely to come from simply amplifying this resource. Ultimately, a more radical solution is required.

Once again, our instincts suggest that it is the AMBIT community of practice that will offer the way forward. To achieve the penetration required, what is required is a much more devolved and "viral" approach to training (or sharing of knowledge and practice) than the current "market model" can supply—one that will have to make more use of the principle of reciprocity rather than relying primarily on financial transactions ("If you can afford this, we can sell it to you"). We note, for instance, reports of the powerful impact upon a team of having regular visitors/observers attending its key meetings. Although generally these visitors are expressly there for their own benefit—to observe and learn about interesting, innovative, or "best" practice—they may not be fully aware of the fact that their observer status also has a significant (and in our experience very positive) influence on the team they are observing. Workers in a team that regularly accepts visitors report how these observers have encouraged them to "raise their game"—to practice much more explicitly in keeping with their agreed intentions. Over time, they agree, this has profoundly helped to shift aspirational practice into everyday practice, which continues even when the visitors are not there. Would reciprocal visiting for observation/demonstration or peer-to-peer supervision from neighboring AMBIT-influenced teams offer a viable model for service improvement that would approach cost neutrality? These sorts of opportunities will require engagement from the wider community, and almost certainly cannot be driven from a central authority, but they do seem to us to be important challenges and potential opportunities for the future.

That we are sharing our dilemmas about how to move forward should, we hope, come as no surprise to a reader at this point in the book. We hope that the materials provided here will, at the very least, give food for thought for teams that are engaged in this difficult work, and perhaps some structure within which they can apply these ideas, but more than anything we hope to evoke their willingness to join in constructing the next paths ahead.

Last words: Return to purpose

This book is about helping to improve the wellbeing of extremely vulnerable people, whose needs have frequently been left unmet by family, society, and helping services. This is also—perhaps especially—the case in highly developed first-world countries, whose traditional social networks have perhaps been eroded even more than elsewhere. We believe that AMBIT offers a promising approach to address the lack of trusting relationships that characterize the frail social networks that our clients inhabit, and also the often fraught world of professionalized help. This applies both within teams and across the networks that have been developed to support them (but so often appear to do the reverse, in spite of good intentions). Above all, AMBIT rests on the idea that all the players in this drama are learners, and that all can contribute in building more sensitive, more robust, and more helpful relationships in the future—but only if what is to be learned is created under conditions of trust. Many people are working in these contexts but without trust, and in such conditions learning barely occurs, or cannot be remembered or recalled in timely ways. If AMBIT makes a small contribution toward creating the crucial conditions of trust, then it will have paid its way. We need each other for this, but we also need to record where we have been, and where we are going.

We have pointed out that if AMBIT is true to its ambition, then this book should be outdated before it goes into print. If this is not the case, then it will have stopped adapting to new evidence and sharing outbreaks of new learning from local teams solving specific problems. The online AMBIT manual (visit https://manuals.annafreud.org and then follow the links to AMBIT), where the "live" version of AMBIT is recorded, is constantly updated, and is stewarded by an editorial team. We urge readers to visit the website and to spend a little time learning how to navigate around it; there is much there that we hope will be of value. Access to it has always been, and will continue to be, free.

References

Fixsen, D. L., Naoom, S. F., Blase, K. A., Friedman, R. M., & Wallace, F. (2005).
Implementation Research: A synthesis of the literature (Tampa, FL: University of South Florida, Louis de la Parte Florida Mental Health Institute, the National Implementation Research Network), http://ctndisseminationlibrary.org/PDF/nirnmonograph.pdf, accessed 27 Jan. 2017.

Fonagy, P., Gergely, G., Jurist, E., & Target, M. (2002). *Affect Regulation, Mentalization, and the Development of the Self* (New York, NY: Other Press).

Fuggle, P., Bevington, D., Cracknell, L., Hanley, J., Hare, S., Lincoln, J., … Zlotowitz, S. (2015). The Adolescent Mentalization-based Integrative Treatment (AMBIT) approach to outcome evaluation and manualization: Adopting a learning organization approach. *Clinical Child Psychology and Psychiatry* 20: 419–35. doi: 10.1177/1359104514521640

Griffiths, H., Noble, A., Duffy, F., & Schwannauer, M. (2016). Innovations in Practice: Evaluating clinical outcome and service utilization in an AMBIT-trained Tier 4 child and adolescent mental health service. *Child and Adolescent Mental Health* doi: 10.1111/camh.12181 [epub ahead of print]

Grol, R., & Grimshaw, J. (2003). From best evidence to best practice: Effective implementation of change in patients' care. *Lancet* 362: 1225–30. doi: 10.1016/S0140-6736(03)14546-1

Jensen, C. D., Cushing, C. C., Aylward, B. S., Craig, J. T., Sorell, D. M., & Steele, R. G. (2011). Effectiveness of motivational interviewing interventions for adolescent substance use behavior change: A meta-analytic review. *Journal of Consulting and Clinical Psychology* 79: 433–40. doi: 10.1037/a0023992

Jones, M., Hopkins, K., Kyrke-Smith, R., Davies, R., Vostanis, P., & Wolpert, M. (2013). *Current View Tool Completion Guide* (London, UK: CAMHS Press), https://www.ucl.ac.uk/ebpu/docs/publication_files/current_view, accessed 27 Jan. 2017.

Law, D. (2013). *Goals and Goal Based Outcomes (GBOs): Some useful information* (London, UK: CAMHS Press), https://www.ucl.ac.uk/ebpu/docs/publication_files/GBOs_Booklet, accessed 27 Jan. 2017.

Miller, R., Freeman, T., Davidson, D., & Glasby, J. (2015). *An Adult Social Care Compendium of Approaches and Tools for Organisational Change* (Birmingham, UK: Health Services Management Centre, University of Birmingham), http://www.download.bham.ac.uk/socsci/hsmc/hsmc-flip-book/ssrc-hsmc_flip.html, accessed 27 Jan. 2017.

Rossouw, T. I., & Fonagy, P. (2012). Mentalization-based treatment for self-harm in adolescents: A randomized controlled trial. *Journal of the American Academy of Child and Adolescent Psychiatry* 51: 1304–13. doi: 10.1016/j.jaac.2012.09.018

Spence, S. H., Donovan, C., & Brechman-Toussaint, M. (2000). The treatment of childhood social phobia: The effectiveness of a social skills training-based, cognitive-behavioural intervention, with and without parental involvement. *Journal of Child Psychology and Psychiatry* 41: 713–26. doi: 10.1111/1469-7610.00659

Weisz, J. R., & Gray, J. S. (2008). Evidence-based psychotherapy for children and adolescents: Data from the present and a model for the future. *Child and Adolescent Mental Health* 13: 54–65. doi: 10.1111/j.1475-3588.2007.00475.x

West, M. A. (2012). *Effective Teamwork: Practical Lessons from Organizational Research* (3rd edn, Chichester, UK: British Psychological Society/John Wiley).

Williams, N. J., & Glisson, C. (2014). Testing a theory of organizational culture, climate and youth outcomes in child welfare systems: A United States national study. *Child Abuse and Neglect* 38: 757–67. doi: 10.1016/j.chiabu.2013.09.003

Index

Notes:
Tables, figures, and boxes are indicated by an italic *t*, *f*, and *b* following the page number.
vs. indicates a comparison
The following abbreviations have been used in this index
    AMBIT   Adaptive Mentalization-Based Integrative Treatment
    CAMHS   Child and Adolescent Mental Health Services

accountability, networks/networking, 233–4
achieving states of calm, holding the balance in mentalizing, 132
action definition, Dis-Integration Grid, 243
active planning, 67–122, 383
  advantages, 67–70
    case study, 68
  clients with intention change, 97–120
    group types, 98
    planned work problems, 98–101
  common process barriers *see* active planning, common process barriers
  elements of, 99*f*
  ending phase, 91–7
    aide memoires, 97
    gradually diminishing contact, 97
    handovers, 96
    introduction at beginning, 91–3
    predicting turbulence, 94–5
    relapse prevention planning, 95–6
    Team around the Client (Child), 96
    therapeutic bargain, 93–4
  initial phase *see* active planning, initial phase (getting started)
  intervention phase, 86–90
    AMBIT manual, in, 88–90
    client needs, 86
    evidence-based interventions, 86–8
    reformulating, 72*t*
    reviewing, 72*t*
    working to plan, 72*t*
  maintenance phase, 91
  mapping, 69, 70–97, 72*t*
  standard case management, 70–3, 70*f*, 72*t*
  team culture as, 101
active planning, common process barriers, 101–20, 103–5*t*
  assessment, 103*t*
  engagement, 102–10, 103*t*
    broadcasting intentions, 109–10
    sensitive attunement, 102, 105–9, 106*f*
  formulation and goal-setting, 104*t*, 110–18

    co-construction of plan (waymark agreement), 117–18
    direct linking between, 110–17
  intervention, 104*t*
  review system, 104*t*
  risk assessment, 103*t*
active planning, initial phase (getting started), 72*t*, 73–85
  assessment, 72*t*, 80–3
    across multiple domains, 80–1
    AMBIT Integrative Measure (AIM) assessment, 81–3
  engagement, 72*t*, 73–80
    communication channels, 79
    setting for, 79–80
    Team around the Worker, 73–9
    worker/service introduction, 73
  formulation, 72*t*, 85
  goal-setting, 72*t*
  risk assessment, 83–5
    contents of, 84–5
    systemic approach to, 83–4
Active Planning Map (Egg and Triangle), 112, 115–17, 115*f*
adaptability, AMBIT, ix–x
Adaptive Mentalization-Based Integrative Treatment *see* AMBIT
adaptive training, core curriculum *vs.*, 387–8
ADHD (attention-deficit hyperactivity disorder), 322
adhesive workers, mentalizing stance, 148–9
Adolescent Community Reinforcement Approach, 274
Adolescent Multi-Agency Specialist Service (AMASS), 343–6, 380
adolescent outreach team, CAMHS, 329–32
Adult Psychiatric Morbidity Survey, 2
advice giving, 89
advocacy, 266
affective mentalizing, cognitive mentalizing *vs.*, 48–9

INDEX

affordable training, available training vs., 388–9
agency collaboration, mentalizing, 361–2
agency respect, creation of mentalizing networks, 224
aide memoires, active planning, ending phase, 97
AIM cards, 82–3, 95
aims (destinations), 111
alternative outcomes, clients, working with, 140–1
AMASS (Adolescent Multi-Agency Specialist Service), 343–6, 380
AMBIT
  client groups, 98
  client's life areas, 234–5
  competencies in team learning, 270–1, 272*b*
  definitions, viii–xi
  development of, viii–xi
  diagnosis *see* AMBIT diagnosis
  Dis-Integration Grid *see* Dis-Integration Grid
  dissemination of, 374–5, 383–6
  evaluation of, 375–7
  evidence for, 374–5, 375–81
    evaluation of, 375–7
    evidence-informed approach, 379–81
  future work, 374–91
  geographical use, 327, 351
  keyworkers, 260–1
  learning system as, 29–30, 381–3
    learning at work, 21
    web-based development, 382–3
  localized content *vs.* core content, 286–7
  main principles, ix–x
  mentalizing stance *see* mentalizing stance
  model development, 377–8
  multi-agency networks/networking *see* multi-agency networks/networking
  online manual *see* AMBIT online manual
  as open system, 30
  positioning theory, 230
  Preparation, Reflection, Evaluation and Planning, 385–6
  principled stance, 21
  resilience recognition, 234
  response variation to, 204–5
  seen as imposition, 204
  service improvements, 357–8
  specific manualized interventions, 159–61, 160*b*
    basic theory, 159–60
    key session structure, 159–60
    practice steps, 159–60
  systems change, 351–73
  teams *see* AMBIT teams
  THRIVE framework and, 366–7
  trainees' intentions, 386–90
    barriers, 387
    challenges, 387
    outcomes, 387
    team strengths, 386
    training needs, 386–7
  training
    adaptive training *vs.* core curriculum, 387–8
    affordable *vs.* available training, 388–9
    four-day team training, 384
  web-based treatment manuals, 284–8
  whole-service design, 358–62
    mentalizing in agency collaboration, 361–2
    professional systems, 358–60
  whole-system change, 367–70
    examples, 368–70
    networks/networking absence, 367–8
  working with client, 21
  working with networks/networking, 21
  working with team, 21
AMBIT Competency Scale, 289
AMBIT diagnosis, 6–19
  hard-to-reach people, 10–13
  learning at work, 16–1719
  networks/networking complexity, 6–10
    case study, 7–8
  working with worry, 14–16
AMBIT Integrative Measure (AIM)
  assessment, 81–3, 203, 377–8
  AIM cards, 82–3, 95
AMBIT online manual, xii, 276–7, 284–5, 285*f*
  active planning, intervention phase, 88–90
  best forms of help, 287–8
  training cost reductionn, 288
  training material, 384
AMBIT Practice Audit Tool (APrAT), 202
  reflective tools in team learning, 290
AMBIT Practice Questionnaire (APQ), 289
AMBIT Pro-Gram, 202, 238–41, 239*f*
  client perception of people, 239
  developmental use, 239–40
  networks/networking knowledge, 240
  as starting point, 240–1
AMBIT stance, 25–9
  client–worker relationship, 26
  evidence-based practice *vs.* local practice and expertise, 27–8
  imbalance recognition, 28–9
  scaffolding existing relationships *vs.* risk management, 27
  teamworking, 26
  working across multiple domains, 26–7
AMBIT teams, 21, 30–4, 327–50
  Adolescent Multi-Agency Specialist Service, 343–6, 380
  Cambridgeshire Child and Adolescent Substance Use Service, 161, 346–8

INDEX

CAMHS adolescent outreach team, 329–32
community youth-led service, 335–6
competencies, reflective tools in team learning, 289–90
Darwin Unit, 332–5
inpatient care, 332–5
intensive treatment service, 341–2
Lothian CAMHS, 341–2
MAC-UK, 335–6
multi-agency teams, 343–6
numbers in, 328
requirements in task, 328
resource limitation, 328
shared values, 328
specialist residential care, 336–40, 340*t*
types of, 327–9
Yellowstone Boys and Girls Ranch, 336–40, 340*t*
see also team building
AMBIT wheel, 20, 22–9, 22*f*
AMBIT stance *see* AMBIT stance
balance and, 23
learning at work, 24
mentalizing (center wheel), 24
structure, 24–9
whole-systems thinking, 22–3
working with client, 24
working with networks/networking, 24
working with team, 24
Anna Freud National Centre for Children and Families, ix–x, 382
THRIVE framework *see* THRIVE framework
anxiety
AMBIT as team approach, 32–3
clients, over, 293
APQ (AMBIT Practice Questionnaire), 289
APrAT *see* AMBIT Practice Audit Tool (APrAT)
ARC (Availability, Responsiveness and Continuity) model, 173–4, 268
assertiveness, 126
graded, teamworking, 198–9
assessment, standard case management, 70
attachment
internal working models of, 12
mentalizing, 45
attention-deficit hyperactivity disorder (ADHD), 322
attunement, 99
sensitive *see* sensitive attunement
automatic mentalizing, controlled *vs.*, 46–7
autonomy, teamworking, 171–2, 171*f*
availability, case study (YPSUS), 316
Availability, Responsiveness and Continuity (ARC) model, 173–4, 268

available training, affordable training *vs.*, 388–9
awareness of problems, 5

balance, AMBIT wheel, 23
barriers, AMBIT training, 387
Bateson, Gregory, 69
beginning, introduction at, 91–3
behind the scenes monitoring, 127
beliefs, neutralizing, 132
Better Health Outcomes for Children and Young People, 4
borderline personality disorder (BPD), 45
boundaries
definitions, 192–3
mentalizing stance, 156–8
no-touch, 157–8
Bowlby, John, 149
BPD (borderline personality disorder), 45
broadcasting intentions
case study (YPSUS), 318–19
engagement, 109–10
holding the balance in mentalizing, 132
mentalizing stance, 155–6
one's intentions, 266–7
worker's own, 100
broadcasting problems, 99
Building Communities from the Inside Out (Kretzmann and McKnight), 370–1
burned-out workers, 167
Burnham, John, 88

calm, achieving states of, 132
Cambridgeshire Child and Adolescent Substance Use Service (CASUS), 161, 346–8
CAMHS *see* Child and Adolescent Mental Health Services (CAMHS)
care
trajectory of, 147–8
trust promotion, 58–9
Care Quality Commission, 4–5
case discussion length, Thinking Together, 186–7
case examples/studies
active planning, 68
AMBIT diagnosis, 14–15
AMBIT networks/networking complexity, 7–8
balance *vs.* unbalance, 143–4
client–worker relationship, team support, 183–4
Dis-Integration Grid, 245, 246*t*, 247
hard-to-reach people, 10–11
networks/networking, 210–11, 250–1
practice-based evidence *vs.* evidence-based practice, 279–80
Team around the Client (Child), 37–8
Team around the Worker, 78–9
team learning, 17–18

INDEX

case study (YPSUS), 299–326
  ethical considerations, 299
  interview, 300–12
  learning at work, 325–6
  method, 299–300
  networks/networking, 322–5
    client problems, 322–3
    confusion, 323
    dis-integration assessment, 323–5
    teamworking, 320–2
  worker commentary, 312–26
  working with client, 313–20
    availability, 316
    end of, 320
    intention broadcasting, 318–19
    mentalizing promotion, 316–17
    relationship building, 313–14
    relationship repairing, 319–20
    trust, 314–16
CASUS (Cambridgeshire Child and Adolescent Substance Use Service), 161, 346–8
CAT (cognitive analytic therapy), 111–12
Catch-up Crew, 17–19
center wheel, AMBIT wheel, 24
challenges
  AMBIT training, 387
  clients, working with *see* clients, working with
  mentalizing stance, 162–4, 163*f*
challenging decisions, connecting conservations, 253–4
change
  clients, working with, 140–1
  sustaining (maintenance phase), 72*t*
checking, mentalizing loop, 135–6
Child and Adolescent Mental Health Services (CAMHS), 170, 351
  adolescent outreach team, 329–32
  demand *vs.* resources, 354–5
  function and responsibilities, 354
  Lothian, 341–2
  mental health problems, 355
  Review, 3, 4
  service reorganization, 356–7
  services fit for purpose, 355
Children and Young People's Health Outcomes Forum, 3–4
Children and Young People's Health Outcome Strategy, 3–4
Children and Young People's Improving Access to Psychological Therapies (CYP IAPT), 120, 377
children's homes, geographic position, 15–16
Children's Trusts, 215
client(s)
  AMBIT as team approach, 31
  life areas in AMBIT, 234–5
  needs in active planning, intervention phase, 86
  outcomes in team learning, 268–70
  perception of people, Pro-Gram, 239
  perceptions in evidence-based practice, 278–9
  problems in case study (YPSUS), 322–3
  relationship building, 32
  workers' anxiety about, 293
client groups, AMBIT, 98
client-rated outcome measure, AMBIT Integrative Measure (AIM) assessment, 82–3
clients, working with, 123–69
  balance *vs.* unbalance, 143–6, 145*f*
  change, 140–1
  limitations and challenges, 164–8
    non-mentalizing, 164–5
    outcomes, 167–8
    overwhelmed/burned-out worker, 167
  mentalizing in different contexts, 141–3
    creative arts, 142
    location, 141
    playful modeling, 142–3
  mentalizing loop, 134–8, 135–6, 135*f*
    checking, 135–6
    noticing and naming, 136–8
  mentalizing stance, 124–34
    holding the balance, 132–4
    non-mentalizing punctuation/ termination, 126–30
    not-knowing (curiosity/ inquisitiveness), 125–6
    reinforcing positive mentalizing, 130–2
  mentalizing the moment, 138–41
    video analogy, 138
client–worker relationship, xi, 157
  AMBIT, 21
  AMBIT stance, 26
  AMBIT wheel, 24
  case study (YPSUS) *see* case study (YPSUS)
  positioning theory, 248
  team support, 181–2, 183–4
    case study, 183–4
cognitive analytic therapy (CAT), 111–12
cognitive–behavioral work, 89
cognitive mentalizing, affective mentalizing *vs.*, 48–9
collaboration
  AMBIT, x
  Marking the Task, 191
colleague intentions, creation of mentalizing networks, 224–5
common process barriers *see* active planning, common process barriers
communication channels
  engagement, 79

psychotherapeutic *see* psychotherapeutic communication system
social *see* social communication
communication, trust in, 51–4
  stimulation of, 53*b*
  see also epistemic trust
communities, mentalizing learning, 44
community of practice, team learning, 290–1
community youth-led service, 335–6
competency frameworks, 270–1, 271*t*
components of practice, 87
confidentiality, 157
  networks/networking, 258–9
confident not-knowing, 293
conflict, persistent in teams, 173
confusion, case study (YPSUS), 323
connectedness, team building, 34
connecting conversations, 251–6
  aspects of, 252–4
  purpose of, 251–2
  system transformation, 256–7
  techniques, 254–6
    help-seeking, 255–6
    joining, 254–5
    preparation, 254
    use of self, 255–6
  see also Dis-Integration Grid
connection to team, keyworkers, 180
constructs, 266
context for team, Team around the Worker, 73–5
context-specific nature of mentalizing, 49–50
contingent care, 157
controlled mentalizing, automatic *vs.*, 46–7
conventional (paper-based) treatment manuals, 273–4
conversations
  connecting *see* connecting conversations
  importance in Marking the Task, 190
co-production, intervention manuals, 275–7
core content of AMBIT, localized content *vs.*, 286–7
core curriculum, adaptive training *vs.*, 387–8
creative arts, mentalizing in different contexts, 142
Crew Resource Management, 199
crisis contingencies
  considerations/protocols, 118
  planning, 84, 89
cross-agency approach
  service provision problems, 352–4
  see also Child and Adolescent Mental Health Services (CAMHS)
Csibra, Gergely, 52
culture
  of curiosity, 277–8
  definition, 223
  mentalizing learning, 44
  organizational, teams, 173–4

positive, teams, 173
curiosity
  mentalizing, 125–6
  networks/networking, 227–8
  sensitive attunement in engagement, 102
Current View, 377
CUSS, 199, 200*t*
CYP IAPT (Children and Young People's Improving Access to Psychological Therapies), 120, 377

Darwin Unit, 332–5
data entry, 269
demand, resources *vs.* in CAMHS, 354–5
dependence, teamworking, 171–2, 171*f*
deployment-focused model development, 378
destinations (aims), 111
developmental science, AMBIT, 379
developmental use of Pro-Gram, 239–40
dialogue, discussions *vs.*, 267
disagreements, teams, 175
disconnection, feelings of, 361
discussions, dialogue *vs.*, 267
dis-integration
  AMBIT in multi-agency networks/networking, 217–20
  assessment, case study (YPSUS), 323–5
  work delivery, 9
Dis-Integration Grid, 202–3, 242–7, 243*t*, 324–5
  action definition, 243
  case example, 245, 246*t*, 247
  jargon avoidance, 244–5
  networks/networking definition, 244
  problem definition, 243
  states of mind, 245
  worker definition, 243
  see also connecting conversations
divergent ideas about solutions in teams, 9
duties, positioning theory, 229–30

educational–vocational training, 89
Egg and Triangle (Active Planning Map), 112, 115–17, 115*f*
emergency procedures, 89
ending phase, 72*t*
ending phase, active planning *see* active planning
engagement
  initial phase (getting started), 72*t*
  standard case management, 70
enthusiasm, lack of, 278
epistemic hypervigilance, 56
  social environment adaptation, 63*b*
epistemic mistrust, 55*b*, 56
epistemic trust, 52–3, 53*b*, 58–9
  creation of mentalizing networks, 223

ethical considerations, case study (YPSUS), 299
evaluation of AMBIT, 375–7
Every Child Matters, 3, 215
evidence-based interventions, 86–8
evidence-based practice, 264
    AMBIT, 379
    local practice and expertise vs., 27–8
    planning, 99
    practice-based evidence vs., 277–80, 277f
        blending of, 279–80
        case study, 279–80
        client perceptions, 278–9
        culture of curiosity, 277–8
        enthusiasm lack, 278
        intervention manuals, 278
evidence-based psychological treatments, effectiveness, 29
evidence, respect for, 87
expertise, team learning, 293
explicit learning, 265
explicit mentalizing, 106
exposing in team learning, 292
external mentalizing, internal mentalizing vs., 47–8

Facebook, 213
failure of therapy, 269
families
    AMBIT wheel, 23
    mentalizing learning, 44
    multi-family work, 90
    relationships vs. networks/networking, 222
    work with, 89
feedback, 269
    learning from, 177
The Fifth Discipline (Senge), 266
fight or flight response, 47, 49–50
focal ranking, 88
forensic settings, AMBIT, 368–70, 369
formulation
    initial phase (getting started), 72t, 85
    standard case management, 71
four-day team training, AMBIT, 384
free access, AMBIT, x
frontline practice, detailed aspects, 294
function of CAMHS, 354
funding, provision of, 6
Future in Mind: Promoting, Protecting and Improving Children and Young People's Mental Health and Wellbeing, 4, 214, 354–5

gang affiliations, 236–7
Gergely, György, 52
Getting Advice, THRIVE framework, 362, 364
Getting Help, THRIVE framework, 364
Getting More Help, THRIVE framework, 365

Getting Risk Support, THRIVE framework, 365, 366
getting started, active planning *see* active planning, initial phase (getting started)
Glisson, Charles, 173, 267–8
global ranking, 87–8
goals *see* waymarks (goals)
good enough parents, 12–3
good ideas, Thinking Together, 185
graded assertiveness, teamworking, 198–9
gradually diminishing contact, active planning, ending phase, 97
group supervision, Adolescent Multi-Agency Specialist Service, 344–5
group work, 89

Hampstead Child Adaptation Measure, 81–2
handovers, 96
hard-to-reach people
    AMBIT diagnosis, 10–13
    multi-agency working, 228
    social dysfunction patterns, 64
help
    AMBIT, ix–x
    mentalizing stance, 149–50, 151f, 152f
    rejection of, 11–12, 13
    seeking in connecting conservations, 255–6
hierarchical systems, mentalizing networks, 223–4
holding the balance, 132–4
honeytraps, 148–9
hostels, 15–16
hyperlinks, 286
hypermentalizing, 46, 51
hypervigilence, epistemic *see* epistemic hypervigilance

ideas, shared in team learning, 282–4
imbalance recognition, AMBIT stance, 28–9
IMP (integrative multimodal practice), viii
implementation science, Learning at Work, 263–4
inadequate support, 5
individual relationships, 34–8
individual workers, networks/networking, 230–1
infant learning, mentalizing, 43–5
information demands, Thinking Together, 186
inherent risks, solutions, 15–16
initial phase, active planning *see* active planning, initial phase (getting started)
inpatient care, 332–5
inquiry, 266
inquisitiveness
    mentalizing, 125–6
    sensitive attunement in engagement, 102

institutional ostensive cues, 224
integration responsibility, multi-agency networks/networking vs., 231–5, 232f
integrative multimodal practice (IMP), viii
intelligent membranes, 156–8
Intensive Quality Assurance (IQA), 274–5
intensive treatment service, 341–2
intentions
  broadcasting of see broadcasting intentions
  of colleague, creation of mentalizing networks, 224–5
internal mentalizing, external mentalizing vs., 47–8
internal working models of attachment, 12
interpretation, understanding vs., 111
intervention manuals, 278
  co-production, 275–7
intervention phase, active planning see active planning
intervention (work) plan, 71
interventions
  evidence-based, 86–8
  failure, 215
  fidelity, manualizing, 273–5
  teams, AMBIT wheel, 23
interviews, case study (YPSUS), 300–12
introduction at beginning, active planning, ending phase, 91–3
IQA (Intensive Quality Assurance), 274–5

jargon avoidance, Dis-Integration Grid, 244–5
joining, connecting conservations, 254–5
joint agency plans, positioning theory, 248–9

key session structure, 159–60
keyworkers
  alternative perspective of client, 180
  AMBIT, 260–1
  client relationships, 151, 180
  connection to team, 180
  development, 178–80
  engagement, 75–7
  integrated into teams, 36–7
  large networks/networking, 36
  mentalizing, 178–80
  new workers as, 77
  strong feelings in, 178
kick-start mentalizing, 20, 127, 129, 190–1
Korzybski, Alfred, 69
Kretzmann, J P, 370–1

language learning, mentalizing learning vs., 43–4
large training programs, AMBIT, 368
lead agency identification, 249

leadership, creation of mentalizing networks, 223
learning
  explicit, 265
  infants, mentalizing, 43–5
Learning at Work, 153, 263–98
  Adolescent Multi-Agency Specialist Service, 345–6
  AMBIT, 21
  AMBIT diagnosis, 16–1719
  AMBIT wheel, 24
  case study (YPSUS), 325–6
  definition, 263
  implementation science, 263–4
  knowledge and theory, 266–77
    learning organizations, 266–7
    learning teams, 266–7
  participation, 263–6
  see also team learning
learning organizations, 265, 266–7
Learning What Works, 153
limitations, clients, working with see clients, working with
living skills, 89
localized content of AMBIT, core content vs., 286–7
local practice and expertise, evidence-based practice vs., 27–8
local reports of practice change, AMBIT, 381
local service evaluations, AMBIT, 380
location
  children's homes, 15–16
  mentalizing in different contexts, 141
  sensitive attunement in engagement, 105–6
Lothian Child and Adolescent Mental Health Services (CAMHS), 341–2
low-hanging fruit, 158–9

MAC-UK, 335–6
maintenance phase
  active planning, 91
  sustaining change, 72t
Making Help Work, 153
maltreatment, mentalizing learning effects, 44–5
manualizers/manualizing, 283
  team working see team(s)/teamworking
manuals, intervention see intervention manuals
mapping
  networks/networking, 238–41
  see also AMBIT Pro-Gram
  team building, 33
map-reading analogy, 105
marking the task, Thinking Together, 188, 189–93
Marlborough Family Service, viii

MBT (mentalization-based treatment), 45, 89–90, 111–12
MBT-A (mentalization-based treatment for adolescents), 376
McKnight, J L, 370–1
measurements, emphasis on, 119
membranes, intelligent, 156–8
The Mental Health and Psychological Well-Being of Children and Young People (UK Department of Health), 3
mental illness/mental health disorders
  CAMHS, 355
  culture, role of, 62–5
  diagnosis, 55
  trust/mistrust generation, 54–62
    see also psychotherapeutic communication system
mentalization-based treatment (MBT), 45, 89–90, 111–12
mentalization-based treatment for adolescents (MBT-A), 376
mentalizing, 42–51, 165–6
  advantages, 124
  agency collaboration, 361–2
  AMBIT wheel, 24
  attachment, 45
  clients, working with *see* clients, working with
  context-/relationship-specific nature, 49–50
  context-specific nature, 49–50
  definition, 20, 42–3
  in different contexts *see* clients, working with
  difficulties in, 46
  emergence of imbalanced modes, 50–1
  explicit, 106
  holding the balance, 132–4
  infant learning, 43–5
  keyworkers, 178–80
  kick-start, 20, 127, 129, 190–1
  learning *vs.* language learning, 43–4
  loop *see* clients, working with
  multidimensional nature, 45–9
    affective *vs.* cognitive, 48–9
    automatic *vs.* controlled, 46–7
    internal *vs.* external, 47–8
    self *vs.* others, 47
  networks/networking *see* networks/networking
  other people, 43
  playful modeling, 142–3
  pretend mode, 51, 64
  promotion of, case study (YPSUS), 316–17
  psychic equivalence, 50, 64
  stance *see* mentalizing stance
  as support system, 64
  team culture, 205–6
  teamworking, 175–6
  teleological mode, 50–1, 64
  workers' capacity, 100
mentalizing letter, 112–15
mentalizing loop *see* clients, working with
mentalizing stance, 146–64
  adhesive workers, 148–9
  boundaries, 156–8
  broadcasting intentions, 155–6
  challenge and support, 162–4, 163*f*
  clients, working with *see* clients, working with
  help, 149–50, 151*f*, 152*f*
  honeytrap, 148–9
  implicit to explicit intentions, 154–5
  intelligent membranes, 156–8
  low-hanging fruit, 158–9
  parallel processes, 151–4
  risk management, 162
  trajectory of care, 147–8
  welcome and contingent care, 146–7
  see also clients, working with
Mentalizing the Moment
  clients, working with *see* clients, working with
  Thinking Together, 188, 194–6
mental models, sharing of, 282
mental states, automatic assumptions about, 46
mind, states of, 245
mistrust
  epistemic, 55*b*, 56
  generation
    in mental illness, 54–62
    trauma, 54
  social communication in, 55*b*
mobile phones, 182–3, 213
momentum maintenance, teamworking, 206–7
motivational work, 90
MST *see* multisystemic therapy (MST)
multi-agency networks/networking, 18–19, 214–20
  AMBIT, 6–77, 216–20
    dis-integration, 217–20
    working in multiple domains, 216–17
  collaborations, 215
  hard-to-reach people, 228
  integration responsibility *vs.*, 231–5, 232*f*
  present system, 214–16
multi-agency teams, 343–6
multi-domain working *see* multi-agency networks/networking
multi-family work, 90
multiple domains
  assessment, 80–1
  working in, 216–17
    AMBIT stance, 26–7

multisystemic therapy (MST), 273–5
  fidelity to manualized models, 274
Munro, Eileen, 146, 216

naming, mentalizing loop, 136–8
National Service Framework for Children, Young People and Maternity Services, 3
navigational aids, 68
NEET (not in employment, education or training), 322
negative feedback, 219
networks/networking, 210–62
  accountability, 233–4
  Adolescent Multi-Agency Specialist Service, 345
  AMBIT, 21
  AMBIT diagnosis *see* AMBIT diagnosis
  AMBIT wheel, 24
  case study, 7–8, 210–11
    see also case study (YPSUS)
  connecting conversations *see* connecting conversations
  definitions, 210–11, 213–14
  Dis-Integration Grid *see* Dis-Integration Grid
  family relationships *vs.*, 222
  importance of, 220–2
    responsiveness, 221
    trust, 221
  individual workers, 230–1
  keyworkers, 36
  knowledge of, 240
  limitations and challenges, 257–61
    confidentiality, 258–9
    privileging client contact, 257–8
    time constraints, 259–60
  mentalizing networks, 222–7, 227–8
    agency respect, 224
    colleague's intentions, 224–5
    culture, definition of, 223
    curiosity and, 227–8
    epistemic trust, 223
    hierarchical systems, 223–4
    institutional ostensive cues, 224
    leadership, 223
    non-mentalizing *vs.*, 224–6
    peer-to-peer networks/networking, 224
  multi-agency *see* multi-agency networks/networking
  positioning theory *see* positioning theory
  problems in, 249–51
    case study, 250–1
    collaboration, lack of, 215–16
    lead agency identification, 249
    personal responsibility, 249–50
  professional *see* professional networks/networking
  sculpting of, 241–2

techniques and skills, 235–57
  explaining network to client, 237–8
  mapping networks/networking, 238–41
    see also AMBIT Pro-Gram
  Pro-Gram *see* AMBIT Pro-Gram
  un-service-centric stance, 235–7
  whole-system change, AMBIT and, 367–8
neutralizing thoughts and beliefs, 132
new practice introduction, team building, 33–4
New Ways of Working for Psychiatrists, 214
new workers as keyworkers, 77
No Health Without Mental Health: A cross-Governmental mental health outcomes strategy for people of all ages, 3
non-learning teams, characters, 267
non-mentalizing, 164–5
  mentalizing *vs.*, 224–6
  punctuation/termination, 126–30
    kick-start mentalizing, 20, 127, 129, 190–1
    pause/reflect method, 128
    Stop! Stop! technique, 129–30
    therapist's use of self, 129–30
non-professional social networks/networking, 214
normative social expectations, 62–3
noticing, mentalizing loop, 136–8
not in employment, education or training (NEET), 322
not-knowing, mentalizing, 125–6
no-touch boundaries, 157–8

open-source approach
  AMBIT, x
  projects, 126
  team learning, 291–2
ordinary practice, connecting conservations, 252–3
organizational culture, teams, 173–4
organizational research, AMBIT, 379–80
ostensive cues, 53
  institutional, creation of mentalizing networks, 224
outcomes/outcome measures
  alternative, 140–1
  AMBIT training, 387
  clients, working with, 140–1, 167–8
  well-validated measures, 119
overwhelmed workers, 167

PACE, 199, 200t
parallel processes, mentalizing stance, 151–4
parents
  "good enough," 12–13
  mentalizing learning effects, 44–5
pause/reflect method, non-mentalizing punctuation/termination, 128
peer-to-peer networks/networking, 224
persistent conflict, teams, 173

personal responsibility, networks/
     networking, 249–50
perspective, sensitivity to, 80
p factor, 56–7
   resilience vs., 59b
pharmacological interventions, 90
physical health matters, 90
planned work problems, active
     planning, 98–101
plans, 118
   co-construction of, 117–18
   towards goals, holding the balance in
     mentalizing, 132
POD system, 382–3
positioning theory, 229–31, 247–51
   AMBIT, 230
   client–worker relationship, 248
   definition, 229
   joint agency plan, 248–9
   rights and duties, 229–30
   social systems, 229
positive cultures, teams, 173
positive mentalizing, reinforcing, 130–2
practice
   components of, 87
   evidence-based see evidence-based practice
practice steps, AMBIT, specific manualized
     interventions, 159–60
Preparation, Reflection, Evaluation and
     Planning (PREP), 385–6
press response, state of services, 2
pretend mode thinking, 51, 64, 170, 226–7
principled stance, AMBIT, 21
privileging client contact, networks/
     networking, 257–8
problem definition, Dis-Integration
     Grid, 243
problems, awareness of, 5
professional languages, 74
professional networks/networking, 90, 214–15
   size of, 218–19
Pro-Gram see AMBIT Pro-Gram
*The Protection of Children in
     England: A progress report*, 214
provision of funding, 6
pseudomentalizing, 51
psychiatrists, 8
psychic equivalence thinking, 50, 64, 170, 226
psychoanalysis, 8
psychopathology, 57b
psychosocial interventions, 56–7
psychotherapeutic communication
     system, 60–2
   content teaching and learning, 60–1
   robust mentalizing re-emergence, 61
   social learning re-emergence, 61–2
psychotherapy, 59
punctuality, 157

quality improvement
   models, 378
   team learning, 267–8

re-cognition, 110
reflective tools, team learning, 288–90
reformulating, intervention phase (working
     together), 72t
reinforcing positive mentalizing, 130–2
relapse prevention, 90
   active planning, ending phase, 95–6
   active planning, maintenance phase, 91
relationship(s)
   building, case study (YPSUS), 313–14
   improvement, Adolescent Multi-Agency
     Specialist Service, 343–4
   repairing, case study (YPSUS), 319–20
   scaffolding existing, 27
relationship(s), AMBIT as team approach, 31
relationship(s), individual, 34–8
relationship-specific nature of
     mentalizing, 49–50
remote experts, 278
research, organizational, 379–80
residential care, specialist, 336–40, 340t
resilience, 57–9
   lack of, 56
   p factor vs., 59b
   promotion of, 58
   recognition in AMBIT, 234
   social communication, 58
resistance management, Marking the
     Task, 191–2
resources
   demand vs. in CAMHS, 354–5
   limitation in AMBIT teams, 328
responsibilities
   CAMHS, 354
   personal, networks/networking, 249–50
responsiveness, networks/networking, 221
Returning to Purpose, 188, 196–7
reviewing
   intervention phase (working together), 72t
   progress measures, 118–20
rights, positioning theory, 229–30
ripples analogy, 187–8, 188f
risk management
   mentalizing stance, 162
   scaffolding existing relationships vs., 27
risks, 85
   inherent in solutions, 15–16
   tolerance of, 16
robust mentalizing re-emergence, 61
role theory, 229

scaffolding existing relationships, 27
scales, 289
scribes, 283

INDEX | 403

secure units, 369
self
   exposure, 109
   therapist's use of, 129–30
   use of, 255–6
Senge, Peter, 265, 266, 282
sensitive attunement, 266
   engagement, 102, 105–9, 106f
sensitivity, sustaining, 132
service(s)
   fit for purpose, 355
   fragmentation in client frustration, 361–2
   integration in THRIVE framework, 365–6
   reorganization in CAMHS, 356–7
   state of, 2–5
service provision problems, 352–8
   cross-agency approach, 352–4
SES (socioeconomic status), 58
session-by-session measures, 120
setting of, engagement, 79–80
shared ideas, team learning, 282–4
shared values, AMBIT teams, 328
shepherding, 232–3
social communication
   mistrust of, 55b, 57b
   resilience, 58
social dysfunction patterns, 64
social-ecological work, 90
social environment adaptation, 63b
social expectations, normative, 62–3
social learning re-emergence, 61–2
social networks, active planning, ending phase, 92
social systems, positioning theory, 229
socioeconomic status (SES), 58
sociology, 8
solutions, inherent risks, 15–16
specialist expert service provision, 161
specialist residential care, 336–40, 340t
sphere of influence, connecting conservations, 253
staff leave, 32
standard case management, 70–3, 70f, 72t
START criteria, 197
states of mind, 245
Stating the Case, 188, 193–4
status updates, 102
Stop! Stop! technique, 129–30
storytelling
   Stating the Case, 192
   Thinking Together, 186
subsistence support, 90
substance use disorder, 90
supervision
   group, Adolescent Multi-Agency Specialist Service, 344–5
   teamworking, 201–3

support
   inadequate, 5
   mentalizing stance, 162–4, 163f
sustainability planning
   ending phase, 72t
   standard case management, 71
sustaining change (maintenance phase), 72t
sustaining sensitivity, holding the balance in mentalizing, 132
Syed, Matthew, 198
systemic approach, risk assessment, 83–4
systemic thinking, 229–31
system transformation, connecting conservations, 256–7

TAM (Therapist Adherence Measure) scores, 274
task requirements, AMBIT teams, 328
TAU/Usual Care, 275
team(s)/teamworking, 8–9, 170–209
   AMBIT see AMBIT teams
   AMBIT stance, 26
   AMBIT wheel, 24
   autonomy, 171–2, 171f
   case study (YPSUS), 320–2
   client behavior, help in, 181–2, 183–4
   climate/culture, 172–5
      active planning, 101
      AMBIT as team approach, 32
      mentalizing, 205–6
   context for, 73–5
   dependence, 171–2, 171f
   graded assertiveness, 198–9
   keyworkers
      connection to, 180
      development, 178–80
   knowledge/theory, 172–7
      mentalizing, 175–6
      team climate/culture, 172–5
   learning in see Learning at Work; team learning
   limitations/challenges, 204–7
      AMBIT as imposition, 204
      AMBIT, variation in response to, 204–5
      momentum maintenance, 206–7
      team culture, 205–6
   manualizing, 271–7
      definition, 272–3
      intervention fidelity, 273–5
   mobile phones, 182–3
   shared approach to challenges, 264–5
solutions
   divergent ideas about, 9
   responsibility for, 10
strengths, AMBIT training, 386
supervision, 201–3
Thinking Together see Thinking Together

Team around the Client (Child), 34–6, 37*f*, 74, 215
  active planning, ending phase, 96
  reduce number of professionals, 36
  see also individual relationships
Team around the Worker, 34–5, 37*f*, 178
  case history, 78–9
  engagement, 73–9
  see also individual relationships
team building, 33–4
team learning, 266–7
  AMBIT competencies, 270–1, 272*b*
  client outcomes, 268–70
  development, 176–7
  importance of, 16–17
  live issues, 281
  manualize regularly, 281–2
  non-learning, features, 267
  quality improvement, 267–8
  staff experience, 292–4
  techniques and skills, 280–92
    community of practice, 290–1
    open-source approach, 291–2
    reflective tools, 288–90
    shared ideas, 282–4
    web-based treatment manuals, 284–8
    working things out, 280–4
  time constraints, 283–4
teleological thinking, 50–1, 64, 170, 227
Therapist Adherence Measure (TAM) scores, 274
therapy, failure of, 269
Thinking Together, 184–203, 201–2, 321–2
  Marking the Task, 188, 189–93
  Mentalizing the Moment, 188, 194–6
  necessity of, 185–7
  requests for, 189–90
  Returning to Purpose, 188, 196–7
  ripples analogy, 187–8, 188*f*
  Stating the Case, 188, 193–4
thoughts, neutralizing, 132
THRIVE framework, 352, 362–7, 363*f*, 376–7
  AMBIT and, 366–7
  Getting Advice, 362, 364
  Getting Help, 364
  Getting More Help, 365
  Getting Risk Support, 365, 366
  service integration, 365–6
TiddlyManuals, 284–5
time constraints
  networks/networking, 259–60
  team learning, 283–4, 292
timekeeping, 157
Together We Stand (NHS Health Advisory Service), 353–4
tolerance of risk, 16
training
  affordable *vs.* available, 388–9

  cost reduction with AMBIT online manual, 288
  needs, 386–7
Train the Trainer approach, 385
trajectory of care, 147–8
trauma
  mentalizing learning effects, 44–5
  mistrust, generation of, 54
trust
  case study (YPSUS), 314–16
  communication in, 51–4
    see also epistemic trust
  development, 54
  epistemic *see* epistemic trust
  generation in mental illness, 54–62
  networks/networking, 221
  promotion by caregiving, 58–9
  in therapy, 59–60
turbulence, active planning, ending phase, 94–5

understanding, interpretation *vs.*, 111
un-service-centric stance, 235–7
use of self, connecting conservations, 255–6

values, shared by AMBIT teams, 328
video analogy, mentalizing the moment, 138

waymarks (goals), 111
  agreements to, 117–18
  planning towards, 132
  setting of, 120
    initial phase (getting started), 72*t*
    standard case management, 71
web-based treatment manuals, 284–8
  development, 382–3
Weisz, John, viii, 21, 29, 87, 159, 264, 269, 275, 356–7, 378
welcome and contingent care, mentalizing stance, 146–7
welfare and education network, AMBIT wheel, 23
West Aboriginal Child Health Survey, 58
whole-system change, AMBIT and, 367–8
whole-systems thinking, AMBIT wheel, 22–3
Wolpert, Miranda, 362
workers
  activity, 126
  burned-out, 167
  client assumptions about, 238
  client relationship *see* client–worker relationship
  commentary in case study (YPSUS), 312–26
  definition, Dis-Integration Grid, 243
  individuals in networks/networking, 230–1
  intentions in broadcasting, 100
  overwhelmed, 167
  perspective, Team around the Worker, 78–9

worker/service introduction, engagement, 73
working parties, state of services, 3
Working Together to Safeguard Children, 214
Working with Myself, 153
Working with your Client, 153
Working with your Network, 153
World Wide Web, 213

worrying work, 14–16
wrong questions, Thinking Together, 185

Yellowstone Boys and Girls Ranch (YBGR), 336–40, 340*t*
Youth Offending Services, 215–16
YPSUS team, 321